EDI DEVELOPMENT STUDIES

NF

Labor Markets in an Era of Adjustment

Volume 1

Issues Papers

Edited by

**Susan Horton
Ravi Kanbur
Dipak Mazumdar**

The World Bank
Washington, D. C.

Copyright © 1994
The International Bank for Reconstruction
and Development / THE WORLD BANK
1818 H Street, N.W.
Washington, D.C. 20433, U.S.A.

The Economic Development Institute (EDI) was established by the World Bank in 1955 to train officials concerned with development planning, policymaking, investment analysis, and project implementation in member developing countries. At present the substance of the EDI's work emphasizes macroeconomic and sectoral economic policy analysis. Through a variety of courses, seminars, and workshops, most of which are given overseas in cooperation with local institutions, the EDI seeks to sharpen analytical skills used in policy analysis and to broaden understanding of the experience of individual countries with economic development. Although the EDI's publications are designed to support its training activities, many are of interest to a much broader audience. EDI materials, including any findings, interpretations, and conclusions, are entirely those of the authors and should not be attributed in any manner to the World Bank, to its affiliated organizations, or to members of its Board of Executive Directors or the countries they represent.

Because of the informality of this series and to make the publication available with the least possible delay, the manuscript has not been edited as fully as would be the case with a more formal document, and the World Bank accepts no responsibility for errors. Some sources cited in this book may be informal documents that are not readily available.

The material in this publication is copyrighted. Requests for permission to reproduce portions of it should be sent to the Office of the Publisher at the address shown in the copyright notice above. The World Bank encourages dissemination of its work and will normally give permission promptly and, when the reproduction is for noncommercial purposes, without asking a fee. Permission to copy portions for classroom use is granted through the Copyright Clearance Center Inc., Suite 910, Rosewood Drive, Danvers, Massachusetts 01923, U. S. A.

The backlist of publications by the World Bank is shown in the annual *Index of Publications*, which is available from Distribution Unit, Office of the Publisher, The World Bank, 1818 H Street, N.W., Washington, D.C. 20433, U.S.A., or from Publications, Banque mondiale, 66, avenue d'Iéna, 75116 Paris, France.

Susan Horton is an associate professor of economics at the University of Toronto; Ravi Kanbur is the World Bank's resident representative in Ghana; and Dipak Mazumdar is a labor markets specialist in the World Bank's Office of the Chief Economist, Africa.

Library of Congress Cataloging-in-Publication Data

Horton, Susan.
    Labor markets in an era of adjustment / Susan Horton, Ravi Kanbur,
Dipak Mazumdar.
        p.   cm.—(EDI development studies)
    Includes bibliographical references.
    Contents: v. 1. Issues papers—v. 2. Case studies.
    ISBN 0-8213-2680-5 (v.1).—ISBN 0-8213-2681-3 (v. 2)
    1. Labor market—Developing countries—Congresses. 2. Structural
adjustment (Economic policy)—Developing countries—Congresses.
3. Labor market—Developing countries—Case studies—Congresses.
4. Structural adjustment (Economic policy)—Developing countries—
Case studies—Congresses. I. Kanbur, S.M. Ravi.   II. Mazumdar,
Dipak, 1932–   . III. Title. IV. Series.
HD5852
331.12'09172'6—dc20   93-34978
                                                  CIP

CONTENTS

VOLUME 1. ISSUES PAPERS

iii

VOLUME 2: CASE STUDIES

FOREWORD

This two-volume study is the result of a series of five conferences organized by the Economic Development Institute of the World Bank in collaboration with the University of Toronto and Warwick University and supported by the Overseas Development Administration of the United Kingdom and the governments of Canada and Ireland.

It comprises the research papers presented at the conferences and revised in light of comments and suggestions by the participants as well as by other experts in the field. Various chapters have been presented in seminars for World Bank staff and at the annual meetings of the American Economic Association.

Amnon Golan, Director
Economic Development Institute

ACKNOWLEDGMENTS

This book is the result of a large research project that was initiated by Ravi Kanbur and Dipak Mazumdar early in 1988. They were subsequently joined by Susan Horton, who had at that time begun to do work on a similar theme for Bolivia.

The research was facilitated by a series of five conferences: three at Warwick University and two at the University of Toronto. The editors would like to thank the universities for their support and the following organizations for providing funding: the Overseas Development Administration of the United Kingdom and the governments of Canada and of Ireland for their support through trust funds established at the World Bank.

Many people participated in the conferences. Some presented papers, others provided useful comments, and all contributed to the progress of the research. In addition to the authors, these included (with their affiliation at the time): A. Berry, D. Benjamin, M. Faig, and Y. Kotowitz (University of Toronto); P. Brixen, L. Haddad, M. Johnson, J. MacKinnon, A. McKay, S. Nath, G. Pyatt, and J. Round (Warwick University); A. Chhibber, J. Daniel, L. Fox, C. Grootaert, T. King, J. Newman, A. van Adams, and M. Walton (World Bank); A. Atsain (University of Abidjan), C. Bean (London School of Economics), J. Bradley (ESRI, Dublin), G. Fields and E. Thorbecke (Cornell University), N. Gregory (ODA), T. Besley, P. Horsnell, S. Kheng-Kok, J. Knight, C. Yves, and A. Zegeye (Oxford University), S. Morley (Vanderbilt University), N. N'geno (University of Nairobi), A. Plourde (University of Ottawa), B. Renison (USAID), G. Rodgers (ILO), B. Salome and D. Turnham (OECD), J. Svejnaar (University of Pittsburgh), R. van der Hoeven (UNICEF), K. Yao (CIRES, Abidjan), and Z. A. Yusof (Malaysian Institute of Economic Research).

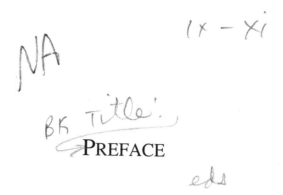

PREFACE

Our interest in undertaking a project on structural adjustment and labor markets in developing countries arose from our perception of a gap in the existing literature. A good deal of work had been done on structural adjustment and poverty, but without work on the labor market little was known about how the effects of structural adjustment were transmitted to the poor, most of whom depend heavily on labor market earnings. At the same time some policymakers and international institutions seem to believe that labor market rigidities are an obstacle to structural adjustment, and several developing countries have implemented rather draconian policies to regulate their labor markets. However few empirical studies of developing countries exist to justify such policies.

At the start of the project we invited researchers to tell us what the existing theory and studies from developed countries suggested about adjustment and labor markets. We then commissioned a series of theory papers to extend the literature to developing countries, looking at topics such as structural adjustment and poverty, the effects on women, the political economy aspects, the long-run effects of adjustment, and so on. At the same time we began twelve country studies to examine the effects of adjustment on labor markets. The country studies took longer and, as a result, were enriched by insights from the theory papers, which were completed earlier.

In choosing countries to study, we wanted to have as wide a geographic coverage as possible. Data availability proved to be one limitation. We felt that it was essential to have access to household labor-force survey data over time (corresponding to the adjustment period) for the countries concerned. Without these data, the effects on women, on income distribution, on real wages, and on unemployment could not easily be studied. Existing international compilations (primarily the ILO *Yearbook of Labour Statistics*) have somewhat uneven coverage since not all countries report and the data they publish are for a mix of household surveys and establishment surveys. Data constraints were most serious for Africa, where very few countries had repeated labor force surveys at different times. The final sample of countries included five from Latin America, three from Asia, one from North Africa and the Middle East, and three from Sub-Saharan Africa.

At the outset we were not aware of different "patterns" of adjustment. In the course of the research, however, the countries fell into four groups of three. One group (the Republic of Korea, Malaysia, and Thailand) reflected what might be termed an "East Asian" pattern of adjustment, with short, sharp recessions and a resumption of fast growth of GDP (more than 5 percent per year). Another group (Bolivia, Chile, and Ghana) undertook "severe" adjustment. These economies had had more serious problems in the 1970s and 1980s, experiencing either sharp falls in GDP in some years, or prolonged stagnation or decline. Real wages fell more than 50 percent in the course of adjustment, and in the case of Chile there was high unemployment (more than 25 percent at the worst points). A third group of countries (Brazil, Costa Rica, and Kenya) might be described as having undergone "partial" adjustment, where adjustment was less painful than in the Asian case but the resumption of growth was also less strong. The final group (Argentina, Côte d'Ivoire, and Egypt) represent "frustrated" adjustment, in that adjustment was delayed for a number of reasons—for example, stop-go cycles in Argentina, difficulties in devaluing because of membership in the franc zone for Côte d'Ivoire, and the later onset of problems for Egypt, as an oil exporter.

The research suggested that labor markets in developing countries were in fact working quite well to permit structural adjustment. Three important conclusions were reached: real wages were more flexible than generally supposed, which would support adjustment; labor reallocation across sectors has been more or less in the desired direction; and labor market institutions such as unions and minimum wages, often argued to be an impediment to adjustment, have more subtle effects on the workings of labor market—a finding that is worthy of further study.

As occurs in all research projects, we discovered other gaps in the literature and topics that seemed worthy of attention but that did not fit within the scope of the existing effort. Much more could be learned about labor markets in developing countries by constructing time series from regular labor force surveys. In some countries, particularly the richer countries in Asia and Latin America, these series have already been put together, but the same is not true for the poorer countries. Time series for key variables are very important since fluctuations and cycles in the economy render one-year "snapshots" derived from a single survey quite misleading. A great deal of work also remains to be done in such areas as quantifying changes in income distribution over time, analyzing the effect of structural adjustment on women, and exploring the effects of labor market institutions in developing countries.

LABOR MARKETS IN AN ERA OF ADJUSTMENT: AN OVERVIEW

Susan Horton
Ravi Kanbur
Dipak Mazumdar

Issues and Country Studies

Labor markets play a central role in determining the macroeconomic success of stabilization and adjustment policies and in mediating the impact of these policies on the population's standards of living, in particular the poor. The 7 issues papers and 12 country studies in these volumes examine the different aspects of this interaction between labor markets and adjustment. The object of this chapter is to provide an overview and to draw out general conclusions, policy lessons, and areas for further research.

Issues

To start with, let us define what we mean by adjustment and by labor markets. Under adjustment we include both stabilization and structural adjustment. Following convention, by stabilization we mean the reduction of national expenditure to bring it in line with national income or output, usually following external shocks. By structural adjustment we mean attempts to increase national income or output through more efficient use of resources. Of course, a myriad of macro policy instruments, such as exchange rates, monetary policy, and fiscal policy, are available to achieve these goals, which may sometimes be stated in terms of inflation, balance of payments, and growth targets.

The links between instruments and targets, however, almost always touch on labor markets and their operation.

A labor market is a mechanism for matching the supply and demand of the factor of production labor, through the terms of the contract between buyer and seller. As many different types of labor exist, differentiated by skill, location, gender, and so on, many different labor markets exist, but these markets are linked with each other because the conditions in one can influence the workings of another. The system of interlinked individual labor markets in a country can be called the labor market. The labor market is itself linked to other markets in the economy: it influences their workings and is in turn influenced by them.

The terms of the contract between buyers and sellers in a labor market can vary, from wage payment in markets for unskilled labor to complex packages of remuneration and benefits over time in markets for skilled labor. The markets can vary in structure, from many buyers and many sellers to small groups of buyers and sellers. Some analysts talk of internal labor markets within large firms. National policy and regulation affect the workings of the labor market, and the labor market in turn produces institutions that become important in setting national policy. While any individual labor market may be small, the outcomes in the labor market as a whole can influence macroeconomic conditions in the economy. Since the outcomes determine the payment to labor, they also affect the distribution of income in the economy.

Policymakers are often interested in knowing whether a country's labor market is "working well," and what can be done to "improve" its workings. But what does it mean to say that the labor market is working well? As always, a general characterization is difficult. The most general statement we can make is in the context of a competitive general equilibrium model of the economy. In this stylized setting, we know that if every other market operates in the manner of classical competitive markets, then if the labor market also operates in this manner the economy will achieve a Pareto optimal outcome. Thus, in this framework and under these conditions what is meant by the labor market working well is clear: it is that the labor market is working like a classical competitive market where price adjusts to equate supply and demand. In most practical settings, this is indeed the test that is applied, and discussion of policy and regulation is highly colored by the use of this benchmark. However, the slightest reflection should reveal how fragile this benchmark is, and how severe and unrealistic are the conditions under which it is viable, as in reality there is no guarantee that other markets are themselves working like classical competitive markets, and a Pareto optimal outcome may not satisfy distributional criteria for evaluating the economic system as a whole.

Since the search for any general characterization is likely to prove futile, the best way to approach the analysis is with a more specific notion of what is being asked of the labor market, given the structure of other markets in the economic system and the particular economic policy problem under consideration. The particular policy problems we focus on here are those of stabilization and structural adjustment through the use of macroeconomic policy instruments.

We discuss stabilization first. The role of the labor market here is to ensure that the reduction in national expenditure takes place without inducing a substantial reduction in national output. The basic mechanisms are well known. As national expenditure falls there will be downward pressure on output prices if output markets behave like classical competitive markets. This downward pressure on output prices will lead to cutbacks in production, and hence in the demand for labor. If the price of labor falls in response to this reduced demand, then this reduction in cost will help maintain the level of production. If the price of labor falls sufficiently in relation to the original fall in output prices, under certain conditions there need be no fall in total output at all. To the extent that the real wage does not fall this far, total output will be lower than it otherwise would be and, because of unemployment, the wage bill will be distributed more unequally than it otherwise would be.

In this framework, therefore, the test for whether the labor market was working well would focus on whether the real wage fell sufficiently to maintain employment and output in the face of a reduction in total national expenditures (vol. 1, chapters 1 and 3). Clearly, labor market institutions are relevant here. If the labor market is unionized, and the union cares more about the real wage of employed members than about the number of the unemployed, then bargaining between the union and employers will lead to a real wage that is too high for maintaining employment and output (vol. 1, chapter 7). The extent to which the union can indeed be sanguine about the unemployed will in turn depend on the nature and extent of unemployment benefits. Wage indexation is also relevant. To the extent that automatic wage adjustments, mandated by national law or agreed by employers as part of a long-term contract, stop the real wage from falling, unemployment and output loss will occur (vol. 1, chapter 4). Also important is how much of the labor market is covered by these adjustments.

Although a fall in demand will lead to unemployment in a particular labor market if the real wage in that market does not fall, at the macroeconomic level the real wage is also one of the determinants of aggregate demand. The mechanism (as developed by Taylor 1988, for example) depends on the assumption that the propensity to save is markedly lower for wage earners than for recipients of profits. If falling real wages are accompanied by a fall in the share of wages in national income, the aggregate demand will fall. We may see persistent unemployment despite large falls in real wages. Thus, the conclusion to be drawn from the coexistence of these phenomena is not necessarily that the labor market is not working well, and that if only real wages fell even further unemployment would go down, but that beyond a certain point the macroeconomic consequences of real wage declines may lead to an additional cost of adjustment that relies too heavily on labor markets.

Another case where observed unemployment does not necessarily mean that the labor market is not working well is where output markets do not behave like classical competitive markets. When competition in product markets is imperfect, unemployment may result even if labor markets are competitive with flexible real wages (vol. 1, chapter 1). With persistent unemployment, therefore, the finger of blame can point to at least one of three factors: imperfectly competitive product markets, aggregate demand feedback from real wages, or labor markets not working well. One cannot automatically assume that the root cause is the latter.

Let us turn now to the role of labor markets in the process of structural adjustment. Structural adjustment has many components, but at its heart is a shift in the composition of national output toward the production of exportables and import-competing output (tradables) through the use of relative price instruments such as the exchange rate. Clearly, such a shift in the pattern of production requires a corresponding shift in factors of production toward certain sectors, and it is the labor market through which the sectoral composition of labor use is altered. The general issue to which this gives rise is the nature and extent of reallocations between different labor markets. Essentially, what is required is for labor to flow to the production of tradables, that is, to flow to those labor markets that serve the production of tradables. This may require reallocation across firms in the same area, across the formal/informal or covered/uncovered divide, or across regions.

In principle, this reallocation could take place through a number of mechanisms, but economic analysis focuses on the role of temporary wage differentials in attracting labor to markets where demand is high. Note, however, that the very reallocation to which the differentials give rise will tend to mitigate the differentials. If the wage differentials are constrained between limits because of institutional factors, standard results on the impact of changes on the relative output price in the composition of employment and output will not occur (vol. 1, chapter 2). The same would happen if gender differences led to significant misallocation of labor (vol. 1, chapter 6). Movements in relative wages can therefore be a deceptive test of whether the labor market is working well. Concentrating directly on the nature and extent of reallocation between output sectors is far better. The faster this reallocation, the faster the desired adjustment in national output. However, labor is only one of the factors of production, and one must take care before one pronounces that because labor reallocation has not taken place, the labor market is not working well. If markets for complementary inputs (for example, credit) are not playing their role, the labor market may be hampered in achieving the desired reallocation of labor, and therefore of output.

Whatever the role of the labor market in achieving the macroeconomic objectives of stabilization and structural adjustment, how the labor market responds to macroeconomic instruments will certainly determine the distribution of income in the economy. At the simplest level, if stabilization necessitates a period of high unemployment because of downwardly rigid wages, then inequality will increase, and perhaps poverty will increase more than if real wages had fallen sufficiently to maintain employment. The extent and nature of the reallocation of labor across sectors will also influence the distribution of income. If, for example, in the initial situation the poor are concentrated in sectors producing tradables, then the increase in wages necessary to attract labor to those sectors will reduce poverty on this count in the short to medium run, although what happens in the long run depends on how markets for other factors operate. One can conduct a systematic analysis of the impact of adjustment on poverty in the presence of a variety of labor market structures (vol. 1, chapter 3). To the extent that the labor market is segmented along gender lines, the distribution of income will also be affected (vol. 1, chapter 6).

Economists now realize that stabilization and structural adjustment policies, although designed to achieve macroeconomic balance in the short and medium term, will have long-run consequences through their impact on investment. There is a similar impact on human capital investment. To the extent that investment in human capital is affected by changes in relative wages, short-run policies (via their effects on labor markets) will also have long-run consequences (vol. 1, chapter 5).

Country Studies

The interactions between labor markets and adjustment thus throw up a number of interesting issues and questions. The answers to many of these questions will be context and country specific. The issue papers in this symposium take up specific conceptual matters and develop or review the analysis on areas highlighted in this section. The country studies, however, are at the heart of this symposium, since they insert reality into the conceptual framework. Each country study author was asked first to give a brief account of the adjustment process: the nature of the shock, the policy responses, and the macroeconomic outcomes. The authors were then asked to give an account of the relevant characteristics of the labor market, for example, labor force composition, wage differentials, and wage setting mechanisms. Armed with these two accounts, the studies then assess the labor market's role in the adjustment process, paying due attention to institutional features. With these basics, the authors were also asked to evaluate the impact of adjustment, as mediated by the labor market, on poverty and on women. Finally, they were invited to consider the long-run consequences of labor market adjustment.

This symposium contains 12 country studies: four from Africa (of which three are from Sub-Saharan Africa), five from Latin America, and three from Asia. The countries span a range of different income levels (using the World Bank's classification), ranging from two low-income countries (Ghana and Kenya), seven lower-middle-income countries (Bolivia, Chile, Costa Rica, Côte d'Ivoire, Egypt, Malaysia, and Thailand), and three upper-middle-income countries (Argentina, Brazil, and the Republic of Korea). The countries also span a range of adjustment experience.

Not all the country studies address all the issues, sometimes because particular issues were important in particular countries but not in others, and sometimes due to data limitations. Almost all the Latin countries, many of those in Southeast Asia, and some in North Africa have periodic labor force surveys, although the data from these vary in terms of accessibility and amount of previous analysis. However, few labor force surveys cover the rural sector (exceptions are Kenya, although the survey is infrequent, and Thailand for occasional years). To the authors' knowledge, Sub-Saharan Africa has no regular labor force surveys, and Kenya is the only country with comparable household surveys for a year in the 1970s and a year in the 1980s. The two other Sub-Saharan African studies rely on cross-sectional data for the 1980s from the World Bank Living Standards Surveys. Data from these surveys have the advantage of covering rural areas, and with some ingenuity (for example, using information on length of tenure in current job or length of residence in current location) can be used to shed light on some changes that have occurred in the labor market over time.

In addition to labor force surveys, many countries have other data from employment and earnings surveys, collected usually at the establishment level. These series tend to cover mainly the formal sector and not a representative sample of households, and can sometimes be misleading, especially during a period of substantial sectoral shifts and declines in formal sector employment (see, for example, Lavy and Newman 1989 on the Côte d'Ivoire). The Bolivian case study similarly points out discrepancies between the real wage and the unemployment series from household surveys as compared to establishment surveys.

The 12 country studies pull together a wealth of information. This is particularly useful given the dearth of centralized international reporting of labor data. The International Labour Organisation's (ILO's) regional subdivisions do collate and report information within the respective regions (Latin America, Africa, and Asia). However, the ILO yearbook, for example, the basis for Johnson's 1986 work, is spotty in terms of country coverage and seems to rely on establishment survey results rather than the (arguably) more reliable household survey data. The country studies here contain not only whatever aggregate data are available, but in many cases also contain original econometric analyses (both micro and macro) of the data.

Although the workings of the labor market have been well studied for some countries, there are relatively few comparative studies of the effects of the crisis of the late 1970s and the 1980s. Fallon and Riveros (1988), ILO (1987), and Johnson (1986) compare a range of countries, Ghai (1987) and JASPA (1988) examine African countries, and some work on Latin America is available, for example, by Tokman (1984) and Riveros (1989), and by the Programa Regional del Empleo para America Latina y el Caribe (PREALC). Investigators have also examined the public sector labor force (Lindauer and others 1988). The present set of studies tries to cover a broad range of countries, including some that had not been studied much previously. Although structural adjustment is by no means complete in these countries, enough years of data have been accumulated since the onset of crisis and adjustment, that it may be timely to assess experience so far. As such, the country studies may provide a valuable basis for generalization.

Varieties of Adjustment Experience

Before drawing conclusions on the role of labor markets in adjustment on the basis of our case studies, it is useful to consider the nature of the adjustment that has taken place in these countries. Although quantifying the type or success of adjustment is hard, we suggest that our 12 countries fall into four groups of three. One group consists of the three Asian countries in the sample, which have by and large had short and successful adjustments (based on previously relatively outward-oriented economies). A second group consists of three countries that had previously had strongly inward-oriented economies that undertook severe and painful adjustment (Bolivia, Chile, and Ghana). The remaining countries all undertook less severe adjustments than the second group, but with less immediate success than the Asian group. These six countries form somewhat of a continuum, but three of them (Brazil, Costa Rica, and Kenya) had moderate success in adjusting without requiring major policy reversals, and the last three (Argentina, Côte d'Ivoire, and Egypt) had somewhat less success (in the case of Egypt as an oil exporter, efforts to adjust began only very late in the time period under study).

Tables 1 and 2 summarize information on two key economic variables: GDP growth rates (the most frequently used indicator of economic performance) and real effective exchange rate (one possible indicator of relative prices key to the adjustment process). As table 1 shows, the Asian countries have had occasional less successful years, but in general exhibit growth rates of 5 percent per annum or greater, and no years of negative growth. Of the "severe adjustment" countries, Chile and Ghana exhibit economic problems dating back to the 1970s, with large negative growth of GDP in some years, but since 1983 each country has grown at close to or more than 5 percent in three of the following years. Bolivia (the other country in the group) encountered economic problems later (bolstered by hydrocarbon exports in the 1970s), and experienced the longest span without positive growth of all the sample countries. Economic recovery there remains weak. Brazil, Costa Rica, and Kenya (characterized here as "moderate adjustment" countries) appear to resume reasonable growth rates of GDP after the worst years (around 1980–82), although their year-to-year growth rates following adjustment are more variable than those of the Asian countries.The remaining three cases (Argentina, Côte d'Ivoire, and Egypt, characterized here as "less successful adjustment" countries) exhibit rather heterogeneous

Table 1 Growth Rates of GDP, 1970/71–1986/87

(constant prices)

Country	1970-71	1971-72	1972-73	1973-74	1974-75	1975-76	1976-77	1977-78	1978-79	1979-80	1980-81	1981-82	1982-83	1983-84	1984-85	1985-86	1986-87
Argentina	3.4	1.9	3.2	6.3	-0.7	-0.2	6.4	-3.2	7.0	1.5	-6.7	-4.9	3.0	2.6	-4.5	5.5	2.0
Bolivia	4.9	5.8	6.7	5.1	6.6	6.1	4.2	3.4	0.0	-0.6	0.9	-4.9	-6.5	-0.3	-0.2	-2.9	2.2
Brazil	12.3	10.9	13.5	9.7	9.9	9.7	2.9	4.9	6.8	9.3	-4.4	0.6	-3.5	5.1	8.3	7.6	3.6
Chile	9.0	-1.2	-5.6	0.1	-12.9	3.5	9.9	8.3	7.8	5.5	-14.1	-0.1	6.3	2.4	5.7	5.7	n.a.
Costa Rica	6.8	8.2	7.7	5.5	2.1	5.5	8.9	6.3	4.9	0.8	-2.3	-7.3	2.9	8.0	0.7	5.5	5.4
Côte d'Ivoire	n.a.	n.a.	n.a.	n.a.	n.a.	12.0	4.7	9.9	5.2	6.3	1.4	3.0	0.0	-8.9	n.a.	n.a.	n.a.
Egypt	n.a.	n.a.	0.8	2.7	9.1	15.3	13.5	5.9	6.2	10.3	3.8	10.1	7.6	6.2	6.7	2.7	2.5
Ghana	5.6	-2.5	15.3	3.4	-12.9	3.5	2.3	8.5	-3.2	0.0	-1.8	-7.2	0.2	2.6	5.1	5.2	4.8
Rep. of Kenya	6.9	9.5	6.8	1.5	3.4	7.0	9.4	9.0	3.8	5.6	3.7	0.6	2.7	2.0	3.8	5.2	5.8
Korea	9.2	5.9	5.4	14.4	7.9	6.5	13.2	10.9	9.7	7.4	9.8	6.7	7.3	11.8	9.4	6.9	12.4
Malaysia	7.1	9.4	11.7	8.3	0.8	11.6	7.8	6.7	9.3	7.4	6.9	5.9	6.3	7.8	9.9	1.2	5.2
Thailand	n.a.	5.0	4.1	9.8	4.8	9.4	9.9	10.4	5.3	4.8	6.3	4.1	7.3	7.1	3.5	5.0	7.1

n.a. = not available

Sources: Calculated from IMF, *International Financial Statistics* (various years) except Bolivia data from country study.

Table 2 Real Effective Exchange Rate, 1976–86
(index, 1980 = 100)

Country	1976	1977	1978	1979	1980	1981	1982	1983	1984	1985	1986
Argentina	n.a.	n.a.	54.5	76.7	100.0	91.1	50.6	42.7	49.7	44.0	44.1
Bolivia	n.a.	n.a.	87.3	91.6	100.0	125.9	136.6	125.4	162.6	279.7	82.2
Brazil	n.a.	n.a.	122.8	112.5	100.0	121.5	128.4	104.2	104.2	100.1	94.4
Chile	93.7	102.1	85.2	86.1	100.0	118.0	106.7	86.8	85.3	68.8	58.2
Costa Rica	91.4	90.0	86.6	90.9	100.0	63.5	72.5	83.4	81.9	80.9	72.7
Côte d'Ivoire	n.a.	n.a.	89.1	98.0	100.0	85.7	78.2	75.2	72.0	72.2	84.5
Egypt	n.a.	n.a.	114.1	92.6	100.0	106.0	118.3	133.7	156.0	164.0	156.4
Ghana	n.a.	n.a.	96.8	76.5	100.0	222.4	278.1	186.9	72.2	52.5	30.2
Kenya	94.2	97.3	104.2	101.0	100.0	96.7	100.3	95.0	101.7	100.3	87.0
Korea, Rep. of	n.a.	n.a.	97.6	107.4	100.0	104.4	106.9	102.7	101.3	95.5	80.6
Malaysia	106.5	105.9	101.4	105.8	100.0	100.4	106.7	111.8	116.1	110.3	92.6
Thailand	n.a.	n.a.	91.2	92.4	100.0	102.8	105.8	108.6	107.2	95.3	85.0

n.a. = not available
Note: Increase implies appreciation.
Sources: Calculated from IMF data.

behavior. Argentina has continual stop-and-go cycles dating back to at least 1974. Côte d'Ivoire encountered problems in the 1980s after successful growth in the 1970s, but its ability to adjust has been limited by its membership in the West African Monetary Union. Finally, Egypt, as an oil exporter only, began to experience a growth slowdown after 1985.

As the time pattern of growth rates in table 1 show, the timing of adjustment was somewhat different in the various countries. Figure 1 shows the sequence of events described in the country studies. The years 1978 and 1982 were obviously watershed years (corresponding to the second oil price shock and start of the rise in real interest rates in one case, and to the onset of the debt crisis as signaled by inability to pay in Brazil and Mexico in the other). Some of the variation depends on price collapses in different commodity markets (coffee, cocoa, and tin affected different countries in the sample), as well as good or bad harvests and weather, particularly for the African countries. At least three countries had begun adjustment in the mid 1970s (Brazil, Chile, and Kenya), and Argentina had also made some efforts in this direction. (Of course, countries such as Korea and Brazil had made structural adjustments earlier still, changing their trade regimes.) After 1982 all the countries in the sample undertook some form of stabilization and/or structural adjustment.

Quantifying adjustment policy efforts or their success is somewhat difficult. The real effective exchange rate (REER) may provide some useful information, insofar as structural adjustment attempts to change relative prices, and the exchange rate is a key price. However, one encounters some problems in interpreting these data. First, some countries may experience policy outcomes that differ from their intentions (for example, Côte d'Ivoire recently tried to mimic a devaluation, but due to changes in other currencies the value of Côte d'Ivoire's currency actually appreciated). Second, there is no benchmark as to what the equilibrium real exchange rate should be. Some countries therefore appear to have succeeded in deep currency depreciations, but from previously highly distorted rates, whereas others appear to have been less successful, but because the previous rate was less distorted.

Figure 1 Timing of Adjustment Efforts

	1970	1971	1972	1973	1974	1975	1976	1977	1978	1979	1980	1981	1982	1983	1984	1985	1986	1987	1988
Argentina							deregulation of economy under military							pre-election ease-up		series of failed SAs		stabilization/ SA	weak growth
Bolivia			reasonable growth					lending ends	failed SA										
Brazil				SA under military								stabilization					stabilization crisis		
Chile				deregulation/ SA by military		stabilization		policies reversed					financial crisis			stabilization and export-led recovery			
Costa Rica										crisis onset: efforts to spend way out of crisis			stabili-zation/SA			major SA			
Côte d'Ivoire								coffee boom ends		problems begin		stabilization lending dries up					further SA efforts hampered by exchange rate		
Egypt	good	growth (oil windfall, aid remittances)											unsuccessful SA						
Ghana			long-run problems									drought		stabili-zation/SA	drought		SA takes hold		
Kenya				structural adjustment began end of coffee boom								devaluation trade policy shift		resumed fast growth	drought				
Korea, Rep. of	fast growth light industry			focus on heavy industry						brief recession and adjustment		spend way out of crisis		resumed fast growth		short severe recession		recovery	
Malaysia					commodity boom														
Thailand													recession, devaluations, change in trade regime				resumed fast growth		

Note: SA = structural adjustment
Source: Country studies.

Table 2 provides some information on REERs. Of the three countries with the least success in adjustment, two also failed to achieve real currency depreciations after 1982 (Egypt's currency appreciated quite sharply), and the third country (Argentina) did not sustain depreciations. Most of the other countries for which data are available achieved some depreciation of their currency: Kenya after the 1981 devaluation and reforms (although the policy may have begun to slip in 1986), Bolivia after the 1985 policy change, Chile after the 1984 stabilization, Costa Rica after the major structural adjustment efforts in 1984, Malaysia after the onset of the 1984 recession, and Ghana after the economic recovery program began in 1983. With this background on the nature of the adjustment experience in the 12 countries, we turn now to labor markets and their role in the adjustment process.

The Role of Labor Markets during Adjustment

The country studies all address the issue of how well labor markets worked during adjustment. The discussion here is organized as follows: first, aggregate real wages and unemployment are examined, then the effect of distributive conflicts and the ensuing macro-tradeoffs are discussed, third, sectoral employment shifts and relative wage are examined, and finally, the role of labor market institutions is dealt with.

Unemployment and Real Wages

Tables 3 and 4 summarize country experience as regards unemployment and real wage trends for the 12 country studies. Unemployment series are available for nine of the countries studied (they are not available for the three countries in Sub-Saharan Africa). As the definition of unemployment varies across countries, cross-country comparisons require some caution. Most of the countries do show cyclical or trend increases in unemployment related to periods of recession and stabilization (see also figure 1). Chile exhibits the most dramatic unemployment, with unemployment levels of over 10 percent in all the years from 1976 (when the series begins) until 1987, reaching a peak of 26 percent in 1982. Understanding how the rate could remain so high for so long in the absence of unemployment benefits is difficult. At the other extreme, Korea's exceptionally low unemployment rate despite the large shocks it encountered as an oil-importing open economy is noteworthy.

Several of the studies discuss the composition of the unemployed and generally confirm the "luxury unemployment" hypothesis, whereby those openly unemployed are more frequently secondary household workers (that is, not household heads) and are often the more educated. Egypt represents an extreme case where a national survey found that 76 percent of the unemployed were new entrants to the labor force, and 74 percent had a high school education or above. Educated female unemployment is a particular problem in Egypt, as few opportunities are available outside the government sector. Of the female unemployed, 97 percent were new entrants to the labor force and 96 percent had a high school education or above. In Thailand, unemployment is highest among those with a vocational education, and unemployment of university graduates rose in the 1980s, when government employment growth slowed dramatically. Likewise in Malaysia, the educated unemployed phenomenon has changed over time, from unemployed high school graduates to unemployed college graduates, and as in Egypt, educated unemployment is concentrated among women. The Costa Rica and Bolivia studies both document another feature of the composition of the unemployed, namely, an increase in the share of heads of households and of job leavers among the unemployed in crisis years.

In most of the countries, weak labor demand did not result only in unemployment. Underemployment increased, although this is hard to measure (Argentina, Bolivia, and Costa Rica studies provide data and show that it has generally moved with the unemployment rate). Participation rates also changed, and informalization increased. Only Bolivia and Chile used formal emergency employment programs, but many of the countries bolstered public employment at least as a temporary measure during the crisis until fiscal stabilization measures dictated cuts in public sector employment.

Changes in participation rates can affect the measurement of unemployment. However, researchers do not agree as to whether the added or the discouraged worker effect will predominate. (The added worker effect is where the income effect of lower earnings during recessions leads to the household supplying additional labor. The

Table 3 Unemployment Rates, 1979–89
(percent)

Country	1970	1971	1972	1973	1974	1975	1976	1977	1978	1979	1980	1981	1982	1983	1984	1985	1986	1987	1988	1989
Argentina	n.a.	n.a.	n.a.	n.a.	4.2	3.4	4.8	3.3	3.3	2.5	2.5	4.8	5.3	4.7	4.6	6.1	5.2	5.6	6.1	n.a.
Bolivia	n.a.	n.a.	n.a.	n.a.	n.a	n.a.	n.a.	n.a.	n.a.	n.a.	7.5	6.2	7.5	8.2	6.6	5.7	4.2	5.9	11.5	10.7
Brazil	n.a.	n.a.	n.a.	n.a.	n.a..	n.a.	n.a.	n.a.	-6.8	6.4	6.3	7.9	6.3	6.7	7.1	5.3	3.6	3.8	n.a.	n.a.
Chile	n.a.	n.a.	n.a.	n.a.	n.a.	n.a.	17.4	16.9	17.9	17.0	15.0	25.0	26.2	21.4	19.0	13.6	10.9	7.2	n.a.	n.a.
Costa Rica	n.a.	n.a.	n.a.	n.a.	n.a.	n.a.	6.2	4.6	4.5	4.9	5.9	8.8	9.4	9.0	n.a.	6.9	5.9	5.6	5.5	n.a.
Côte d'Ivoire	n.a.	n.a.	n.a.	n.a.	n.a.	n.a.	n.a.	n.a.	n.a.	n.a.	2.5	n.a.	n.a.	n.a.	n.a.	2.8	2.5	n.a.	n.a.	n.a.
Egypt	2.4	1.8	1.5	4.7	2.3	2.5	n.a.	3.1	3.6	4.6	5.2	5.4	5.7	6.6	6.0	n.a.	n.a.	n.a.	6.8	n.a.
Ghana	n.a.	n.a.	n.a.	n.a.	n.a.	n.a.	n.a.	n.a.	n.a.	n.a.	n.a.	n.a.	n.a.	n.a.	n.a.	n.a.	n.a.	n.a.	n.a.	n.a.
Kenya	n.a.	n.a.	n.a.	n.a.	n.a.	n.a.	n.a.	6.1	n.a.	n.a.	n.a.	n.a.	n.a.	n.a.	n.a.	n.a.	6.9	n.a.	n.a.	n.a.
Korea, Rep. of [a]	4.5	4.5	4.5	4.0	4.1	4.1	3.9	3.8	3.2	3.8	5.2	4.5	4.3	4.1	3.8	4.0	3.8	3.1	2.5	n.a.
Malaysia	7.6	n.a.	n.a.	n.a.	6.7	n.a.	n.a.	n.a.	6.3	5.7	5.7	5.0	4.7	5.5	6.3	7.6	8.5	8.2	n.a.	n.a.
Thailand	n.a.	n.a.	n.a.	n.a.	n.a.	0.4	0.8	0.8	0.7	0.9	0.9	0.9	3.6	1.9	2.3	3.7	3.5	5.8	n.a.	n.a.

n.a. = not available

a. Manufacturing only.

Sources: Argentina, Bolivia, Chile, Costa Rica, Kenya: country studies. Brazil: Riveros (1989). Côte d'Ivoire: 1980 census; Fields (1990). Egypt: population census. Korea: Bank of Korea, *Principal Economic Indicators.* Malaysia: Wong (1985) for the 1970s; Fifth Malaysia Plan 1986–90 for 1980; World Bank economic reports for 1981–89. Thailand: *Statistical Yearbook* (various years).

Table 4 Real Wages Indices, 1970–88
(index, 1980 = 100)

Country	1970	1971	1972	1973	1974	1975	1976	1977	1978	1979	1980	1981	1982	1983	1984	1985	1986	1987	1988
Argentina	108	112	105	115	129	124	80	74	77	86	100	91	80	97	106	87	82	72	n.a.
Bolivia	100	114	113	118	94	86	98	107	108	110	100	80	56**	42	36	55	34	42	n.a.
Brazil	79	n.a.	n.a.	n.a.	n.a.	84	85	89	94	95	100	109	122	113	105	113	122	106	n.a.
Chile	110	n.a.	n.a.	n.a.	n.a.	63	72	82	91	100	100	114	133	95	89	76	73	71	n.a.
Costa Rica[a]	n.a.	n.a.	n.a.	n.a.	n.a.	n.a.	80	96	97	105	100	85	63	77	n.a.	92	95	n.a.	n.a.
Costa Rica[b]	n.a.	n.a.	n.a.	n.a.	n.a.	n.a.	n.a.	n.a.	n.a.	n.a.	100	84	65	77	n.a.	93	97	n.a.	n.a.
*Côte d'Ivoire	n.a.	n.a.	n.a.	n.a.	n.a.	n.a.	n.a.	n.a.	n.a.	n.a.	100	n.a.	n.a.	n.a.	n.a.	115	n.a.	n.a.	n.a.
*Egypt[c]	n.a.	n.a.		89	92	73	79	92	89	105	100	103	104	108	118	120	103	91	n.a.
*Egypt[d]	n.a.	n.a.		93	96	86	88	109	100	103	100	105	108	104	108	101	92	84	n.a.
*Egypt[e]	n.a.	n.a.		125	109	104	105	104	103	103	100	108	109	98	96	89	75	69	n.a.
*Ghana	n.a.	n.a.	n.a.	n.a.	n.a.	n.a.	n.a.	n.a.	113	93	100	59	53	41	60	87	141	n.a.	n.a.
*Kenya[f]	n.a.	n.a.	n.a.	n.a.	88	86	89	87	90	91	100	90	81	79	80	78	79	82	84
*Kenya[g]	n.a.	n.a.	n.a.	n.a.	106	103	114	109	110	106	100	96	85	84	81	78	83	80	81
Korea, Rep. of	44	45	46	53	57	58	68	82	96	105	100	99	106	115	122	130	139	150	168
Malaysia	83	83	80	71	76	80	85	87	89	95	100	106	111	118	125	135	133	130	127

n.a. = not available
* Denotes data from employment and earnings surveys or household surveys.
** Denotes possible break in series.

a. Paid workers (employees).   c. Private sector.   e. Government.   g. Public sector.
b. All workers.   d. Public enterprises.   f. Private sector.

Sources: Argentina, Bolivia, Chile, Costa Rica, Egypt, Ghana, Kenya: country studies. Brazil: Riveros (1989). Côte d'Ivoire: Lavy and Newman (1989). Korea: Bank of Korea, *Principal Economic Indicators.* Malaysia: Department of Statistics, Industrial Surveys for 1968–74; Department of Statistics, Monthly Industrial Statistics for 1975–87.

discouraged worker effect is where the substitution effect of lower wages during recessions decreases household labor supply.) Three of the studies discuss the issue and suggest that the added worker effect predominated in Costa Rica during the crisis and the discouraged worker effect in Bolivia. In Argentina the authors argue that the discouraged worker effect prevailed in the 1970s and the added worker effect in the 1980s, although they do not explain the change. One complication in interpreting the data is that most countries have also observed a trend increase in female labor force participation rates (the Bolivia, Costa Rica, Kenya, Korea, and Malaysia studies all mention this). Thus, separating trends in female labor force participation over time from temporary fluctuations in response to economic crisis is not easy.

A final form of quantity adjustment involved a shift from formal to informal sector employment. As employees lost their jobs, one option in the absence of unemployment compensation was to become self-employed, and likewise output, and thus employment, often shifted from large formal sector firms to smaller informal sector ones. This is again a difficult topic on which to obtain data, and studies often define the informal sector differently. Tokman (1984) and others have studied the phenomenon extensively for Latin America. The Bolivia case study argues that informalization was an important method of labor market adjustment. In Argentina, although the authors state that the informal sector was less important than elsewhere in Latin America, nonwage employment grew faster than wage employment in nontradables in all three periods considered (the 1960s, the 1970s, and the 1980s), and in both manufacturing and agriculture nonwage employment grew faster in two of the three periods. In Brazil the main shift was into the unprotected employee sector (those without signed contracts) rather than into self employment.

Informalization has been less well documented in Africa. The Côte d'Ivoire study, however, does mention a shift between formal and informal establishments in manufacturing, and the authors of the Kenya paper argue that a similar employment shift occurred in Kenya, where employment in the informal sector grew 11 percent in 1988 when wage employment growth slowed. There is also similar evidence for Asia. In Malaysia the trend rise in employees as a proportion of the labor force was reversed during the short recession. In Korea the trend toward an increased employment share in large firms in manufacturing was arrested in the early 1980s, and the proportion of women who were regular employees, as opposed to temporary or casual, likewise reversed its upward trend.

Real wage behavior, perhaps more than unemployment rates, differentiates the country groups discussed earlier (note that the wage data available are for the formal sector except for the Latin countries). The Asian countries show a fairly steady advance in real wages, with brief interruptions during the recession (although the authors stress the importance of these real wage slowdowns in allowing productivity to stay ahead of real wage growth and ensuring declining unit costs). The severe adjustment countries show dramatic wage fluctuations, with wages at their lowest less than 50 percent of the peak, and with real wage declines far greater than the fall in GDP. Real wages in Ghana recovered by 1986, are still not back to peak levels in Chile, and are continuing to fall in Bolivia. The other countries are somewhat intermediate: in two of the three moderate adjustment countries (Brazil and Costa Rica) there are gains between the start and end of the time series, albeit less marked than for the Asian countries, and Kenya has a wage decline in the public sector, but private wages are closer to holding their own. The difference between Kenya and the other countries in this group is probably due to population pressure. Finally, the less successful adjustment countries show a less severe wage decline than the severe adjustment ones, perhaps explaining a little of the political opposition to such severe adjustments. However, one must be somewhat cautious in interpreting the real wage data, particularly in cases where it is not from household survey data, because of the employment composition issue. Earnings functions can be helpful in this regard.

How can we interpret the evidence discussed above, and what can we infer about labor market workings? As discussed earlier, there are three possible explanations as to why unemployment may persist during stabilization. The first is that the labor market is not working well because of real wage rigidity. The evidence presented by the case studies certainly does not favor the view that real wages were rigid, and therefore led to unemployment. Even for Chile, where unemployment was highest and persisted the longest, real wages fell dramatically. Real wages have also been flexible in Brazil and Argentina, despite wage indexation. Devereux (vol. 1, chapter 4) argues that the failure of disinflation plans in these countries is due more to inappropriate and noncredible fiscal policies. The effect of wage indexation is only to magnify and lengthen the inflation response. Some critics might still argue that real wages did not fall fast enough, but a good case for this remains to be made. If the inflexible real wage explanation is inappropriate because of the observed severe falls in real wages, this leaves the other two explanations: aggregate demand feedback from declining real wages and output market imperfections.

The wage level enters the system as a determinant of aggregate demand through its effect on the distribution of private income. The mechanism depends crucially on the assumption (generally valid empirically) that the propensity to save is markedly lower for wage earners than for recipients of profits. If the share of wages in total disposable income falls, for example, savings in the economy increase, and aggregate demand will fall unless there is an offsetting increase in investment or government spending. These ideas are implicit in the works of Keynes and Kalecki, and have recently been discussed in the context of developing countries' stabilization and adjustment problems by Taylor (1988) and others.

Taylor distinguishes between what he calls "exhilarationist" and "stagnationist" economic scenarios. In the former, output is constrained by bottlenecks related to a short supply of capital. Real wage cuts leading to a higher profit share will increase the supply of savings, and may translate into higher investment. In the stagnationist economic scenario, however, the binding constraint on output growth is the low level of consumer demand relative to capacity. A fall in the share of wages in these conditions leads to stagnation. It is possible for an economy to start from an exhilarationist position, but then slip into a stagnationist position as wage share falls steeply.

The existence of a dual labor market, with a distinctly lower wage level in one sector compared to the other, reinforces the conclusions drawn from the model with a homogeneous labor market. Consider the case of a recession with a fall in labor demand in the formal sector. Although the typical scenario as analyzed in the country studies is that a fall in wages occurs, sometimes fairly drastic, this is not always the case. In Malaysia the average earnings of workers in the formal sector actually increased because those most recently hired and at the lower spectrum of wages and skills were laid off first. In all cases, however, the workers displaced from the formal sector as well as those entering the labor force entered the informal sector in growing numbers. The share of total employment at the lower wage levels increased significantly. For the economy as a whole, therefore, average wages fell faster and to a greater extent than in the formal sector.

Does the stagnationist hypothesis still hold if we allow for the possibility of exports? In the traditional model of the small open economy (such as the one reviewed in vol. 1, chapter 3) it will not hold unless wages are rigid downward in both the tradable and the nontradable sectors. As demand contracts, with wage rigidity in the nontradable sector, unemployment will occur in this sector, but if wages are flexible in the tradable sector, costs will fall in tradables. However, the small open economy model assumes unlimited demand for tradables at the going product price, thus the unemployed labor will be absorbed in the more profitable tradable sector. Total demand will be restored to its initial level with a larger share of GDP accounted for by tradables. However, even if there are wage rigidities in both sectors, the profitability of the tradable sector needed to attract resources can still be achieved by a real devaluation that increases the ratio of the prices of tradables to the prices of nontradables (P_T/P_N). This is why in the textbooks devaluation is sometimes called an alternative to wage flexibility.

The Asian and Latin American country studies provide sharp contrasts as concerns the role of wages and devaluation in macro demand contraction. Korea, for example, depended on continuous nominal devaluation of its currency over a long period of time as well as maxi devaluations during periods of severe external shock. As an export-oriented economy, Korea had to increase its competitiveness by reducing its unit labor costs in dollar terms. Due to the rapid growth of labor productivity, the response to external shocks was to hold constant real wages rather than requiring a wage decline. The combination of a maxi devaluation and temporarily preventing wages from rising with productivity led to a very quick recovery of exports.

At the same time, since the slowdown in real wage growth was so short, there was no significant deflationary impact in the domestic market.

Another factor important in recovery was government policies to counter the increase in nonwage costs following devaluation. Because of its important role in the finance of large-scale industry, the government was to some extent able to offset the increase in the cost of borrowed foreign capital caused by devaluation by offering cheap, subsidized credit to businesses. An important feature of the Korean case of adjustment to the shocks was that exports increased rapidly in Korea despite the rise in wages.

The last point touches on a general point about the role of wage flexibility in adjustment. In Southeast Asian economies the share of wages in value added is typically one-third or a little more (according to Riveros 1989, it is closer to 40 percent in Latin America). Thus, changes in capital costs are often as important in determining competitiveness as changes in wage levels. The course of events leading up to the recession in Malaysia in the mid-1980s, and the subsequent adjustments triggering recovery, illustrate the point vividly. Unlike Korea, Malaysia is an oil exporter. In the early 1980s, government spending in Malaysia increased enormously, partly to bolster an attempt to prolong the boom associated with the oil boom. The resultant pressure on external competitiveness came from three sources: (a) wages increased, even after employment growth had slowed down; (b) interest rates increased sharply as demand for private capital funds competed with the public demand; and (c) the currency appreciated in real terms because the capital account was uncontrolled, and there was a massive inflow of capital to finance the budget deficit.

The loss of competitiveness created an external imbalance that could only be corrected through a sharp recession. Malaysia was fortunate, however, in that all the relevant factor markets showed remarkable flexibility. As wages fell from their early 1980s level, the interest rate fell to a level that was nearly a third of its peak, and there was a sharp depreciation of the currency. Clearly the "collapse" of all the factor markets was instrumental in making the recession short-lived. Of course, the improvement in the world economy was a factor triggering the recovery, but it was the gain in competitiveness fed by the downwardly flexible wages, interest rates, and exchange rates that allowed Malaysia to seize the opportunity in the second half of the 1980s.

The Latin American studies illustrate almost the opposite case in terms of the effects of real wages on demand, with Bolivia providing the clearest example. The fall in real wages in the 1980s was twice the size of the fall in real GDP. Even by the end of the decade, real wages and employment showed little sign of any recovery. The fall in the share of wages must have depressed the domestic market considerably. At the same time, despite the real value of the currency falling to less than a third of the 1985 level, there was no sign of export-led recovery. Evidently the market structure for favoring large shifts to export did not exist in Bolivia.

By contrast, another Latin American country, Costa Rica, hints at the existence of a basic structure of links to the world market, and also illustrates the advantages of an institutional mechanism that limits the direction of wage deflation. Real wages fell between 1980–82 as indexation tied to past inflation failed to protect workers as inflation accelerated. In mid-1982, when stabilization was instituted, real wages turned upward again as inflation decelerated. By 1986, real wages had regained their 1980 value. The short period to which the real wage decline was confined might have helped to stabilize the domestic aggregate demand. At the same time, the decline in the dollar price of exportables, helped by the fall in real wages and the devaluation of 1980, was instrumental in improving the export situation. Thus, two factors helped Costa Rica to stage a recovery in the post-1982 period. Market links were important in ensuring that the fall in the real value of the currency and in wage costs had the desirable impact on exports. More surprisingly, indexation was significant in engineering the initial fall in real wages and in limiting the period of wage stagnation.

Another instance of sharp deflation caused by a fall in the share of wages in GDP comes from the case of Chile during the drastic policies of stabilization pushed through by the military *junta* after the fall of the Allende regime. This case illustrates the importance of product markets in the process of adjustment. Although extreme, it is worth discussing because, as Ramos (1980, p. 468) points out: "other countries may simply be experiencing in slow motion (stagflation) what Chile experienced all at once (hyperstagflation)."

In October 1973, the *junta* freed prices that had been controlled under the previous socialist regimes, but unlike Germany after World War II, Chile did not have a monetary reform to put a cap on the freed inflationary prices. Inflation immediately accelerated to 90 percent during the month of October alone. Although prices moderated after October, they continued to increase at rates higher than 300 percent in 1974 and 1975, clearly overshooting by a good deal the expected equilibrium level.

On the labor front, the *junta's* policy was to separate wage readjustments from the freezing of prices to prevent a wage-price spiral. It postponed adjustment of wages by several months. When it did take place, it was consistent with a much lower rate of inflation. Thus, real wages dropped sharply, and by 1975 stood at nearly half their pre-Allende level. Astonishingly, the real wage decline was accompanied not only by high rates of inflation, but also by a rapidly increasing rate of unemployment, which climbed from 3 percent in the first half of 1973 to 10 percent in 1974 and 19 percent in the first half of 1976. The rise in unemployment was, as one would expect, associated with a sharp decline in industrial output, at least until the end of 1975 (the index of industrial output halved between end-1973 and end-1975).

What explains the coexistence of a high inflation rate, falling real wages, and declining output? The crux of the problem would seem to be the inflationary expectations and noncompetitive behavior in the product market. There was clearly no demand pressure because consumer demand fell very early with the fall in real wages, and demand contraction intensified as real wages fell and unemployment increased at a high rate. Nor was there any cost pressure, for "whereas the prices of imported inputs in the last quarter of 1973 rose to 30 times and wages rose 14 times their 1969 levels, product prices rose to 40 times their 1969 levels upon being freed in October 1973" (Ramos 1980, p. 472). Prices seem to have increased in anticipation of much higher demand and cost pressures than actually existed. "Producers seem to have set prices to balance supply and demand not as of the moment, but in three months' time so to speak" (Ramos 1980). The anticipated increase could be on the side of money demand, or in terms of unforeseen wage adjustments, devaluation, and a rise in input costs.

The continuation of inflationary price increases in the face of serious disequilibrium in the product market with producers unable to sell their products is a difficult proposition to explain in terms of textbook economics, and indeed came as a surprise to policymakers. A major factor in the continuation of the process was that price setters were not penalized soon enough for their erroneous expectations because of the massive increase in the share of profits that the fall in real wages entailed.

The inflationary expectation was finally broken when the currency was revalued in 1976, when the balance of payments situation reversed, showing a net surplus, and tariff reductions were undertaken for reasons connected with the economy's long-run development. The downward jolt these measures gave to the prices of both inputs and final goods seems to have fueled the recovery after 1976. Prices finally began growing less than the money supply, with output rising, unemployment falling, and real wages rising much more than total output.

Problems of Distributive Conflicts

The availability of enough evidence to suggest that wages have been flexible in many countries during the periods of adjustment does not imply that distributive conflicts have not been major issues in several countries. The country studies show that in Latin America, in particular, the conflict between maintaining or increasing labor's share of output and achieving external balance has been an important factor in the limited success of stabilization policies. Countries, of course, differ in the importance of distributive conflict in their economic history. Apart from differences in labor market institutions, the economy's structure seems to be critical in some cases.

One factor that seems to be important is whether or not food is an important tradable. The case of Argentina is a good example that shows how the different objectives could be in conflict when basic foods in the workers' consumption budget (cereals, meats, and so on) are tradable goods, and the government does not interfere significantly with the domestic prices of these commodities. In this case there is a close relationship between the exchange rate and the product wage in the economy's nontradable sector. Currency devaluations lead to increases in the domestic price of food, which in turn leads to upward pressure on money wages. Such an increase will not affect product wages in the tradable sector, since product prices of traded goods would also have increased in the domestic market, but other things being equal, the product wage in the nontradable sector will increase. In this case a conflict of interests arises between the producers of nontradables and the workers employed in this sector.

This exchange rate wage tradeoff, taken together with the nontradable sector's more powerful political position because of its urban location, has given rise to the wage cycle documented in the country study. When external markets for Argentina's food exports are strong, the currency tends to slide into overvaluation, which helps increase real wages without hurting profitability in the urban nontradable sector and fiscal balance in the public urban nontradable sector. However, when the external terms of trade weaken, devaluation is imperative to ease the problem of external imbalance, and various forces are set in motion that depress real wages to protect profitability. In Argentina, as in much of Latin America, bursts of inflation have often been the mechanism for reducing real wages.

Note that not all countries have a large proportion of their wage goods or food as tradables as Argentina does. In particular, in many Asian economies (including the two in our sample, Korea and Malaysia) rice, although an internationally traded good, is more like a nontradable because of government price policies. In these countries, the government plays a dual role in the rice market. On the one hand, it buys rice from the farmers at a high procurement price to help support the level of earnings in this sector. On the other hand, it distributes the rice through its retail outlets at a subsidized price for the benefit of, for the most part, urban consumers. The financial deficit caused by the difference between the buying and selling price of rice is covered by the central government's overall budget. Thus, although the government imports rice to supplement the amount procured from local farmers, the domestic price of rice is insulated from the border price. This important wage good is, in effect, a nontradable. The problem analyzed above, which stems from an inverse relationship between the external value of the currency and the price of the wage good, does not exist for such economies (although the fiscal issue does).

The supply of capital may also lead to a tradeoff between wages and the exchange rate. Let us assume that the growth of output is constrained by the supply of capital (savings) rather than by demand (in other words, the economic scenario is an exhilarationist one). The share of wages in value added has a direct effect on total savings, and hence on the growth rate of output. The exchange rate also affects output growth from two angles. First, the higher the value of the currency, the greater the trade deficit that, if it can be sustained, increases foreign savings (borrowing) in the economy. Second, a higher value of the currency reduces the cost of intermediate inputs, and effectively increases the marginal impact of savings on output growth.

An exchange rate/wage tradeoff exists in the sense that a given rate of savings (and growth rate) could be achieved with different pairs of values of the exchange rate and the wage share; the higher the latter, the higher must the degree of overvaluation be. Government policy affects both the exchange rate and the wage share through its determination of the rate of growth of the money supply, and hence the rate of inflation. With indexation rules determining both exchange rate and wage adjustments, lags in the system mean that a higher rate of inflation achieves both a higher rate of overvaluation and a lower share of wages. Thus, an equilibrium relationship exists that connects the rate of inflation, the value of the exchange rate, the wage share, and the real growth rate of the economy.

The case of Brazil illustrates the key problems and constraints in this system. During 1967–83, Brazil followed a policy of stepping up the growth rate by expanding the money supply. This led to a rise in the rate of inflation and a fall in the share of wages. The associated increase in the real exchange rate and the fall in the share of wages both increased real output growth by increasing foreign and domestic savings and reducing the domestic cost of imported inputs. The mechanism for bringing about this change worked as long as changes in the values of the relevant variables were sustainable. The feasibility of a fall in the share of wages depended on the existence of an authoritarian political system. Similarly, the appreciation of the currency meant an increase in the trade deficit that could only be financed by foreign borrowing. The persistent increase in foreign debt was one of the costs of this strategy of boosting the real rate of growth.

The first oil shock of the mid-1970s meant, in effect, a change in the parameters of the Brazilian production function, so that at the old values of the variables, output growth was depressed. At the same time the import bill increased sharply. The government's response to this situation was to undertake a program of import substitution in capital and intermediate goods, financed by stepped up foreign borrowing. The second oil shock and the increase in interest rates finally made this policy unsustainable. The debt burden had reached a level when further foreign borrowing was no longer an option to maintain an overvalued currency. A new element in the situation was the change in the political system. It was no longer easy to reduce the share of wages with a higher rate of inflation. The country study discusses the distributional conflicts in more detail.

Thus, two barriers prevented achievement of a higher real savings rate to counteract the effect of the deterioration of the external terms of trade. The government could not continue to overvalue the currency nor to depress wages. Nor could these be changed with a higher rate of inflation in such a way that a new equilibrium set of values of the relevant variables could be achieved. This was at the heart of the failure of stabilization efforts in the 1980s. One way out would have been if total factor productivity growth could have been increased to a sufficient degree, but evidently the Brazilian economy was unable to achieve this goal. On the contrary, the country study indicates that labor productivity actually fell as labor hoarding in the formal tradable sector increased significantly in response to the deteriorating employment situation. The contrast with Korea's experience is striking. The country study documents the enormous importance of total factor productivity growth in the Korean economy's successful adjustment to the oil price shocks. Because of the increase in total factor productivity, the required decline in the share of wages could be achieved with a negligible decrease in the absolute level of real wages, and the increase in the cost of imported inputs due to devaluation could be largely offset.

Sectoral Employment Shifts and Relative Wages

Sectoral employment shifts are a key part of structural adjustment, and Edwards and Edwards (vol. 1, chapter 2) discuss these in a basic two-sector two-factor dependent economy model in the presence of labor market distortions. They examine four different scenarios plus the basic competitive case. In the basic model, standard results apply and labor would tend to benefit from trade liberalization, which the authors define as tariff cuts: the effects of devaluation, which usually accompanies adjustment, are not considered. Even if economywide wage rigidity is allowed for, the authors argue that trade liberalization will result in unemployment in the short run where capital is immobile. However, in the longer run, if importables are the less labor-intensive sector, starting from an initial condition of unemployment, trade liberalization will increase total employment in the economy.

The authors then take the case where only the importable sector is covered by a minimum wage. In the short run there will be lower employment in importables and higher employment in exportables, but employment in nontradables and total employment is ambiguous. They conclude that: "In the presence of labor market distortions, trade liberalization policies usually considered to be beneficial may generate nontrivial (short run) unemployment problems." This conclusion holds also in the third variant considered, that of capital account liberalization.

The fourth and final case considered is where wage distortions in importables are related to the degree of tariff protection. In the short run, trade liberalization increases unemployment and depresses wages in the economy's other sectors. Although some of this would disappear in the long run, the scenario highlights possible political economy conflicts. Labor, "the factor of production that is supposed to gain from freer trade, is negatively affected in the short run, and the long run gains are hard to perceive when compared to the initially distorted situation of the economy."

The country studies provide information on wages and employment by various sectoral groupings: economic sectors (agriculture, manufacturing, construction, and so on), formal/informal, public/private, tradable/nontradable, and occasionally even finer categories such as importable/exportable/nontradable. They also provide some information on skill groups. How formal/informal or skilled/unskilled categorizations correspond to the tradable/nontradable distinction that is of key interest is not always clearly specified in the country studies, and varies between countries (the Brazil study provides the most complete breakdown). One important problem in many of the studies is that the agriculture sector is an important component of tradables, but no agricultural wage data over time exist for the Latin American countries, and neither agricultural wage nor employment data over time exist for the African countries.

Let us consider sectoral employment first, and then sectoral relative wages. Table 5 provides information on employment shifts by sector of GDP for 8 of the 12 countries in the study (the ILO Yearbook does not have data for the other four countries). The ILO Yearbook reports sectoral employment data by 10 sectoral groups, which are here further grouped into primary, manufacturing, utilities and construction, and tertiary. This classification is used on the assumption that, roughly speaking, primary and manufactured goods are tradable, whereas the output of the construction, utilities, and tertiary sectors are not. Obviously this grouping is rather crude, and the Costa Rica and Argentina studies provide more detailed information on the tradable/nontradable shift, even to the extent of comparing employment in the traditional and nontraditional export sectors (Costa Rica).

The debt crisis years had clear effects on structural transformation in the countries studied, in that the usual changes accompanying development either halted or reversed in all cases. In Brazil, Costa Rica, Korea, Malaysia, and Thailand (the Asian and partial adjustment countries), the manufacturing share declined somewhat during stabilization, but then resumed growth. The recovery is strongest in Korea. The data series for Malaysia and Thailand both end before recovery sets in strongly. In Chile and Bolivia, declines in the manufacturing share were more striking. These were reversed under structural adjustment in Chile, but not as yet in Bolivia. The data series for Egypt stops before economic problems intensified, but a decline in the share of manufacturing employment is already evident.

The ILO Yearbook does not contain data on sectoral employment trends for Sub-Saharan Africa, but the country studies contain some information. The Kenya country study argues that urban employment figures suggest that the manufacturing share stagnated after 1978. Data for the formal sector for the Côte d'Ivoire suggest a large decrease in modern manufacturing employment despite subsidies.

The debt crisis slowed the transition out of agriculture for most countries, and for Bolivia, Côte d'Ivoire, and Ghana shifts back into agriculture are evident. The ILO data for Bolivia show that although the primary share overall declined, the agriculture share increased in the worst years (1982–83) and stagnated thereafter. In the Côte d'Ivoire a shift back into agriculture occurred (based on labor force transition behavior). In Ghana, the capital city, Accra, changed from being the destination of 46.5 percent of migrants prior to 1970 to being the source of 60.0 percent of recent migrants in 1982–87. Even in the higher-income countries, agriculture played an important role in absorbing labor market entrants: one-third of new jobs in Malaysia during the 1986–87 recession were in agriculture, and agricultural employment grew as fast as total employment in Chile in the successful adjustment period after 1985.

The Argentina and Costa Rica studies both examine employment shifts between the tradable and nontradable sectors. Argentina has seen a secular trend toward increased employment in nontradables, and Costa Rica has seen a similar trend out of exportables. As Argentina did not have a sustained adjustment program, this trend continued in the 1980s, but in Costa Rica adjustment arrested, but did not reverse, the trend. However, the study authors find some cause for optimism in the growth of the small, nontraditional export sector.

A useful exercise is to examine sectoral wage data in conjunction with sectoral employment figures. Simple theory suggests that the effect of structural adjustment policies should lead to a relative increase in wages in tradables to encourage labor movement (unless markets are so frictionless that the reallocation does not require price signals). However, employment shifts may also cause changes in

Table 5 Employment by Sector, 1971–89

(percentage of total employment)

Country/sector	1971	1972	1973	1974	1975	1976	1977	1978	1979	1980	1981	1982	1983	1984	1985	1986	1987	1988	1989
Bolivia																			
Primary	53.7	53.1	52.6	52.2	51.6	50.9	50.5	50.2	49.4	50.9	51.0	50.9	52.1	51.9	51.5	50.0	49.9	50.0	50.0
Manufacturing	8.8	8.8	8.9	9.0	9.0	9.1	9.2	9.3	9.4	10.3	10.0	9.1	8.9	8.8	8.7	7.0	7.1	7.1	7.1
Utilities and construction	4.3	4.7	5.0	5.5	5.9	6.4	6.4	6.5	6.5	5.9	5.1	3.7	3.7	3.3	3.2	3.1	3.2	3.2	3.2
Tertiary	33.2	33.4	33.5	33.3	33.4	33.6	34.2	34.1	34.7	32.9	33.9	36.3	35.2	36.0	36.5	39.9	39.8	39.8	39.8
Brazil																			
Primary[a]	n.a.	n.a.	n.a.	n.a.	n.a.	n.a.	n.a.	n.a.	n.a.	n.a.	29.3	29.5	27.1	29.8	28.5	25.8	24.6	n.a.	n.a.
Manufacturing[b]	n.a.	n.a.	n.a.	n.a.	n.a.	n.a.	n.a.	n.a.	n.a.	n.a.	24.7	23.4	14.0	14.2	14.7	16.2	15.7	n.a.	n.a.
Utilities and construction	n.a.	n.a.	n.a.	n.a.	n.a.	n.a.	n.a.	n.a.	n.a.	n.a.	n.a.	n.a.	11.4	7.5	7.4	8.0	8.1	n.a.	n.a.
Tertiary	n.a.	n.a.	n.a.	n.a.	n.a.	n.a.	n.a.	n.a.	n.a.	n.a.	46.1	47.1	47.6	48.4	49.3	50.0	51.6	n.a.	n.a.
Chile																			
Primary	n.a.	n.a.	n.a.	n.a.	24.6	20.6	21.1	20.2	19.3	18.5	17.5*	18.1	17.7	18.0*	22.5	22.8	22.9	22.3	21.7
Manufacturing	n.a.	n.a.	n.a.	n.a.	16.8	16.8	16.7	16.3	16.5	16.1	15.5	12.7	12.6	13.8*	13.3	13.6	15.1	15.7	16.9
Utilities and construction	n.a.	n.a.	n.a.	n.a.	5.3	4.8	4.7	4.8	5.1	5.4	6.0*	3.7	3.6	4.4*	4.6	5.4	5.8	7.1	7.3
Tertiary	n.a.	n.a.	n.a.	n.a.	52.6	57.4	57.2	58.5	58.9	59.8	60.7*	65.4	66.0	63.7*	59.6	58.2	56.0	54.8	54.1
Costa Rica																			
Primary	n.a.	n.a.	38.2	n.a.	n.a.	34.8	33.0	30.4	28.9	27.4	27.6	30.0	28.2	30.0[d]	27.3	26.9*	28.1	28.1	26.2
Manufacturing	n.a.	n.a.	12.9	n.a.	n.a.	14.6	15.8	15.2	16.5	16.3	15.4	15.2	16.6	15.2[d]	15.9	17.1*	17.5	16.7	18.8
Utilities and construction	n.a.	n.a.	6.9	n.a.	n.a.	6.5	6.4	7.4	8.2	7.8	6.7	5.7	5.1	4.9[d]	5.1	5.8*	5.9	5.9	6.2
Tertiary[c]	n.a.	n.a.	42.0	n.a.	n.a.	44.0	44.8	47.0	47.7	48.5	50.3	49.1	50.1	49.9[d]	51.7	50.2*	48.5	49.3	48.8
Egypt																			
Primary	54.2	53.8	51.5	47.6	49.1	n.a.	45.8	42.5	42.1	42.6	40.5	39.3	41.3	40.9	n.a.	n.a.	n.a.	n.a.	n.a.
Manufacturing	12.5	12.8	14.1	15.3	14.3	n.a.	14.7	15.1	16.0	14.7	15.9	15.3	14.7	13.9	n.a.	n.a.	n.a.	n.a.	n.a.
Utilities and construction	2.7	2.8	3.3	3.1	3.2	n.a.	4.2	4.8	5.4	5.2	5.9	6.3	6.2	5.9	n.a.	n.a.	n.a.	n.a.	n.a.
Tertiary	30.6	30.6	31.0	33.5	33.3	n.a.	35.3	37.6	36.5	37.5	37.8	39.1	37.8	39.3	n.a.	n.a.	n.a.	n.a.	n.a.

Korea																			
Primary	49.4	51.1	50.4	48.6	46.4	45.1	42.6	39.2	36.6	34.9	35.1	32.8	30.5	28.1	26.0	24.8	23.0	21.5	20.1
Manufacturing	13.3	13.7	15.9	17.4	18.6	21.3	21.6	22.4	22.9	21.7	20.4	21.1	22.5	23.2	23.4	24.7	27.0	27.7	27.6
Utilities and construction	3.7	4.1	3.6	4.2	4.6	4.5	5.1	6.3	6.5	6.4	6.5	6.0	6.0	6.5	6.4	6.0	5.9	6.4	6.8
Tertiary[c]	33.7	31.0	30.0	29.8	30.4	29.0	30.7	32.1	34.1	37.0	38.0	40.1	41.1	42.2	44.3	44.5	44.1	44.5	45.5
Malaysia																			
Primary	n.a.	n.a.	n.a.	n.a.	n.a.	n.a.	n.a.	n.a.	n.a.	38.2	36.8	32.1	32.9	31.3	31.1	31.3	31.4	n.a.	n.a.
Manufacturing	n.a.	n.a.	n.a.	n.a.	n.a.	n.a.	n.a.	n.a.	n.a.	16.1	16.1	15.5	17.0	15.4	15.0	15.2	15.5	n.a.	n.a.
Utilities and construction	n.a.	n.a.	n.a.	n.a.	n.a.	n.a.	n.a.	n.a.	n.a.	7.1	8.3	7.9	8.9	8.9	8.0	7.0	6.2	n.a.	n.a.
Tertiary	n.a.	n.a.	n.a.	n.a.	n.a.	n.a.	n.a.	n.a.	n.a.	38.7	38.8	44.4	45.2	45.0	45.5	46.5	46.8	n.a.	n.a.
Thailand[d]																			
Primary	79.3	72.9	72.6	65.7	73.1	75.9	73.7	73.8	n.a.	70.9	64.5	61.9*	63.4	64.9	63.9	63.9	n.a.	n.a.	n.a.
Manufacturing	4.0	7.7	7.0	9.9	7.5	6.2	6.5	6.8	n.a.	7.9	9.2	10.2*	9.6	9.2	9.4	9.1	n.a.	n.a.	n.a.
Utilities and construction	1.2	1.7	1.8	2.0	1.4	1.5	1.9	1.7	n.a.	2.2	3.3	3.2*	3.2	3.3	3.2	3.1	n.a.	n.a.	n.a.
Tertiary[c]	15.5	17.7	18.5	22.4	18.0	16.3	17.9	17.7	n.a.	18.9	22.9	24.7*	23.8	22.6	23.5	23.8	n.a.	n.a.	n.a.

n.a. = not available

* Change in sample or methodology. See ILO (1989).

a. Excludes mining.

b. Includes mining.

c. Includes utilities.

d. November not July (usual).

Note: For Thailand, repair and installation services are included in manufacturing, sanitary services are included in manufacturing, unpaid family workers working less than 20 hours were excluded. The primary sector throughout includes agriculture and mining, the tertiary sector includes commerce, transport, banks, services, and other. Figures may not sum exactly to 100 percent due to rounding.

Source: ILO (various years), author's calculations.

relative wages. In practice, structural adjustment has been associated with labor shedding from government and from formal sector activities (either due to reduced tariff protection or the removal of job security legislation). As workers cannot remain unemployed for long in developing countries due to the lack of unemployment benefits, labor has tended to move to sectors with flexible entry, frequently the informal sector or agriculture. The crowding of labor in these sectors may have also depressed relative wages in the short run. Thus, relative wages in nontradable sectors with easy entry (for example, commerce, services) may have been depressed both directly due to exchange rate changes and indirectly due to labor crowding, while wages in tradable sectors with easy entry (for example, agriculture) could go in either direction in the short run due to opposing effects. Furthermore, changes in labor force composition within sectors can obscure trends. Sectors losing labor may experience increases in aggregate wages due to the loss of workers with the lowest levels of human capital and seniority. The latter effect can be dealt with by the use of earnings functions as discussed later.

All the studies (except Côte d'Ivoire and Thailand) provide some information on the changes in relative wages, whether between economic sectors, formal/informal sector, tradable/nontradable, or skill categories. Table 6 summarizes the results by broad GDP sectoral categories for seven countries, and table 7 shows the results by tradables/nontradables for two countries and for the public/private sectors for five countries. The data in table 6 are for agriculture, manufacturing, construction, and service sector wages, where available. As construction is the largest component of the group utilities plus construction, and services are similarly the largest component of the tertiary group, the sectoral wage data in table 6 correspond reasonably well to the sectoral employment data of table 5. In general, relative wage changes did support structural adjustment objectives, although this is not necessarily true for each country and every sector.

In Ghana relative wages increased in agriculture and mining, sectors featuring heavily in the Economic Recovery Program (see table 6 and the Ghana study). In Egypt relative wages increased in agriculture (see table 6 and the Egypt study) largely because other

Table 6 Real Wage Indices by GNP Sectoral Classification, 1970–89
(index, 1980 = 100)

Country/sector	1970	1971	1972	1973	1974	1975	1976	1977	1978	1979	1980	1981	1982	1983	1984	1985	1986	1987	1988	1989
Bolivia																				
Manufacturing	98	111	112	121	97	96	112	109	109	112	100	*	81[a]	114[a]	136[a]	52[a]	59[a]	n.a.	n.a.	n.a.
Construction	83	98	96	90	80	74	90	95	95	108	100	*	85[a]	47[a]	93[a]	52[a]	74[a]	n.a.	n.a.	n.a.
Services	125	128	125	130	109	88	95	115	111	105	100	*	63[a]	57[a]	104[a]	46[a]	72[a]	n.a.	n.a.	n.a.
Chile																				
Manufacturing	114	135	93	50	54	72	80	85	102	108	100	132	147	112	101	85	79	81	86	n.a.
Total	112	118	104	58	56	63	72	81	91	100	100	114	133	95	89	76	73	71	72	n.a.
Egypt[b]																				
Agriculture	n.a.	n.a.	n.a.	48	53	63	75	84	87	97	100	115	129	139	157	158	140	116	n.a.	n.a.
Manufacturing[c]	n.a.	n.a.	n.a.	74	82	79	85	100	99	100	100	107	113	118	132	124	110	99	n.a.	n.a.
Construction	n.a.	n.a.	n.a.	64	81	95	104	110	108	112	100	97	93	85	85	90	85	74	n.a.	n.a.
Services[c]	n.a.	n.a.	n.a.	80	80	77	82	85	112	107	100	101	101	99	104	126	101	86	n.a.	n.a.
Ghana																				
Manufacturing	n.a.	n.a.	n.a.	n.a.	n.a.	n.a.	n.a.	n.a.	121	85	100	71	64	46	85	92	153	n.a.	n.a.	n.a.
Construction	n.a.	n.a.	n.a.	n.a.	n.a.	n.a.	n.a.	n.a.	115	91	100	65	54	61	67	188	175	n.a.	n.a.	n.a.
Services	n.a.	n.a.	n.a.	n.a.	n.a.	n.a.	n.a.	n.a.	116	92	100	57	49	36	55	70	131	n.a.	n.a.	n.a.
Kenya[b]																				
Manufacturing	n.a.	n.a.	n.a.	n.a.	119	107	106	103	103	97	100	90	852	85	83	81	81	84	87	84
Construction	n.a.	n.a.	n.a.	n.a.	93	93	95	92	97	90	100	92	69	69	68	66	64	71	66	67
Services	n.a.	n.a.	n.a.	n.a.	99	88	96	90	87	93	100	90	79	79	84	83	86	91	88	90
Korea																				
Agriculture	50	61	64	68	73	76	81	89	93	99	100	107	114	120	138	146	n.a.	n.a.	n.a.	n.a.
Manufacturing	45	47	49	53	57	58	68	82	96	105	100	99	106	115	121	130	n.a.	n.a.	n.a.	n.a.
Rubber	30	77	76	82	86	71	86	91	93	97	100	92	93	92	92	91	95	99	n.a.	n.a.
Oil palm	64	61	63	66	73	73	76	80	88	96	100	107	103	101	106	110	111	108	n.a.	n.a.
Manufacturing	83	83	80	71	76	78	84	88	89	96	100	106	111	119	125	135	133	129	n.a.	n.a.
Construction	86	87	89	92	82	90	94	96	97	100	n.a.	112	122	126	126	128	129	124	n.a.	n.a.

n.a. = not available
* Break in series
a. March 1982 = 100.
b. Private sector only (separate series for public sector available).
c. Enterprises of 10 and more workers.
Note: Definitions of sectors may not be identical across countries. Data for Bolivia and Chile are household surveys, the rest are employment and earnings surveys.
Source: Country studies.

Table 7 Real Wage Indices by Tradable/Nontradable and Public/Private Sectors, 1970–89

Country/sector	1970	1971	1972	1973	1974	1975	1976	1977	1978	1979	1980	1981	1982	1983	1984	1985	1986	1987	1988	1989
Tradable and nontradable (ratio of average wages)																				
Argentina																				
Tradables/nontradables	0.89	0.91	0.91	0.88	0.93	0.92	0.93	0.94	0.91	0.93	0.89	0.91	0.91	0.95	0.96	0.97	0.96	n.a.	n.a.	n.a.
Potentially traded/nontradables	1.04	1.04	1.03	1.00	1.05	1.02	1.04	1.04	1.01	1.04	0.99	1.03	1.03	1.05	1.10	1.10	1.12	n.a.	n.a.	n.a.
Costa Rica*																				
Export/nontradables	n.a.	n.a.	n.a.	n.a.	n.a.	n.a.	0.92	0.93	0.87	0.68	0.83	0.83	0.91	0.97	n.a.	0.90	n.a.	0.75	0.78	n.a.
Imports/nontradables	n.a.	n.a.	n.a.	n.a.	n.a.	n.a.	0.98	1.01	1.09	1.05	0.96	1.10	0.98	1.05	n.a.	1.03	n.a.	0.96	1.00	n.a.
Public/nontradables	n.a.	n.a.	n.a.	n.a.	n.a.	n.a.	1.20	1.34	1.19	1.15	1.03	1.13	1.15	1.18	n.a.	1.08	n.a.	1.03	1.01	n.a.
Public and private (index, 1980 = 100)																				
Brazil																				
Private**	n.a.	n.a.	n.a.	n.a.	n.a.	n.a.	n.a.	n.a.	n.a.	n.a.	100	107	114	106	99	105	117	108	95	n.a.
Public	n.a.	n.a.	n.a.	n.a.	n.a.	n.a.	n.a.	n.a.	n.a.	n.a.	100	97	103	86	78	99	116	n.a.	n.a.	n.a.
Egypt																				
Private	n.a.	n.a.	n.a.	89	92	73	79	92	89	104	100	103	104	108	118	120	103	91	n.a.	n.a.
Public	n.a.	n.a.	n.a.	125	109	104	105	109	104	103	100	108	109	98	96	89	75	69	n.a.	n.a.
Public entities	n.a.	n.a.	n.a.	93	96	86	88	95	100	103	100	105	108	103	108	101	92	84	n.a.	n.a.
Ghana																				
Private	n.a.	n.a.	n.a.	n.a.	n.a.	n.a.	n.a.	n.a.	116	95	100	53	56	38	69	89	115	n.a.	n.a.	n.a.
Public	n.a.	n.a.	n.a.	n.a.	n.a.	n.a.	n.a.	n.a.	113	92	100	61	52	41	58	86	147	n.a.	n.a.	n.a.
Kenya																				
Private	n.a.	n.a.	n.a.	n.a.	88	86	89	87	90	90	100	90	81	79	80	78	79	82	84	85
Public	n.a.	n.a.	n.a.	n.a.	106	103	114	109	110	106	100	96	85	84	81	78	83	80	81	81
Costa Rica*																				
Private	n.a.	n.a.	n.a.	n.a.	n.a.	n.a.	n.a.	n.a.	n.a.	n.a.	100	82	63	79	n.a.	96	n.a.	108	105	n.a.
Public	n.a.	n.a.	n.a.	n.a.	n.a.	n.a.	n.a.	n.a.	n.a.	n.a.	100	94	71	91	101	101	n.a.	115	106	n.a.

n.a. = not available
* Adjusted for human capital
** São Paulo
Source: Country studies.

sectors were unable to adjust employment. In Bolivia manufacturing wages did relatively badly, which is consistent with falling employment (table 5). In Chile manufacturing wages increased relative to average wages (table 6), again consistent with an increasing share of employment. In Malaysia manufacturing and construction wages tended to increase during the recession. The Argentina study found that relative wages had tended to increase in nontradables during 1940–62 (vol. 2, chapter 1), but that the failed structural adjustment attempts since then had at least managed to arrest the trend. In Costa Rica relative wages in importables and nontradables fell during the 1980–82 recession, but recovered faster during the ensuing adjustment period, thus maintaining their relative position overall during the period (table 7).

Government wages (table 7) seem to have fallen universally during adjustment due to pressures on government expenditures (although some country study authors suggest that the trends were different in the central government and in the parastatals). This is documented in the Brazil, Costa Rica, Egypt, Ghana, and Kenya studies. The Bolivia study also provides evidence on falling relative wages in government, and the Malaysia study states that government wages rose less rapidly than in other sectors. The government sector generally consists of nontradables. Thus changes in sectoral wages seem to have generally supported structural adjustment aims, and also corroborate the trends in employment.

Six of the country studies also examine trends in the formal/informal wage differential. Here wage trends are likely to reflect not only goods prices, but also the effects of crowding discussed earlier. The country studies suggest that the patterns also depend on institutions in place in individual countries. For example, the formal sector is generally better able to protect itself during anticipated inflation, provided that institutional mechanisms provide full compensation for inflation. The informal sector, however, is less tightly bound by wage freezes, and in periods of unanticipated inflation informal wages are more closely tied to the goods market. In countries where the informal sector thrives because of distortions in the formal economy, Ghana, for example, structural adjustment may remove rents, and therefore benefit the formal sector.

Crowding seems to have been important in the early 1980s recession in Brazil, Chile, and Costa Rica, when the informal sector did relatively worse. In Korea also the formal/informal earnings gap widened during recessions, probably because of a composition effect (the formal sector shed the lower paid workers). However, in the Bolivian hyperinflation and during the Brazilian heterodox stabilization under the Cruzado Plan, where a price freeze was combined with strong demand, informal sector earnings improved relative to formal sector earnings. The Malaysian evidence is somewhat mixed, as men's and women's wages performed oppositely. The wages of self-employed men rose faster than employee wages during the whole period (partly explained by the increase in education of the self-employed). Employed women fared better during the boom, but then their wages fell relative to those of the self-employed during the recession (the Malaysian results are from earnings functions, not aggregate wages, unlike the results for the other countries). The author of the Malaysia study suggests that this indicates the existence of pockets of women employed in the informal sector that did not participate in the boom affecting the rest of the economy.

Finally, a couple of studies mention skill differentials. These narrowed during inflation and the first structural adjustment period in Chile (1970–76) and never recovered. In Egypt white collar/blue collar differentials narrowed throughout the oil boom and continued to narrow through the recession, perhaps due to slower growth in the public sector.

Some further information on earnings can be obtained from analyzing earnings functions (table 8). Altogether six of the case studies present earnings functions, of which four have separate functions for years before and after the onset of structural adjustment (Bolivia, Costa Rica, Kenya, and Malaysia). Two other African country studies present earnings functions for a single year (Côte d'Ivoire and Ghana), although the Ghana study divides the sample by length of job tenure, which is an ingenious way to get some information on changes in the labor market. Thus, in five cases (that is, all but the Côte d'Ivoire), one can get additional information on changes in sectoral, male/female, and formal/informal differentials purged of the effect of changes in human capital characteristics within sectors. Such a correction is important during a period of large structural change (see, for example, Lavy and Newman's 1989 work on the Côte d'Ivoire), or when participation rates change greatly.

The two Latin American countries exhibit changes in the earnings functions, both rather similar. The coefficient of determination (R^2) falls in both cases, and the size of the coefficients of characteristics associated with the formal sector declines, particularly in Bolivia (namely, the coefficients on education and experience, and for Bolivia being male, being married, and working in the formal sector). One possible explanation is that labor market institutions, and hence segmentation, were perhaps strongest in Latin America, and have weakened somewhat during adjustment (this was an explicit aim of Bolivia's adjustment program).

Earnings functions for the other countries also show changes consistent with adjustment: in Ghana the returns to urban location, working in the service sector, and being a union member declines, and the mining coefficient increases. Kenya is an exception. The authors argue that Kenyan labor markets did not adjust, and the coefficients on formal sector characteristics (age, being male, working in the formal sector, and working in Nairobi) increase.

For Ghana, earnings functions suggested a relatively well-working labor market, which complemented the findings from the few trend data available. Men's and women's hourly earnings were not too dissimilar (although total earnings differed), first and second jobs had similar hourly earnings (except in agriculture), and there was a premium for seasonal labor.

For the Côte d'Ivoire data were available for two consecutive years, including some repeated data on the same individuals. Participation and employment transition equations were estimated rather than earnings functions. The panel data showed that labor market transitions generally were toward sectors favored by adjustment, particularly agriculture, and that within manufacturing there was a shift toward the informal sector. As regards the probability of leaving employment, this was higher for women, lower for the services, higher for construction, and lower for the more educated. Likewise higher levels of education had a positive effect on the probability of entering

Table 8 Changes in Earnings Functions Over Time: Coefficients for Selected Independent Variables, Selected Years

Country	Year	Employment characteristic	Independent variable					R^2
			Schooling	Experience	Experience^2	Women (dummy)	Other variables included	
Bolivia	1981		.122	.053	-.000640	-.327	unmarried, informal,	.478
	1988		.0951	.0322	-.000308	-.234	3 cities	.253
Côte d'Ivoire	1985		.207	.053	-.082	-.002	nationality, years technical educational	.585
Costa Rica	1980	paid workers	.1348	.0505	-.00063	.3318	n.a.	.472
		all workers	.1325	.0464	-.00055	-.3217	n.a.	.402
	1988	paid workers	.123	.03911	-.00045	-.1945	n.a.	.356
		all workers	.113	.03911	-.00045	-.1945	n.a.	.251
Ghana	1987–88	tenure > 5	.110[a]	.011	-.0001	-.268	region, sector, formal,	.278
		tenure < 5	.085[a]	.027	-.0003	.272	urban, others	.281
Kenya[b]	1977–78		.0073 (.0033S^2)	.0759^c	-.0008^c	-.1188	occupation, city,	.413
	1986		-.0222 (.0057S^2)	.0784^c	-.0008^c	-.1587	age, education	.537
Malaysia[c]	1970	Malay men	.142	.093	-.0012	n.a.	n.a.	.451
		Malay women	.147	.071	-.0011	n.a.	n.a.	.421
		Chinese men	.139	.110	-.001	n.a.	n.a.	.521
		Chinese women	.133	.680	-.0007	n.a.	n.a.	.437
	1987	Malay men	.171	.111	-.0014	n.a.	n.a.	.439
		Malay women	.196	.110	-.0016	n.a.	n.a.	.421
		Chinese men	.153	.098	-.0012	n.a.	n.a.	.437
		Chinese women	.152	.076	-.0009	n.a.	n.a.	.326

n.a. = not available
a. Secondary school dummy.
b. Urban only.
c. Age.
Sources: Country studies, except Côte d'Ivoire source is van der Gaag and Vijverberg (1989).

employment, in contrast to the results for Asia and Latin America, where structural adjustment often adversely affected earnings and unemployment for the educated. Unemployment could be relatively persistent: of those seeking employment in 1985, 81 percent were still unemployed in 1986, although 42 percent of the original group had stopped looking. Finally, the study had some interesting results on the effects of crop price indexes on work behavior in rural areas. Increases in these indexes had a positive effect on work supply both for those who were working and in school in the first of the two survey years, but a negative effect on work supply for those in full-time education in the first year. In other words, crop price increases could increase effort, but not at the expense of interrupting human capital acquisition, an interesting finding.

The use of earnings functions is obviously a useful direction for further work on labor markets and adjustment, and in this respect the technique of dividing the sample (as used in the Ghana study) seems a promising way of teasing out trends from a single cross-section of data, which might be particularly useful for African countries.

Labor Market Institutions

Two issues papers deal with labor market institutions, Devereux's on wage indexation (vol. 1, chapter 4) and Nelson's on political economy issues (vol. 1, chapter 7). The latter paper focuses on the effect of unionism, both private and public, on labor market flexibility. It also discusses economic and political factors that affect how militant or cooperative labor movements are likely to be.

Nelson argues the existence of theoretical reasons that explain why unions in developing countries might be more militant than in developed ones. The relationship between union organization and militancy is an inverted U-shape: weak unions exhibit a low level of militancy, and very strong centralized unions are also less militant as they can no longer consider only sectoral gains. Developing country unions fall in the middle, with some strongly organized sectors, but no strong central union body. Unions in most developing countries do not fit the corporatist model, where wage gains are traded off for better employment security and where labor may take account of the macro impact of sectoral wage demands. Another feature of unions in developing countries is the greater role of public sector unions due to the greater share of public sector employment in total formal employment. A feature of the public sector is the greater difficulty experienced in laying off workers and the large severance payments offered.

Economic factors may affect labor's intransigence: they tend to show more concern for wages during upswings and more concern for employment protection during downswings, although unions foreseeing times getting worse may try to grab what they can early in the downswing. Political factors also matter: authoritarian regimes tend to use coercion more than democratic regimes, with some exceptions on both sides. The stage of the electoral cycle matters, as does labor's role in the political and party process. Labor may be attached to one party in a polarized system, or have access to more than one party in a more open system, or be largely excluded from the political arena. Likewise the regime's degree of stability matters, with new democracies in particular being susceptible to the revolution of rising expectations. Nelson makes the important point that successful adjustment in the long run not only requires investor confidence in the government's long-run ability to fulfill its promises, but also the confidence of the labor movement. The degree of equity in a society may be an important ingredient in sustaining such confidence.

The Latin American country studies dwell at length on labor market institutions: unions, indexation, minimum wages, legislation on benefits and job security, and segmentation. For the African countries these institutions receive less coverage in the country studies, although they do exist. As the Kenya study shows, however, it is one thing for the institutions to exist, and another for them to be effective, and their force tends to be weakened by the highly elastic labor supply to urban areas in Africa. It is also likely that the much lower proportion of urbanization and of formal sector employment makes a difference. The Asian countries have some similar institutions (two-year wage contracts in Malaysia and the same kind of long-term contract/temporary labor division in Korea as in Brazil). However, the role of unions in Asia is clearly very different from their role in Latin America and Africa.

The five Latin American country studies provide an interesting contrast in terms of the alleged effect of labor market institutions in causing rigidities in the labor market. In three of the countries (Argentina, Brazil, and Costa Rica) the institutions remain strong despite the economic crisis, whereas in the other two (Bolivia and Chile) they have been substantially weakened and/or dismantled. Some of the country authors criticize these institutions. For Argentina and Brazil they argue that they impeded adjustment and labor market mobility, and in Chile they receive partial blame for the painful nature of the recession and ensuing high unemployment. At the same time the Bolivian and Costa Rican cases are interesting counterpoints. In Costa Rica labor institutions survived relatively unscathed, for example, over 500 minimum wages are legislated, and are generally enforced, which did not prevent moderate adjustment. In Bolivia much labor legislation was dismantled and large-scale labor shedding occurred without as yet strong recovery. To some extent it seems that labor market institutions are often a symptom of underlying political and economic difficulties, which make adjustment difficult, and the institutions are unfairly blamed for causing problems.

The Brazil study describes labor market institutions in some detail. Unions are very strong (in the form in which they reemerged during the democratization period from the late 1970s onward), and are linked to political parties along the lines of the corporatist state discussed by Nelson. They combine strong plant-level organization with a previously legislated strong centralized structure, which allows them to transmit bargains struck at the best organized plants to national level. Wage indexation is perhaps the most sophisticated in Latin America, with monthly adjustments. Job security legislation used to be an important hindrance to mobility, but the setting up in 1964 of a fund (to which employers contribute) to provide severance pay has eased the problem. Tradables predominantly hire formal sector (that is, signed contract), unionized workers, whereas nontradables hire all types of workers, formal and informal, unionized and nonunionized.

Argentina has many of the same institutions. The author links union strength to inward-oriented economic policy, since the oligopolistic nature of employers demands an equally centralized representation for labor. The author also mentions a compulsory wage policy, whereby bargains struck by the unions are obligatory for all firms, which he argues harmed small firms. One difference from the Brazil case is that the main exportable in Argentina is food, and unionization is therefore concentrated in nontradables or importables. This arguably has been a major hindrance in changing the relative price of tradables and nontradables.

One difference in Costa Rica is that although legislation is equally strong, unions are relatively weak, having been broken in an unsuccessful face-off with Standard Fruit in the 1970s. Wage indexation in Costa Rica, far from being an impediment to desirable relative price changes, is given much of the credit for allowing a real wage decline at a critical point following devaluation. Since indexation was imperfect, real wages fell, but by an apparently impartial mechanism. This tactic, however, can only be used infrequently, and Brazil, for example, is no longer able to make such gains from unanticipated inflation.

Two Latin American countries undertook major labor market reforms. Chile between 1973 and 1975 eliminated unions and job security and removed much of the force from minimum wages, benefits, and wage indexation mechanisms (the government actually cheated on the price index used for wage indexation). However, the author argues that lack of labor legislation during 1973–79 was detrimental to growth because employers feared that the law, once reinstated, would be unduly favorable to labor. Bolivia, the other Latin American severe adjustment case, likewise removed similar institutions, with the exception that wage indexation had never been particularly important and had not survived the hyperinflation as an institution. Job tenure was ended and job security reduced, thus allowing labor shedding. The government stepped out of previously centralized wage bargaining. In both Bolivia and Chile the public sector shed a substantial amount of labor, equal to 25 percent of Bolivia's public sector labor force and 3 percent of Chile's total labor force (the author does not specify as to whether total urban or total urban plus rural is meant).

Comparisons between the Latin American countries in terms of the success of adjustment are instructive. Contrasting, for example, the relatively successful adjustment in Costa Rica and the problematic one in Bolivia, evidently dismantling labor institutions is neither necessary (Costa Rica) nor sufficient (Bolivia) for successful adjustment. Another interesting comparison is between Brazil and Costa Rica. In Brazil large political-economic tensions exist, such that consensus over the division of output is lacking, which causes continual inflationary tendencies (tensions that similarly pushed Bolivia over the brink into hyperinflation). Although wage indexation has sometimes been blamed for perpetuating Brazil's inflation, it is more a symptom of the defensive ability of one of the groups engaged in underlying conflict. In Costa Rica, by contrast, a higher degree of social consensus allowed a union-backed president to undertake some of the painful initial steps toward successful adjustment, in which wage indexation actually helped the process.

The Asian countries also have institutional structures in the labor market. The Korean government has followed a highly interventionist policy with respect to unions. The right to strike was banned in 1971 and only recently reinstated, and unions need government permission to undertake collective bargaining. The author argues that wage and productivity trends and their consequent effect on unit costs has been crucial in Korea's export success. In this respect the government was heavily involved in ensuring that wages did not get ahead of productivity, and at the same time that workers did share in the fruits of higher productivity. Increasing union autonomy and increasing strikes in the late 1980s may herald a change in the so far virtuous productivity and wage nexus in Korea.

In Malaysia union power is similarly limited. The level of unionization is low, less than 25 percent in manufacturing, and unions are banned in some sectors. Paradoxically unions are strongest in the plantation sector, where wages stagnated in the 1980s. Malaysia has relatively long (three-year) wage contracts, which may have hindered adjustment. Unions in Thailand are also weak except in the public sector. In both Malaysia and Korea the importance of bonuses in earnings (around 30 percent of pay in Korea and 15 percent in Malaysia) has been argued to cause flexibility, since earnings and profits are related. Latin American countries also have bonuses, but less related to productivity and profits than to Christmas, seniority, and so on.

Although studies of Latin American countries frequently blame labor market segmentation (formal/informal) as a problem, some kinds of segmentation also exist in the Asian countries. In Korea labor is divided into permanent, temporary, and casual, and much labor market adjustment falls upon the casual and temporary workers, particularly women. Another type of segmentation between large and small firms is also quite marked in Korea, and small firms tend to pick up the slack during recessionary periods. Segmentation also seems to persist over time, although taking the form of a widening gap in the human capital levels of large as compared to small firms, rather than a widening of wage differentials.

Finally public sector employment and adjustment is a topic worthy of separate study in its own right. The growth of public sector employment as an initial response to economic crisis is mentioned in many of the studies (all of the Latin American studies, Egypt, and Malaysia). The eventual need to shed public sector labor was a difficult undertaking. Bolivia, Chile, Costa Rica, and Ghana have bitten the bullet, Argentina has been unable to; and in Egypt, Kenya, and Malaysia adjustment took the form of a substantial slowdown in government hiring. In the latter three countries one consequence discussed was a rise in educated unemployment, particularly of women in Egypt and Malaysia, where educated women have few private sector alternatives. The relative decline in public sector wages observed in almost all the countries reflects the greater difficulty of adjusting labor quantity in the public than the private sector.

Consequences of Labor Market Adjustment

Labor market adjustment has consequences for income distribution and poverty, and on long-run growth. The country study authors were asked to consider these, paying particular attention to the role of women in labor markets.

Income Distribution

As Addison and Demery show (vol. 1, chapter 3), theoretical discussion of the effects of adjustment on poverty yields ambiguous predictions. Their paper begins with the standard Salter-Swan account of expenditure reduction and expenditure switching, and works out wage and employment effects, assuming competitive labor markets. These wage and employment effects are then fed through a poverty index, but yield ambiguous predictions.

The rest of the paper examines how these effects are modified by the introduction of different labor market imperfections. The first case is where there exists an economywide "quantity rationing" framework, that is, unemployment can persist. In this case the discussion of poverty becomes more complicated, since one must consider poverty among those employed in tradables, those employed in nontradables, and those unemployed. In this case although a devaluation may increase poverty because it shifts workers to the tradable sector, where greater poverty is assumed, and because it lowers the real wage, it will decrease poverty because of the unemployment reduction. Thus, ambiguity in predictions persists, but of a different type than before.

The paper then moves on to discuss partial labor market imperfections, dividing the labor market into a formal and an informal sector. The analysis is similar to that by Edwards (1988) and Edwards and Edwards (vol. 1, chapter 2). The authors consider different types of wage inflexibility and trace out the consequences for sectoral employment, wages, and unemployment. These are again fed through a poverty index. Ambiguity is again the order of the day, although the analysis does illuminate the different components.

A third variant is where barriers exist to entry into the formal labor market. Here Addison and Demery (vol. 1, chapter 3) argue that an expenditure switching policy is quite likely to reduce poverty if barriers to entry into nontradables or tradables exist.

The fourth and final case is where labor market imperfections exist in both sectors, and the authors distinguish between unemployment and employment in informal tradables, formal tradables, informal nontradables, and formal nontradables. They follow through the real wage and labor allocation consequences of expenditure switching, and again feed them through the poverty index. They conclude that the effects of switching under these assumptions seem to be the most promising as far as poverty reduction is concerned.

Tracing the effect of adjustment on poverty and income distribution empirically is no easier than doing so theoretically.

Asking the counterfactual question as to what happened during adjustment as compared to what would have happened otherwise is difficult, as many countries were on unsustainable courses. The data available also affect the conclusions that one can reach. It is usually more difficult to obtain information on overall economywide changes in income distribution from nationwide income-expenditure surveys than to obtain results on the urban distribution of earned income from labor force surveys. However, if real wages fall by more than GDP and urban-rural differentials change, then the latter data only tell part of the story.

We focus here on relative earnings distribution. Several studies also document increases in poverty, unsurprising as a consequence of economic crisis. For Africa almost no time series data exist with which to make comparisons. The Kenya study does cite UNICEF's finding that the share of the bottom 10 percent declined. For Egypt no distribution data are available after 1981/82. Changes in urban-rural income differentials are of great interest in the case of Africa and are the focus of studies elsewhere (Jamal and Weeks 1987), but country studies here lacked the data to examine the issue.

In Latin America income distribution is a key issue related to the political economy of the economic growth process, and all the studies provided data. Brazil's income distribution has long been of interest given that inequality increased during the long boom "economic miracle" period between 1967 and 1974, when there was a type of structural adjustment as the economy became more open. Some improvement in income distribution is evident between 1974 and 1981, with a worsening during the recession and stabilization (1981–85), and since then a slight recovery. One interesting finding is that interregional equality increased during structural adjustment, which hit harder at the more affluent urbanized south than the more rural northeast.

For Chile the pattern was somewhat similar, but more exaggerated, with a sharp increase in 1974–76 accompanying the start of adjustment, the Gini remaining constant during 1976–79, increasing again in 1979–84, and since then decreasing slightly, but to a level much higher than at any time during 1960–74. It is not surprising that distribution worsened so much, given the massive cuts in real wages and the very high unemployment levels. The measured changes may be offset somewhat by changes in social expenditures. In Argentina income distribution also worsened during the stop-go cycles (although the only data available are for income earners in Buenos Aires during 1974–88). The top two deciles gained at the expense of all others.

For Bolivia and Costa Rica data are more scanty and knowing exactly what happened is harder. In Costa Rica inequality may have increased between 1971 and 1983 (before adjustment), but after the onset of adjustment different data sources give conflicting trends. For Bolivia the data are also not very good, but suggest a possible improvement between 1982–85, when informal sector wages rose relatively during the hyperinflation, but by 1988 distribution had reverted back to 1982 levels.

In Asia, income distribution may have improved in Malaysia and worsened in both Thailand and Korea. In Malaysia resources were put into agriculture, including food agriculture, whereas in Korea policy focused for at least some of the period on heavy industry, and in Thailand little was done about the problem of urban primacy (concentration in Bangkok).

Women and Labor Market Adjustment

Much of the literature on women and structural adjustment has concentrated on the effects of structural adjustment on women. Collier and others (vol. 1, chapter 6), using evidence from Africa, examine the opposite issue, namely, how women's economic mobility may affect the success of adjustment. They argue that women face constraints not only in the labor market and in access to education, but also in credit markets, which may affect adjustment. In particular, women in Africa are frequently concentrated in food production. The authors present three possible cases relevant to adjustment. Food may be a tradable, in which case its output should expand with adjustment; it may be a nontradable, in which case output should contract; or it might be nontradable in rural areas but tradable in urban areas, in which case food marketing (again frequently a female preserve, at least in West Africa) would need to expand. If food crops are to contract, this requires a reallocation of women's labor into other activities, and if they are to expand, this requires women's access to credit. In either case, constraints on women's flexibility will hinder the success of structural adjustment.

Collier and others therefore urge that government policies should focus on relaxing constraints to women's economic activities. Another reason cited in favor of this strategy is that it also improves household income security if higher women's incomes offset the loss of men's jobs in the formal or government sectors during adjustment, although they do not consider the potential costs involved, such as women's responsibilities for children.

The paper by Collier and others also discusses women in South Asia, again focusing on women as participants in, rather than victims of, structural adjustment. It deals with both rural and urban activities of women, and draws somewhat on the earlier experiences of women in export-oriented industries in East Asia. Bardhan sees structural adjustment as potentially altering the existing U-shaped pattern of female labor force participation with education: in South Asia women tend to participate either with very low education in menial and low-productivity activities, or in high-skilled, high-education activities. The author argues that adjustment may increase the demand for labor-intensive industry output, requiring women workers with medium education, with resulting beneficial effects on reduced fertility and increased incentives for female education. Adjustment may also involve costs for women, such as those where the male family members or the whole family migrate, and the costs imposed particularly on women's time when social infrastructure deteriorates. Like Collier, she sees a role for government in relaxing the constraints on women's activity. Labor market legislation aimed at protecting women has ended up tending to exclude them from the formal sector. Bardhan foresees benefits to women in selective deregulation of some sectors in India, such as electronics.

Another aspect of the paper by Collier and others focuses rather more on the effects of structural adjustment on women. In Latin America, studies on women seem to focus mainly on labor force participation, and little information is available on trends in relative earnings. Women's labor force participation has been increasing, partly due to sectoral shifts, in particular, increased employment in the service sector, but largely due to higher participation within sectors.

The participation increases vary somewhat across countries. The authors undertake econometric analysis for Chile, which suggests that unemployment that accompanies structural adjustment does not have differential effects on discouraging female and male labor force participation. One interesting avenue they suggest for future work is to examine how increased female participation fits in with the trend in much of Latin America toward increased informalization of the labor force.

The country studies concentrate more on the effects of structural adjustment on women. As Collier and others argue, the effects are likely to depend on the preceding sectoral distribution of women workers and on the effect on participation rates. However, the likelihood exists that women workers' more tenuous attachment to the labor force means that they are more likely to lose jobs during periods of labor shedding. The country studies do not give a single story, although there seems to be a lot of evidence of adverse impacts, but the data are not very complete. Even for the United States, where data are available, understanding how male/female wages, for example, had changed over time due to changes in female labor force participation was difficult. For the developing countries female labor force participation has exhibited trend changes plus cyclical responses due to crisis. Tracing the effects on women's welfare is even harder if most women live in households with men. Although the effects on female-headed households are less ambiguous to interpret from the data, this was a topic well beyond the scope of the country studies.

The Ghana study documents that women suffered rather more from structural adjustment than men as they were concentrated in the informal sector, which tended to absorb excess labor. Women are also predominantly in food crop agriculture, whereas resources have gone instead to cash crops. In Côte d'Ivoire, insofar as education had a positive effect on the probability of remaining in employment or of entering employment, and women tend to have less education, they are likely to have faced disadvantages. The Egypt study documents an adverse effect on women due to the lengthening queue for government employment, and the more limited private sector alternatives available to women.

In Bolivia the male/female differential fell between 1981 and 1987 as measured from earnings functions, although aggregate data suggest the opposite (the difference is perhaps explained by changes in participation rates). Although anecdotal evidence suggested that labor shedding from the formal sector was to the detriment of women, who are more costly workers in terms of benefits, this may have been offset by much of the employment loss being focused in mining, a male-dominated sector. In Costa Rica the male/female earnings differential increased during the crisis and decreased thereafter, which the authors attribute to rising female participation during the crisis (added worker effect), where the female entrants were less well qualified. In both Bolivia and Chile the emergency employment schemes explicitly targeted male workers, at least initially, and in Chile public sector hiring in the early part of the crisis also favored men.

In Malaysia some evidence suggests that women lost ground during the recession due to the firing of labor in a weaker position in the labor market; however, a trend increase in female wages is evident over the 1970s and 1980s. The relative earnings of Malay women in particular increased between 1970 and 1984, and the returns to female education and experience rose absolutely and relative to the same returns for men. However, these gains were all reversed in the 1984–87 recession. Nevertheless, Malaysia differs from some of the other countries studied in that women are a higher proportion of wage employment than of self-employment, and are concentrated in some export industries, such as electronics. In Korea women are at a disadvantage, crowded into low paying, white collar sectors, and providing a disproportionately high share of family workers, the most disadvantaged group in the labor force. Female participation rates are also surprisingly low in Korea compared to other East and Southeast Asian countries. Women also tended to lose out in the recession. Whereas male employment shifted continuously toward the permanent category, this proportion declined for women during the recession.

Effects on Long-Run Growth

Most of the issues papers focus on demand side effects of adjustment and the labor market. Buffie's (vol. 1, chapter 5), by contrast, highlights the supply side consequences of fiscal contraction, and hence the impacts on long-run growth. Demand side complications are abstracted from by assuming that the economy is small and open. Two traded goods, agricultural exports and manufactures, are produced using labor and capital. Manufacturing also requires an intermediate input, which is supplied by the public sector. Labor employed in the public sector and in manufacturing is paid a higher than competitive wage, and the rest of the labor is underemployed in agriculture. Buffie assumes a fixed wage differential between the modern and the informal/agricultural sectors. Capital accumulation dynamics are also modeled.

Human capital is modeled by distinguishing between skilled and unskilled labor. Skilled labor growth is determined by human capital investment by the government. If factors are complementary, then the productivity of unskilled labor declines when investment is cut, as does the productivity of capital. Overall, Buffie shows that disinvestment in human capital leads to capital decumulation. The paper suggests two broad policy lessons. First, productive government investments in human capital should be protected, which requires broadening the tax base. Second, a more gradual approach to adjustment is likely to entail fewer adverse impacts on productive investments vital for long-run growth.

To some extent the topic of adjustment and long-run growth is a difficult one to study empirically, since many countries are still grappling with short- and medium-term issues, but some of the studies provide information on investment, in particular, human capital investment, as discussed by Buffie. The Kenya and Côte d'Ivoire studies discuss falling investment, but do not blame labor markets. The Argentina study throws the blame for stop-go cycles onto the labor market's inability to allow prices of tradables to rise relatively in a sustained way, thereby harming long-run growth. Similarly, in Chile a lack of labor legislation and fears of a return to previous laws that favored labor are assigned the blame for lack of investment.

As regards human capital investments, the Costa Rica study documents a sharp drop in school enrollment during the crisis, especially at the secondary and technical levels, with likely adverse effects on growth and distribution. By contrast, no such effect was predicted from cross-section regressions for the Côte d'Ivoire. In Asia where short-run problems of adjustment have been largely solved, the studies had more room to focus on long-run issues. The Malaysia and Korea studies examine changing returns to education, and the Thai study examines potential labor market skill mismatch issues.

Conclusion

This overview has summarized theoretical predictions and country study experience on two important topics related to labor markets and adjustment. First, how well have labor markets functioned, and have they assisted or impeded macro adjustment efforts? Second, what were the effects of some of these adjustments on the labor market?

With respect to the issue of labor market functioning, labor markets have at least three allocative functions: they match workers to employment in such a way that overall unemployment levels and real wages matter; they allocate workers between sectors, and match worker skills to job requirements so that relative wages and employment matter, both for economic sectors and for skill categories; and they provide incentives for intertemporal allocation of resources, specifically for human capital accumulation in education and firm-specific training. Applying these three criteria to the often descriptive country studies to assess how well or how badly labor markets performed is not easy. By and large individual country authors argue that the labor markets performed well, although authors of the studies for the big three Latin American countries, Argentina, Brazil, and Chile, were more critical.

Theory suggests that labor market rigidities are only one of three possible reasons for unemployment. With the exception of Chile, the countries have not had prolonged unemployment despite severe recession, however, cyclical increases have occurred. This fits with the presumption that in developing countries without unemployment insurance schemes, unemployment is not an option for primary household earners unless the household is unusually wealthy. The evidence on real wages casts considerable doubt on theoretical concerns about aggregate real wage rigidity and labor market inflexibility as a hindrance to adjustment. Real wage declines have been dramatic, and often far greater than the fall in GDP. For some countries the real wage declines may have been excessively large and led to a fall in domestic demand, which inhibited recovery.

With regard to the sectoral employment shifts, these have generally been in the desired direction, that is, toward tradables, although this has generally meant that agricultural employment has increased relatively and manufacturing employment declined in all but the most successful countries. Shifts of employment into services and commerce are, however, indicative of weak GDP growth, and hence growth of labor demand. Sectoral wage changes have also been largely in the appropriate direction, although little information is available on agricultural wages. The decline in relative government wages is one factor causing relative wages in nontradables to decline.

Finally, on the intertemporal aspect, the evidence is a little more mixed. In Costa Rica the evidence showed that the recession had induced decreases in school enrollment, whereas in Côte d'Ivoire econometric results suggested that increases in crop prices, which would help adjustment, would not lead to parents pulling their children out of school. Earnings functions for Bolivia, Costa Rica, and Malaysia showed that returns to all formal sector characteristics including education and experience declined during adjustment, and in that government relative wages declined universally, and government tends predominantly to hire the more educated, this would decrease the incentives to acquire schooling. The country studies did not discuss another human capital issue, namely international migration, although for at least three of the countries—Côte d'Ivoire, Egypt, and Ghana—this was important.

The country studies also explicitly discussed labor market institutions, thought to be a source of rigidity. One possible interpretation is that where these institutions lack binding force, whether because of elastic labor supply (Africa) or weak unions (Asia and perhaps Costa Rica), they were not perceived as obstacles to adjustment. Nevertheless, dismantling of the institutions and weakening of the unions as in Bolivia does not seem to be sufficient to ensure recovery, in that country imperfections in the functioning of the capital market seem to bear at least part of the responsibility for poor growth. The authors also argued here that labor market institutions in Latin America often receive the blame, whereas they are only the symptoms of underlying political economy problems detrimental to growth.

Turning now to the second broad topic, the outcomes of labor market adjustment, the authors had some difficulties in separating how far outcomes were due to structural adjustment, how far due to recession, and how far due to pre-existing trends. Severe adjustment, as in the case of Chile with high unemployment and sharp falls in real wages in an economy where urban employment predominates, can be very adverse to income distribution. Perhaps Brazil's worsening during the 1964–79 structural change period has some parallels, as does Korea's heavy industry phase. That is, unless countries make explicit provision for poorer groups, for example, the emphasis on food crop agriculture in Malaysia, structural change can worsen income distribution, although some of the changes, such as improved rural-urban relative income and possible improvement in informal/formal relative income, might militate in the opposite direction. Country-specific factors—success of indexation, wage and price freezes—also affect distribution. The effects on distribution also depend on the level of the GDP. No data are available for Africa to test this hypothesis, but it seems plausible that improving rural-urban terms of trade and abolishing rents from price distortions as part of adjustment programs could improve income distribution nationally.

The effects on women might be somewhat country specific, depending whether women were in tradables or not, but women are likely to face adverse effects of the employment shrinkages in some sectors due to their weaker attachment to the labor market. The country studies generally confirmed this. Finally, the effects on long-term growth were adverse, but not directly attributable to labor market malfunctioning.

Where should one go from here? One issue is that the apparently benign conclusion that labor shifted into tradables masks that in response to structural adjustment, labor has moved in the direction opposite to that usually associated with economic development. Labor has shifted back into agriculture, out of manufacturing, and out of the public sector, although one might argue that this latter sector was too large given the level of development reached. Recession plus adjustment has also resulted in an increase in informalization, increased use of casual labor, decreased worker benefits, and declines in skill and possibly education differentials. These trends are observed even in the most successful adjustment cases in Asia. Developing countries have long resisted being relegated to the role of primary producers in the international economic order, and it is unlikely that structural adjustment entailing further shifts of labor into agriculture would be highly sustainable.

As regards possible further research, country study and some issues paper authors pointed the finger of blame for adjustment problems onto the capital market and possible price rigidities in the output market. Another possibly fruitful topic is that of the role of labor market institutions, unions, and the political economy; something worth examining before launching into a wholesale advocacy of dismantling such institutions. Finally, as in all empirical research, better data are needed. One useful step would be to improve international collation of labor force statistics, clearly separating the results from household surveys from those of establishment surveys. Another would be to encourage further analysis of, and increased accessibility to, labor force surveys, which tend to be more expensive to analyze, but arguably yield more reliable results.

References

Dutt, A. K. 1984. "Stagnation, Income Distribution and Monopoly Power." *Cambridge Journal of Economics* 8(1): 25–40.

Edwards, S. 1988. "Terms of Trade, Tariffs and the Labor Market Adjustment in Developing Countries." *World Bank Economic Review* 2(2): 165–185.

Fallon, P. R., and L. A. Riveros. 1988. "Macroeconomic Adjustment and Labor Market Response: A Review of the Recent Experience in LDCs." Washington, D.C.: World Bank. Draft, processed.

Fields, G. 1990. "Labor Market Policy and Structural Adjustment in Côte d'Ivoire." Ithaca, New York: Cornell University. Draft.

Ghai, D. 1987. *Economic Growth, Structural Change and Labor Absorption in Africa: 1960–85.* Discussion Paper No. 1.

Geneva: United Nations Research Institute for Social Development.

Horton, S., R. Kanbur, and D. Mazumdar. 1988. "Labor Markets in an Era of Adjustment: A Project Proposal." Washington, D.C.: World Bank, Economic Development Institute. Processed.

ILO (International Labour Organisation). 1987. *World Recession and Global Interdependence: Effects on Employment, Poverty and Policy Formation in Developing Countries.* Geneva: ILO World Employment Program.

_____. Various years. *Yearbook of Labour Statistics.* Geneva: ILO.

_____. 1989. *Yearbook of Labour Statistics.* Geneva: ILO.

Jamal, V., and J. Weeks. 1987. *Rural-Urban Income Trends in Sub-Saharan Africa.* World Employment Programme Labor Market Analysis and Employment Planning Working Paper No. 18 (WEP 2–43/WP.18). Geneva: ILO

JASPA (Jobs and Skills Program for Africa). 1988. *Africa Employment Report 1988.* Addis Ababa: ILO.

Johnson, O. E. G. 1986. "Labor Markets, External Developments, and Unemployment in Developing Countries." Washington, D.C.: IMF Staff Studies for the *World Economic Outlook.*

Lavy, V., and J. Newman. 1989. "Wage Rigidity: Micro Evidence on Labor Market Adjustment in the Modern Sector." *World Bank Economic Review* 1(1): 97–117.

Lindauer, D. L., O. A. Meesook, and P. Suebsaeng. 1988. "Government Wage Policy in Africa: Some Findings and Policy Issues." *World Bank Research Observer* 3(1): 1–26.

Ramos, J. R. 1980. "The Economics of Hyperstagflation: Stabilization Policy in Post 1973 Chile." *Journal of Development Economics* 7(4): 467–88.

Riveros, L. 1989. "Recession, Adjustment and the Performance of Urban Labor Markets in Latin America." Washington, D.C.: World Bank. Processed.

Taylor, L. 1988. *Varieties of Stabilization Experiences Towards Sensible Macroeconomics in the Third World.* Oxford, U.K.: Clarendon Press.

Tokman, V. E. 1984. "The Employment Crisis in Latin America." *International Labor Review* 123.

van der Gaag and Vijverberg. 1989. "Wage Determinants in Côte d'Ivoire: Experience, Credentials, and Human Capital." *Economic Development and Cultural Change* 37: 371–381.

Wong, P. K. 1985. "Economic Development and Labor Market Changes in Peninsular Malaysia." Working Paper No. 12. Kuala Lumpur and Canberra. ASEAN-Australia Joint Research Project.

1

RECENT DEVELOPMENTS IN THE DEVELOPED-COUNTRY LITERATURE ON LABOR MARKETS AND THE IMPLICATIONS FOR DEVELOPING COUNTRIES

Jean-Paul Azam

In an era of adjustment, the labor market plays a central role as it determines the properties of the macroeconomic equilibrium and the way it reacts to major policy changes. The process of adjustment comprises two main changes that macroeconomic policies try to achieve:

(i) a cut in aggregate demand (stabilization), aimed at reducing the twin deficits of the government budget and the balance of payments;

(ii) an attempt at depreciating the real exchange rate, aimed at providing the incentives for the reallocation of factors of production, including mainly labor, from the sectors producing nontraded goods to the sectors producing traded goods (structural adjustment).

The labor market is involved in these two processes. The extent of its imperfections, as compared to the textbook competitive labor market, determines whether the demand shocks resulting from (i) will result in increased unemployment, and whether nominal instruments like the devaluation of the nominal exchange rate can be used to

This paper benefited from comments by Edward Buffie, Sebastian Edwards, Chris Heady, Ravi Kanbur, and A. McKay as well as from stimulating discussions with Jean-Yves Lesueur and Bentley MacLeod. But they are not responsible in any way for this paper, including its shortcomings.

effect the changes in relative prices involved in (ii). This pair of questions has in common the issue of the interaction between nominal and real variables.

In the Western world of industrialized countries, macroeconomics started as an attempt to explain why nominal variables like the quantity of money or the exchange rate affect real variables, and more particularly the levels of aggregate output and employment, and how they could be used within a macroeconomic policy package to fight the depression of the 1930s. This was the central message of Keynes's *General Theory,* and it has been extended and refined by several generations of Keynesian economists. This viewpoint has been challenged by various brands of "classical" economists who do not believe that nominal shocks can have noticeable real effects.

Today the aims of macroeconomic policies have changed, with the fight against inflation and the balance of payments deficit coming to the forefront, while the problems of unemployment tend to be given a secondary importance from the point of view of macroeconomic policy and are more and more regarded as microeconomic problems. This is especially true for LDCs who had to enter into the adjustment process after the commodities booms of the late 1970s, and the debt resulting from the expectation errors that followed.

Nevertheless, the precise way in which macroeconomic policy works cannot be modeled unless assumptions about the labor market are carefully specified (Bruce and Purvis 1985; Marston 1985; Edwards 1988). In particular, the role of changes in the level of aggregate income in the adjustment mechanisms depends crucially on whether the labor market is fully competitive, or whether there is some unemployment.

Moreover, the question of the relationships between macroeconomic policies and the real economy has taken a new turn recently under the name of the social consequences of macroeconomic policies. One may regard unemployment as one particular indicator of poverty, among many other indicators that might be more relevant in many less developed countries. Then, one can view the issue of the effects of macroeconomic policies on the poor, especially in LDCs, as an extension of this basic question (Demery and Addison 1987; Kanbur 1987; Azam, Chambas, and

Guillaumont 1989). It would be void if monetary policy or devaluation had no real effects. Instead of limiting the analysis to the possible effects of macroeconomic policies on unemployment, the aforementioned authors extend the list of the relevant indicators that might be affected.

The aim of this paper is to present the recent development of the literature on labor markets and the macroeconomy in developed countries, and to bring out some of their implications for LDCs. Of course, labor markets have very different characteristics in different parts of the world. In developed countries (DCs) they display contrasted stylized facts: while real wages seem to be insensitive to the cycle in Europe, they seem to react to macroeconomic fluctuations in North America. The contrast seems even sharper when dealing with LDCs. While labor markets seem fairly competitive in many Asian countries, one observes an evident segmentation in Latin America, with strong trade unions in the urban segment of the market and a less organized rural sector. In Africa, a very large share of the labor force is in the rural sector and wage labor plays a minor role, mainly in the plantation sector or the formal urban sector. Nevertheless, the theoretical developments in the DC literature provide useful insights for analyzing labor markets in LDCs, provided these developments are suitably adapted to the structural characteristics of the different economies.

I begin with a brief account of the historical and logical steps that were taken until the 1970s for dismissing the Keynesian wisdom. Various brands of the Phillips Curve and the credibility issue in the monetary policy game are discussed. These models are then compared with a "New-Structuralist" assumption. In the next section of the paper I examine the main models that have been put forward to explain unemployment until the 1970s, including implicit contracts, trade unions, and efficiency wage models. I discuss their implications for macroeconomic policy, and their possible adaptations to the special problems of LDCs. Most of these models yield predictions that leave little room for nominal shocks to have real effects, and as such are not Keynesian, despite their ability to explain unemployment. Finally, the paper focuses on two new theories that challenge the once dominant "New Classical" doctrine: the "New Keynesian" approach and the insider-outsider approach.

The Dismissal of the Keynesian Wisdom

The dominant view after the Second World War was that nominal variables like the quantity of money and the exchange rate could be used for macroeconomic policy, and especially for maintaining full employment. The corollary of this belief is that contractionary policies, which are typical of stabilization policies (in the modern sense), are bound to entail increased unemployment.

The gradual dismissal of this Keynesian wisdom has led to the view that one can use contractionary policies to fight inflation or balance of payments deficits, without fears of undesirable real consequences. To reach this position, several steps were taken in the 1960s and the 1970s, corresponding to logical steps in the construction of a model with better microeconomic foundations. The main points of this theoretical path—40 years of macroeconomic research in a nutshell—will now be presented.

We can decompose this movement from Keynes to Lucas (1973) in four ways of modeling the wage-setting process. No particular innovations are involved on the demand side of the labor market. The common assumption in this respect is what Keynes called the "First Postulate of the Classics," namely that firms are on their demand curve (that is that the level of employment is determined where the marginal product of labor is equal to the real wage rate). In log-linear terms, this common assumption can be written:

$$d = a - b \, (w - p), \qquad (1)$$

where d is the (log of) labor demand, w and p the nominal wage and price of output, respectively, and a and b are positive constants. This assumption has remained nearly unchallenged for 40 years. The main exception was the so-called "disequilibrium approach," starting from Patinkin (1965, chap. 13) and Clower (1965), and reaching its maturity with the works of Barro and Grossman (1971, 1976) and Malinvaud (1977). This school assumes that both the nominal wage and the nominal price of output are rigid in the short-run, so that firms can be held off their labor demand curve when they are constrained by insufficient outlets on the goods market. In such a state of excess supply, the demand for labor depends on the demand for goods and is different from (1). This theory has been applied successfully in Soviet-type economies (Portes 1981). It has been adapted to the controlled economies of the South by Berthélemy and Gagey (1984), Azam (1986) and Bevan et al. (1987). I do not present it here.

The Road from Keynes to Lucas

Then, given (1), the "classical" approach assumes that the wage rate adjusts quickly to maintain equilibrium:

$$d = s, \tag{2}$$

where s is the supply of labor, which we regard as exogenous for the sake of simplicity. In this case, macroeconomic policy, or more generally nominal shocks, which we capture as changes in p, have no real effects, but are passed on as changes in w. The equilibrium real wage is:

$$w - p = (a - s)/b. \tag{3}$$

Keynes (1936) reverses this causal chain, from the supply of labor to the equilibrium wage rate, and assumes instead that the latter is given exogenously:

$$w = w^k. \tag{4}$$

One then gets an unemployment equilibrium, with the level of employment (and hence of output) given by:

$$d = a + bp - bw^k. \tag{5}$$

Nominal shocks have real effects, as any change in p affects d.

But assumption (4) seems a bit crude. It cannot cope with periods of inflation, where wages and prices chase each other. Even Keynes did not push it too far, and in 1940 replaced it by a wage-setting rule based on expectations:

$$w - p^e = c, \tag{6}$$

where c is a constant, and p^e the price level expected by the workers to prevail during the period for which w has been decided. It means that the wage rate is determined in advance, with a view to maintain a given purchasing power. In this formulation, the nominal rigidity implied by the first Keynesian equation (4) above is in fact explained by a real rigidity (a purchasing power target), with imperfect information.

Substituting (6) into (1), one gets:

$$d = n + b\,(p - p^e). \tag{7}$$

Then, a change in p only has real effects if it is unexpected (that is, if it entails a change in the expectation error $p-p^e$). Keynes trusted inflation to perform such a trick. He advocated it as a means to finance the war effort. But this innovation of Keynes's remained unnoticed for a long time, as economists all over the world were struggling to try to absorb the *General Theory* and could not spare attention for this one.

The main stream did absorb Phillips's (1958) empirical result, which can be written for the sake of simplicity as the following wage-setting rule:

$$w = c - g\,(s - d). \tag{8}$$

No room is allowed for expectations, and the unemployment rate (s-d) plays a part instead. This may be regarded as a compromise between the first Keynesian view and the classical approach, with the nominal wage moving slowly in response to excess demand. Despite this extra bit of flexibility, nominal shocks remain powerful under this assumption, as can be seen by substituting (8) into (1), which yields:

$$d = x + zp, \tag{9}$$

where x and z are constants.

But the Phillips Curve (8) seemed *ad hoc;* it implies that workers suffer from money illusion, determining the wage rate without taking into account its purchasing power, as influenced by p. Friedman (1968) and Phelps (1968) corrected this point. Probably without realizing it, they offered a synthesis of Keynes (1940) and Phillips. Their wage-setting equation is essentially:

$$w - p^e = c - g\,(s - d). \tag{10}$$

This is in essence what is known as the "expectations augmented Phillips Curve." The policy conclusion entailed by this change of assumption is basically what we found above:

$$d = x + z\,(p - p^e). \tag{11}$$

Then again, nominal shocks only have real effects if they are unexpected: if changes in p translate into changes in $p-p^e$. But the difference from Keynes is that Friedman did not trust inflation to perform such a trick, except maybe in the short-run.

Rational Expectations and Macroeconomic Policy

Lucas (1972, 1973) made the last step in this process, formalizing Friedman's distrust of inflation as a means to promote full employment. He used Muth's (1961) theory of rational expectations.

The basic element of the rational expectations hypothesis is that agents use optimally any information they have in order to form expectations. Assuming away costs of processing information, expectation errors are not functions of the information available to the agent when he forms his expectations. Otherwise, the agent would use this functional relationship to improve the accuracy of his expectations. Then, in the simplest case, one can write the equation describing the formation of expectations as:

$$p = p^e + e, \text{ with } E\,(e\,/\,I) = 0, \tag{12}$$

where e is the expectation error (or nominal surprise), regarded as a random variable, and $E(e/I)$ is the mathematical expectation of e conditional upon all available information, noted I.

Then, combining the demand for labor function (1), the wage-setting equation (10), and the expectations formation equation (12), one can solve for the level of employment and the real wage rate:

$$d = x + ze, \tag{13}$$

$$w - p = h - ke, \tag{14}$$

where h and k are positive constants. Then, any positive nominal surprise, like an unexpected inflation hike brought about by a positive money supply shock or an unexpected devaluation, entails a reduction in the real cost of labor and an increase in the level of employment and output.

This result cannot be used systematically by macroeconomic policy since e is a random variable that the government does not control. Random policy shocks have real effects, while systematic macroeconomic policy has only nominal effects. Therefore, provided it is well announced and well understood by private agents, a contractionary demand policy of the type required by the stabilization policies of the 1980s can be pursued without entailing unemployment.

As Kydland and Prescott (1977) and Barro and Gordon (1983) point out, there is a credibility problem, which makes macroeconomic policy more tricky than the above picture shows. The cause of this problem is that it might not be in the interest of the government to actually do what it says if the private agents believe it, so that smart agents will not believe the government in the first place. (In a dynamic context, this is known as the "time consistency" problem.) This can be illustrated simply as follows.

Assume that the government has the following utility function:

$$u^g = d - p^2. \tag{15}$$

The reasons why the utility of the government is positively affected by the level of employment (and hence of income) are fairly obvious.

They range from the desire to fight unemployment to the desire to get tax revenues as high as possible, if tax receipts are an increasing function of national income. The second term in this utility function is a simple way of capturing the government dislike for price changes because of their possible political impacts (social unrest, and so on) or for other reasons.

Then if the government announces its choice of p and is believed by the people, so that $p^e=p$, it reaches the utility level $x-p^2$, as can be checked using equations (11) and (15). In this case, the government's optimum choice is p=0. But this is not the best result that the government can obtain if it announces p=0 and is believed by the private agents. For in this event, the government's problem becomes:

$$\max_p d - p^2 \qquad (16)$$

$$\text{s. t. } d = x + zp.$$

His optimal choice is:

$$p = z / 2. \qquad (17)$$

The government has a clear incentive to cheat and to pursue an inflationary policy when the private sector expects a stable price level. But smart private agents will soon realize this point and will not believe the government when it claims to pursue a stable price policy.

In order to grasp systematically the strategic choices involved in this problem, let us write it in a simple game form. The choice of the government is to select p=0 or p=z/2. The choice faced by the private agent is between $p^e=0$ and $p^e=z/2$. To complete the model, we need to specify the utility function of the private agent, and for the sake of simplicity, we assume it to be:

$$u^P = - (p - p^e)^2. \qquad (18)$$

This is a simplified way of capturing the fact that any expectation error will lead the private agent to act differently from what he would have done optimally with full information.

The game can now be summarized by the matrix of Table 1.1. In each cell of the matrix, the first entry represents the private agent's level of utility and the second one that of the government, when both players choose the corresponding pair of values of p and p^e.

The Pareto equilibrium of this game is the North-West pair of strategies, where $p=p^e=0$. But this equilibrium is not credible, as the North-East cell is preferable for the government, as seen above. Therefore, the smart private agent will not get trapped in believing that the government will keep its word, and he will choose the second row of the matrix. Knowing that, the government will choose the inflationary policy. In other words, the South-East cell is the Nash equilibrium of this game.

A particularly bad outcome is the South-West cell, where the government pursues an anti-inflationary policy, while the private sector does not believe it. This illustrates the social costs caused by the credibility constraint and may shed some light on recent policy failures in Latin America and elsewhere. It may be viewed as the case where the government engages in an active adjustment policy, but the private sector does not believe it to be sustainable. Sargent (1986) presents a historical discussion of the credibility issue. He shows how some political leaders have overcome this problem and succeeded in stopping hyperinflation in Austria, Hungary, Germany, and Poland in the 1920s.

Because of this credibility constraint, the optimum outcome is not likely to emerge from the monetary policy game, and the most

Table 1.1 The Monetary Policy Game

		The government	
		$p = 0$	$p = z/2$
The private agent	$p^e = 0$	$0 ; x$	$-z^2/4 ; x + z^2/4$
	$p^e = z/2$	$-z^2/4 ; x - z^2/2$	$0 ; x - z^2/4$

plausible outcome is the noncooperative Nash equilibrium with fully expected positive inflation. The source of this inefficiency is that the government cannot convince the private sector of its willingness to pursue the noninflationary policy. The way out is to obtain a credible commitment from the government, removing from it the possibility of breaking its word and pursuing an active monetary policy. A solution is to have a constitution forbidding the use of expansionary monetary policy or devaluation of the nominal exchange rate (Andersen 1989). In Africa, this is in essence what the rules of the Franc Zone do for member countries (Guillaumont and Guillaumont 1984; Frimpong-Ansah 1990).

Once regarded as a desirable policy choice to fight unemployment, inflation has become an undesirable side effect of an institutional framework where the government possesses too many policy instruments or too much discretion to use them. There is then a built-in inflationary bias in the macroeconomic policy game, which raises the credibility issue when it comes to the adjustment policies that were so common in LDCs in the 1980s. Perhaps many governments regard an agreement with the IMF as a means to enhance the credibility of an announced adjustment policy.

The introduction of "heterodox" elements in a stabilization package (wage and price freezes, exchange rate pegging, and so on) may strengthen credibility, as illustrated by Blejer and Cheasty (1988) in their study of stabilization programs in Argentina, Bolivia, Brazil, and Israel in 1985-86. But, in all cases, a necessary basis for credibility of a restrictive policy is internal consistency, as shown in various Latin American cases by Dornbush (1982b), Corbo and de Melo (1987); and Kiguel and Liviatan (1988).

It is not certain that this whole framework is appropriate for discussing the problems of LDCs. The relevance for these countries of equation (1), which is the common thread of all of the models discussed above, has been questioned in the literature.

Are Phillips Curves Positively Sloped in the South?

Milton Friedman (1977) raised the issue of the positively sloped Phillips Curve for the developed countries in his Nobel lecture. In his mind, the higher the rate of inflation, the less efficient the markets for coordinating the actions of the various agents and hence the lower the efficiency of the economy as a whole. Azam (1988) extends this idea.

The reasons invoked here are very different and are based on the structural characteristics of some LDCs. One of the features that distinguishes most LDCs from DCs is the preponderance of agriculture in the former. This difference has been exploited by Nugent and Glezakos (1982) to produce a Phillips Curve with a positive slope, which can explain the negative relationship that is consistently found in empirical analyses of the impact of inflation on the rate of growth of national income (Kormendi and Meguire 1985; Fry and Lilien 1986).

The first point is that the agricultural production takes place within a yearly seasonal cycle. Labor is applied nearly all year long, while output is obtained only at the end of the season. Production decisions, and hence hiring decisions, are made on the basis of the price of the product that is expected to prevail at the end of the season, rather than on the basis of the observed price. In this case, it is logical to assume the following demand for labor function:

$$d = a - b \ (w - p^e), \qquad (19)$$

where p^e represents the price expected by the landlord or the farmer who makes the hiring decision (we neglect discounting here for simplicity).

The wage-setting equations presented earlier assume that the labor market is fairly developed since they imply that the wage rate is determined for a given period of time, on the basis of the expected price level, and so on, and not as a spot price. In LDCs, however, labor is often hired for a short period on the street-corner labor market. The worker does not need to make sophisticated decisions based on expectations since the wage rate is a spot price determined by supply and demand on a day-to-day basis. Then, it is reasonable to assume that labor supply depends on the observed real wage rate:

$$s = c + f \ (w - p \ ), \qquad (20)$$

where c and f are positive constants.

Assume that competitive equilibrium prevails on this market, in agreement with the comments made earlier:

$$s = d. \tag{21}$$

We can now solve this three equation system, by eliminating w, to get the equilibrium level of employment:

$$d = x + z \, (\, p^e - p), \tag{22}$$

where x and z are positive constants, different from the ones used above. In this model expectation error remains the fundamental determinant of employment and output. But here it affects the level of employment negatively, whereas it had a positive impact above. Now unexpected inflation leads to a contraction of activity and not to an expansion as in the developed-country models above.

A related but different reason for a positively sloped Phillips Curve can be found in the models produced by the "Neo-Structuralists" in the debates over the contractionary impact of devaluation (Lizondo and Montiel 1989). Some of these models (Taylor 1983; van Wijnbergen 1983; and Buffie 1984) emphasize the role of working capital in the labor demand function and use it to show a possible channel whereby devaluation may have a contractionary effect. In fact, this assumption finds its roots in the wages fund doctrine of the classics. See Pasinetti (1960) on Ricardo.

The idea is again that output takes time to come by, while labor must be paid before the product is sold. Therefore, the wages fund has to be advanced by the farmers or the landlords. The Neo-Structuralists allow for the possibility of borrowing the funds from the banking sector or the curb market, so that the relevant rate of interest will be involved in the transmission mechanism. It can be described simply as follows. The marginal cost of hiring a worker is the wage rate *plus* the interest cost of advancing it. These two costs determine the demand for labor. Then, provided the money supply is not perfectly elastic, an increase in the price level, caused for example by a devaluation, implies a reduction in the real supply of credit and hence an increase in the relevant interest rate and a fall in the demand for labor. This is known as the "Cavallo effect." In reduced form, the aggregate demand for labor is:

$$d = k - w, \tag{23}$$

where k is the (log of the) wages fund, which we regard here as exogenous, without bothering to specify how it is financed. We could make it a function of p without changing the result, provided its elasticity is less than one.

If one adopts again the labor supply function (20) and the equilibrium condition (21), one gets an equilibrium employment function that reads:

$$d = g + h (k - p), \tag{24}$$

where g and h are positive constants, unrelated to the ones above. Then, given the wages fund, the levels of employment and output are decreasing functions of the price level.

These two instances show that the real effects of nominal variables are as important for LDCs as they are for DCs, but they may lead to quite different conclusions. The relative importance of agriculture in national income seems to be a crucial factor in determining the relevance of the Phillips Curve in LDCs.

We have seen above a series of models predicting that nominal variables (here p) may affect real variables (here d), irrespective of expectations, while others restrict this occurrence to cases where the nominal shock is unexpected. The next sections are devoted to a deeper understanding of the assumptions that can lead to these two different predictions. I present various theories that provide microeconomic foundations for the existence of unemployment, but that restrict the power of nominal variables to affect the level of employment to the cases of expectation errors.

Alternative Explanations of Unemployment

Several theories were presented in the 1970s and the 1980s to explain unemployment. I restrict my attention here to theories in which expected changes in nominal variables do not affect the level of employment.

The Implicit Labor Contract Approach

A new class of models was introduced simultaneously by Baily (1974), Gordon (1974), and Azariadis (1975). As Azariadis made especially clear, this theory was not meant to explain unemployment, but why the discontinuation of an employment relationship between an employer and his employee takes the form of layoffs rather than quits (Azariadis 1975, p. 1201). These models explain unemployment only when asymmetric information is assumed (Grossman and Hart 1981). They have not attracted much support from specialists (Layard and Bean 1988). Therefore, we only present briefly the main points of this approach in the case of symmetric information. The following simple exercise captures the essence of this theory.

Assume that the firm can find itself in two states of the world: good (or *status quo)* and bad, with probabilities q and l-q. We assume symmetric information, so that both the firm and the worker are able *ex post* to observe whether good or bad has happened, and no cheating is possible. But the contract has to be accepted or rejected before the state of the world is known. It stipulates that, in the good case, the worker gets a wage w. He derives from it a utility level u(w $/p^e$), u(.) being increasing, strictly concave, and differentiable. In the bad case, the worker keeps his job with probability r, getting then a wage w^B and utility u(w^B/p^e) x; with probability (l-r), in the bad case, he is laid off and gets nothing. In this simple model, the worker's expected utility if he accepts the contract with the firm is:

$$V = q \, u \, (\, w \, / \, p^e \,) + (\, 1 - q \,) \, r \, u \, (\, w^B \, / \, p^e \,). \qquad (25)$$

Next assume that the worker believes to have an outside opportunity of getting an expected utility level V^R, which we call his reservation utility. The worker quits instead of accepting the contract with the firm, unless:

$$V \geq V^R. \qquad (26)$$

Then the firm seeks to minimize the expected cost of the contract acceptable by the worker hired:

$$\min_{w,w^B} \quad q\,w + (1-q)\,r\,w^B, \text{ s.t. } (26). \tag{27}$$

The first order conditions from this problem yield:

$$u'\,(w/p^e) = u'\,(w^B/p^e), \tag{28}$$

which implies $w = w^B$, irrespective of the value of r (the probability of keeping one's job). This exercise thus shows that the contract between the firm and the worker does not make the wage rate contingent on the good or bad state of the world in which the firm happens to be *ex post*. It follows that in the bad state of the world, the firm has to fire a fraction (1-r) of its work force, rather than offer a general wage cut. This result relies heavily on the worker perceiving that he has outside opportunities, warranting his reservation utility. If we assume that in equilibrium this reservation utility is equal to the expected utility from contracts obtainable elsewhere, the constraint (26) only states that the worker must be offered an equal deal by all firms that are liable to hire him.

This theory explains why workers are laid off in bad states of the world, rather than being pushed to quit by being offered a wage cut. But it is felt that it is not an approach to unemployment theory, which should explain why some workers do not get contracts at all. Second, it is fairly obvious that this model determines a rigid *real* wage (in terms of p^e) and not a level of the nominal wage. Any effect of nominal variables in this setting would again result from expectation error. The same comment applies to the next theory.

The Monopoly Power of the Collective Worker

In the Western world, there are institutions that give monopoly power to the workers taken collectively (for example, trade unions). These institutions have been much studied in the literature (McDonald and Solow 1981; Oswald 1982). In other countries where the government intervenes quite directly to determine the legal minimum wage (like in France), or in times of tight incomes policy (for example, the United Kingdom in the 1970s), the monopoly power of the worker comes through the ballot box: one may vote for a high wage government (left wing ?) or for a low wage government (right wing?).

Assume that the representative worker knows that the probability of his getting a job is a decreasing function of the wage rate: $q(w)$, $q'<0$. For the sake of simplicity, assume that $p=p^e=1$, since it is perfectly clear that we are dealing with the *real* wage. If this worker is representative, $q(.)$ is the ratio of the demand for labor function to the supply of labor function.

Next assume that the worker reaches a utility level $u(w)$ if he gets a job at the going wage; he gets u^0 if he is unemployed, which represents the utility of the forced leisure, plus unemployment benefits, if any, and so on. We assume that these outside opportunities yield a lower utility level than getting a job in the relevant range.

Then the worker's expected utility is:

$$v(w) = q(w) u(w) + (1 - q(w)) u^0. \qquad (29)$$

Under standard conditions, this function $v(w)$ is concave and single peaked. Therefore, if w is determined by majority voting, within the union or at the general election, it maximizes the utility of the median voter. For him, we have $v'(w) = 0$, that is:

$$q(w) = -q'(w) (u(w) - u^0) / u'(w). \qquad (30)$$

Regarding $q(w)$ as the rate of employment, it is higher the higher the elasticity of $q(w)$, the smaller the utility level yielded by outside opportunities u^0, and the lower the marginal utility of w. In other words, it is higher, the higher the risk involved in a wage increase, and the lower the benefit. Hence, full employment is not bound to come out of the ballot box. The reason for this is that given the power to choose, the representative worker may want to trade off an increase in the wage rate for a slight increase in the probability of being sacked.

When regarding q(w) as the ratio of the demand for and supply of labor functions, we implicitly assume that firms select at random the workers to be fired. All workers have the same probability of losing their job. However, in the real world, the rationing rules for allocating jobs are different, and seniority matters. In British terms, the rule is "last in, first out." This changes slightly the predictions of the model since the median voter has a lower probability of being sacked than does more junior colleagues, and this tends to push the chosen wage upward, as compared with the simple model above (Grossman 1983). For an opposing view, see Oswald (1986).

Trade union models of the kind sketched above have been applied to LDCs to explain urban unemployment and wage determination in the formal sector. Calvo (1978) assumes a different utility function for the union. McDonald and Solow (1985) have extended their 1981 model to the case of dual labor markets, a common feature in LDCs (Mazumdar 1983; Fields 1987). Heady (1987) has tested the relevance of this type of model against efficiency-wage models, to be discussed below, using disaggregated data on the manufacturing sector in Colombia. He found that the former outperform the latter in the majority of industries. It is a commonly held view that unions matter more in Latin America than in other LDCs. However, they play a part even in Africa (Ahiauzu 1985; Dompierre 1986). The wage-setting institutions of some Latin American economies (and Jamaica) are contrasted to the working of the labor market in the East Asian newly industrialized countries (NICs) by Fields and Wan (1989). They emphasize the costs of trade unions and labor market distortions in the former.

But the median voter argument must be amended for countries that are not under democratic rule. The theory I present next was in fact applied in the reverse order: built for LDCs, it was adapted later to the DCs.

Efficiency Wage Models

The efficiency wage theory was initially meant to apply to LDCs (Leibenstein 1957; Mirrlees 1975; Stiglitz 1974, 1976), and then adapted for DCs (Calvo 1979; Calvo and Wellisz 1979; Salop 1979; Solow 1979).

THE BASIC ARGUMENT. If the level of the wage rate affects the productivity of workers, then it may be in the firm's interest to raise the wage rate above the market clearing level and to refuse to cut wages, despite the resulting unemployment. Assume that the level of effort of the representative worker is an increasing function of the real wage as perceived by him, $e(w/p^e)$ ($e'>0$ and $e(v) = 0$ for $v \le v^0$, and e (v) > 0 for $v>v^0$). Measuring the effective quantity of labor used by the firm by the effort level e(.) of the representative worker *times* the number of workers n, and assuming a production function f(.) (increasing, differentiable, and concave), we assume that the firm seeks to maximize profits:

$$\max_{n,w} p\, f\, (e\, (w/p^e)\, n) - w\, n. \qquad (31)$$

The first order conditions can be arranged in such a way that they provide first a wage-setting equation:

$$(w/p^e)\, e'\, (w/p^e)\, /\, e\, (w/p^e) = 1, \qquad (32)$$

sometimes called the "Solow condition." It says that the marginal effort level per unit of real wage must be equal to the average one. Equation (32) gives w as a function of p^e only, like equation (6) used above to illustrate the assumption in Keynes (1940).

Second, denoting v* the value of the real wage that is the solution to (32), we obtain from the first order conditions that employment equation:

$$n = f^{\,'-1}\, (v^*\, p^e\, /\, p)\, /\, e\, (v^*). \qquad (33)$$

Given v*, it is again a function of p only if it affects expectation error $((p^e/p)-1)$.

When Leibenstein initiated this theory, he had in mind the relationships between high real wages and the level of nutrition, health, and so on of the workers, which in turn affects positively their productivity. Subsequently, researchers have been extremely creative to diversify the channels whereby the level of remuneration can affect productivity. Following Katz (1986) one can distinguish five approaches that are not exclusive. The most exciting is probably the shirking model (Calvo 1979; Shapiro and Stiglitz 1984) since it raises a fundamental question regarding the relationships between employer and employee, especially for the societies predominantly based on wage labor.

THE SHIRKING MODEL. In the wage relationship, there is an important element of moral hazard arising from the costs of monitoring an employee's effort. It is difficult to establish whether a worker (1) worked honestly and productively, or (2) worked honestly but without significant results because of independent events like the breakdown of a machine, or (3) shirked (that is, did not even try to produce anything). If actual work has some disutility for the worker and shirking has a good probability of passing unnoticed, the worker may try to get the wage paid without spending any effort. What makes things even worse is that the employer may have an incentive to accuse the worker of shirking, even if he has worked honestly, in order to get the product without paying the wage.

We can summarize this problem by putting it under a simple game form, as in Table 1.2. Assume that the worker produces y in a unit of time, if he works, while he incurs a disutility level t; if he does not work, he produces nothing at no subjective cost. The employer gets the product y, if it exists, and may pay the worker a wage w<y (in real terms), unless the employer accuses him of shirking. There is no possibility of establishing whether such an accusation is right or wrong. We assume that the balance of power within the firm is such that in the latter case, the employer gets away with the output, and without paying the wage. This is obviously a pretty rough assumption. It is meant to bring out dramatically the possible outcomes of the wage relationship.

The matrix in Table 1.2 summarizes all the possible payoffs for the two agents, with the firm getting the first entry in each cell, and the worker the second one, knowing that the alternatives are: work or shirk for the worker, and pay or accuse, for the firm.

This game is obviously a dead end: the worker has an incentive to shirk, and the firm has an incentive to accuse (both are "moral

Table 1.2 The Wage Labor Game

The worker

		Work	Shirk
The employer	Pay	y-w ; w-t.	-w ; w.
	Accuse	y ; -t.	0 ; 0.

hazard" problems). Therefore, while the optimum is in the North-West cell, the Nash equilibrium is in the South-East cell, with no employment and no output.

As usual with these types of games, the predictions become less dramatic when we go from the world of one-shot games to the world of repeated games with a long horizon and discounting. Moreover, there are institutions in the Western world to avoid some of the consequences of this game. Casual observation suggests that wage employment is the dominant mode of employment, and that employers and employees spend more time, on average, in the factory than in the court.

Shapiro and Stiglitz (1984) show how firms have an incentive to increase wage above the market-clearing wage, as a "worker discipline device." The idea is simple. If there is full employment with the same wage paid to all workers, the incentive for shirking is strong. When caught shirking, the worker can be fired at no cost to him since he is bound to find immediately a new equivalent job. Then to improve the productivity of workers, firms must try and offer better wages than do their competitors, in order for the workers to face a prospect of some loss when caught shirking. But then all the firms pay a wage above the full employment level, and the resulting unemployment is a sufficient penalty, in equilibrium, to deter shirking.

A powerful criticism of this analysis is the so-called "bonding argument": if workers were asked to pay a fee for their job, so that they would have to pay again if fired, to get a new job, then that would provide enough of a deterrent against shirking, removing the need for equilibrium unemployment. Table 1.2 provides a clue explaining why such a scheme may not work: it would increase too much the incentive for the firm to accuse the worker and collect the job fee (Eaton and White 1983).

The shirking issue has been raised in relation to the drop in living standards of civil servants and public employees in LDCs that pursued an adjustment program in the 1980s (Lindauer, Meesook, and Suebsaeng 1988). Signs of such a decline are moonlighting, as studied by van der Gaag, Stelcner, and Vijverberg (1989) in the cases of Côte d'Ivoire and Peru, and increased corruption (Klitgaard 1989). But Besley and McLaren (1990) have expressed theoretical doubts about the possibility of controlling corruption by increasing wages.

Extensions of this model have shed new light on other interesting issues in work organization—such as the roles of reputation, hierarchy, and so on. (Calvo and Wellisz 1979; Malcomson 1984; MacLeod and Malcomson 1988). It is interesting to note how institutions are involved in the solutions suggested to this problem. The same applies, to an even larger extent, to the literature dealing with the same kind of issues in LDCs. Another strategy has been followed in LDCs to explain how a market for labor could develop despite this shirking problem, but without postulating that labor remuneration has to take the form of a wage payment. It is well known that the wage system is not widespread in the developing world (Sen 1975). In agrarian societies the system of sharecropping is often more common. Much has been written to explain this phenomenon (Quibria and Rashid 1986; Otsuka and Hayami 1988). One strand of this literature is directly related to the shirking issue; sharecropping arrangements are regarded as risk-sharing contracts that take care of some of the moral hazard aspect of the problem. If he shirks, then the sharecropper will not get a given wage, but only a share of the output. This share is smaller the more shirking he has done. Such a self-punishment mechanism may deter shirking.

Hence, this whole literature can provide underpinnings for the analysis of dual labor markets à la Harris-Todaro, for some countries at least: in the rural areas there may be sharecropping with little open unemployment, and in towns the modern sector pays high wages, at the cost of a positive level of unemployment. In each case the shirking problem is taken care of in a specific way determined by structural factors. The next type of efficiency wage model also has something to say on dual labor markets.

THE LABOR TURNOVER MODEL. Stiglitz (1974) for LDCs and Salop (1979) for DCs have studied models where the efficiency wage mechanism is based on labor turnover costs. There are costs associated with hiring a new worker (training costs, for example), so hiring a new worker can reduce the productivity of the whole firm.

Salop (1979) assumes that the rate of turnover faced by a firm is a decreasing function of the wage it pays, relative to the expected wage available elsewhere. The latter is the average wage times the rate of employment, regarded as the probability of getting another job after quitting the firm. Hence, firms have an incentive to increase their wage offer above the market clearing wage in order to reduce the turnover costs. In a symmetric equilibrium, all the firms pay the same wage, but a positive rate of unemployment makes the expected outside wage low enough to reduce the rate of turnover at its equilibrium level.

Another dimension is added to this model in its applications to LDCs since the turnover rate depends not only on the wage paid by the firm relative to the expected wage in the industry, but also relative to the rural wage. Then the model explains both urban unemployment and the urban-rural wage gap (Stiglitz 1974, 1982; Basu 1984).

OTHER MODELS. Other rationales have been used in the literature to explain efficiency wage effects (Akerlof and Yellen 1986; Katz 1986). There is the adverse selection model, which applies to a world of heterogeneous workers, where the firm has no clues about the quality of each job applicant. If it picks at random from the pool of applicants, the firm has an incentive to offer better than average wages, in order to attract a high proportion of applicants with above average ability. Akerlof (1982) has presented a sociological model, where a higher wage is regarded as a "gift" from the firm, which the work force feels like reciprocating by a "gift" of higher work norms. This idea is close to Mauss's theory of the "potlatch" in anthropology (Mauss 1954). Leibenstein (1978) links his X-efficiency theory with the efficiency wage approach, involving as well psychological and sociological elements. Lastly, there is the "union threat model," where the firm tries to keep unions at bay by paying high wages (Katz 1986).

THE NUTRITIONAL MODEL. As mentioned above, the efficiency wage theory involved initially the nutrition-productivity relation (Leibenstein 1957; Bliss and Stern 1978). Recent empirical studies have confirmed that this relation is significant in some countries (Behrman, Deolalikar, and Wolfe 1988; Sahn and Alderman 1988).

Dasgupta and Ray (1986) have presented an extension of the efficiency wage model for LDCs where such a relation plays an important part. In this case what really matters is food consumption, which determines the productivity of a worker, rather than the wage rate *per se.* For rural people with some land, the consumption level will depend not only on the wage income, but also on the product of the own farm. Landless laborers will depend entirely on their wage income to buy their food. Hence, for lack of better information, an employer has more chances of hiring a well-fed and hence productive worker if he hires somebody who owns some land rather than a landless laborer whose nutritional status depends on his unobservable recent work history.

The existence of landed laborers in the job market creates a form of downward flexibility of the wage rate that may squeeze landless laborers out of the market. Landed laborers can remain productive even if the wage rate falls below what is required for buying the amount of food necessary for maintaining productivity since they can get some food from their own farm production. On the other hand, landless laborers become unproductive at such low levels of the wage rate and so lose any chance of getting a job. Hence, inequality of land ownership might explain in some cases rural unemployment with a flexible real wage.

Sahn and Alderman (1988) have tested an aspect of this theory on data from Sri Lanka. They show that land ownership gives a competitive advantage in the labor market. But it shows up as a wage premium rather than in the form of unemployment of the landless with a uniform wage.

All the models of this section may explain equilibrium unemployment in DCs or LDCs. But they rest on "real rigidity" since they determine the real wage and the rate of unemployment. The only room that is left for nominal shocks to affect real variables, and in particular the level of employment, is expectation errors, as in the Friedman-Lucas analysis.

Because the rational expectations hypothesis has superseded the old adaptive expectations assumption in the minds of economists, one does not trust expectation errors for explaining systematic and persistent effects of aggregate demand on output and employment. Two research strategies have evolved from this fact. One has been to find other, nonmonetary explanations of output fluctuations, and this has given rise to the "real business cycle" theory (Long and Plosser 1983); the alternative has been to introduce in the analysis some specific elements of imperfect competition. Then money and aggregate demand recover their earlier theoretical importance.

The Impact of Nominal Shocks

Many economists feel unhappy with the view that nominal shocks can have only unsystematic, short-lived effects on the real economy. Moreover, policy-oriented applied macroeconomists neglect the subtleties of recent theoretical developments and use old-fashioned models where money affects output systematically (Mankiw 1988; Malinvaud 1989). A theoretical vacuum was therefore needing to be filled. I will discuss two recent attempts to reconcile the well-established Keynesian predictions with the assumption of rational behavior of economic agents.

The New Keynesian Approach

The New Keynesian approach emphasizes the imperfections of the *goods market,* while giving up the old Keynesian emphasis on nominal wage rigidity. As such, it falls somewhat outside the scope of this paper. Nevertheless, it is worth reviewing briefly for two reasons. First, it is an important complement to the real models of unemployment seen above, which can be used to introduce in them systematic effects of nominal variables (Akerlof and Yellen 1985, 1986). Second, it meets old themes of the development economics literature, which can be usefully revived on this basis.

The New Keynesian approach abandons the assumption of perfect competition and uses instead models of monopolistic competition. Hart (1982), who gives an important part to income distribution issues (between wages and profits), and Weitzman (1982) are the recent forerunners of this approach. Weitzman makes the point that if there were no increasing returns to scale, dismissed workers would set up a new firm instead of becoming unemployed. See as well Blanchard and Kiyotaki (1987).

The first point of this set of models is that in a world of monopolistic competition, the private costs of nonoptimal behavior may be very small. This refutes a critique of Keynesian models by Lucas (1972, 1973). According to him, there are "$500 bills lying on the sidewalk"—in other words, opportunities for mutually advantageous trade that are not exploited. The "PAYM insight" shows that only a few cents are left on the sidewalk by nominal rigidities (Parkin 1985; Akerlof and Yellen 1985; Mankiw 1986).

We can check that the loss involved in slight deviations from optimal behavior by firms in monopolisitic competition is small. Denote $r(p)$ the profit of a monopolistic firm that sets price p, and denote p^* the optimal price—that is, $r'(p^*)=0$. Notice that the profit function of a competitive firm is not differentiable with respect to price at the equilibrium point: if the firm raises its price, sales jump to zero (Akerlof and Yellen 1985).

Then using a Taylor expansion about p^*, one finds:

$$r(p) = r(p^*) + (p - p^*) r'(p^*) + (p - p^*)^2 r''(p^*) / 2. \tag{34}$$

Using the definition of p^*, one can compute the approximate amount of profit lost by setting the price p instead of the optimal price p^*:

$$r(p^*) - r(p) = - (p - p^*)^2 r''(p^*) / 2. \tag{35}$$

For small deviations of p from p^*, this loss can be quite small, if $r(p)$ is quite "flat at the top." Therefore, it can be "near rational" to leave prices unchanged in response to small nominal shocks. Akerlof and Yellen (1985) combine this insight with an efficiency wage model to generate Keynesian results.

If there exist small costs of changing prices, called "menu costs" in this literature (for example, costs of printing new menus and catalogs, or of changing price tags), it may not be worth changing the price of the product when the optimal price changes a little because the second-order potential gain (35) is not enough for compensating the menu costs.

This result bears directly on the question of nominal rigidities. Assume, for example, that the quantity of money is increased by x percent and that aggregate nominal demand is proportional to the money supply. If menu costs deter the firms from changing their price, then real aggregate demand increases by x percent and so does output. We thus find a Keynesian effect of a nominal variable on the real economy.

It is a well-known result that output is lower under monopolistic competition than under perfect competition. Blanchard and Kiyotaki (1987) extend this result by showing first that this outcome can be viewed as a consequence of an externality in the process of price setting, which explains why the private benefit from cutting the prices differs from the social benefit (see as well Weitzman 1982). Assume that the demand curve facing the monopolistically competitive firm is:

$$y = f(p/p^a) \, m/p^a, \tag{36}$$

where f(-) is a decreasing function, with elasticity larger than one, p is the price charged by the firm for its product, p^a is the average price in the economy, and m is the money supply. Blanchard and Kiyotaki provide the microeconomic foundation for such a demand function (see Dixit and Stiglitz 1977). If there are enough firms in the economy, the average price level is like a public good since the choice made by each firm taken in isolation has a negligible impact on it, while it is determined by the combined decisions of all the firms.

Hence, a small price cut by the firm would have only a small impact on the demand for its product and by definition would entail a cut in expected profit in the Cournot-Nash equilibrium. But if all the firms were to cut their prices simultaneously, relative prices would remain unaffected, and real balances would increase proportionately. Then real demand and the real profit of each firm would increase, assuming that the nominal wage fell in the same proportion. Therefore, the inefficiency entailed by monopolistic competition can be regarded as a coordination failure. If instead of thinking like Cournot-Nash, taking as given the prices chosen by the other firms, each firm was making the Kantian assumption that all other firms are going to do the same move as it does (Laffont 1975), then a price cut would leave relative prices unchanged, would increase profits, and would imply a Pareto improvement.

This argument can be translated into dynamic terms by taking staggered contracts into account (Taylor 1980; Blanchard 1983, 1986). If firms fix their prices at discrete intervals, and if price revisions are made without synchronization, then nominal price changes entail relative price changes, at least for a transitional period. This can slow down the transition between two steady-state levels of nominal prices in which relative prices may be identical. As the first movers incur a transitional loss of competitiveness when increasing their price, they may prefer to adjust their price only partially and wait until all the other firms have done some price adjustment to carry on the process. Some nominal price inertia results.

Now add menu costs and assume that the government increases the money supply. For each firm in isolation, the outward shift of the demand curve might not be enough to warrant a price increase because of menu costs. But then, if no firm increases its price, the increase in the money supply turns into an increase in real output demand, and hence entails an increase in output (and welfare). If all firms were behaving in the Kantian fashion, they would all raise their price, and this would make it profitable for each of them to incur the menu costs. Money would then be neutral. Moreover, Blanchard and Kiyotaki (1987) show that this type of model may have multiple Nash equilibria—for example, one in which no firm adjusts its price and one in which all firms do (see as well Rotemberg 1987). In Weitzman (1982) there is a continuum of equilibria.

One of the problems with the menu costs approach to nominal price rigidity is that it assumes implicitly that it is more costly to change prices than to change output levels. Greenwald and Stiglitz

(1989) solve it by assuming that firms are risk averse and that the effects of price changes are more uncertain than are the effects of output change.

This type of analysis of the externalities involved in monopolistic competition, with the Keynesian consequences that they imply for the design of macroeconomic policy, is related to a founding debate in the development economics literature. Rosenstein-Rodan (1943), Nurkse (1953), and Scitovsky (1954) discussed underdevelopment as an equilibrium point with suboptimal output level in terms close to the ones presented above to explain the inefficiency of monopolistic competition. The externality brought out by this literature was expressed in terms of income rather than in terms of prices. Each firm in isolation has no incentive to expand its production because only a fraction of the income distributed by the firm would turn into increased demand for its product. But if all firms were expanding simultaneously, then the increased income distributed by the firms would translate into increased demands for the various products and would make the expansion profitable for all. This argument, which led to the so-called "balanced growth" doctrine, could be expressed rigorously using models of monopolistic competition like the ones sketched above. Basu (1984) presents an attempt at clarifying Nurkse's analysis with the help of conjectural equilibria.

Murphy, Schleifer, and Vishny (1989a, 1989b) have tackled the issue of industrialization using models of monopolistic competition of the type discussed here, assuming increasing returns to scale. Although their models mainly deal with long-run matters, they meet some shorter-run issues. For example, they have an "Anti-Dutch Disease" result, whereby a primary export boom may pull an expansion of the industrial sector, provided the distribution of income is right, boosting demand (Murphy, Schleifer, and Vishny 1989a). Similarly, van Wijnbergen (1988) uses a monopolistic competition model to discuss the role of "heterodox" measures to solve the credibility problem of a stabilization policy. Temporary price controls thus may be a device to avoid the coordination failure described above, and the resulting inflation inertia.

While the New Keynesian line of research tries to reconcile Keynesian results with rational behavior by explaining nominal price rigidities or inertia, the insider-outsider approach looks rather for inertia of quantities. It accepts the Friedman-Lucas point that only unexpected nominal shocks can have real effects, but it shows why these effects can persist for a long time.

The Insider-Outsider Approach

The standard neo-classical approach to the demand for labor assumes that the balance of power within the firm is well defined, with the management pursuing the interest of the owners, and the workers doing what they are told. The insider-outsider approach recognizes that incumbent workers (the insiders) can influence the hiring and firing decisions of the firm. Lindbeck and Snower (1986, 1987a, 1987b, 1988) have investigated the consequences of various costs that protect insiders from the competition of outsiders (unemployed workers), and the sorts of rent-seeking activities that they can use to increase these costs, and hence the rent that they are able to extract.

Two basic elements drive a wedge between the wage paid to insiders and the reservation wage of the outsiders. First, there are various costs for hiring (advertising vacancies, selecting the workers, training them, and so on) and for firing (severance pay, legal action, and so on). Second, insiders possess a know-how that outsiders need to acquire, and this entails a productivity differential. If a ($0<a<1$) denotes the productivity of an outsider as a fraction of the productivity of an insider, c the result of the various hiring and firing costs, and w^0 the reservation wage of the outsiders, then employing an insider is more profitable for the firm than hiring an outsider provided that the insider's wage w^I satisfies:

$$w^I \le (w^0 + c) / a. \qquad (37)$$

Lindbeck and Snower assume that the insiders have the power to capture this potential rent ($w^I - w^0$), while leaving the outsiders unemployed. They also assume that they can manipulate c, a, and to some extent w^0, to try and make it as large as possible (without forcing the firm to close down). To increase c, they can enforce high training costs by complicating the training process and increasing the required qualifications, and they can raise firing costs by imposing long and costly legal procedures, and so on. To reduce a, they can harass entrants, refuse to cooperate with them, and disrupt training. Lastly, they can increase the reservation wage of the outsiders with a "stick" and a "carrot": the implicit threat of harassment to increase the disutility of work and the prospect of getting a high wage, if there is a nonzero probability of becoming an insider in the future. The unionization of the insiders can enhance their power, but it is not necessary for generating the main results of the model.

This theory offers an explanation of unemployment, and it has important consequences for macroeconomic dynamics and the effect of nominal shocks on output and unemployment. In its simple form, it implies a ratchet effect, or *hysteresis effect*. As the model determines real variables, its equilibrium can only be disturbed by unexpected nominal shocks. But then the model explains the persistence of the effects. For example, if some insiders are fired after an unexpected negative shock and lose rapidly their status (becoming outsiders), then the economy settles at this new equilibrium level with a lower level of employment than in the preshock equilibrium, even after the shock itself has disappeared.

Begg (1988) presents a model where insiders decide on the wage rates for themselves, and for entrants, in an overlapping generation framework resulting in perfect hysteresis (that is, no tendency for the economy to return to its previous equilibrium once disturbed).

Blanchard and Summers (1986) discuss the importance of membership rules and of objective functions for the group of insiders, which may be unionized or not. The crucial elements of the membership rule are the training time it takes to make an entrant an insider and the time during which a dismissed worker can keep his status of insider. The longer the latter, the more the model behaves stochastically like a classical model, with the level of employment being basically white noise. The faster one becomes an outsider after being fired, the more the model resembles a random walk, with no tendency to return to a previous equilibrium point.

Various attempts have been made to test "outsiders' ineffectiveness" (Layard and Bean 1988). Layard and Nickell (1987) show that the long-term unemployed exert less downward pressure on wages than do the other unemployed. In his study of Australia, Gregory (1986) was one of the first to produce a result of this kind. But the insider-outsider approach is generally regarded as especially suited for the European context (Blanchard and Summers 1986; Fitoussi and Phelps 1988). Applications of this theory to LDCs are yet to come, but would probably be appropriate for some Latin American countries.

In empirical terms, this model stresses the importance of testing for unit root in autoregressive models of aggregates like GDP or the unemployment rate. Perfect hysteresis implies a unit root, while dynamic stability requires a smaller value. This issue has launched a new debate on how to describe the main dynamic characteristics of a macroeconomic series. For a long time the dominant picture was that of irregular cycles around a trend. The random walk description, however, yields a vision where series have spells of small random fluctuations about a given level, which may change abruptly after a series of unexpected shocks in the same direction. These two views are now challenged from a "Keynesian" viewpoint, which regards macroeconomic fluctuations as lapses from a potential (full employment) level (de Long and Summers 1988). In this case the aim of macroeconomic theory is to explain output gaps, rather than cycles around a trend or the persistence of shocks.

Conclusion

I have presented a broad picture of the recent developments in the DC literature on labor markets and the macroeconomy, and I have drawn out some of their implications for LDCs. My emphasis is on the impact of adjustment policies, especially the impact of nominal shocks (monetary policy, devaluation, and so on).

The discussion of the Phillips Curve type of model has brought out the credibility issue in the macroeconomic policy game. But doubts have been reported about the applicability of this whole framework to LDCs. The preponderance of agriculture (with the annual period of production that it entails) and the role of working capital raise the possibility of an upward sloping Phillips Curve.

When presenting the microeconomic models of unemployment, I have noted that the union model could be of use for some LDCs, depending on their level of development and on the democratic character of their political regime. Extending the models to dual labor markets is an important step when applying any model of the labor market to LDCs. The efficiency-wage type of model deals with a wide range of issues relevant for LDCs. The nutrition-productivity model sheds light on rural unemployment, the turnover model can be applied to urban unemployment, and the shirking model brings out some fundamental aspects of the employer-employee relationship in a world of costly monitoring of effort. The shirking model can be used to explain both the role of unemployment in the segment of the labor market where the institution of wage labor prevails, and the fact that this institution can be replaced by sharecropping in different contexts.

The New Keynesian literature follows a path begun a long time ago by founding fathers of development economics. It could provide a renewed framework to revive these themes. Although the insider-outsider approach was developed to analyze European problems, it yields two useful points for the analysis of developing countries. The first one is simply an enrichment of the analysis of trade unions and other types of collusive behaviors of workers. The second is more methodological since this type of model is so deeply rooted in European realities. The point is that specific models can sometimes be more useful than "universal" ones. Analyzing "continent-specific," or even "country-specific," theoretical models can be a fruitful endeavor.

There is much room for crossfertilization between the DC and LDC literature on labor markets and the macroeconomy, especially at the applied level. The literature of LDCs has developed issues and methods of its own, but it seems promising to try and test the theories presented above on data from LDCs, after adapting them appropriately. Only a few such attempts can be found so far in the literature.

References

Ahiauzu, A.I. 1985. "Ideology, Culture, and Trade Union Behavior: The Nigerian Case." *The Developing Economies* 23: 281-295.

Akerlof, G. 1982. "Labor Contracts as Partial Gift Exchange." *Quarterly Journal of Economics* 97: 543-569.

Akerlof, G., and J. Yellen. 1985. "A near-Rational Model of the Business Cycle with Wage and Price Inertia." *Quarterly Journal of Economics* 100: 823-838.

_____. 1986. "Introduction." In G. Akerlof, and J. Yellen, eds., *Efficiency Wage Models of the Labor Market.* Cambridge: Cambridge University Press.

Andersen, T.M. 1989. "Credibility of Policy Announcements: The Output and Inflation Costs of Disinflationary Policies." *European Economic Review* 33: 13-30.

Azam, J-P. 1986. "L'approvisionnement en Biens de Consommation et l'Effort de Production dans un PED: Analyse Théorique." Clermont-Ferrand: CERDI unpublished.

_____. 1988. "A Neo-Structuralist Model of Inflation and Unemployment." In D. Laussel, W. Marois, and A. Soubeyran, eds., *Monetary Theory and Policy.* Berlin: Springer-Verlag.

Azam, J-P., et al. 1989. *The Impact of Macroeconomic Policies on the Rural Poor.* UNDP Policy Discussion Paper. New York: United Nations.

Azariadis, C. 1975. "Implicit Contracts and Underemployment Equilibria." *Journal of Political Economy* 83: 1183-1202.

Baily, M.N. 1974. "Wages and Unemployment Under Uncertain Demand." *Review of Economic Studies* 41: 37-50.

Barro, R.J., and D.B. Gordon. 1983. "A Positive Theory of Monetary Policy in a Natural Rate Model. *Journal of Political Economy* 91: 589-610.

Barro, R.J., and H.I. Grossman. 1971. "A General Disequilibrium Model of Income and Employment." *American Economic Review* 61: 82-93.

_____. 1976. *Money, Employment, and Inflation.* Cambridge: Cambridge University Press.

Basu, K. 1984. *The Less Developed Economy.* Oxford: Basil Blackwell.

Begg, D.K.H. 1988. "Hysteresis, Market Forces, and the Role of Policy in a Dynamic Game with Insiders and Outsiders." *Oxford Economic Papers* 40: 587-609.

Behrman, J.R., A.B. Deolalikar, and B.L. Wolfe. 1988. "Nutrients: Impacts and Determinants." *World Bank Economic Review* 2: 299-320.

Berthélemy, J-C., and F. Cagey. 1984. "Elasticité-prix de l'offre agricole dans les pays en développement: Une note sur la rationalité des agriculteurs dans un contexte non-walrassien." *Annales de l'INSEE,* 55/56, 203-220.

Besley, T., and J. McLaren. 1990. "Tax Compliance and Corruption Deterrence: The Role of Wage Incentive." Discussion Paper 44, J.M. Olin Program. Princeton, N.J.: Princeton University Press.

Bevan, D.L., et al. 1987. "Peasant Supply Response in Rationed Economies." *World Development* 15: 431-439.

Blanchard, O-J. 1983. "Price Asynchronization and Price Level Inertia." In R. Dornbusch and M.H. Simonsen, eds., *Inflation, Debt, and Indexation.* Cambridge, Mass.: MIT Press.

——————. 1986. "The Wage-Price Spiral." *Quarterly Journal of Economics* 101: 543-566.

Blanchard, O-J., and L.H. Summers. 1986. "Hysteresis and the European Unemployment Problem." *NBER Macroeconomics Annual 1986,* 15-78.

Blanchard, O-J., and N. Kiyotaki. 1987. "Monopolistic Competition and the Effects of Aggregate Demand." *American Economic Review* 77: 647-666.

Blejer, M.I., and A. Cheasty. 1988. "High Inflation, Heterodox Stabilization, and Fiscal Policy." *World Development* 16: 867-881.

Bliss, C.J., and N.H. Stern. 1978. "Productivity, Wages, and Nutrition, I: Theory." *Journal of Development Economics* 5: 331-362.

Bruce, N., and D. Purvis. 1985. "The Specification and Influence of Goods and Factor Markets in Open Economy Macroeconomic

Models." In R.W. Jones and P.B. Kenen, eds., *Handbook of International Economics*, pp. 808-857. New York: North-Holland.

Buffie, E. F. 1984. "Financial Repression, the New Structuralists, and Stabilization Policy in Semi-Industrialized Economies." *Journal of Development Economics* 14: 305-322.

Calvo, G. A. 1978. "Urban Unemployment and Wage Determination in LDCs: Trade Unions in the Harris-Todaro Model." *International Economic Review* 19: 65-81.

_____. 1979. "Quasi-Walrasian Theories of Unemployment. *American Economic Review Proceedings* 69: 102-107.

Calvo, G. A., and S. Wellisz. 1979. "Hierarchy, Ability, and Income Distribution." *Journal of Political Economy* 87: 991-1010.

Clower, R. W. 1965. "The Keynesian Counterrevolution: A Theoretical Appraisal." In F. Hahn and F. Brechling, eds., *The Theory of Interest Rates*. London: Macmillan.

Corbo, V., and J. de Melo. 1987. "Lessons from the Southern Cone Policy Reform." *World Bank Research Observer* 2: 111-142.

Dasgupta, P., and D. Ray. 1986. "Inequality as a Determinant of Malnutrition and Unemployment: Theory." *Economic Journal* 96: 1011-1034.

De Long, J. B., and L. H. Summers. 1988. "How Does Macroeconomic Policy Affect Output?" *Brookings Papers on Economic Activity* 2: 433-480.

Demery, L. and T. Addison. 1987. "Stabilization Policy and Income Distribution in Developing Countries." *World Development* 15: 1483-1498.

Dixit, A., and J. E. Stiglitz. 1977. "Monopolistic Competition and Optimum Product Diversity." *American Economic Review* 67: 376-414.

Dompierre, M. B. 1986. "The Role of Unions in African Economic Development." *The Developing Economies* 24: 71-85.

Dornbusch, R. 1982b. "Stabilization Policies in Developing Countries: What Have We Learned?" *World Development* 10: 701-708.

Eaton, C., and W.D. White. 1983. "The Economy of High Wages: An Agency Problem." *Economica* 50: 175-181.

Edwards, S. 1988. "Terms of Trade, Tariffs, and Labor Market Adjustment in Developing Countries." *World Bank Economic Review* 2: 165-185.

Fields, G.S. 1987 "Public Policy and the Labor Market in Developing Countries." In D. Newbery and N. Stern, eds., *The Theory of Taxation for Developing Countries*, pp. 264-277. A World Bank Research Publication. Oxford: Oxford University Press.

Fields, G.S., and H. Wan, Jr. 1989. "Wage-Setting Institutions and Economic Growth." *World Development* 17: 1471-1483.

Fitoussi, J-P., and E.S. Phelps. 1988. *The Slump in Europe.* Oxford: Basil Blackwell.

Friedman, M. 1968. "The Role of Monetary Policy." *American Economic Review* 58: 1-17.

_____. 1977. *Inflation and Unemployment.* London: Institute of Economic Affairs.

Frimpong-Ansah, J.H. 1990. "The Prospects of a Monetary Union in the Context of ECOWAS." In R. Agarwala, ed., *Proceedings of the Workshop on Regional Integration and Cooperation in Sub-Saharan Africa.* Washington, D.C.: World Bank.

Fry, M.J., and D.M. Lilien. 1986. "Monetary Policy Responses to Exogenous Shocks." *American Economic Review Proceedings* 76: 79-83.

Gordon, D.F. 1974. "A Neo-Classical Theory of Keynesian Unemployment." *Economic Inquiry* 12: 431-459.

Greenwald, B., and J.E. Stiglitz. 1989. "Toward a Theory of Rigidities." *American Economic Review Proceedings* 79: 364-369.

Gregory, R.G. 1986. "Wages Policy and Unemployment in Australia." *Economica* 53 (Supplement): S53-S74.

Grossman, G.M. 1983. "Union Wages, Temporary Layoffs, and Seniority." *American Economic Review* 73: 277-290.

Grossman, S., and O. Hart. 1981. "Implicit Contracts, Moral Hazard and Unemployment." *American Economic Review* 71: 301-307.

Guillaumont, P., and S. Guillaumont. 1984. *Zone Franc et Développement Africain*. Paris: Economica.

Hart, O. 1982. "A Model of Imperfect Competition with Keynesian Features." *Quarterly Journal of Economics* 97: 109-1138.

Heady, C. 1987. "Alternative Theories of Wages in Less Developed Countries: An Empirical test." *Journal of Development Studies*. 24: 5-15.

Kanbur, S.M.R. 1987. "Structural Adjustment, Macroeconomic Adjustment, and Poverty: A Methodology for Analysis." *World Development* 15: 1515-1526.

Katz, L. 1986. "Efficiency Wage Theories: A Partial Evaluation." *NBER Macroeconomics Annual, 1986.*

Keynes, J.M. 1936. *The General Theory of Employment, Interest, and Money*. London: MacMillan.

_____. 1940. *How to Pay for the War*. London: MacMillan.

Kiguel, M.A., and N. Liviatan. 1988. "Inflationary Rigidities and Orthodox Stabilization Policies: Lessons from Latin America." *World Bank Economic Review* 2: 273-298.

Klitgaard, R. 1989. "Incentive Myopia." *World Development* 17: 447-459.

Kormendi, R.C., and P. Meguire. 1985. "Macroeconomic Determinants of Growth: Cross-Country Evidence." *Journal of Monetary Economics* 16: 141-163.

Kydland, F.E., and E.C. Prescott. 1977. "Rules Rather than Discretion: The Inconsistency of Optimal Plans." *Journal of Political Economy* 85: 473-491.

Laffont, J-J. 1975. "Macroeconomic Constraints, Economic Efficiency and Ethics: An Introduction to Kantian Economics." *Economica* 42: 430-437.

Layard, R., and C. Bean. 1988. "Why Does Unemployment Persist?" Discussion Paper 321. London: Centre for Labour Economics, London School of Economics.

Layard, R., and S. Nickell. 1987. "The Labour Market." In R. Dornbush and R. Layard, eds., *The Performance of the British Economy.* Oxford: Oxford University Press.

Leibenstein, H. 1957. "The Theory of Underemployment in Densely Populated Backward Areas." Reprinted in 1986. In G.A. Akerlof and J.L. Yellen, eds., *Efficiency Wage Models of the Labor Market,* 22-40. Cambridge: Cambridge University Press.

_____. 1978. *General X-Efficiency Theory & Economic Development.* New York: Oxford University Press.

Lindauer, D.L., O.A. Meesook, and P. Suebsaeng. 1988. "Government Wage Policy in Africa: Some Findings and Policy Issues." *World Bank Research Observer* 3: 1-25.

Lindbeck, A., and D.J. Snower. 1986. "Wage Rigidity, Union Activity and Unemployment." In W. Beckerman, ed., *Wage Rigidity and Unemployment,* 97-125. Baltimore: The Johns Hopkins University Press.

_____. 1987a. "Efficiency Wages Versus Insiders and Outsiders." *European Economic Review* 31: 407-416.

_____. 1987b. "Strike and Lock-Out Threats and Fiscal Policy." *Oxford Economic Papers* 39: 760-784.

_____. 1988. "Cooperation, Harassment, and Involuntary Unemployment: An Insider-Outsider Approach." *American Economic Review* 78: 167-188.

Lizondo, J.S., and P.J. Montiel. 1989. "Contractionary Devaluation in Developing Countries." *IMF Staff Papers,* 182-227.

Long, J.B., and C.I. Plosser. 1983. "Real Business Cycles." *Journal of Political Economy* 91: 39-69.

Lucas, R.E., Jr. 1972. "Expectations and the Neutrality of Money." *Journal of Economic Theory* 4: 103-104.

_____. 1973. "Some International Evidence on Output-Inflation Trade-offs." *American Economic Review* 63: 326-334.

Malcomson, J.M. 1984. "Work Incentives, Hierarchy, and Internal Labor Markets." *Journal of Political Economy* 92: 486-507.

Malinvaud, E. 1977. *The Theory of Unemployment Reconsidered.* Oxford: Basil Blackwell.

_____. 1989. "Observation in Macroeconomic Theory Building." *European Economic Review* 33: 205-223.

Mankiw, N.G. 1985. "Small Menu Costs and large Business Cycles: A Macroeconomic Model of Monopoly." *Quarterly Journal of Economics* 100: 528-539.

_____. 1988. "Recent Development in Macroeconomics: A Very Quick Refresher Course." *Journal of Money, Credit and Banking* 20: 436-449.

Marston, R.C. 1985. "Stabilization Policies in Open Economies." In R.W. Jones and P.B. Kenen, eds., *Handbook of International Economics.* Vol. 2. Amsterdam: North-Holland.

Mauss, M. 1954. *The Gift: Forms and Functions of Exchange in Archaic Societies.* London: Cohen and West.

Mazumdar, D. 1983. "Segmented Labor Markets in LDCs." *American Economic Review* 73, no.2 (May): 254-259.

McDonald, I.M., and R.M. Solow. 1981. "Wage Bargaining and Employment." *American Economic Review* 71: 896-908.

_____. 1985. "Wages and Employment in a Segmented Labor Market." *Quarterly Journal of Economics* 100: 1115-1141.

MacLeod, W.B., and J.M. Malcomson. 1988. "Reputation and Hierarchy in Dynamic Models of Employment." *Journal of Political Economy* 96: 832-854.

Mirrlees, J.A. 1975. "A Pure Theory of Underdeveloped Economies." In L. Reynolds, ed., *Agriculture in Development Theory.* New Haven: Yale University Press.

Murphy, K.M., A. Shleifer, and R.W. Vishny. 1989a. "Income Distribution, Market Size, and Industrialization." *Quarterly Journal of Economics* 104: 537-564.

_____. 1989b. "Industrialization and the Big Push." *Journal of Political Economy* 97: 1003-1026.

Muth, J.F. 1961. "Rational Expectations and the Theory of Price Movements." *Econometrica* 29: 315-335.

Nugent, J.B., and C. Glezakos. 1982. "Phillips Curves in Developing Countries: The Latin American Case." *Economic Development and Cultural Change* 30, 2 (January): 321-334.

Nurkse, R. 1953. *Problems of Capital Formation in Underdeveloped Countries.* Oxford: Basil Blackwell.

Oswald, A.J. 1982. "The Microeconomic Theory of the Trade Union." *Economic Journal* 92: 576-595.

_____. 1986. "Is Wage Rigidity Caused by 'Lay-offs by Seniority'?" In W. Beckerman, ed., *Wage Rigidity and Unemployment*, 77-95. Baltimore: Johns Hopkins University Press.

Otsuka, K., and Y. Hayami. 1988. "Theories of Share Tenancy: A Critical Survey." *Economic Development and Cultural Change*, vol.37, no.1 (October): 31-68.

Parkin, M. 1986. "The Output-Inflation Trade-off When Prices Are Costly to Change." *Journal of Political Economy* 94: 200-224.

Pasinetti, L.L. 1960. "A Mathematical Formulation of the Ricardian System." *Review of Economic Studies* 27: 78-98.

Patinkin, D. 1965. *Money, Interest and Prices: An Integration of Monetary and Value Theory.* New York: Harper & Row.

Phelps, E.S. 1968. Money Wage Dynamics and Labor Market Equilibrium." *Journal of Political Economy* 76: 687-711.

Phillips, A.W. 1958. "The Relation Between Unemployment and the Rate of Change of Money Wage Rates in the United Kingdom, 1861-1957." *Economica* 25: 283-299.

Portes, R. 1981. "Macroeconomic Equilibrium and Disequilibrium in Centrally Planned Economies." *Economic Inquiry* 19: 559-578.

Quibria, M.G., and S. Rashid. 1986. "Sharecropping in Dual Agrarian Economies: A Synthesis." *Oxford Economic Papers* 38: 94-111.

Rosenstein-Rodan, P.N. 1943. "Problems of Industrialization in Eastern and South-Eastern Europe." *Economic Journal* 53: 202-211.

Rotemberg, J.J. 1987. "The New Keynesian Microfoundations." *NBER Macroeconomics Annual 1987*, 69-104.

Sahn, D.E., and H. Alderman. 1988. "The Effects of Human Capital on Wages and the Determinants of Labor Supply in a Developing Country." *Journal of Development Economics* 29: 157-183.

Salop, S.C. 1979. "A Model of the Natural Rate of Unemployment." *American Economic Review* 69: 117-125.

Sargent, T. 1986. *Rational Expectations and Inflation*. New York: Harper & Row.

Scitovsky, T. 1954. "Two Concepts of External Economies." *Journal of Political Economy* 17, vol 62, no. 2: 143-151.

Sen, A.K. 1975. *Employment, Technology and Development*. Oxford: Clarendon Press.

Shapiro, S., and J.E. Stiglitz. 1984. "Equilibrium Unemployment as a Worker Discipline Device." *American Economic Review* 74: 433-444.

Solow, R.M. 1979. "Another Possible Source of Wage Stickiness." *Journal of Macroeconomics* 1: 79-82.

Stiglitz, J.E. 1974. "Alternative Theories of Wage Determination and Unemployment in LDCs: The Labor Turnover Model." *Quarterly Journal of Economics* 88: 194-227.

_____. 1976. "The Efficiency Wage Hypothesis, Surplus Labour, and the Distribution of Income in LDCs." *Oxford Economic Papers* 28: 185-207.

_____. 1982 "Alternative Theories of Wage Determination and Unemployment: The Efficiency Wage Model." In M. Gersovitz, C.F. Diaz-Alejandro, G. Ranis, and M.R. Rozensweig, eds., *The Theory and Experience of Economic Development, Essays in Honor of Sir W.A. Lewis*, London: George Allen and Unwin, 78-106.

Taylor, J.B. 1980a. "Aggregate Dynamics and Staggered Contracts." *Journal of Political Economy* 88: 1-24.

_____. 1980b. "Staggered Wage Setting in a Macro Model." *American Economic Review*, Papers and proceedings 69: 108-113.

Taylor, L. 1983. *Structuralist Macroeconomics*. New York: Basic Books.

van der Gaag, J., M. Stelcner, and W. Vijverberg. 1989. "Wage Differentials and Moonlighting by Civil Servants: Evidence from Côte d'Ivoire and Peru." *World Bank Economic Review* 3: 67-95.

van Wijnbergen, S. 1983. "Credit Policy, Inflation and Growth in a Financially Repressed Economy." *Journal of Development Economics* 13: 45-65.

_____. 1988. "Monopolistic Competition, Credibility, and the Output Costs of Disinflation Programs." *Journal of Development Economics* 29: 375-398.

Weitzman, M.L. 1982. "Increasing Returns and the Foundations of Unemployment Theory." *Economic Journal* 92: 787-804.

2

LABOR MARKET DISTORTIONS AND STRUCTURAL ADJUSTMENT IN DEVELOPING COUNTRIES

Alejandra Cox Edwards
Sebastian Edwards

Most "official" plans to deal with the debt crisis contemplate significant economic reforms in the developing countries. In particular, the Baker plan, the Brady plan, and the programs sponsored by the International Monetary Fund and the World Bank include as one of their key components significant reforms to open up these economies to the rest of the world. In fact, a reform of their trade regime is one of the most important policy prescriptions now being considered by the authorities of the developing nations.[1]

In spite of clear theoretical arguments and of the insistence with which trade liberalization is pushed by the multilateral agencies, many countries vehemently resist it. Why? If trade reform is as desirable as economists have argued, why do we see so few sustained efforts at opening up the developing countries? There is no doubt that trade liberalization entails adjustment costs that often take the form of increased aggregate unemployment. But why do these costs induce so

We are grateful to John Knight, Ravi Kanbur, Miguel Savastano, Ed Buffie, and Luis Riveros for their helpful comments. Alejandra C. Edwards acknowledges support from the California State University–Long Beach Research Office. Sebastian Edwards acknowledges support from UCLA's Academic Senate and from the National Science Foundation.

1. Most World Bank structural adjustment loans (SALs) have had a trade liberalization component as a condition for releasing funds (Thomas 1989).

much resistance, particularly in light of the expectation of future social benefits? Why does the road to protectionism, which also entails an adjustment process, appear so much smoother?

Surprisingly, most of the policy literature on structural reform and liberalization of the external sector has tended to sidestep the question of unemployment.[2] Moreover, in those studies that take the simple Heckscher-Ohlin model as a benchmark, the issue is completely nonexistent. In fact, according to the simplest textbook approach, in a small developing economy with capital-intensive imports, fully mobile factors of production, and flexible prices, the reduction of import tariffs will have no effect on total employment even in the short run. In this setup the only labor market effects of trade liberalization will be a reallocation of labor out of the importables sector and an increase in the real wage rate.[3] In reality, however, there are reasons why these textbook conditions will not hold, and why tariff reforms can lower employment in the short run. In fact, existing historical evidence suggests that in many cases trade liberalization reforms have been associated with short-run increases in unemployment (Edwards 1990).

The Ricardo-Viner model with real wage rigidity provides the simplest framework for illustrating the possible short-run employment consequences of a tariff reform. In this model capital is, in the short run, fixed to its sector of origin; only slowly through time (and possibly via investment) can capital be reallocated. Contrary to the more traditional textbook case with fully flexible prices and resource movements, a tariff reduction in this more realistic setting can lower the *equilibrium* real wage rate required to maintain full employment. However, if for some reason the economy's labor market is distorted— due to a government imposed minimum wage, or to the existence of indexation clauses—there will be downward inflexibility of real wages, and the required reduction in the wage rate will not take place. As a

---

2. There are, however, a few exceptions. Krueger (1983) discusses the empirical relation between trade orientation and employment in the long run; Michaely, Choksi, and Papageorgiou (1986) deal with the employment effects of trade reforms, and Edwards (1990) examines the unemployment ramifications of a cross section of liberalization attempts.

3. This result, of course, is what is predicted by the Stolper-Samuelson theorem under the (plausible) assumption that imports are relatively capital intensive.

result of this rigidity, some of the labor force will become unemployed.

Labor markets play a crucial role in determining the success of liberalization policies. This paper provides a theoretical survey of the ways labor markets can react to structural adjustment reforms. More specifically, we provide a typology of different labor market configurations and investigate how two main liberalization policies—a reduction of import tariffs and the relaxation of capital controls—will affect the level of aggregate employment and the rate of unemployment. Our analysis is based on the employment implications of several models.[4]

We start with a brief discussion of the standard Australian or dependent economy model with flexible wages and prices. Its deficiencies are pointed out. This model provides a benchmark case that is then used to discuss different extensions. In the second section we discuss labor market distortions in the form of wage rigidities. Here we make a distinction between economy-wide and sector-specific wage rigidity. Capital is assumed to be sector specific, and our focus is on short-run situations. The third section of the paper incorporates an intertemporal dimension and deals with both the employment effects of relaxing capital controls and the employment implications of anticipated trade liberalization reforms. We then relax the standard trade theory assumption of a fixed labor supply and consider a model with upward-sloping labor supply and queuing. In this fourth section we pay closer attention to the initial labor market conditions of a typical protected economy. We assume that, along with trade protection, the economy is characterized by labor unions or some other institutionalized form of labor protection.[5] Ironically, the factor of production that is supposed to gain from freer trade is actually gaining from trade restrictions. Needless to say, it is not the entire labor force that benefits from protectionism but only the more organized sectors. It is perhaps within this setting that the resistance to trade liberalization can be better understood.

---

4. We survey and summarize a number of existing models including some we have used in our previous work such as Cox-Edwards (1986) and Edwards (1988, 1990).

5. Labor unions have a stronger negotiating power and sometimes even monopsony power in a closed economy.

Tariff Liberalization and Labor Market Adjustment in the Standard Australian Model

We will now discuss the way in which a tariff liberalization reform affects the labor market in the standard Australian model with flexible prices and no market distortions.[6] These results will then be compared later in the paper with those obtained from alternative specifications of the labor market.

Consider the case of a small country that produces and consumes three goods: importables (M), exportables (X), and nontradables (N).[7] Households consume all three goods and maximize a utility function subject to a constraint that states that the value of expenditure does not exceed income. There are a large number of identical producers, and perfect competition prevails in the goods markets. Firms are assumed to maximize profits subject to existing technology and to the available factors of production: labor, capital, and natural resources.[8] In addition to consumers and producers, there is a government that imposes a tariff on imports. Following traditional trade theory, it is assumed that the revenue from the tariff is handed back to consumers in a lump-sum fashion.[9] There are no other taxes and no government

---

6. This model has a long tradition in international trade theory. See Mussa (1974) and Dornbush (1974, 1980). Edwards (1988) provides a diagrammatical discussion of this standard model.

7. The distinction between two types of tradable goods (X and M) and a nontradable good (N) is analytically convenient, and it is at the very core of modern open economy macroeconomics. In practice, however, it is not easy to determine which goods are actually tradables and which are nontradables. Indeed, statistics for the vast majority of countries do not make such a distinction. Although this practical difficulty does not invalidate the usefulness of the dependent economy model, it does imply that analysts and policymakers should be particularly careful (and creative) when using this model. At the simplest level it can be argued that (at least) a large percentage of the services sector of an economy is constituted by nontradables. The importance of this nontradable sector will vary across countries. For instance, some authors have argued that, strictly speaking, in the case of Uruguay there are no nontradables: at least for Argentinean consumers all Uruguayan goods are tradable.

8. Alternatively, we can assume that there are two factors only—capital and labor—and that capital is sector specific in the short run. In fact, this formulation is much simpler than the one used in this section. On three-factor models of international trade, see Leamer (1987).

9. For a model where the government uses tariff proceeds to finance its own consumption, see Edwards (1989a).

spending on goods or services. Finally, we use the price of exportables as the numeraire.

Denoting the revenue function by R, the expenditure function by E, the price of nontradables relative to exportables by q, and that of importables relative to exportables by p, the equilibrium in this simple economy can be represented by the following set of equations (where a subindex refers to a partial derivative):

$$R(1,p,q;L,K,G) + \tau(E_p - R_p) = E(1,p,q,U),\qquad(1)$$

$$E_q = R_q,\qquad(2)$$

$$p = p^* + \tau.\qquad(3)$$

where L, K, and G are labor, capital, and natural resources, respectively, τ is the specific import tariff, (E_p-R_p) are imports, and U is total utility.[10] Equation (1) is the budget constraint and establishes that total income—stemming from factors' income and government transfers—has to equal expenditure. Equation (2) is the nontradables equilibrium condition. Equation (3) establishes the relation between the domestic price of importables and the import tariff τ.

As in most traditional trade models, we assume that factors supplies—and in particular the supply of labor—are inelastic.[11] The initial labor market equilibrium is illustrated in Figure 2.1 where the horizontal axis measures total labor available in the economy, and the vertical axis depicts the wage rate in terms of exportables. Schedule L_T denotes the demand for labor by the tradable goods sector and is equal to the horizontal sum of the demand for labor by the exportables sector, (schedule L_X), and the demand for labor by the importables sector. Demand for labor by the nontradable goods sector is shown by schedule L_N. The initial equilibrium is characterized by full employment and a wage rate equal to w_0. At this position O_TL_A

---

10. For a detailed exposition of traditional trade theory using duality, see Dixit and Norman (1980).

11. We relax this assumption later in our analysis of queuing models. See also Edwards (1990).

labor is used in the production of exportables, $L_A L_B$ labor is employed in the production of importables, and $O_N L_B$ labor is used in the production of nontradables. Assume that in the short run only labor can move across sectors, although in the long run all three factors are mobile. However, since our main interest is on the short-run consequences of structural reform, most of our discussion will focus on the Ricardo-Viner case with factor specificity.

Consider now a tariff liberalization reform that reduces the import tariff and thus causes a reduction in the domestic price of importables. In this simple general equilibrium framework, this reform will affect a number of variables including relative prices. With regard to employment, the tariff reduction will provoke changes in the allocation of labor across sectors.

In order to track down the full effect of the reform on the labor market, it is first necessary to determine the effect of the reduction in tariffs on the price of nontradable goods. Only then will we be able to know the direction of the shift of schedule L_N in Figure 2.1. From the manipulation of equations (1) to (3), it is easy to show that the direction in which the price of nontradables will change is going to depend on the assumptions made regarding substitutability in demand and on the magnitude of the income effect. Assuming that the three goods are gross substitutes in consumption and that the income effect does not exceed the substitution effect, the price of nontradables as a result of the tariff reform will fall relative to that of exportables: that is, $dq/d\tau > 0$.[12]

The labor market adjustment process under these assumptions is illustrated in Figure 2.2. The reduction in the tariffs will result in a lower domestic price of importables, generating a downward shift of the L_T curve (with the L_X curve constant). The new L_T' curve will intersect the L_N curve at R. However, since the reduction in the world price of importables will also result in a *decline* in the price of nontradables (relative to exports), this is not the final equilibrium. As a consequence of the decline of q, L_N will shift downward (by less than the shift in L_T), and the final short-run equilibrium will be achieved at

---

12. For a formal and more complete analysis of the effects of tariff reforms and terms of trade disturbances on the equilibrium real exchange rate, see Edwards and van Wijnbergen (1989).

Figure 2.1 Standard Dependent Economy Model: Labor Market Equilibrium

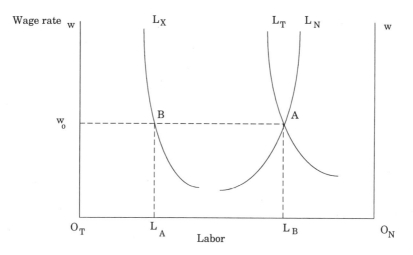

Figure 2.2 Standard Dependent Economy Model: Trade Liberalization

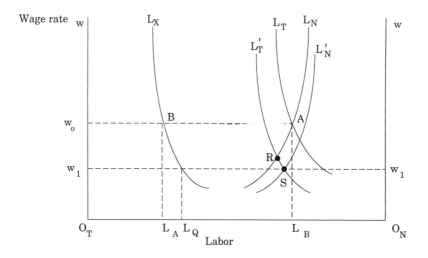

S with a lower wage rate w_1. In this new equilibrium, production of exportables has increased, with labor used by this sector increasing by $L_A L_Q$. The production of nontradables may either increase or decrease, and production of importables will fall. In the case depicted in Figure 2.2, labor has moved out of the importables sector and into the exportables and nontradables sectors.

What has happened to factor rewards in the short run? Wages have declined in terms of exportables (from w_0 to w_1 in Figure 2.2). Wages have also declined in terms of nontradables because the vertical distance between the L_N and L'_N curves is smaller than the reduction in w from w_0 to w_1. Wages, however, have increased relative to importables because the domestic price of these goods has fallen by more than the decline in wages. In the exportables sector, the real return to the sector-specific factors has increased. However, the real return to these fixed factors in the importables and nontradables sectors could either increase or decrease.[13]

Thus, in the standard Ricardo-Viner model with wage flexibility a tariff liberalization reform will have the following short-run effects on production, prices, and factor rewards: (1) production of exportables will increase; (2) production of importables will decrease; (3) production of nontradables may increase or decrease; (4) prices of nontradables will decrease; (5) wages will increase in terms of importables and decrease in terms of exportables and nontradables; (6) the real return to the sector-specific factors allocated to the exportables sector will increase relative to all goods; (7) the real return to factors specific to the importables sector will decrease relative to importables but could increase or decrease relative to the other goods; and (8) the real return to factors specific to the nontradables sector will increase relative to nontradable goods but either increase or decrease relative to the other two goods.

Until now we have assumed that the main difference between the short- and long-run effects of a trade liberalization is that, in the short run, capital and natural resources are locked in their sector of origin. As time passes, however, capital will slowly move between sectors. To

---

13. Formally, the real return on the sector-specific factors allocated to the importables sector will decrease in terms of importables and could increase or decrease in terms of the other two goods. See Edwards (1988).

simplify the exposition, let us assume that the movement of capital does not require the use of resources. However, the analysis could be modified by introducing a "moving industry," which uses labor and a specific factor, as in Mussa (1978). The transition period will be characterized by factors moving between sectors, until the new long-run equilibrium (that is, post trade liberalization) capital-labor ratios, and production levels are attained.

The analysis of the long-run equilibrium when the three factors are mobile can be rather complicated. The reason, of course, is that with three factors the concept of factor intensities becomes somewhat ambiguous. However, as Leamer (1987) has shown, if we assume that a particular sector is more intensive in a factor relative to both of the other factors, then the Stolper-Samuelson theorem will still hold.[14] In terms of our discussion, if we assume that the importables sector is the least labor intensive sector, relative to both capital and natural resources, then we can conclude that in the long run real wages will increase, as occurred in the two-factors case in Edwards (1988).

Although the dependent economy framework presented here provides a useful starting point for analyzing the way in which a trade reform affects the labor market, it has a number of shortcomings. Perhaps the most important one is the assumption of factor price flexibility. In many developing nations there exists some kind of (real) wage rigidity. A second shortcoming of this model is that it ignores all intertemporal considerations. Within this framework it is not possible to analyze issues related to restrictions to capital movements or to the way in which the level of employment reacts to anticipated changes in tariffs. A third limitation of this standard formulation is that it assumes, within the tradition of trade theory, that the labor supply is completely inelastic. Finally, the assumption of no-search activities on behalf of workers is also quite stringent and unrealistic. The models presented in the following sections attempt to overcome some of these limitations.

---

14. A formal and detailed discussion of the long-run case is given in Edwards (1990).

Sector-Specific Human Capital

So far we have referred to labor as a homogeneous factor. However, for the type of question we are studying, the results would not be qualitatively changed if we allowed for differences in general human capital. In fact, we could easily incorporate differences in general human capital by introducing the distinction between units of labor and the number of workers. That is, some workers would have embodied more units of labor than others. However, if we assume the existence of sector-specific or industry-specific human capital (Oi 1962), our conclusions would be affected because in that case labor mobility would be costly.

One of the consequences of a trade liberalization reform is that it wipes out entire industries, destroying the value of industry-specific human capital. This loss of productive factors, in different degrees, has to be considered as part of the adjustment costs of trade liberalization. In practice, this cost translates into a type of unemployment that reflects differences between the market value of a given worker's human capital and the same worker's perception of what that value is, based on his or her recent experience and expectations. This type of phenomenon affects the experienced groups of the labor force most negatively.

Moreover, the change in relative prices brought about by a trade liberalization changes not only the market value of sector-specific human capital, but also the geographical allocation of labor demand. Thus, mobility costs associated with labor reallocation across areas can become an additional barrier to full employment immediately after a trade reform takes place. In fact, the labor economics literature has given attention to this type of adjustment barrier in an effort to explain wage differentials and unemployment across geographical areas or sectors of economic activity (Topel 1986). These ideas, although not yet applied to the question of trade reform, can be very useful in an empirical analysis of trade liberalization experiences.

Wage Rigidities and Labor Market Adjustment

The previous discussion followed the traditional Australian model of international trade, which assumes that all factor prices, including wages, are perfectly flexible. However, this is a simplifying assumption that does not correspond to reality in many developing countries where minimum wage laws or other types of rigidities affect the whole economy or some parts of it.[15] In the past ten years or so, a number of international trade models that assume some type of factor price rigidity have been developed (Brecher 1974; Bruce and Purvis 1984). These useful models have added considerable realism to the analysis, but most of them have concentrated on the case in which the economy produces only two goods. They have not addressed specifically the way in which trade liberalization reforms will affect aggregate employment.

In this section we extend these results to the three-goods model and discuss the effects of tariff liberalization under both economy-wide and sector-specific wage rigidities stemming from exogenously imposed minimum wages. Again the analysis concentrates on the short-run case in which capital and natural resources are locked into their sector of origin. Although the discussion emphasizes the case of minimum wages, it is also useful for understanding the effects on employment of other mechanisms widely applied in developing countries, such as wage indexation arrangements, and disequilibrium real wages set by powerful labor unions.

Economy-wide Wage Rigidities

Consider first the case of an economy-wide minimum wage. In order to facilitate the diagrammatical exposition, this minimum wage is assumed to be expressed in terms of our numeraire (exportables).[16] The incorporation of an economy-wide minimum wage into the analysis requires that we modify the model given by equations (1) to (3). Specifically, we now need to define a "restricted" revenue function that considers the existence of wage rigidities and initial unemployment such as:

---

15. For a review of practices used in different countries to determine minimum wages, see Starr (1981).

16. The results we present are fairly sensitive to this assumption. Edwards (1990) discusses in detail how using different price indexes to set the minimum wage will affect the results from the model.

$$\overline{R}\left(\overline{W},p,q;V\right)=\max_{S,L}\left\{\left(S_X+qS_N+pS_M\right)-\overline{W}L\right\} \tag{4}$$

where $\overline{W}$, is the minimum wage; L is employment; S_i, i=X,M,N, refers to output of exportables, importables, and nontradables, respectively; and V refers to the vector of nonlabor (flexible-price) factors of production.[17] This restricted revenue function can be conveniently written in the following way:

$$\overline{R}=\overline{R}\left(1,p,q,L\left(1,p,q,\overline{W}\right)\right) \tag{5}$$

were L( ) is an employment function (Neary 1985).

In this case the nontradable market equilibrium condition also has to incorporate in an explicit way the existence of wage rigidity and of initial unemployment. This is done by computing the supply of nontradables as the derivative of the restricted revenue function relative to the price of nontradables q:

$$\overline{R}_q=E_q \tag{6}$$

The nature of the initial labor market equilibrium is now captured by Figure 2.3, which is similar to Figure 2.1. Demand for labor by the tradable goods sector (L_T) is equal to the horizontal sum of the demand for labor by the exportables sector (L_X), and the demand for labor by the importables sector (L_M, not shown). Demand for labor by the nontradables sector is given by the L_N schedule. If there is a minimum wage rate equal to $\overline{W}$, unemployment of magnitude U' will result; the amount of labor demanded by the nontradables sector is now determined by the minimum wage and is equal to $O_N L_N^1$.[18]

---

17. See Neary (1985) for a detailed discussion of the properties of restricted revenue functions.

18. Notice, however, that if the minimum wage is fixed in terms of the importable good, the tariff reform will not generate any unemployment. In order for the wage rate to remain constant in terms of M, it will have to decline in terms of the exportable. See Edwards (1990).

Figure 2.3 Economy-Wide Minimum Wage: Unemployment

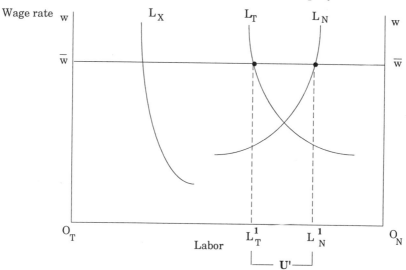

Figure 2.4 shows that when labor is the only mobile factor, and there is a minimum wage in real terms (expressed in terms of the exportables), a tariff reduction will result in an *increase* in unemployment which is given by U". As shown in the previous

Figure 2.4 Economy-Wide Minimum Wage: Trade Liberalization

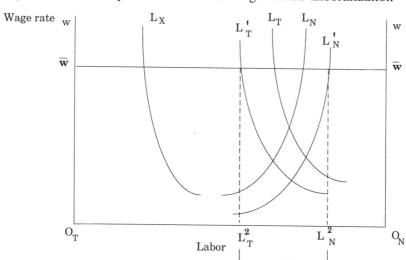

section, the reason for this is the decline in the (real) wage that a trade liberalization will require in order to maintain the prereform level of employment. If, due to institutional factors, this reduction cannot take place, the adjustment will occur via quantities, and total employment will be reduced. The extent of the change in employment will in turn depend on: the magnitude of the tariff reduction, the amount by which the price of nontradables goes down, and the employment elasticities in the different sectors.

Formally, the effect of a tariff change on total employment is given by the expression:

$$\frac{dL}{d\tau} = L_p + L_q \left(\frac{dq}{d\tau} \right) \tag{7}$$

where Lp and Lq are the derivatives of the employment function with respect to the domestic price of importables and the relative price of nontradables respectively, and where (dq/dτ) is the "real exchange rate effect" of the tariff change. Within our Ricardo-Viner framework with initial unemployment, both Lp and Lq are positive, indicating that increases in domestic prices will result in higher employment.[19] On the other hand, under the most plausible assumptions, (dq/dτ) will be positive, indicating that a tariff increase (liberalization) will result in a real exchange rate appreciation (depreciation). Consequently, equation (7) as a whole has a positive sign, implying that with rigid (real) wages and factor specificity a trade liberalization reform will result in unemployment.

What will happen in the long run? In this case all factors will move across sectors, and the interpretation of terms Lp and Lq in equation (7) will be more complicated and will be related to the direction of the Rybczynski effects. Formally:

---

19. In the case of full factor mobility, it is rather difficult to sign these derivatives.

$$L_p = \frac{-R_{pL}}{R_{LL}}$$

$$L_q = \frac{-R_{qL}}{R_{LL}}$$

(8)

where R_{LL} is the slope of the marginal product of labor schedule and is negative. R_{pL} and R_{qL}, on the other hand, are Rybczynski terms that capture what will happen to output of M and N (R_p and R_q, respectively) if there is an increase in the labor force. Their sign is undetermined *a priori* and depends on relative factor intensities, which are difficult to determine in our 3x3 model. However, as Leamer (1987) has shown, if nontradables is the most labor intensive sector—with respect to capital and to natural resources—R_{qL} will be positive. This means that R_{pL} can be either positive or negative. A necessary (although not sufficient) condition for it to be positive is that importables is the second most labor intensive sector. If we assume that R_{pL} is also positive, then we will obtain the result in which a tariff liberalization reduces employment. If, however, importables is the least labor intensive sector (as measured with respect to both of the other factors), R_{pL} will be negative, and we can obtain the more standard result where, starting from an initial condition of unemployment, a trade liberalization reform will increase total employment in the economy.

Sector-Specific Wage Rate Rigidity

In most countries wage rigidity is not generalized. Rather, it affects a subgroup of sectors in the economy. In this subsection we will briefly use our diagrammatic apparatus to analyze two cases where the above-equilibrium wage affects only one sector in the economy.[20]

---

20. The formal analysis of a sector-specific wage rate rigidity is somewhat complicated. See Edwards (1990).

CASE 1: SECTOR-SPECIFIC WAGE RIGIDITY WITH NO UNEMPLOYMENT. This configuration of the labor market has recently been used by Burda and Sachs (1987) to analyze the structure of unemployment in Germany. It is assumed that one sector, say nontradables, is subject to an above-equilibrium wage rate, and that the wage rate in the rest of the economy—the so-called uncovered sector—takes the level required to ensure full employment in the economy as a whole. The initial conditions under these assumptions are summarized in Figure 2.5, where $\overline{W}_N$ is the minimum wage in the protected sector (the nontradables sector), and W_T is the wage rate in the uncovered (tradables) sector. Employment in tradables is equal to the distance O_TA, and employment in nontradables is equal to O_NA.

Under these conditions, and assuming that capital and natural resources are sector-specific, a trade liberalization reform will increase the wage gap between the protected and the uncovered sectors, reduce employment in nontradables and importables, and increase employment and output in exportables (see Figure 2.6).

Figure 2.5 Sector-Specific Wage Rigidity and Full Employment

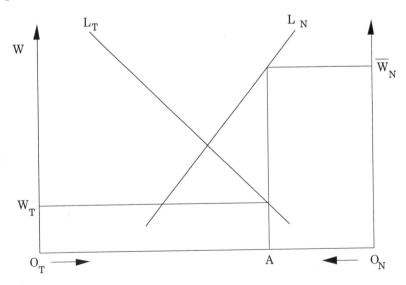

Figure 2.6 Sector-Specific Wage Rigidity and Trade Liberalization

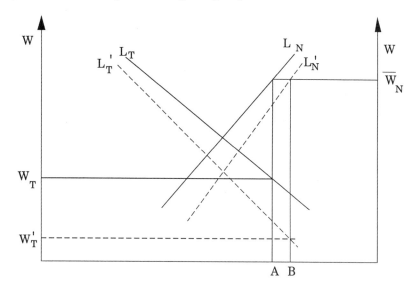

The main limitation of this approach is that it is characterized by a nonequilibrium wage rate differential $(\overline{W}_T - W_N)$ that can only be maintained if there are severe barriers to entry to the protected sector. Only in this way can it be reconciled having a major distortion in the labor market, in the form of intersectoral wage differentials, and no unemployment. An elegant way of solving this problem is by introducing, as we do below, a Harris-Todaro type of mechanism to generate an equilibrium wage rate differential.

CASE 2: SECTOR-SPECIFIC MINIMUM WAGES WITH UNEMPLOYMENT. Consider now the case where there is a binding minimum wage in the importables sector only. In order to analyze this case, the diagrams used previously must be somewhat modified. Figure 2.7 is similar to Figure 2.5 except that in Figure 2.7 total labor used in the importables sector is measured from the righthand side origin O_M. The wage rate $\overline{W}_M$ is the minimum wage in the importables sector (say, manufacturing); $\overline{L}_M$ is employment in this sector. Curve qq is a rectangular hyperbola known as the Harris-Todaro locus, along which the following equation is satisfied:

Figure 2.7 Sector-Specific Wage Rigidity and Unemployment

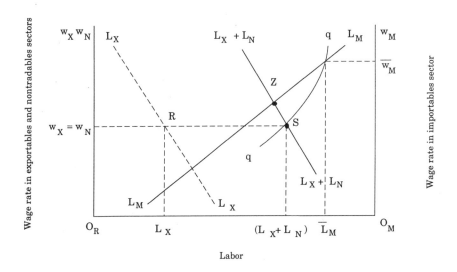

Labor

$$W_N = W_X = \frac{\overline{L}_M}{\overline{L}_M + U} \, \overline{W}_M \, , \tag{9}$$

where U is the equilibrium level of employment.[21] In the absence of a minimum wage, equilibrium is attained at point Z. With a minimum wage, however, the intersection of $(L_X + L_N)$ with qq at point S gives the wage rate in the uncovered (no minimum wage) sectors, employment in each sector, and total unemployment. The distance $O_R L_X$ is total employment in the exportables sector; the distance $L_X(L_X+L_N)$ is employment in nontradables; the distance $(L_X+L_N)\overline{L}_M$ is the initial equilibrium level of unemployment; and the distance $O_M \overline{L}_M$ is employment in the covered sector.[22]

---

21. This is based on Harris and Todaro (1970) and Harberger (1971). For the use of this framework in the context of a two-sector economy, see Corden and Findlay (1975) and Neary (1981). The discussion that follows draws from Edwards (1988).

22. There is an important difference between this type of minimum wage model in which total availability of labor to the economy is given and models with an upward sloping aggregate supply of labor.

The short-run (with capital immobile across sectors) effects of a reduction in the world price of importables are illustrated in Figure 2.8. As a result of the decline in the world price of importables, demand for labor in that sector shifts downward. At the given minimum wage, $\overline{W}_M$, total demand for labor in the importables sector will decline. The new demand for labor in the importables sector (not drawn) will intersect $\overline{W}_M$ at A. A new rectangular hyperbola q'q' passes through this point, and labor demanded by the importables sector is now reduced to $O_M\overline{L}_M{}'$.

What will happen to wages and employment in the uncovered sectors and to unemployment? Under the assumption that the price of nontradables remains constant, curve (L_X+L_N) remains at its original location, and point B, given by the intersection of q'q' and (L_X+L_N), is the new equilibrium. This position is characterized by a lower wage and higher employment in the uncovered sectors. As discussed above, however, the reduction of tariffs will affect the price of nontradables and (L_X+L_N) will not remain constant. Under the assumptions discussed before, the lower tariffs will generate a reduction in the price of nontradables, which is, however, smaller than the decline in the price of importables. As a result, in the final short-run equilibrium, (L_X+L_N) will shift downward to (L_X+L_N) (not drawn). The intersection of $(L_X+L_N)'$ and the q'q' rectangular hyperbola at point C is the final equilibrium when capital is locked in its sector of origin.

Under the given assumptions, the post-tariff-reduction equilibrium is characterized by the following: (1) lower employment in the sector covered by the minimum wage (importables); (2) lower wages in the uncovered sectors, expressed in terms of exportables; (3) either higher or lower equilibrium unemployment; (4) either lower or higher employment in nontradables; and (5) higher employment and production in exportables.[23]

Not surprisingly, a tariff liberalization in the case of partial minimum wage coverage generates a different outcome than that obtained in the case of an economy-wide minimum wage. First, under

23. In this setting, unemployment is given by $U = L_M(\overline{W}_M/W_N{-}1)$. Because L_M declines and $\overline{W}_M/W_N$ goes up, it is not possible to know *a priori* which way U will go. The final direction will depend on the elasticities of demand for labor in each sector.

partial coverage, there is an increase in production and employment in exportables. Second, employment in nontradables may also increase. In the short run, the reduction in tariffs can result in a decline in the equilibrium level of unemployment in the case of partial minimum wage coverage, whereas greater unemployment always results after such a policy in the case of an economy-wide minimum wage. This illustrates an important finding: in the presence of labor market distortions, trade liberalization policies usually considered to be beneficial may general nontrivial (short-run) unemployment problems.

What will happen in the long run in the presence of this type of sector-specific minimum wage? In the short run, after the domestic price of importables has gone down, the real return to (sector-specific) capital will be different across sectors. The reduction in tariffs reduces the return to capital in the importables (manufacturing) sector and increases it in the exportables and nontradables sectors. Of course, this situation with different real returns to capital cannot continue in the long run. As time goes by, capital will be reallocated, moving out of importables and into the other sectors. In terms of Figure 2.8, this means that L_M will shift further downward—and with it the rectangular

Figure 2.8 Sector-Specific Wage Rigidity, Unemployment, and Trade Liberalization

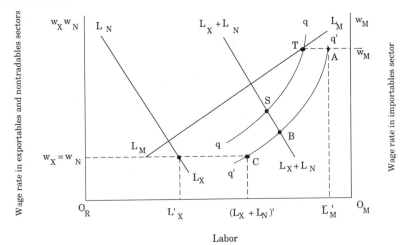

hyperbola qq—while demand for labor in the uncovered sectors will shift upward. Moreover, these curves will shift in such a way that the final outcome will be characterized by a higher equilibrium wage in the absence of wage rigidities.

The final long-run equilibrium must satisfy two conditions: the return to capital must be equalized across sectors, and the labor market must be in equilibrium in the sense that $W_N = W_X = \left\lceil \bar{L}_M / \left(\bar{L}_M + U\right)\right\rceil \bar{W}_M$. As capital is reallocated, employment in the importables sector declines and employment in the exportables and nontradables sectors increases in relation to the short-run levels depicted in Figure 2.8. It is not possible, however to know *a priori* whether wages in the uncovered sectors (nontradables and exportables) will be higher or lower in the long run than their initial levels. This will depend on the elasticities of substitution and on the relation between the slopes of the L_M, qq, and $(L_X + L_N)$ curves.

The Liberalization of the Capital Account, Anticipated Tariffs, and Employment

The preceding framework has ignored intertemporal decisions and thus cannot handle issues such as the employment effects of relaxing capital controls or the employment consequences of an anticipated change in tariffs. The purpose of this section is to extend the dependent economy model to an intertemporal setting and to investigate how the presence of more than one period modifies the results from the static model analyzed before.[24]

The Intertemporal Dependent Economy Model

The simplest way to incorporate intertemporal aspects is by considering the existence of two periods: the present (period 1) and the future (period 2). If we now want to look at capital account liberalization, we must assume that initially there are capital controls that are reflected in a differential between the domestic real interest

---

24. The discussion that follows focuses on the role of intertemporal substitution in consumption. Some macroeconomic models that became popular in the 1970s also emphasized intertemporal substitution in the supply of labor. However, recent empirical work by Altonji (1982) and Mankiw et al. (1985) have shown that this type of effect is not empirically relevant.

rate (r) and the foreign real interest rate (r*). As before, it is assumed that there are many producers and identical consumers, and that perfect competition prevails. The labor market is distorted by a minimum wage $\overline{w}$, which we first assume is in effect in both periods.

In this 2-period model, consumers maximize utility subject to their intertemporal budget constraint, whereas firms maximize profits subject to the existing constant returns to scale technology, availability of factors of production, and the predetermined minimum wage. Assuming that the utility function is time separable, with each subutility function homothetic and identical, the representative consumer problem can be stated as follows:

$$\max \quad V\left[u\left(c_N, c_X, c_M\right); U\left(C_N, C_X, C_M\right)\right],$$

subject to:

$$c_X + pc_M + qc_N + \delta\left(C_X + PC_M + QC_N\right) \leq \text{Wealth}, \qquad (10)$$

where the lower-case letters refer to the first-period variables and the upper-case letters refer to second-period variables. The price of exportables has been taken to be the numeraire, (for example, $p_X = P_X = 1$). V is the intertemporal welfare function; u and U are periods 1 and 2 subutility functions assumed to be homothetic and identical. c_X, c_M, c_N, (C_X, C_M, and C_N) are consumption of X, M, and N in period 1 (period 2). q and Q, and p and P are the prices of nontradables and importables relative to exportables faced by consumers in periods 1 and 2, and they are inclusive of the tariff on M. δ is the domestic discount factor equal to $(1+r)^{-1}$. Since there is a tax on foreign borrowing, the domestic real interest rate r is higher than the world interest rate. The differences between these two rates is given by the tax (σ) on capital movements: $r = r^* + \sigma$.

Wealth is the discounted sum of consumers' income in both periods. Income, in turn, is given by: (1) income from labor services; (2) income from the renting of capital stock and natural resources that consumers own to domestic firms; and (3) income obtained from government transfers. These transfers, in turn, correspond to the government's revenue from tariffs and from taxes on capital flows in each period. The solution to the consumers' optimizing problem is conveniently summarized by the following intertemporal expenditure function:

$$E = E\left(\pi(1,p,q), \delta^* \Pi(1,P,Q), V\right), \tag{11}$$

where π and Π are exact price indexes for periods 1 and 2. Under the assumptions of homotheticity and separability, these price indexes correspond to unit expenditure functions (Svensson and Razin 1983; Edwards and van Wijnbergen 1986). Given our assumption of a time separable utility function, total expenditure in periods 1 and 2 are always substitutes.

As before, the producers' maximization problem can be summarized with the aid of restricted revenue functions, which give us the maximum revenue that firms can obtain after making all the optimal decisions in terms of hiring and production given the distortion in the labor market (Neary 1985). Denoting r and R as periods 1 and 2 restricted revenue functions, we have:

$$r = r\left(1,p,q,\ell\left(1,p,q,\overline{w}\right)\right) \tag{12}$$

and

$$R = R\left(1,P,Q,L\left(1,P,Q,\overline{W}\right)\right) \tag{13}$$

where $\ell(\ )$ and $L(\ )$ are employment functions in periods 1 and 2.

The complete model is then given by the following set of equations (where subindexes refer to partial derivatives with respect to that variable):

$$r\left(1,p,q,\ell(1,p,q,\overline{w})\right) + \delta R\left(1,P,Q,L\left(1,P,Q,\overline{W}\right)\right)$$
$$+ TRANS = E\left(\pi\ (1,p,q), \delta \Pi(1,P,Q), V\right) \tag{14}$$

$$TRANS = bCA + \tau^1 M^1 + \delta \tau^2 M^2 \tag{15}$$

$$b = \delta^* - \delta \tag{16}$$

$$CA = R - \Pi E_{\delta\Pi} \tag{17}$$

$$r_q = E_q \tag{18}$$

$$R_Q = E_Q \tag{19}$$

$$p = p^* + \tau^1; \quad P = P^* + \tau^2 \tag{20}$$

$$M^1 = (E_p - r_p); \quad M^2 = (E_P - R_P). \tag{21}$$

Equation (14), the intertemporal budget constraint, says that the present value of income (the lefthand side) has to equal the present value of expenditure (the righthand side). TRANS, the present value of government transfers to the public, is given by equation (15). Here bCA is the present value of the tax on foreign borrowing, where b is the present value of the tax per unit borrowed and is equal to (δ*-δ), and CA is the current account in period 2, which is defined in equation (17) as period 2 income minus expenditure. Since in this model there is no investment, the current account is equal to savings in each period. Finally, $\tau^1 M^1$ and $\delta\tau^2 M^2$ in equation (15) are revenues from import tariffs; τ^i is the tariff rate in period i, and M^i are imports in i and are defined in equation (21) as the excess demand for importables in each period. Equations (18) and (19) state that the nontradables goods market has to clear in each period; r_q and R_Q are the quantities produced of these goods, and E_q and E_Q are quantities demanded.

An important characteristic of this model is that there is initial unemployment. In fact, we can think of Figure 2.3 as capturing the initial conditions prevailing in the labor market in each period. The model assumes that the minimum wage ($\overline{w}$) is expressed in terms of the numeraire and is in effect in both periods. Of course, this need not be the case, and we can easily handle the case where there is a minimum wage in one period only.

In the rest of this section we will illustrate the functioning of this model for the case of two liberalization policies: (1) the relaxation of capital controls and (2) an anticipated tariff liberalization. In order to facilitate the discussion, in each case we will make some simplifying assumptions that will allow us to focus on the problem at hand.

Capital Account Liberalization and Employment

The model presented in equations (14) through (21) is very general and can be used to analyze how a number of structural adjustment policies will affect welfare, output, and employment. In this subsection we will focus on the employment effects of reducing capital controls under a set of simplifying assumptions.[25] In particular we will assume that:

(1)   the minimum wage is in effect during period 1 only;[26]

(2)   there are no import tariffs in either period.

The only distortions in the economy under analysis are a minimum wage in period 1 and a tax on foreign borrowing.

A reduction in the extent of capital controls implies that the domestic discount factor δ increases, moving closer to its international level δ^*. As a result of this the consumption rate of interest $\delta\Pi/\pi$ will increase, making current consumption relatively more attractive than future consumption. Thus, households will substitute expenditure into the present. Since some of this increase in expenditure in period 1 will fall on nontradables, there will be an incipient excess demand for N, which will result in an increase in the price of N in that period (q). This means that the period-1 real exchange rate will experience an equilibrium appreciation as a result of the liberalization of the capital account (Edwards 1989b). This, in turn, will shift the demand for labor in the N sector upward, generating an increase in employment in period 1. This effect will be reinforced by the positive welfare effect of reducing the existing distortion on foreign borrowing.

In a Ricardo-Viner framework with sector-specific capital and natural resources, this is the final effect of a capital account reform. However, if we assume that capital and natural resources can move

---

25. The liberalization of capital controls has played an important role in recent reform programs in the Southern Cone of Latin America and in Korea.

26. This assumption is also made by Svensson (1984) in a different context.

across sectors, we will have additional indirect affects that will shift further the labor demand schedules. The direction and magnitude of these induced shifts will depend on the sign of the Rybczynski effects. If we assume that the nontradable sector (N) is the most labor intensive of all sectors and that the importable sector (M) is the least labor intensive, the final effect of a capital account reform will be an increase in period-1 employment. See Edwards (1989b) for a formal expression. This labor market adjustment is captured in Figure 2.9 where the shift of L_N to L'_N is the result of the (impact) real exchange rate effect of a higher δ, and the shift of L'_N to L''_N and of L_T to L'_T are the consequences of the reallocation of the cooperative factors.

Under our assumptions, the optimal government policy would be to impose a *small* subsidy on foreign borrowing. A small subsidy on external borrowing would result in higher consumption, and thus employment, in period 1. Since initially employment in this period was "too low," the small subsidy would tend to correct this distortion.

Figure 2.9 Capital Account Liberalization

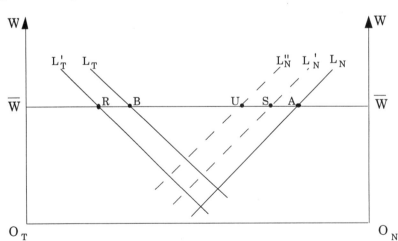

The magnitude of this subsidy will be given by:

$$b^* = \frac{r_\ell \ell_q \left(\dfrac{dq}{db}\right) + \delta^* R_L L_Q \left(\dfrac{dQ}{db}\right)}{-\Pi^2 E_{\Pi\Pi} + \Pi E_{\pi\Pi} \pi_q \left(\dfrac{dq}{db}\right) + \delta \Pi E_{\Pi\Pi} \Pi_Q \left(\dfrac{dQ}{db}\right)} \; , \qquad (22)$$

where r_ℓ and R_L are the marginal product of labor in periods 1 and 2. ℓ_q and L_Q are the derivatives of each period employment function with respect to that period's relative price of nontradables and, as before, are equal to:

$$\ell_q = \frac{-r_{q\ell}}{r_{\ell\ell}}; \; L_Q = \frac{-R_{QL}}{R_{LL}} \; .$$

R_{LL} and $r_{\ell\ell}$ are, in turn, the slopes of the marginal product of labor schedules for N and are negative; $r_{q\ell}$ and R_{QL} are the Rybczynski terms that capture what will happen to output of N (r_q and R_Q) when there is an increase in labor supply. Under our assumptions of labor intensities, they are positive. Finally (dq/db) and (dQ/db) are the "real exchange" rate effects of the capital account liberalization. They measure the reaction of the equilibrium relative prices of N to a lowering of the tax on foreign borrowing and are positive (Edwards 1989b).

Anticipated Tariff Reform and Employment

The model developed in this section can be used to analyze how the expectations or anticipations of a tariff reform—that is, a reduction in τ^2—will affect employment in an economy with initial unemployment. As in the case of capital account liberalization, the main channel through which these anticipations will generate an effect will be the intertemporal substitution of expenditure and its effects on the real exchange rate. To the extent that an anticipated tariff reform postpones current expenditure, we will observe, in the Ricardo-Viner case, a reduction in the price of nontradables in the current period, q, and a decline in employment.

Formally, under Ricardo-Viner assumptions of sector-specific capital and natural resources, the aggregate employment effects of an anticipated tariff reform are given by:

$$\text{period 1:} \quad \frac{d\ell}{d\tau^2} = \ell_q \left(\frac{dq}{d\tau^2} \right) \tag{23}$$

$$\text{period 2:} \quad \frac{dL}{d\tau^2} = L_P + L_Q \left(\frac{dQ}{d\tau^2} \right). \tag{24}$$

These expressions capture several important results. First, as can be seen from equation (23), a future (anticipated) tariff reform will affect employment in period 1, when the reform has not taken place yet. This effect takes place exclusively through the change in period-1 real exchange rate, which is induced by the future tariff reform. Edwards (1989b) has shown that under plausible assumptions a future tariff liberalization will result in a real exchange depreciation: that is, $dq/d\tau^2$ > 0.[27] Under Ricardo-Viner assumptions, ℓq is positive and thus $d\ell/d\tau^2$ in equation (23) is also positive.[28] This means that a future tariff reform will result in a *decline* in today's aggregate employment.

Second, according to equation (24), there will be two channels through which an anticipated tariff reform will affect period-2 aggregate employment. The first one, captured by the term L_P, is the direct effect that, under Ricardo-Viner assumptions, will be positive. The second channel is given by the term $L_Q(dQ/d\tau^2)$ and operates via changes in the equilibrium real exchange rate in period 2. Under the most plausible assumptions, a tariff reform will result in a real exchange rate depreciation in the period when the reform actually takes place: that is, $(dQ/d\tau^2)$ > 0. Given that under Ricardo-Viner assumptions L_Q is also positive, expression (24) will by unambiguously positive. If capital and natural resources are sector

---

27. The conditions required for this result are that all goods are substitutes in consumption and that the income effects do not offset the substitution effect.

28. Remember that l_q is the derivative of the employment function with respect to the price of nontradables. In a Ricardo-Viner setting, the only effect of a change in q is a parallel shift in the L_N schedule.

spccific, an anticipated tariff reform will increase unemployment in periods 1 and 2.

If instead of a Ricardo-Viner setting we assume that capital and natural resources can move freely across sectors, the interpretation of equations (23) and (24) will be different. As said before, the signs of ℓ_q and L_Q will then depend on the Rybczynski terms and thus on relative factor intensities.

Trade Restrictions, Labor Market Protection, and Elastic Labor Supply

One of the shortcomings of the dependent economy model is that it assumes an inelastic labor supply. Here we relax this assumption and introduce a different type of involuntary unemployment. In the dependent economy model there is also no connection between the level of the minimum wage and the trade orientation of the economy. Here we assume that there is some form of institutional wage protection (unions, government, or other) that becomes stronger in an economy that is more closed to the rest of the world.[29] Thus, the minimum wage that prevails for the importables sector tends to be relatively higher when there are high trade restrictions. In order to maintain our presentation at a simple level, we greatly simplify other aspects of the problem, concentrating on a one-period partial equilibrium representation. This, however, proves sufficient for our purposes.

Consider, once again, a three-goods economy with exportables (X), importables (M), and nontradables (N). We now assume that there *is* a minimum wage that affects only one sector. More specifically, we assume that the importables sector (M) is subject to a minimum wage and that wages are market determined in the nontradables (N) and exportables (X) sectors. In order to simplify the exposition, we consider only two factors: capital and labor. While capital is fixed in its sector or origin in the short run, it is perfectly mobile in the long run.

---

29. Monopsony power will tend to increase in the same way as monopoly power under trade protection.

We relax the assumption that labor supply is inelastic by considering the existence of a distribution of labor supply prices, and by assuming that labor force participation is determined by the market wage. Since wages in the M sector are higher than in the rest of the economy, labor supply to that sector exceeds demand. We assume for simplicity that firms in the M sector select the workers they employ randomly (that is, in a way that is not correlated with labor supply prices) from the pool of applicants As a result, some potential workers would be willing to take a "protected" job but are unwilling to settle for a lower wage in the N or X sectors.

This situation is described in Figure 2.10, where schedule L_S represents a labor supply derived from a linear distribution of supply wages. At the minimum wage (W_M), employment in M is equal to $L_M < L_S(W_M)$. By assumption, employment in M is a random sample of $L_S(W_M)$, which implies that the labor supply to the rest of the labor market (L_s') is a fraction $(1-L_M/L_S(W_M))$ of the original supply L_S. The interaction between labor demand in X and N, denoted by (L_N+L_X) in Figure 2.10, and the "residual" labor supply to those sectors will determine the free segment wage $W_f = W_N = W_X$ and the level of employment in X (L_X) and N(L_N). Individuals with supply price above W_f and below W_M are voluntarily unemployed with respect to X and N and involuntarily unemployed with respect to M. We refer to this group as *quasi-voluntary unemployed* (U^{qv}). With a linear distribution of supply prices, the amount of quasi-voluntary unemployment is given by:

$$U^{qv} = \frac{W_M - W_f}{W_M - \underline{W}}(1-\beta)L_s(W_M) \qquad (25)$$

where $\underline{W}$ is the smallest reservation wage for which the supply of labor to the market is positive.

A crucial difference between the current model and the standard dependent economy model is that in this case we will have an equilibrium level of queuing unemployment. In equilibrium, the *expected* wage in the protected segment, for those who choose to queue, will be equal to the alternative wage in the free segment. Figure 2.11 shows the presence of both types of unemployment.

Figure 2.10 Elastic Labor Supply: Quasi Voluntary Unemployment

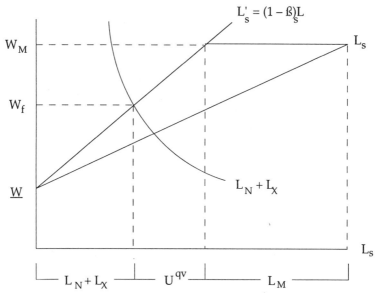

Figure 2.11 Elastic Labor Supply: Queuing Unemployment

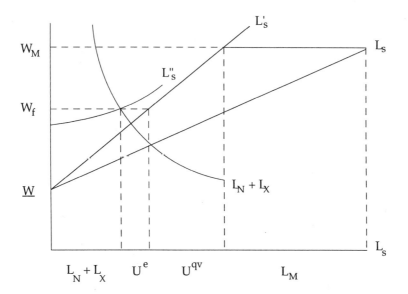

Wage "protection" results in a very elastic labor supply to the "protected" sector (M) and a less elastic labor supply to the rest of the labor market. As a result, the general trend will be for quasi-voluntary unemployment to fall when labor demand increases in the M sector and for the free sector wage to increase when labor demand increases in the N and X sectors.

In what follows, we develop a formal model for analyzing the way in which tariff liberalization will affect unemployment and wages in our framework with upward sloping supply and queuing. We define L_N, L_X, and L_M as the general equilibrium demand functions for labor in the nontradables, exportables, and importables sectors. The aggregate supply of labor to the economy L_S is a function of (real) wages and can be expressed as depending on the wage rate in the importables sector. We call β the proportion of the total labor supply employed in sector M at W_M:

$$\beta = \frac{L_M}{L_S(W_M)} . \qquad (26)$$

The fraction $(1-\beta)$ of individuals with supply price lower or equal to W_M have three alternatives. The first is to become part of the total supply of labor to the nonprotected sectors. We assume, however, that in spite of having jobs in the nonprotected sectors, this group can still apply to jobs in sector M, and it has a probability p of being chosen. The second alternative is to spend the present period queuing, so that the probability of getting a job in sector M increases to γp $(\gamma>1)$. The third alternative is to become voluntarily unemployed with respect to sectors N and X and involuntarily unemployed with respect to M.

Assuming risk neutrality and no unemployment compensation, the present value of the first two alternatives for the marginal worker has to be the same. There will thus be an equilibrium queuing unemployment level for each possible value of W_M. To simplify the notation, we present here the case in which all jobs turn over each period. Thus, the expected wage of applying for a job in M is $(1-p)W_N + pW_M$, whereas the value of queuing is $\gamma p W_M$. Therefore, the equilibrium condition becomes:

$$(1-p)W_f = p(\gamma - 1)W_M \tag{27}$$

with

$$p = \frac{L_M}{L_N + L_X + U^{qv} + \gamma U^e + L_M} \tag{28}$$

where L_N is the number of workers employed in the nontradables sector, L_X is the number of workers employed in the exportables sector, U^{qv} is the level of quasi-voluntary unemployment, U^e is the level of equilibrium queuing unemployment, and L_M is the number of workers employed in the importables sector. Using the expression $u^e = U^e/L_S (W_M)$ for the rate of equilibrium unemployment, and combining expressions (26), (27), and (28), we find:

$$u^e = \frac{W_M}{W_f}\beta - \left(\frac{1-\beta}{\gamma - 1}\right) \tag{29}$$

as well as the effective supply of labor to the nonprotected sectors of the labor market that is equal to:

$$L_S''(W_f) = (1-\beta)L_S(W_f) - \left[\frac{W_M}{W_f}\beta - \left(\frac{1-\beta}{\gamma-1}\right)\right]L_S(W_M). \tag{30}$$

A Reduction in Import Tariffs

A reduction in import tariffs implies a decrease in the domestic price of M relative to X. Additionally, as discussed earlier, the reduction of the import tariffs will affect the relative price of nontradables: if nontradables are substituted with importables and exportables in consumption, the reduction of the tariff will result in a decline in the price of nontradables.[30]

---

30. Notice that if trade liberalization is accompanied by a large amount of foreign aid or foreign credit capable of inducing a large income effect, the impact of the relative price of nontradables may be positive.

Assuming, at least for the short run, that the protected wage W_M remains constant, we expect no change in labor force participation. A reduction in L_M—generated by the reduction in the tariff—with a given L_S (W_M) means that the fraction β defined in (26) falls. In turn, a reduced fraction of workers employed in M increases the quasi-voluntary unemployment and signals a lower probability of finding a protected job, triggering a reduction in queuing unemployment.[31] Thus, labor supply to the free segment will shift downward inducing a reduction in the free sector wage rate W_f. If we now consider the reduction in L_f included by the decline in relative prices of nontradables (the real exchange rate effect), we get an even larger reduction in the nonprotected wage rate W_f.

In order to simplify the presentation in the derivations that follow, we will ignore the change in L_f and estimate the impact on u^e of a change in β induced by a reduction in the extent of trade protection. Since a tariff liberalization will result in a reduction in β, our analysis will deal with the way in which changes in this parameter will affect unemployment and wages in the unprotected sector. Imposing the equilibrium condition in the free market sectors (X and N), we can find how the changes in the demand for labor in the protected sector will affect unemployment and the freely determined wage rate:

$$\frac{du^e}{d\beta} = \frac{1}{\gamma - 1} + \frac{W_M}{W_f} - \beta \frac{W_M}{W_f^2} \frac{dW_f}{d\beta} \qquad (31)$$

with

$$\frac{dW_f}{d\beta} = \frac{L_s(W_f) + \left[\dfrac{W_M}{W_f} + \dfrac{1}{\gamma - 1}\right]L_s(W_M)}{\left(\varepsilon^f - \eta^f\right)L_f/W_f} \geq 0 \qquad (32)$$

where $L_f = L_X + L_N$, ε^f is the elasticity of labor supply to the free sectors of the labor market, and η^f is the elasticity of labor demand to the free sectors.

---

31. See Cox-Edwards (1986).

The wage reduction in the non-protected or free sectors (X and N) induces an increase in labor use in those sectors, but at the same time more potential workers become quasi-voluntary unemployed. Therefore, the immediate effect of trade liberalization is a loss of employment in the M sector; the sector we associate with more "attractive" or "better paid" jobs. This will increase the level of quasi voluntary and queuing unemployment and will exert downward pressure on the level of wages as workers seek employment in the free segment.

The above discussion assumes that the protected wage segments are maintained after the trade liberalization. This is not a fully plausible assumption. In the long run we could indeed expect that trade liberalization would weaken the capability of governments to grant protection to certain sectors of the labor market, and that wages would come down in line with labor market conditions.[32]

What will happen if W_M is reduced? First, β will increase not only through the numerator (depending on η^M) but also through the denominator because aggregate labor force participation will fall with W_M. The magnitude of this fall will depend on ε, the elasticity of labor supply to the market. At the same time, the equilibrium level of queuing unemployment will be affected by changes in β and W_M. This in turn, will affect labor supply to the nonprotected sectors and W_f.

From (29) we have:

$$\frac{du^e}{dW_M} = \frac{\partial U^e}{\partial W_M} + \frac{\partial U^e}{\partial \beta}\frac{\partial \beta}{\partial W_M} + \frac{\partial U^e}{\partial W_f}\frac{\partial W_f}{\partial W_M} \tag{33}$$

---

32. Here we are assuming that the minimum wage affects the importable sector and that its level will be affected by changes in the tariff. However, this does not need to be the case for every country. Indeed, it is possible that in some countries the exportables sector has a protected labor market. This, of course, would change our result.

where:

$$\frac{\partial W_f}{\partial W_M} = \frac{L_M W_M + L_f W_f \dfrac{\varepsilon W_f}{W_M} + (\varepsilon - \eta^M)\dfrac{L_M W_f^2}{W_M}}{\eta^f L_f W_f - L_M W_M} \leq 0. \tag{34}$$

Combining these expressions we obtain:

$$\frac{du^e}{dW_M} = \underset{(+)}{\frac{\beta}{W_f}} + \underset{(-)}{\left[\frac{1}{\gamma-1} + \frac{W_M}{W_f}\right]}(\eta^M - \varepsilon)\frac{\beta}{W_M} -$$

$$\underset{(-)}{\frac{L_M \cdot W_M \cdot \beta}{L_M W_M - \eta^f L_f W_f}\left(\frac{\varepsilon - \eta^M}{W_M} + \frac{W_M}{W_f^2} + \frac{\varepsilon L_f}{L_M W_M}\right)} \tag{34'}$$

For the particular case where $\eta^M = 0$ and $\eta^f = -\infty$ we have that a change in W_M will affect u^e in the following way:

$$\frac{du^e}{dW_M} = \frac{\beta}{W_f}\left[1 - \varepsilon\left(\frac{1}{\gamma-1} + \frac{W_M}{W_f}\right)\right]. \tag{35}$$

Notice that this expression states that a reduction in W_M will generate two offsetting effects on queuing unemployment: with the reduction in W_M, the gains from queuing decrease, but the probability of getting a job in the M sector rises. The higher is ε, the more important is the second (positive) effect. In fact, if

$$\varepsilon < \frac{(\gamma-1)W_M}{(\gamma-1)W_M + W_f} \quad \text{then} \quad \frac{du^e}{dW_M} > 0 . \tag{36}$$

We can then state:

$$\frac{du^e}{dW_M} \begin{cases} > & 0 \quad \text{if} \quad e \approx 0 \\ < & 0 \quad \text{if} \quad e > 1 \end{cases} \tag{37}$$

and for $0 < \varepsilon < 1$ the effect of W_M on queuing unemployment will depend on how close W_M and W_f are at the initial level of W_M. That is, the expression du^e/dW_M will be positive for a very inelastic labor supply and will be negative for an elastic labor supply.

In short, the more time we allow for the adjustment of the labor market (the more elastic is labor supply), the larger will be the reduction in u^e induced by a downward adjustment of the protected sector wage rate W_M. At the same time, the level of quasi-voluntary unemployment will fall as the difference between W_M and W_f shortens:

$$
\frac{dU^{qv}}{dW_M} = \left(\frac{W_f - \underline{W}}{W_M - \underline{W}} \right)(1-\beta) - \frac{U_{qv}}{W_M}\left(\eta^M - \varepsilon\right) \bullet \frac{\beta}{1-\beta}
$$
$$
- \frac{1-\beta}{W_M - \underline{W}} \ \frac{\partial W_f}{\partial W_M} \ \geq \ 0 \ .
$$

(38)

A reduction of tariffs that induces a reduction of employment in the protected sector (importables) will result in higher quasi-voluntary unemployment, lower free sector wages, and higher free sector employment in the short run. In the long run, we assume that the strength of the wage protection weakens and W_M falls. With the reduction of W_M, labor force participation falls, the labor market tightens, quasi-voluntary unemployment falls, and queuing unemployment ultimately falls as the difference between free sector wages and protected wages disappears. To complete the previous analysis, the effect of trade liberalization on labor demand in the free segment would have to be included. In this case, however, the final result will depend on the factor intensities, on the income elasticity of demand for nontradables, and on the size of the income effect generated by the reduction in employment in the importables sector.

In general it is not possible to determine analytically if the average level of wages falls or rises with the trade liberalization effort. This will depend on how distorted the labor market was initially and on how we weight the wage contribution of different groups.

Conclusions

This paper has analyzed a number of international trade models that can deal with the employment consequences of trade reforms. Within the most basic trade framework—Heckscher-Ohlin model—a trade liberalization does not generate any employment problems in a developing nation where exports are labor intensive. In fact, this will be the case whether wages are flexible or rigid. We started by evaluating the standard dependent economy model. However, contrary to traditional treatments, we considered the case where there are three factors of production. This extension introduced some nontrivial problems since in that case it is not possible to determine unequivocally factor intensities. In this setting and assuming wage flexibility, we showed that the short-run effects on production, prices, and factor rewards of a tariff liberalization reform will be as follows: (1) production of exportables will increase; (2) production of importables will decrease; (3) production of nontradables may increase or decrease; (4) prices of nontradables will decrease; (5) wages will increase in terms of importables and decrease in terms of exportables and nontradables; (6) the real return to the sector-specific factors allocated to the exportables sector will increase relative to all goods; (7) the real return to factors specific to the importables will decrease relative to importables but could increase or decrease relative to other goods; and (8) the real return to the factor-specific nontradables sector will increase relative to nontradable goods but could either increase or decrease relative to the other two goods. In the long run, factor rewards are equalized across sectors. Under the assumption that the importables sector is the least labor intensive sector, real wages will increase.

The same model indicates that trade liberalization results in unemployment if wages do not adjust downward. If the wage rigidity is limited to the importables sector only, there will be equilibrium unemployment initially, and a trade liberalization will tend to increase the gap between wages in the importables and the other sectors. The labor force in this case will tend to be reallocated between nontradables and exportables. The effect of trade liberalization on total unemployment is not clear because there are two forces that affect the equilibrium level of unemployment in opposite directions. On the one hand, the probability of finding a "high wage" job is reduced by the reduction in labor demand in the importables sector. On the other hand, the wage in the rest of the labor market falls, reducing the opportunity cost of unemployment.

The effect of capital account liberalization on the labor market was studied using an intertemporal framework. Under the assumption that the economy is distorted by controls to capital mobility and a minimum wage, we find that the removal of capital controls tends to increase employment in nontradables through a positive expenditure effect. In a similar framework we also showed that an anticipated tariff reform can generate a negative effect on the level of employment.

In the last section we paid closer attention to the starting conditions of a typical protected economy. We modified the assumption of a given minimum wage and assumed that the degree of wage distortion in the importables sector was directly related to the degree of trade protection. In this case, one of the implications of trade reform is the consequent reduction of the predetermined wage in the importables sector to a level compatible with market conditions. At the same time, we relax the assumption of a fixed labor supply and thus allow labor force participation to be a function of wages. We define labor force participation as determined by all those workers willing to take a job in the high-wage sector. In this context, we define quasi-voluntary unemployment as that which is involuntary with respect to the importables sector and voluntary with respect to the rest of the labor market. Under these assumptions, the immediate effect of a trade liberalization is a decline in the level of employment in the importables sector, which will increase the level of quasi-voluntary unemployment and will tend to reduce wages in the rest of the economy as some workers seek employment there. In the long run, we expect that trade liberalization would weaken the capability of governments to grant protection to unions or to certain sectors of the labor market and that wages would come down in line with labor market conditions. The structure of the labor market will then change, and the difference between protected wages and free sector wages will tend to disappear, eliminating the distinction between the two types of unemployment described in the text.

In this framework it is clear that wages in the importables sector fall, although it is not clear how aggregate average wages behave. However, it is perhaps in this setting that the opposition to trade liberalization can be better understood. Labor, which is the factor of production that is supposed to gain from freer trade, is negatively affected in the short run. The long-term gains are hard to perceive when compared to the initially distorted situation of the economy.

References

Altonji, J. 1982. "The Intertemporal Substitution Model of Labor Market Fluctuations: An Empirical Analysis." *Review of Economic Studies.* November: 507-522.

Brecher, R.A. 1974. "Minimum Wage Rates and the Theory of International Trade." *Quarterly Journal of Economics* 88 (February): 98-116.

Bruce, N., and D. Purvis. 1985. "The Specification and Influence of Goods and Factor Markets in Open Economy Macroeconomic Models." In R.W. Jones and P.B. Kenen, eds., *Handbook of International Economics*, pp. 808-857. New York: North-Holland.

Burda, M., and J. Sachs. 1987. "Institutional Aspects of Unemployment in Germany." NBER Working Paper. Cambridge, Mass.: National Bureau of Economic Research.

Corden, W.M., and R. Findlay. 1975. "Urban Unemployment, Intersectoral Capital Mobility, and Development Policy." *Economica* 42: 59-78.

Cox-Edwards, A. 1986. "Economic Reform, External Shocks, and the Labor market: Chile, 1974-83." Paper presented at World Bank Conference on Adjustment of Labor Markets in LDCs to External Shocks. June.

Dixit, A., and V. Norman. 1980. *Theory of International Trade.* Cambridge: Cambridge University Press.

Dornbusch, R. 1974. "Tariffs and Nontraded Goods." *Journal of International Economics* 4, no.2 (May): 177-185.

_____. 1980. *Open Economy Macroeconomics.* New York: Basic Books.

Edwards, S. 1988. "Terms of Trade, Tariffs, and Labor Market Adjustment in Developing Countries." *World Bank Economic Review* 2: 165-185.

_____. 1989a. *Real Exchange Rates, Devaluation, and Adjustment.* Cambridge, Mass.: MIT Press.

_____. 1989b. "Tariffs, Capital Controls, and Equilibrium Real Exchange Rates." *Canadian Journal of Economics.*22, no. 1 (February): 79-92.

_____. 1990. "Structural Reforms and Labor Market Adjustment." UCLA Dept. of Economics Working Paper.

Edwards, S., and S. van Wijnbergen. 1986. "The Welfare Effects of Trade and Capital Market Liberalization." *International Economic Review* 27: 1411-1448.

_____. 1989. "Structural Adjustment and Disequilibrium." In H. Chenery and T.N. Srinivasan, eds., *Handbook of Development Economics.* New York: North-Holland.

Harberger, A.C. 1971. "On Measuring the Social Opportunity Cost of Labor." *ILO Review* 103: 559-579.

Harris, J., and M.P. Todaro. 1970. "Migration, Unemployment and Development: A Two-Sector Analysis." *American Economic Review* 60: 126-142.

Krueger, A. 1983. *Trade and Employment in Developing Countries.* Chicago: University of Chicago Press.

Leamer, E. 1987. "Paths of Development in the Three-Factors, N-Goods General Equilibrium Model." *Journal of Political Economy* 95, no. 5 (October): 961-999.

Mankiw, N.G., J. Rotemberg, and L. Summers. 1985. "Intertemporal Substitution in Macroeconomics." *Quarterly Journal of Economics* 100 (February): 225-253.

Michaely, M., A. Choksi, and D. Papageorgiou. 1986. "The Phasing of a Trade Liberalization Policy: Preliminary Evidence."

Paper presented at the Annual Meeting of American Economic Association, New Orleans. December.

Mussa, M.L. 1974. "Tariffs and Distribution of Income: Importance of Factor Specificity, Substitutability, and Intensity in Short and Long Run." *Journal of Political Economy* 82: 1191-1203.

_____. 1978. "Dynamic Adjustment in the Heckscher-Ohlin-Samuelson Model." *Journal of Political Economy* 86: 775-791.

Neary, P. 1981. "On the Harris-Todaro Model with Intersectoral Mobility." *Economica* 48: 219-234.

_____. 1985. "International Factor Mobility, Minimum Wage Rates, and Factor Price Equalization: A Synthesis." *Quarterly Journal of Economics* 100 (August): 551-570.

Oi, W. 1962. "Labor as a Quasi-Fixed Factor." *Journal of Political Economy* 70: 538-555.

Starr, G. 1981. *Minimum Wage Fixing: An International Review of Practices and Problems*. Geneva: International Labor Office.

Svensson, L. 1984. "Oil Prices, Welfare, and the Trade Balance." *Quarterly Journal of Economics* 99: 649-672.

Svensson, L., and A. Razin. 1983. "The Terms of Trade and the Current Account: The Harberger-Laursen-Meltzer Effect." *Journal of Political Economy* 91: 97-125.

Thomas, V. 1989. "Extent of Trade Reforms in the 1980s." Washington, D.C.: World Bank. Processed.

Topel, R. 1986. "Local Labor markets." *Journal of Political Economy* 94, no.3, part 2 (June): S111-143.

3

THE POVERTY EFFECTS OF ADJUSTMENT WITH LABOR MARKET IMPERFECTIONS

Tony Addison
Lionel Demery

Whereas in the not-too-distant past, there seemed only to be voices crying in the wilderness on behalf of the poor in developing countries (voices such as those of Cornia et al. 1987), today bilateral and multilateral donors alike are once again directing their attention to poverty alleviation. Much of this resurrection of interest has emerged from the implementation of adjustment policies in developing countries, since there is a longstanding suspicion that the poor bear a disproportionate burden of the short-run costs of adjustment. Moreover, the emphasis given to market forces in restoring economic growth raises the longer-run question of whether such a process will benefit lower income groups. Much of this has a familiar ring— rekindling debates on trickle down and redistribution with growth.

The poverty/adjustment policy debate, however, has revealed a weakness in orthodox (and, for that matter, nonorthodox) theory: the general lack of understanding about the tradeoff between macroeconomic policy on the one hand and income distribution on the other. Orthodox theory is strictly agnostic about how conventional macroeconomic adjustment packages will affect the poor, even at the highest level of theoretical abstraction. The added complexities introduced by the peculiar characteristics of most developing countries, and by the particularly difficult empirical challenges that the subject raises, all combine to leave the impression that this is a story that remains mostly untold.

The present need is for a simple conceptual framework to guide our thinking. In another paper (Addison and Demery 1989), we build on the earlier work of Cornia, Jolly, and Stewart (1987) by developing the notion of the "meso," which is simply that which comes between the micro and macroeconomies.[1] There are three main components to the meso: markets in which microeconomic units trade (which can be product or factor markets, official, unofficial, or even illegal); economic infrastructure (including the physical infrastructure and other economic services not provided by the market); and social infrastructure (most importantly, health and education services). Understanding how adjustment affects poor households, therefore, requires a two-stage analysis: micro-meso analysis in order to identify how macro policies influence markets and infrastructure; and meso-micro analysis to understand how households (or individuals) are affected by the meso-economic changes that are so induced.

This simple framework is the basis for this paper. We are concerned with only one (albeit generally critical) meso-economic element: the operation of the labor market and how it transmits macro-changes into micro outcomes, notably the effect on poverty. The approach we shall take is first to understand the meso effects of macro policy (identifying its unemployment and real wage consequences), and then to trace how these are likely to affect poverty. Our main preoccupation is with short-run effects, since this accords with most policy priorities. Moreover, the long run is too uncertain—shocks in the future can completely swamp whatever long-run processes are set in motion by current adjustment policies. Consequently, capital will be assumed to be sector specific and fixed in supply. Insofar as sectoral shifts in output occur under adjustment, they are achieved through labor reallocations alone.

The labor market, of course, is central to any consideration of how macroeconomic policies affect poverty, since the poor often rely entirely on their labor services to generate primary incomes. Yet most of the theoretical work to date does little justice to the complex ways in which the labor market might transmit income changes to the poor. The adjustment/ poverty literature generally assumes a fully

---

1. "Meso" is derived from the Greek "mesos" or middle.

competitive labor market, so that it denies potential conflicts of interest among working groups. Our purpose is to introduce, in a relatively simple manner, labor market imperfections into the analysis of adjustment and poverty.

We begin with a brief account of the competitive model and its predictions about the poverty outcomes of adjustment. Wage inflexibility is then introduced in a "disequilibrium" framework, with quantity rationing throughout the labor market, and the poverty effects of policy intervention derived. In dealing with partial labor-market rigidities, the next section assumes that the imperfections, apply only to one sector (which may be tradables or nontradables). We then analyze the case where market imperfections affect both tradables and nontradables. Finally, we discuss the real world applicability of the theoretical cases considered.

The Orthodox Treatment

Our starting point then is the account of macroeconomic adjustment and poverty as given by the standard international trade or "orthodox" model—namely, the "Meade-Salter-Swan" or dependent-economy model.[2] It has provided the theoretical structure for many contributions to the adjustment/poverty literature, including Knight (1976), Corden (1985), Lal (1984, 1988), and Edwards (1988).[3]

The basis of the model is a distinction between traded commodities, whose prices are given in world product markets, and nontraded goods, the prices of which are determined by domestic supply and demand. Both tradables (T) and nontradables (N) are final consumer goods. There are no intermediate goods here. It is assumed that each commodity requires both capital and labor in its production. Capital is sector specific, while homogeneous labor is mobile across the sectors, even during the short run of our policy time frame. In this way we exclude long-run considerations (in which capital may be considered as mobile between sectors) from our analysis. This implies that the rate of return to capital may not be equal in the two sectors. Arbitrage in

---

2. It is also known as the "Australian" model.
3. Corden (1986) considers the model to be particularly suited to developing-country problems. Variants of the model with quantity rationing are reviewed later in this paper.

the labor market, however, ensures that real wages are equalized. Moreover, by assuming that the money wage is fully flexible, full employment is ensured, so that the economy is consistently at its production frontier.

Consider such an economy experiencing an unsustainable balance of trade deficit as depicted in Figure 3.1. Given a level of real absorption of OA in terms of nontradables, and a real exchange rate (defined as the relative price P_n/P_t) of AA', production is at x while expenditure is at y. There is internal balance (there being full employment in the labor market and zero excess demand in the nontradables market), but a balance of trade deficit of xy. If all prices are fully flexible, a policy of disabsorption (for example, cutting government spending or increasing taxes) would restore equilibrium. This would cause a depreciation in the real exchange rate (P_n/P_t falling to BB'), taking both the consumption and production points to z. In the final equilibrium, absorption has to be reduced to OB (valued in nontradables). However, if P_n is inflexible downward, this contractionary policy will not be able to induce the necessary production switching to restore equilibrium. Under such circumstances, the depreciation in the real exchange rate must be brought about through an increase in P_t rather than a fall in P_n as in the previous case. Therefore, a combination of an exchange rate depreciation (taking the real exchange rate to BB') and expenditure reduction (taking absorption to OB) will do the trick.

The "meso" effects of all this can now be considered. A necessary condition for restoring equilibrium (without creating unemployed labor or capital) is to switch production from N to T. It is this production switching that determines the main distributive effects of adjustment.[4] In the short run, output switching can be brought about only by *labor reallocations* from sector N to sector T. Labor market

---

4. We are tracing changes only in the "primary" distribution that are generated by these production effects. The change in absorption (through, for example, cuts in government expenditure) will lead to adjustments in the "secondary" distribution by changing the pattern of income transfers. These are ignored in this paper, although it should be borne in mind that the real wage effects that are derived would need to be modified if expenditure cuts reduced elements of the "social wage."

Figure 3.1

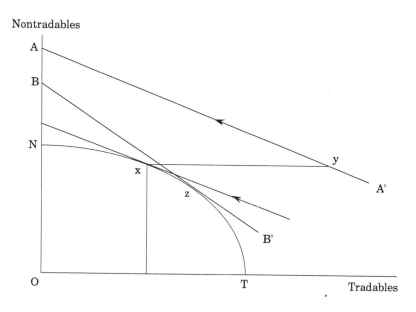

equilibrium is defined when the sum of labor demands in the two sectors equals the (fixed) available supply. This is given by:

$$L_t\left(\frac{W}{P_t}, K_t\right) + L_n\left(\frac{W}{P_n}, K_n\right) = L ,\qquad(1)$$

where W is the nominal wage (which is equal across sectors given the assumption of labor mobility), W/P_i the real product wage (i = t, n), and K_i the (fixed) capital stock in each sector.[5] Following Dornbusch

---

5. A distinction here is made between the real product wage and the real consumption wage. The former, given by W/P_i (i = n, t), deflates the money wage by output price, while the latter divides the money wage by a consumption-based

(1980, p. 98), we note that the equilibrium wage that is established following a devaluation is a linear function of output prices.

$$\dot{W} = a\dot{P}_n + (1-a)\dot{P}_t \qquad 0 < a < 1 \qquad (2)$$

where the dot refers to a percentage change. Rearrangement gives,

$$\dot{W} - \dot{P}_t = -a\left(\dot{P}_t - \dot{P}_n\right)$$
$$\dot{W} - \dot{P}_n = (1-a)\left(\dot{P}_t - \dot{P}_n\right) \qquad (3)$$

It follows from (3) that since $\dot{P}_t > \dot{P}_n$, the real product wage will fall in the tradables sector and rise in nontradables. In this short-run case, production switching is derived solely from the reallocation of labor. To encourage increased employment in the traded sector, the real product wage in that sector *must fall*. By the same token, to discourage employment in sector N, its real product wage must rise. Thus, the effect on the real consumption wage of a devaluation is ambiguous and depends on the relative weights in workers' consumption baskets of traded and nontraded goods. The change in the real consumption wage is given by,

$$\dot{W}_c = \beta\left(\dot{W} - \dot{P}_t\right) + (1-\beta)\left(\dot{W} - \dot{P}_n\right), \qquad (4)$$

where β is the average propensity to consume tradables out of wage income. If workers spend a sufficiently high proportion of their income on nontraded goods, it may be possible to achieve the objectives of adjustment in the short run without reducing the real consumption wage. The condition governing this is simply,

$$\beta < \frac{1}{1 - \left(\dfrac{a}{1-a}\right)} \qquad (5)$$

weighted average of all prices. It is assumed that all workers face the same prices and have the same consumption bundles.

That is, the direction of change in the real consumption wage will depend on the average propensity to consume tradables in relation to the technology parameter, a, which governs the wage response to the change in relative prices. If their average propensity to consume tradables is high, workers will experience a decline in their living standards under adjustment.[6] This is independent of the assumed relative factor intensities.

These short-run labor market repercussions can be illustrated diagramatically. The horizontal axis of Figure 3.2 allocates the total

Figure 3.2

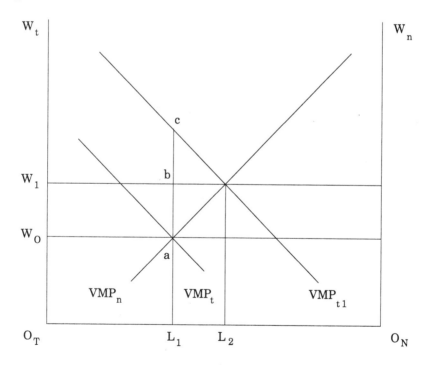

---

6. Note that if *marginal* propensities to consume tradables and nontradables differ out of profits and wages, the indifference map in Figure 3.1 will shift and alter the final equilibrium point (z).

labor supply (O_T-O_N) to the two sectors, measuring labor in tradables from the left and in nontradables from the right. The vertical axis measures the wage and marginal productivity in the two sectors in terms of the nontraded goods. This construction is now well established in the literature (Mussa 1974; Neary 1978; Edwards 1988). The original demand for labor curves (being the value of the respective marginal product of labor curves - VMP) associated with production at x (in Figure 3.1) gives $O_T L_1$ labor in tradables and $O_N L_1$ in nontradables. Given flexible wages, the labor market clears at the wage W_0.

With P_n fixed, the depreciation in the real exchange rate is achieved through devaluation, which raises P_t. Given that wages and marginal products are measured in terms of the nontraded good, the curve VMP_t shifts outward, with VMP_n remaining unchanged. Equilibrium is restored in the labor market at a higher wage (W_1). The increase in the nominal wage (ab) is less than the increase in P_t (ac), so that the movements in the real product wages are in the required direction (as indicated in equation 3). The change in the real consumption wage, therefore, is subject to the orthodox ambiguity, depending on workers' consumption propensities. $L_1 L_2$ workers previously employed in the N sector move into tradables production.

It remains now to demonstrate how these labor market outcomes are likely to affect poverty. But first we must select a poverty index for the purpose. Measures of poverty must reflect both its incidence (as measured by the head count ratio, H), its intensity (indicated by the income-gap ratio, I), and the degree of inequality among the poor. Taking a class of indices developed by Foster, Greer, and Thorbecke (1984), Kanbur (1987) has formally derived the effects of a switching policy on poverty. The poverty index proposed by Foster et al. has the advantage of incorporating all three aspects of poverty. The index is given by,

$$PV_\alpha = \frac{1}{n} \sum_{i=1}^{q} \left(\frac{Y_p - Y_i}{Y_p} \right)^\alpha \qquad (6)$$

where n is the population size, q is the number below the poverty line, Y_p (so that $H=q/n$), and Y_i ($i = 1,..., q$) are the incomes of the poor. α is a policy parameter chosen by the user to reflect his or her aversion to poverty.[7] The larger is α the greater is the weight given in the index to the lowest income earners. Moreover, this index is subgroup decomposable, so that it can be decomposed sectorally (that is, into traded and nontraded sectors).

To derive the poverty effects, Kanbur makes three simplifying assumptions: only wage earners can be poor, thus enabling us to ignore profit income:[8] within-sector income distributions are unchanged, which means that the variance of wage income within tradables and nontradables is not affected by the switching policy;[9] and finally, as workers move from one sector to the other, they assume the income distribution characteristics of the sector of destination.[10] The effects of the change in the real consumption wage and the induced movement of labor between sectors can be combined to yield an estimate for the overall short-run poverty effect of a switching policy, π. This is given as,[11]

$$
\frac{dPV_\alpha}{d\pi} = -\frac{d\Omega_w}{d\pi}\left[x_n\alpha\left(PV_{\alpha-1,n} - PV_{\alpha,n}\right) + x_t\alpha\left(PV_{\alpha-1,t} - PV_{\alpha,t}\right)\right]
$$
$$
+ \frac{dx_t}{d\pi}\left(PV_{\alpha,t} - PV_{\alpha,n}\right) \tag{7}
$$

Ω_w is the induced proportional change in the real consumption wage, and $PV_{j,i}$ gives the respective poverty indices of the sectors ($j = \alpha$, $\alpha-1$, and $i = n, t$). The weights (x_i) refer to the proportions of the

---

7. When $\alpha = 0$, the index is simply the head count ratio; when $\alpha - 1$, $PV_\alpha = HI$; and for $\alpha > 1$, inequality among the poor is reflected in the index.

8. In many developing countries where the poor are often smallholder farmers, or self-employed in the informal sector, this may not be a helpful assumption.

9. Kanbur's analysis simply assumes that mean incomes in tradables rise, and in nontradables fall, with no change in the dispersion around these mean incomes. But the movements in the whole distributions within each group will clearly affect the numbers and intensity of poverty.

10. And this suggests that workers are withdrawn from the sector of origin in a representative manner, implying that the distribution of income there is unchanged following the labor reallocation.

11. This result applies only to marginal changes in the real wage.

wage-earning population in the two sectors. If the real consumption-wage increases ($d\Omega_w/d\pi > 0$), the first term on the righthand side of equation (7) is negative, since $PV_{\alpha-1,i} > PV_{\alpha,i}$. The second term on the right hand side of equation (7) will be positive if poverty is greater in the tradables sector ($PV_{\alpha,t} > PV_{\alpha,n}$), since under switching, labor will be reallocated to tradables ($dx_t/d\pi > 0$).

Therefore, equation 7 shows an additional source of ambiguity in tracing the poverty effects of switching. Even if the real consumption wage rises in the short run (thus excluding the orthodox ambiguity), the net effect on overall poverty remains uncertain. Poverty might increase if poverty in tradables is significantly higher than in nontradables. Similarly, when the real consumption wage is expected to fall, the effect on poverty need not be adverse. If poverty is significantly greater in nontradables (that is, $PV_{n,\alpha} > PV_{t,\alpha}$) and if there is a sufficiently large transfer of labor across the sectors ($dx_t/d\pi$ is large in value), the overall poverty index could decline. This possibility may well have relevance for developing counties. There are therefore two effects of expenditure switching on poverty: the "real wage" effects and the "reallocation" effects. The one may be favorable while the other may not.

An Assessment

Kanbur's account of the poverty effects of adjustment based on the dependent-economy model is particularly useful since it provides a simple structure from which to interpret empirical evidence. And the evidence required by this structure is generally available from household surveys. Consumption patterns (which are critical in determining the direction of the short-run change in the real consumption wage) can be estimated from household data. In addition to this, poverty indices in the various sectors can be computed from the same source (household data) to give a useful indication of whether the reallocative effect is likely to augment or counteract the real wage effect.

However, Kanbur's attempt to derive the poverty repercussions of adjustment has some shortcomings. First, the reallocative effect rests on the assumption that as labor moves from nontradables to tradables it assumes the income distribution characteristics of the sector of destination (that is, the income variance within tradables is assumed to apply to all new entrants to that sector). This would suggest that sections of the work force are poor simply because of the economic circumstances of the sector in which they work, rather than because of their specific individual and household characteristics. If, for example, a household is poor because of a high dependency ratio, simply transferring the household head across sectors is unlikely to offer much relief.

Second, Kanbur ignores income transfers between households, which could figure prominently in any final accounting of what happens to poverty. The labor reallocations of the kind encouraged by expenditure switching are likely (if not certain) to set in motion reverse transfers in cash and kind (from destination sector to origin sector). This is especially noticeable (and possibly more likely) if the reallocation involves geographical migration. Some observers consider that this is happening in many African countries as a result of recent adjustment programs. With switching policies raising returns in agriculture, and a tendency for labor to be reallocated to rural areas, remittances may well have become predominantly rural to urban in direction.[12] Labor reallocations into the T sector therefore might generate a counterflow of remittances back to those remaining in the N sector, and this would modify the income profiles used to derive equation 7.

Assume that real consumption wages fall in the short run, and that $PV_{n,\alpha} > PV_{t,\alpha}$, so that the reallocative effect would decrease overall poverty. One might expect an increase in remittance flows from T to N as a result of labor transfers. This would raise incomes in N and reduce them in T. Since $PV_{n,\alpha} > PV_{t,\alpha}$, this would *ceteris paribus* reduce overall poverty, so that equation 7 would tend to overestimate the poverty effect. If $PV_{n,\alpha} < PV_{t,\alpha}$, the opposite would be the case. However, if poverty were higher in the T sector, it is doubtful that significant remittance flows would result from labor reallocation, and the modifications if any to (7) would probably be minor.

---

12. Jamal (1988a) suggests that as a result of the downturn in real wages during adjustment in Uganda, urban dwellers now make frequent trips back to rural areas to obtain food. Jamal (1988b, p. 799) cites the key role played by (external) remittances in "sustaining living standards in the towns" of Somalia.

A final point concerns the empirical interpretation of Kanbur's results. If workers tend to consume mainly tradable goods, and if poverty is greater in nontradables, the short-run poverty effects of switching will be beneficial. But if the two effects work in opposite directions, we evidently need to know something about labor reallocations before the net effect on poverty can be derived (and this may not be available from household-level data, unless surveys are regularly conducted). Difficulties arise, therefore, in trying to draw inferences from point-in-time household data about how poverty might be affected by adjustment policies.[13] For example, it is tempting to conclude that the poverty effects of adjustment will be beneficial if poverty is greater in the expanding T sector since this sector benefits from the switching policy. But excluding the real wage effect (common to both sectors), the fact that poverty is greater in the T sector means that poverty will *increase* as a result of labor transfers. Workers are simply being encouraged to move to a sector that generally exhibits greater poverty than elsewhere.[14]

Economy-wide Labor Market Imperfections

So far, the analysis of the primary income distributive effects of stabilization has been confined to the switching effects brought about by movements in the real exchange rate. These changes were assumed to be the result of fiscal and monetary contraction alone, or in combination with a currency devaluation (with P_n inflexible downward). The real output effects of these policies were treated as movements along the production frontier (from x to z in Figure 3.1). Increases in the output of tradables could be achieved, therefore, only by reductions in the production of nontradables. This had predictable effects on the distribution of primary incomes under various

---

13. The World Bank is now facing this problem in the design of its project on the social dimensions of adjustment in Africa.

14. For example, in analyzing household data in Côte d'Ivoire, Kanbur (1990, p. 43) concludes that "a shift of relative prices in favor of export crops will tend to benefit poverty" merely on the ground that the incidence of poverty in that sector at the time of the survey was greater than sectors less favored by adjustment. This conclusion is only valid if most of the poor are smallholders and do not rely primarily on wage income. Otherwise, the fact that poverty is greater in tradables would *ceteris paribus* increase poverty during adjustment.

assumptions about workers' consumption patterns. The main difficulty with this theoretical account is that it is ill suited to real world situations in which the initial situation is characterized not only by external deficits, but also by unemployment and internal disequilibrium. In such situations the neo-classical "equilibrium" framework can lead to serious policy mis-specifications. To introduce unemployment, we shall now assume some form of wage rigidity, which combined with rigid P_n will lead to *rationed markets* and involuntary unemployment.

Adjustment with Quantity Rationing

Macro-models for the closed economy under quantity rationing, building on the earlier work of Patinkin (1965) and Clower (1965), were developed by Barro and Grossman (1971) and Malinvaud (1977). More recently, Dixit (1978), Cuddington (1980, 1981), and Neary (1980) have shown that the disequilibrium framework of Barro and Grossman can usefully be applied to open economies. Our use of these approaches is based on Cuddington, Johansson, and Löfgren (1984).

In the short-run version of the basic model, three markets are analyzed: two product markets (tradables and nontradables) and the labor market. Given the small-country assumption, producers of tradables will not face any quantity constraints in their product market, simply because they can sell as much of their output as they wish in the world market at the given price. Similarly, consumers of tradables cannot be constrained in the amount of the product they buy, since any amount of it is available through imports from abroad at the going price. Although (under fixed exchange rates) the domestic price of tradables is fixed, no quantity rations are imposed in the tradables market.

The same, however, cannot be said of the other two markets. Since nontradables are by definition only produced and consumed domestically, the fixed price (P_n) will lead to either buyers or sellers being rationed at the short end of the market. If the price is set too high, leading to excess supply in the nontradables market, suppliers will be able to sell only what is demanded at that price. Producers of N will therefore face a quantity constraint in the market (equal to the level of demand, D_n). Although the price/wage configuration that prevails in the market would lead them to supply a *notional* output of Y_n^*, with rationing they would supply only an effective output of $Y_n = D_n$. If P_n were set too low, an excess demand for nontradables would lead to rationing of consumers. They would be able to buy only what profit-maximizing producers of N were willing to supply, that is, $D_n = Y_n$. Moreover, rationing in one market will lead to further rationing in other markets, so that the firms that are unable to sell Y_n^* in the product market and are obliged to produce only Y_n will reduce their labor demand accordingly. In the labor market, therefore, demand (L_d) will be below its notional level (L_d^*) simply because of a ration in the product market. Similarly, if the wage is set too high, an excess supply of labor would ration households seeking to sell their labor services. They would be able to sell only what the firms are willing to hire. Thus, actual employment would be determined by the demand for labor (L_d), and unemployment would persist.

The central proposition of these models is that the failure of any market to clear will spill over into other markets. Thus, if there is excess supply in the labor market, households constrained in the amount of labor they wish to sell will reduce their demands for commodities, thus affecting product markets. In the same way, firms constrained in a product market (because of excess supply in the market) will be obliged to reduce output and employment. The effective demand for labor, therefore, will be constrained by the fact that firms are rationed in the product market. The net effect of such rationing in labor and nontraded product markets might be a temporary "equilibrium" in which unemployment persists. Given the constraint faced by households in selling labor services, their effective demands for nontradables will be lowered. Faced with this low level of effective demand, firms would be obliged to reduce output. This level of output would then lead to reduced demand for labor, constraining household incomes and demands. And so on. The economy would finally settle at a point where the *effective* demands and supplies in the two markets (labor and nontradables) are equal. But this temporary equilibrium is consistent with the persistence of non-zero excess *notional* demands in any of the two markets.

We shall trace the effects of stabilization with excess supply pervading the labor market—with the wage set too high to clear the market. Two broad cases of unemployment are then distinguished: when the N sector is in excess demand (P_n too low), unemployment is considered "classical" in nature;[15] second, with nontradables in excess supply, "Keynesian" unemployment is said to exist. What are the effects of stabilization policy under such rationed regimes? To trace the poverty effects, we are now no longer simply concerned with the real consumption wage. That preoccupation was justified only under full employment since increases in the real consumption wage inevitably raised labor's real income share. With rationing in the system, changes in the level of labor utilization will also have a profound effect on the wellbeing of the working population. Finally, it should be remembered that with unemployment in the economy, stabilization need not require a reduction in aggregate absorption to reduce the trade deficit. This, in principle, can be achieved through devaluation alone. However, before considering the distributive effects of devaluation, we shall trace briefly the effects of a policy of expenditure reduction. In what follows, we take only the case of Keynesian unemployment, with notional excess supplies in both labor and nontradables markets.

Adjustment under Keynesian Unemployment

FISCAL POLICY. Since the levels of tradables output (Y_t) and employment (L_t) are determined by the firms' profit-maximizing behavior, aggregate demand management policies will have no effect on the sector. This applies even if the government reduces spending on tradables. Firms will simply direct more of their output to foreign demand. The same is not true for nontradables. Decreased government expenditure on nontradables (as part of a fiscal and monetary contraction) will reduce output in the sector according to the familiar multiplier process,

---

15. It is "classical" in the sense that the classical policy prescription of real wage reductions will correct excess supply in the labor market and reduce excess demand in the nontraded goods market.

$$\frac{dY_n}{dG_n} = \frac{1}{1-\left(\frac{dD_n}{dY}\right)P_n} > 0 \qquad (8)$$

where the denominator equals one minus the marginal propensity to spend on nontraded goods.[16] The value of the marginal propensity to consume used in deriving (8) will clearly depend on the income distributive effects that the fiscal contraction causes. If the unemployed spend more (less) on nontradables, the value of the multiplier that is used in calculating the effect of fiscal contraction would need to be adjusted upward (downward). A general fiscal contraction, involving for example a decline in government spending on both tradables and nontradables, will have unambiguously beneficial effects on the trade balance. The reduced spending on tradables will dollar-for-dollar reduce imports of tradables. The decline in spending on nontradables will reduce private-sector demand for imports because of the decline in employment and incomes generated by the nontradables sector.

The effects, then, of fiscal contraction under the assumptions of this fix-price, Keynesian two-sector model are as follows: the trade balance improves; incomes and employment in tradables remain unchanged; although the real consumption wage in nontradables remains constant, the level of employment falls. Kanbur's (1987) representation of expenditure reduction as involving either "additive" or "multiplicative" reductions in incomes for everyone, therefore, misses the key point about the poverty effects of expenditure reduction. General fiscal contraction will not typically lead to an across-the-board decline in incomes. It will leave some incomes largely unaffected, but it will reduce the incomes of others drastically. When it comes to the poverty effects of expenditure reduction, it is critical whether the poor are engaged in sectors that are sensitive to reductions in aggregate demand.

---

16. To derive (8) Cuddington, Johansson, and Löfgren (1984, p. 83) invoke the assumption of weak separability on labor in the utility function "because an increase in employment has two effects: (1) an income effect and (2) an effect on the marginal rate of substitution between consumption and leisure. The assumption that consumption and wealth are weakly separable from leisure/labor ensures that the latter effect vanishes."

DEVALUATION. How are the switching effects of devaluation in the full employment model modified, and what are the implications for income distribution? Devaluation will lower the product wage in the tradables sector and therefore increase Y_t unambiguously. This has a directly beneficial effect on the trade imbalance $(Y_t - D_t)$. But the increased incomes generated (through increased employment and enhanced profits in the tradables sector) will raise the levels of demand D_t and D_n. The increase in D_t will have an adverse effect on the trade imbalance, while the change in D_n will stimulate the production of nontradables.

Two important differences from the basic model emerge in the case of Keynesian unemployment. First, a devaluation will not necessarily improve the balance of trade, the net effect depending on the relative magnitude of the different price and income effects. Second, the increase in Y_t is not at the expense of Y_n, as in the full employment model. Under Keynesian unemployment, both Y_t and Y_n increase as a result of devaluation, this being made possible by a reduction in unemployment. The neat theoretical reasoning employed in the full employment model to trace the primary distributive effects of devaluation no longer applies. With output in both sectors increasing, and with unemployment falling, the net effect on incomes is quite different. Since both W and P_n are fixed (by assumption) and P_t is raised through the devaluation, the real consumption wage certainly declines. This induces the increase in employment in both T and N sectors. So in contrast to the neo-classical equilibrium model analyzed above, the real wage effect is unambiguously adverse in the presence of unemployment. This is because there is now no necessity for the real product wage to increase in the nontradable sector—which was why, so long as sufficient nontradables were consumed by workers, the real consumption wage might have risen.

These labor market effects are illustrated in Figure 3.3. With the wage fixed at W^*, the original level of unemployment in the economy is L_1L_2. In shifting the VMP_t schedule to VMP_{t1}, a devaluation will reduce both the real consumption wage and the level of unemployment (to L_3L_2).

The net effect on labor's real income share, therefore, will depend on the relation between the cut in the real consumption wage and the

Figure 3.3

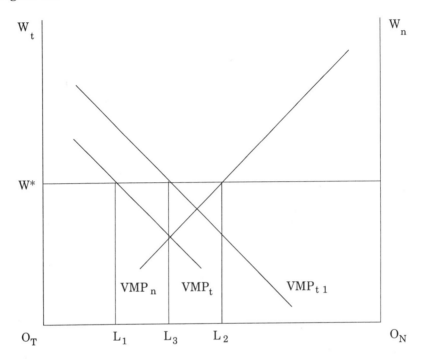

increase in employment. This, in turn, depends on the real wage elasticity of demand for labor. Even if it were shown that labor's share falls as a result of devaluation (with the increase in employment being insufficient to counteract the effect of the real wage decline), there can be no presumption that poverty has increased. In granting employment to the most vulnerable (those who are unemployed or who are underemployed in low-productivity casual labor in the informal sector), a devaluation might reduce the incidence of poverty. This is clear when the poverty effects of these Keynesian meso-economic outcomes are assessed.

In this Keynesian version of the dependent-economy model, overall poverty must be decomposed into *three* components,

$$PV_\alpha = x_n PV_{\alpha,n} + x_t PV_{\alpha,t} + x_u PV_{\alpha,u} . \tag{9}$$

A switching policy π, in inducing a proportionate change in the real consumption wage (Ω_w), will give the following poverty effect:

$$\frac{dPV_\alpha}{d\pi} = \frac{d\Omega_w}{d\pi}\left[x_n\left(\frac{dPV_{\alpha,n}}{d\Omega_w}\right) + x_t\left(\frac{dPV_{\alpha,t}}{d\Omega_w}\right) + x_u\left(\frac{dPV_{\alpha,u}}{d\Omega_w}\right)\right]$$
$$+ PV_{\alpha,n}\left(\frac{dx_n}{d\pi}\right) + PV_{\alpha,t}\left(\frac{dx_t}{d\pi}\right) + PV_{a,u}\left(\frac{dx_u}{d\pi}\right) \tag{10}$$

Under the assumption that $dPV_{\alpha,u} / d\Omega_w = 0$ (which can be interpreted to mean that the change in the real consumption wage does not influence transfers to the unemployed), and given that $dx_n + dx_t = -dx_u$,[17] equation 10 may be rewritten,

$$\frac{dPV_\alpha}{d\pi} = -\frac{d\Omega_w}{d\pi}\left[x_n\alpha\left(PV_{\alpha-1,n} - PV_{\alpha,n}\right) + x_t\alpha\left(PV_{\alpha-1,t} - PV_{\alpha,t}\right)\right]$$
$$+ \frac{dx_t}{d\pi}\left(PV_{\alpha,t} - PV_{\alpha,u}\right) + \frac{dx_n}{d\pi}\left(PV_{\alpha,n} - PV_{\alpha,u}\right) \tag{11}$$

In this Keynesian model, we know that a switching policy reduces the real consumption wage in this short run (so that $d\Omega_w/d\pi < 0$). The first term on the righthand side of equation (11) is therefore positive (the wage effect increasing poverty). It is also clear that $dx_i/d\pi > 0$ ($i = n, t$). If it is assumed that poverty is greater among the unemployed than among those working in either the N or T sectors, the second and third terms (relating to the reallocative effect) are negative. So again the net effect on overall poverty is ambiguous, even though we know that the real wage effect is adverse. The origin of this ambiguity comes from the expansionary effect a devaluation has under these Keynesian assumptions.[18] The effects of adjustment under these assumptions are shown to cause conflicts within the working population that the orthodox model fails to capture. While the employed will find their real incomes declining, the unemployed will unquestionably benefit.

---

17. Recall that $x_n + x_t + x_u = 1$.

18. Some have questioned this beneficial effect by highlighting the possibility of deflationary effects of devaluation (see Demery and Addison 1987, p. 1489-1490)

Before concluding our discussion of the poverty effects of these wage rigidities that apply globally in the labor market, we will compare these outcomes with the orthodox model. In both cases, poverty effects are ambiguous in theory and can be resolved only empirically. But the source of the ambiguity differs. In the orthodox model, both the wage and the reallocative effects are ambiguous (real consumption wages may rise or fall, and poverty may or may not be greater in the T sector). The predictions of the Keynesian model, however, are much firmer since it is certain that the real wage effect will be adverse and that the allocative effect will be beneficial. The ambiguity here derives from the inevitable conflict between these two effects.

Partial Labor Market Imperfections

The preceding analysis assumed that the nominal wage is fixed throughout the labor market. A more realistic approach is to assume that the wage impediment applies only to one section of the labor market (the "formal" labor market), while it is free to clear in the rest of the market (the "informal" sector). Unemployment in the model will not be involuntary since it is assumed that work is always available in the informal labor market at the going wage. If unemployment does exist in such a world, it arises from voluntary search activity.

We shall take two simple cases of partial labor market imperfection in exploring the implications for the poverty effects of adjustment. In the first place, we assume downward rigidity of *nominal* wages in the formal sector. This can be interpreted as a legislated minimum wage fixed in nominal units, and not changed during the period of adjustment. Given the difficulties of enforcing such legislation, the minimum wage cannot be applied throughout the labor market. We consider that the assumption of a fixed nominal wage rather than *real* wage is appropriate for the experiments we are conducting. In most countries experiencing the traumas of adjustment, governments are reluctant to raise minimum wages. Their efforts are directed principally to reducing domestic absorption, and maintaining real wages (albeit in only a section of the labor market) would run counter to this.

Second, we will consider the case in which relatively high wages in the "covered" sector are the result of barriers to entry into employment there.[19] How do the meso-economic outcomes under such assumptions differ from those previously derived?[20] Do these labor market imperfections introduce other conflicts among the working population that the competitive and the simple Keynesian models fail to capture?

Several possibilities exist concerning the type of labor market segmentation that can be assumed in the context of our two-sector (tradable/nontradable) world. The simplest assumption is that one production-sector's labor market is entirely informal, while the other sector operates wholly in a formal labor market. This we explore first. The more complex case, where *both* the formal and informal sectors produce both tradables and nontradables, is considered later.

A Two-Sector Framework

With the labor market divided into its formal and informal sections, a simple theoretical framework is needed to determine labor allocations to these sectors (and to the "unemployed" category), and the level of wages in the two sectors. The Harris-Todaro (1970) framework is a useful starting point for analyzing such situations, and we shall amend Mincer's (1976) more general version in what follows.

Those employed in the covered sector have the advantages of higher wages, bestowed either through a legislated minimum wage or through some form of union-induced barrier to entry into the sector. Those outside must either take employment at the market-determined wage in the informal sector, or opt to be unemployed in the hope of securing a covered job through a full-time job search. With a fixed labor supply (L), it follows that

$$L = L^F + L^I + U \tag{12}$$

---

19. We use the terms "covered," "protected," and "formal" interchangeably in describing the high-wage sector.

20. Throughout this section, we remain within the terms of the dependent-economy model, maintaining the assumption that the economy is a price taker in world markets and that for some unspecified reason P_n is rigid. Devaluation is therefore required in order to depreciate the real exchange rate and restore external balance.

where the superscripts refer to the formal (F) and informal (I) sectors, and U is the level of search unemployment.[21] Equilibrium in such a labor market is given when the expected wage in the protected sector (given by pW^F, where p is the probability of obtaining a formal-sector job) equals the certain wage in the informal sector (W^I). The simplest assumption is that every worker has the same chance of obtaining a formal-sector job when it becomes available. Under this assumption of probabilistic rationing, the probability of obtaining a high-wage job is given by,

$$p = \frac{\delta L^F}{U + \delta L^F} \qquad (13)$$

where δ is the turnover rate in the covered sector. This is a reasonable approximation when labor is homogeneous and when there are no barriers to entry into the sector.[22] If the labor market segmentation is based on other rationing devices (such as education, class, family connections, access to union membership), equation 13 will overstate job probability in the covered sector.[23]

To deal with this in a relatively simple way, we shall introduce a parameter (τ) that reflects these additional factors. With $\tau = 1$, all

---

21. Changes in the real wage are assumed in the model not to influence the size of the labor force. In practice, we would expect some labor-supply response to the real wage effects of adjustment, and in fact Mincer (1976) incorporates this response. However, in the interests of diagrammatic (and algebraic) simplicity, we shall take labor supply as given.

22. This model assumes that workers cannot engage in job search while employed in the low-wage sector. If the F and I sectors are separated geographically, this may be reasonable. But if they are in close geographical proximity, so that some (albeit less effective) job search is feasible while in I-sector employment, the amount of search unemployment predicted by the model will be overstated. However, even when the sectors are separated geographically, workers engaged in the uncovered sector may still have access to covered jobs without necessarily engaging in full-time (unemployed) job search. For example, Mazumdar (1983, p. 257) found evidence in India and Malaysia that the majority of formal sector workers were recruited directly from the rural areas.

23. For example, when employers have imperfect information about worker quality, they can reduce their uncertainty over an applicant's likely productivity by relying on existing workers to introduce and vouch for new workers. Existing workers have most information about their own kin, hence the observed importance of kinship ties in the recruitment process (Mazumdar 1983).

workers stand the same chance of a job in the covered sector, so that workers outside the formal sector compete for formal jobs on an equal footing with those within. But if $\tau = 0$, workers outside the covered sector will find it impossible to obtain such a job. (We can call this the "apartheid" assumption.) For values in between, τ measures the degree of difficulty outside workers face in breaking into formal-sector employment. Equation 13 should therefore be rewritten as,

$$p = \tau \left(\frac{\delta L^F}{U + \delta L^F} \right) \tag{13a}$$

which shows clearly that (13) is only the special case of $\tau = 1$.

Equilibrium unemployment in such labor market is given by,

$$U = L^F \delta \left(\frac{\tau W^F}{W^1} - 1 \right) \tag{14}$$

and the unemployment ratio by,

$$u^F = \frac{U}{L^F} = \delta \left(\frac{\tau W^F}{W^1} - 1 \right) \tag{14a}$$

To illustrate the determination of wages and employment in the two sectors, and the level of unemployment, it is helpful to make the simplifying Harris-Todaro assumptions that $\delta = \tau = 1$. Returning to the apparatus previously employed in Figure 3.2, with a minimum nominal wage of W^{F*} (see Figure 3.4), formal-sector employment is restricted to $O_F L_1$. With both δ and τ equal to unity, employment in the informal sector is given where a rectangular hyperbola (labeled H and drawn through x) intersects VMP^I (at point y). Thus, the informal-sector wage settles at W^I_1, with employment at $O_1 L_2$. $L_2 L_1$ workers opt for search unemployment. It should be kept in mind that the level of unemployment given by the rectangular hyperbola overstates the amount of search unemployment if either δ or τ are less than unity.[24] With this basic framework, we can now investigate the

---

24. This is obvious from equations 14 and 14a. Expositions of this model do not usually make this clear (for example, Edwards 1988).

Figure 3.4

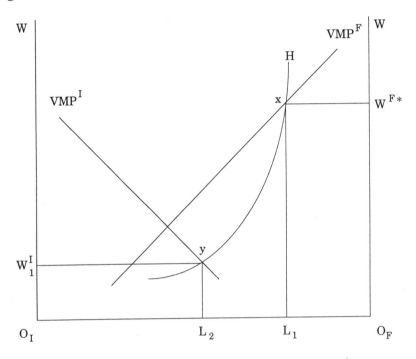

labor market outcomes of an expenditure-switching adjustment
policy.

Wage Inflexibility in Nontradables

Our first case, therefore, is one in which the inflexible nominal
wage applies only to employment in nontradables. In the interests of a
clearer exposition, we drop the F and I superscripts, replacing them
with n and t subscripts respectively. Wages and marginal products are
expressed in terms of nontradables. Since P_n is assumed to be fixed
throughout these exercises (and nontradables are taken to be a
numeraire), the fixed nominal wage can readily be illustrated through
this apparatus. Although this interpretation was open to him, Edwards
(1988) chose to rationalize a fixed (minimum) wage (measured in his
case in terms of exportables) as an approximation of the real
consumption wage, which would be satisfactory so long as workers

consumed mainly the exportable. Since he assumed that the minimum wage applied only in importables, his interpretation was a variant of Dixon's (1988) "pork-pie" effect, according to which workers do not consume any of the product of the sector in which they work. The problem with this interpretation is that it leads to the exclusion of real wage ambiguity that characterizes most orthodox models. If workers consume mostly one commodity, the real wage effect can be predicted.

Consider then the effects of a nominal minimum wage W_n^* in nontradables, restricting employment to $O_N L_1$ (see Figure 3.5). The remainder of the labor force takes up employment in the T (informal) sector at the market-clearing wage, or searches for formal N-sector (higher-wage) employment. Thus, the informal-sector wage settles at W_{t1}, with employment at $O_T L_2$. Given this wage differential, $L_1 L_2$ workers decide to remain unemployed while engaged in a job search.

Figure 3.5

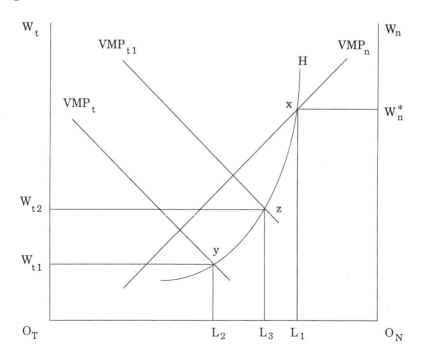

What are the meso-economic effects of adjustment under these circumstances? How does it change this existing equilibrium? As before, an expenditure-switching policy causes VMP_t to shift out (to VMP_{t1}), but leaves the position of VMP_n unchanged. The result is an increase in the informal (T) sector wage to W_{t2}, while L_3L_1 workers opt for search unemployment.

The meso-economic effects of adjustment, therefore, are as follows:

- informal (T) employment rises to O_TL_3;
- formal (N) employment is unchanged;
- unemployment falls to L_3L_1;[25]
- the real consumption wage in the N sector falls;
- the change in the real consumption wage in the T sector is ambiguous and depends on the consumption propensities of workers;[26]
- the real wage-gap narrows.

Maintaining the assumptions made earlier about poverty (only wage-earners and the unemployed are poor, no transfers between sectors, and so on), the short-run poverty effect of adjustment when the minimum nominal wage applies only to nontradables is given by,[27]

$$
\frac{dPV_\alpha}{d\pi} = -\left(\frac{d\Omega_n}{d\pi}\right)x_n\alpha\left(PV_{\alpha-1,n} - PV_{\alpha,n}\right)
$$
$$
-\left(\frac{d\Omega_t}{d\pi}\right)x_t\alpha\left(PV_{\alpha-1,t} - PV_{\alpha,t}\right) \qquad (15)
$$
$$
+\frac{dx_t}{d\pi}\left(PV_{\alpha,t} - PV_{\alpha,u}\right)
$$

---

25. With $\delta = \tau = 1$, equation 14 becomes,

$$
U = L_n\left(\frac{W_n}{W_t} - 1\right).
$$

Since L_n is unchanged and W_n/W_t has fallen, it follows that unemployment will fall during adjustment.

26. This is because the real wage in terms of nontradables has risen, but it has fallen in terms of tradables. The rise in W_t/P_n is less than the increase in P_t/P_n, so that W_t/P_t falls.

27. For convenience, we have dropped the w subscript on Ω but have added the sector subscript. Recall that $dx_n/d\pi = 0$ and that the following results are for small changes in the wage.

The real wage effect on poverty differs between sectors (as compared with the earlier cases). While the real consumption wage in the N sector is certain to fall and therefore to raise poverty (the first term in the righthand side of equation 15), the real consumption wage change in the T sector is subject to the same ambiguity identified earlier (for the competitive case). The net effect on overall poverty of the real wage effect is, therefore, strictly uncertain. But this is combined with a clear-cut reallocative effect. If we maintain the assumption that $PV_{\alpha,t} < PV_{\alpha,u}$, the third term (the reallocative effect) is unambiguously negative.

The partial minimum nominal wage has created conflicts of interest among employed workers in addition to the conflict between the employed and the unemployed. Adjustment could reduce incomes and increase poverty among one group (in this case, workers in the N sector) and raise incomes (reducing poverty) in another (the T-sector workers). The expansion of employment in the T sector also creates opportunities for those previously unemployed and engaged in a job search. Again such conflicts could not be captured in the simple competitive model.

The reallocative effect under these assumptions is poverty reducing (as in the Keynesian case), but the real wage effect is ambiguous (as in the orthodox case). It is clear, then, that the presence of a fixed nominal wage in this section (N) of the labor market does little to remove the theoretical ambiguity surrounding the poverty effects of adjustment. Does it make any difference if the wage rigidity applies only to the tradables sector?

Wage Inflexibility in Tradables

If tradables were produced mainly by "modern" firms and the nontradables sector comprised petty-traders and small-scale producers, it would make more sense to assume that the tradables sector is subject to the labor-market imperfection, while the nontradables wage is flexible. In this case, a minimum wage of W_t^* restricts employment to O_TL_1 in the T sector (see Figure 3.6). The remainder of the labor force takes up employment in the N (informal) sector at the market-clearing wage or searches for formal T-sector (higher wage)

Figure 3.6

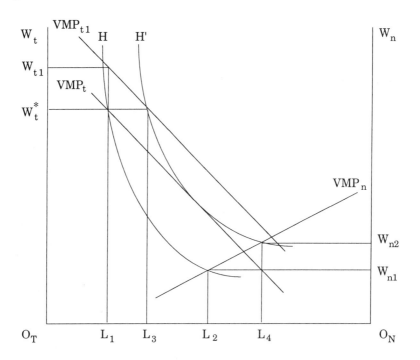

employment. Thus, the informal sector wage settles at W_{n1}, with employment at $O_N L_2$. Search unemployment is $L_1 L_2$.

Assuming that the minimum wage continues to be binding in the T sector, despite the upward shift in the VMP curve, the post adjustment (short-run) equilibrium involves the following changes:[28]

- given the minimum wage, employment will increase in the T sector to $O_T L_3$;[29]
- the market-clearing wage in the N sector will rise (to W_{n2});
- employment in the N sector will fall to $O_N L_4$;

---

28. If VMP_t were to shift out sufficiently, the market-clearing wage could rise above the statutory minimum, thus eradicating any wage difference between the sectors and all search unemployment. This case is not considered. However, it warrants empirical investigation when devaluation is known to have induced a particularly strong tradable output and employment response.

29. Prior to the labor reallocations, the increase in P_t will raise the tradables money wage to W_{t1}. However, the inflow of labor into the sector bids the wage back to the minimum.

- unemployment will fall to L_3L_4;[30]
- the real consumption wage in T will have fallen;
- the real wage change in N will be ambiguous, again depending on consumption patterns;
- the real wage gap will narrow.

The poverty effects of these changes are as follows:

$$\frac{dPV_\alpha}{d\pi} = -\left(\frac{d\Omega_n}{d\pi}\right)x_n\alpha\left(PV_{\alpha-1,n} - PV_{\alpha,n}\right)$$

$$-\left(\frac{d\Omega_t}{d\pi}\right)x_t\alpha\left(PV_{\alpha-1,t} - PV_{\alpha,t}\right) \qquad (16)$$

$$+\frac{dx_t}{d\pi}\left(PV_{\alpha,t} - PV_{\alpha,n}\right) + \frac{dx_u}{d\pi}\left(PV_{\alpha,u} - PV_{\alpha,n}\right)$$

In this case, the tradables real wage effect will increase poverty, while the influence of real consumption wages in nontradables is uncertain. To evaluate the last two terms on the righthand side of equation (16), assumptions must be made about the level of poverty in the sectors. If $PV_{\alpha,t} < PV_{\alpha,n}$ and $PV_{\alpha,u} > PV_{\alpha,n}$, the reallocative effect will be negative and, therefore, will reduce overall poverty.[31] So once again we have an ambiguous real wage effect and an unambiguously beneficial reallocative effect.

In both cases discussed so far in this section, the real consumption wage falls in the formal sector, and its direction of change in the informal sector is ambiguous, regardless of the tradability, or otherwise, of the sectors. This is simply because in the formal sector the nominal wage is unchanged over the short run, so any policy that

---

30. Equation 14 is not as helpful here since under our assumptions it is not readily apparent which direction U takes. Although W_t/W_n falls, L_t rises, so that the unemployment effect appears ambiguous. However, since the expansion in L_t (which is given along the horizontal line at W^*_t) is certain to be greater than the contraction in L_n (which is along the VMP_n curve), it follows that unemployment will fall.

31. Both these assumptions make eminent sense in this model. With the T sector alone having benefited from the nominal minimum wage, one would expect that over time poverty will be lower than elsewhere in the economy. The relatively high level of poverty among the unemployed in such a model is a little more uncertain, especially if the unemployed are dependents of households engaged in the formal sector. See, for example, the Kenyan evidence reported in Collier and Lal (1986).

raises the general price level will reduce real earnings. Those in the informal section of the labor market are likely to do better, especially if they consume mainly nontradables. The unemployment effects of both cases are beneficial since in these circumstances adjustment will reduce the real wage gap between the sectors.

The ambiguity characteristic of the orthodox model is likely to dominate the outcome of these two cases simply because the sector in which the real consumption-wage is certain to fall (that is, in the covered sector) is unlikely to influence the overall poverty index significantly. First, the overall weight of such workers in the total working population (x_F) is unlikely to be large. Second, poverty in the sector (which has benefited from wage support over the years up to adjustment) is likely to be negligible. The uncertain real consumption wage change in the uncovered sector, therefore, is likely to dominate the real wage effect.

The main difference between these imperfect labor market cases and the orthodox cases is to be found in the reallocative effects. Whereas this was ambiguous in the orthodox model, in the two minimum wage cases the reduction in unemployment leads to beneficial reallocative effects under reasonable assumptions about relative poverty levels. Moreover, when the formal sector produces only tradables, the expansion in employment in that sector enables more workers to be covered by the protection that wage rigidity affords, albeit at the cost of a reduction in the real value of that protection.[32]

The Barriers to Entry Case

Until now, we have assumed conveniently that the high wage in a section of the labor market arises through minimum wage legislation with partial coverage. How are the poverty effects amended when the source of the labor market imperfection lies not so much in wage

---

32. The narrowing of the real wage gap between sectors, the fall in unemployment, and the increase in the proportion of workers in the protected sector (at least in the case when the T sector is formal) suggest beneficial effects on *equity* (at least among the working population) since less-favored workers may well gain relative to the favored.

rigidity, as in the existence of barriers to entry into the formal labor market? To represent this case, the level of employment in the formal sector is fixed at L^{F*}, which then results in a relatively high wage offered in the sector. In this way, high formal-sector wages are the *result* of the labor-market imperfection rather than its cause.

With barriers to entry into the formal sector, it makes no sense at all to retain our earlier simplifying assumption that $\tau = 1$. While the entry barriers into formal-sector employment would not entirely frustrate job search on the part of workers outside, it is again helpful to make a simplifying assumption, this time taking $\tau = 0$, or the apartheid case.[33]

Barriers to Entry into Nontradables

Labor market equilibrium when there are barriers to entry into nontradables under the apartheid assumption is illustrated in Figure 3.7. Employment in nontradables is fixed at $O_N L_n^*$, which results in a relatively high (non-market-clearing) wage of W_n. Since there is no possibility of uncovered workers gaining N-sector employment, the H curve becomes vertical through x at L_n^*. The preadjustment level of employment in tradables is at $O_N L_n^*$, at the wage W_{t1}. With no prospect of a covered-sector job, there will be no search unemployment. The outward shift in the VMP_t curve leaves labor allocation entirely unaffected, and causes the tradables wage to rise to W_{t2}.[34] The meso-economic effects of adjustment under these assumptions are:

- no labor reallocations between sectors;
- a fall in the N-sector real consumption wage;
- a rise in the T-sector real consumption wage.[35]

---

33. In denying any returns from job search, we exclude search unemployment in the labor market, and any resource reallocations into and out of the unemployment pool.

34. This labor mobility constraint will obviously damage the adjustment program, since the relative price change will not lead to production switching, with both labor and capital locked in the sectors.

35. We are assuming that $\beta < 1$. If $\beta = 1$, the real wage in tradables would remain unchanged.

Figure 3.7

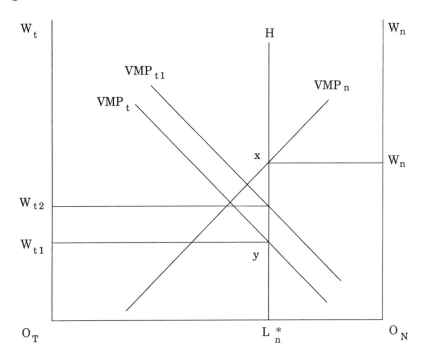

The poverty effects of these labor market outcomes are the simplest yet:

$$\frac{dPV_\alpha}{d\pi} = -\left(\frac{d\Omega_n}{d\pi}\right)x_n\alpha\left(PV_{\alpha-1,n} - PV_{\alpha,n}\right)$$
$$-\left(\frac{d\Omega_t}{d\pi}\right)x_t\alpha\left(PV_{\alpha-1,t} - PV_{\alpha,t}\right) \tag{17}$$

With no reallocative effects, the poverty outcome arises only from real-wage changes, the effect of which is ambiguous, given the opposing changes in the two sectors. Since x_t is likely to be greater than x_n, and since poverty is likely to be greater in the informal sector, the poverty outcome should be favorable.

How critical is the apartheid assumption for these poverty results? As τ rises above zero, the increase in the tradables real consumption wage becomes less likely. Indeed, with $\tau > 0$, strict real-wage ambiguity returns to the T sector, with the direction of its change depending on the relative values of τ and β. The real consumption wage in the tradables sector is more likely to rise the higher is τ and the lower is β. Moreover, with $\tau > 0$, there will be some beneficial unemployment effect of adjustment that we have not picked up under the simplifying apartheid assumption.

Barriers to Entry into Tradables

In dealing with the case when L_t is fixed (at $O_t L_t^*$ in Figure 3.8) as a result of barriers to entry, we continue to maintain the apartheid assumption. The outward shift in the VMP_t curve does not now cause an expansion of employment in T (due to the entry barriers), but rather simply raises W_t (to W_{t2}^* measured in nontradables). By the same token, employment in nontradables also remains unchanged (at $O_N L_t^*$). Adjustment, therefore, leads to the following effects:

Figure 3.8

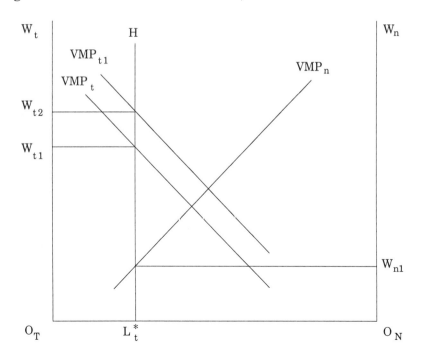

- no labor reallocations;
- a real consumption wage decline in nontradables;
- a real consumption wage increase in tradables.

The poverty effects of these changes are as in the previous case (and as described in equation 17). Here also the real consumption wage in tradables rises, while it falls unambiguously in nontradables. So whereas in the minimum-wage case real consumption wages fell in the protected sector (regardless of whether it was producing N or T) with barriers to entry, the tradables real consumption wage always benefits, regardless of whether it is protected or not.

This suggests that the poverty effects are more likely to be beneficial when there are barriers to entry into nontradables since unprotected workers gain at the expense of protected workers. In the present case, with entry barriers into the T sector, adjustment would probably increase poverty since real consumption wages in the unprotected (N) sector (where most workers are to be found, and where poverty is likely to be greater) will certainly fall. The conflict of interest between different groups of workers is very much highlighted in these entry-barrier cases since some workers definitely gain, while others are sure to lose from expenditure switching.

It should be noted that when $\tau > 0$, ambiguity again surrounds the direction of change in the informal (N) sector real-wage change since the increase in the T-sector wage would encourage an increase in search unemployment, reducing employment in nontradables and driving up the nominal wage there. Again, the higher is τ and the lower is β, the more likely it is that the N-sector wage will not fall. The increase in unemployment would also create some adverse resource-allocative effects on poverty, as workers quit their employment in nontradables to search for coveted T-sector jobs.

Labor Market Imperfections in Both Sectors

Partial Nominal Wage-Rigidity

The previous analysis has assumed that labor market imperfections were neatly located in only one sector. Although there may be cases where the T sector is *predominantly* formal and the N sector predominantly informal (and vice versa), most cases will involve a partial wage-rigidity in *each* sector (Knight 1976). In such circumstances, market arbitrage ensures that tradable and nontradable wages are equalized *within* each of the institutional sectors (formal and informal), but not between them. How might a switching policy affect this labor market?

Labor can now be allocated to one of five categories:
* employment in,
    informal tradable;
    formal tradable;
    informal nontradable;
    formal nontradable;
* unemployed.

To illustrate the effects of switching in such a model, Figure 3.9 is drawn differently from the others. Now we measure employment in the formal sector (in both N and T sectors) from the O_F origin, and in the informal sector from the O_I origin. The demand for labor in the formal sector (VMP^F) is the horizontal sum of the labor demand in nontradables (VMP_n^F) and tradables. Similarly for the informal sector, labor demands in the two production sectors are summed horizontally.

Figure 3.9

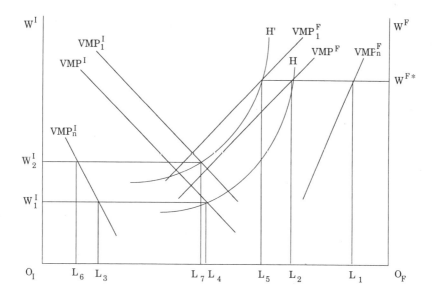

The initial equilibrium is shown with a minimum money-wage of W^F* in the formal sector, employment being $O_F L_1$ in nontradables and $L_1 L_2$ in tradables. The equilibrium wage in the informal sector is at W_1^I, with informal employment being $O_I L_3$ in nontradables and $L_3 L_4$ in tradables. Unemployment is $L_4 L_2$.[36]

A switching policy (in raising P_t) will shift both formal-sector and informal-sector labor demand curves outward, leaving the nontradables components of these unaffected. The new equilibrium gives an increase in the nominal wage in the informal sector to W_2^I, accompanied by a change in tradables employment to $L_1 L_5$ in the formal sector and to $L_6 L_7$ in the informal sector. While employment in formal nontradables remains unchanged, informal nontradables employment declines to $O^I L_6$. Unemployment falls to $L_7 L_5$.

The effects of switching in such a model can be summarized as follows:

- employment in the formal N sector is unchanged;
- employment in the formal T sector increases;
- employment in the informal N sector falls;
- the change employment in the informal T sector is ambiguous;
- unemployment falls;
- real consumption wages in both formal tradables and nontradables falls;
- real consumption wages rise in the informal sector (in both the N and T sectors there).[37]

These are interesting results. While we have the usual certain fall in real consumption wages in the protected sector, the change in real consumption wages elsewhere in the economy is no longer ambiguous, and moreover, it is positive.

Following the usual procedure, we derive the poverty effects of switching as,[38]

---

36. Note that we have restored the assumption that $\delta = \tau = 1$ for this case and have reintroduced the rectangular hyperbola.

37. This follows from the fact that W^I/P_n increases by more than the increase in P_t/P_n, so that W^I/P_t increases as well.

38. Bearing in mind that $d\Omega^F_t/d\pi = d\Omega^F_n/d\pi$ and $d\Omega^I_t/d\pi = d\Omega^I_n/d\pi$.

$$\frac{dPV_\alpha}{d\pi} = -\frac{d\Omega^F}{d\pi}\left[x_n^F\alpha\left(PV_{\alpha-1,n}^F - PV_{\alpha,n}^F\right) + x_t^F\alpha\left(PV_{\alpha-1,t}^F - PV_{\alpha,t}^F\right)\right]$$

$$-\frac{d\Omega^I}{d\pi}\left[x_n^I\alpha\left(PV_{\alpha-1,n}^I - PV_{\alpha,n}^I\right) + x_t^I\alpha\left(PV_{\alpha-1,t}^I - PV_{\alpha,t}^I\right)\right]$$

$$+\frac{dx_t^F}{d\pi}\left(PV_{\alpha,t}^F - PV_{\alpha,t}^I\right) + \frac{dx_n^I}{d\pi}\left(PV_{\alpha,n}^I - PV_{\alpha,t}^I\right) \qquad (18)$$

$$+\frac{dx_u}{d\pi}\left(PV_u - PV_t^I\right)$$

Taking the real wage effects first, the real consumption wage movements in the formal and informal sectors work in opposite directions. The first term on the rhs of (18) is positive, thus increasing poverty, while the second term is negative (real consumption wages rise in the informal sector). Under the reasonable assumption that poverty and the share of employment is greater in the unprotected sector, we can conclude that the real wage effect of switching is beneficial—the fall in real consumption wages in the formal sector being more than compensated by the rise in the informal sector.

The allocative effects are ambiguous in this case. Although under reasonable assumptions about poverty in the sectors ($PV_t^F < PV_t^I$ and $PV_u > PV_t^I$), the third and fifth terms on the righthand side of equation (18) are negative (thus having a beneficial effect on poverty). The fourth term cannot be assessed. If there is little difference between poverty in tradables and nontradables within the informal sector (or if $PV_n^I > PV_t^I$), then the allocative effects will be beneficial.[39]

In sum, the effects of switching under these assumptions seem to be most promising as far as poverty reduction is concerned. The real wage effect in the informal sector (in which poverty might be expected to be relatively high) is favorable, as is the unemployment effect.

---

39. That is, the fourth term is either near zero or negative.

Barriers to Entry in Both Sectors

Figure 3.10 illustrates this last case which we consider, when there are barriers to entry in parts of both the N and T sectors assuming once again apartheid conditions ($\tau = 0$). The original equilibrium is one where there is no search unemployment. Entry barriers restrict employment in the formal sector to $O_F L_1$, with labor demand allocating $O_F L_2$ to nontradables and $L_1 L_2$ to tradables. With the restriction on entry, the initial wage in the formal sector is at W_1^F. The remainder of the work force takes up employment in the informal sector, at a market clearing wage of W_1^I.

Following adjustment, labor reallocations under these circumstances will not take place between the formal and informal sectors, but will be confined to movements out of nontradables into tradables *within* each of the institutional sectors. Specifically, $L_2 L_4$ workers in the formal sector move from the N sector to the T sector, while $L_5 L_3$ informal-sector workers move into tradables. The labor market effects of adjustment under these assumptions may be summarized as:

- an increase (of the same magnitude) in the real consumption wage in both formal and informal sectors;[40]
- reallocations of labor between T and N sectors, but within formal and informal labor markets.

The poverty effect is given by,[41]

$$\frac{dPV_\alpha}{d\pi} = -\left(\frac{d\Omega^F}{d\pi}\right)\left[\begin{matrix} x_n^F\alpha\left(PV_{\alpha-1,n}^F - PV_{\alpha,n}^F\right) + x_t^F\alpha\left(PV_{\alpha-1,t}^F - PV_{\alpha,t}^F\right) \\ + x_n^I\alpha\left(PV_{\alpha-1,n}^I - PV_{\alpha,n}^I\right) + x_t^I\alpha\left(PV_{\alpha-1,t}^I - PV_{\alpha,t}^I\right) \end{matrix}\right] \tag{19}$$
$$+ \frac{dx_t^F}{d\pi}\left(PV_{\alpha,t}^F - PV_{\alpha,n}^F\right) + \frac{dx_t^I}{d\pi}\left(PV_{\alpha,t}^I - PV_{\alpha,n}^I\right)$$

---

40. It should be noted once again that the real wage only rises for cases when $\beta < 1$. Should $\beta = 1$, the real wage will be unchanged.

41. Note that $d\Omega^I = d\Omega^F$, $dx_t^I = -dx_n^I$, and $dx_t^F = -dx_n^F$.

Figure 3.10

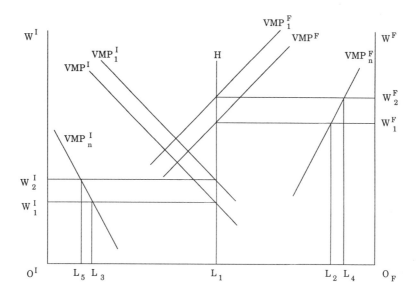

The real wage effect is unambiguously negative, since real consumption wages rise in all four sectors. These favorable real wage effects arise directly from the market imperfection. If there were no barriers to entry, real consumption wage ambiguity (as described in Figure 3.2) would apply. But ambiguity returns to the allocative effects. This depends on whether poverty is greater in tradables than nontradables within each of the institutional sectors. These results hold even for cases when $\tau > 0$.

Conclusions

The implications of adjustment for employment and wages depend on how far the latter respond flexibly to shifts in labor market conditions. The poverty effects of an expenditure switching policy do depend on the characteristics of the labor market—on the nature of imperfections and on their sectoral incidence. The moral is that in designing "poverty-sensitive" adjustment programs, we need to understand how the poverty effects are influenced by different labor market structures. This naturally leads us to ask how flexible labor markets might be in developing countries and thus to the practical relevance of the models presented above. To address this issue properly would require another paper, but the following points can be made.

First, in the developed-country literature much wage inflexibility is attributed to unionization. This factor has been the most influential, among developing areas, in Latin America through the indexation of wage contracts to inflation, and there are certainly cases in the early 1980s where this has contributed to program failure (Reisen 1985; p. 24). For such cases, it would be more appropriate to assume fixed real wages. However, the depression of labor market activity in more recent years has weakened considerably labor's bargaining power, especially where unionization has been lower in expanding sectors as compared with contracting sectors. Incomes polices applied with the cooperation of labor have become increasingly common (as in Mexico). Unionization is not strong in Africa (with the exception of capital-intensive sectors such as mining), and in recent years unions have been more concerned about protecting jobs than in pushing for higher wages (on Kenya see Lal and Collier 1986, p. 165). In East Asia government limitations on worker organization have ensured labor market flexibility.[42] In sum, for most countries (and certainly for those low-income countries), the assumption of real-wage rigidity arising from unionization no longer applies.[43]

Second, in the development literature wage rigidity is more often attributed to the role of government in labor markets, either enforcing minimum wages (as was assumed earlier) or setting public-sector wages without due consideration to labor market conditions. These factors have certainly been more important in Africa and Asia than has unionization. In presenting our models, we assumed that governments fixed a minimum wage before adjustment began. Expressing the minimum wage in terms of nontradables is akin to

---

42. This flexibility was one of the factors behind South Korea's rapid adjustment to the shocks of 1979-80, although it remains to be seen whether the recent growth in union activity will impart rigidity (Aghevli and Marquez-Ruarte, 1985).

43. Edwards (1989, p. 333) found that in 29 episodes of devaluation (mainly in middle-income countries) real agricultural wages tended to fall in a larger number of postdevaluation cases than did real manufacturing wages. This is attributed to differences in indexation possibilities across sectors.

assuming that the government fixes it in money terms, since nontradables were taken as a numeraire. We can justify this on the grounds that while in the past governments set minimum wages with reference to the price basket of all goods, this practice has diminished considerably among adjusting countries. Across Africa, with few exceptions, adjustments in minimum wages have lagged far behind the rate of inflation (ILO 1987, p. 102). Large reductions in real minimum wages have also occurred in some Latin American countries.

Of course, these trends do not imply that all the required real-wage flexibility has been achieved, for the scale of real exchange-rate depreciation required in some countries (particularly Africa) is very considerable indeed, and indices of the real value of minimum wages are very imperfect indicators. But recent studies using micro-level data indicate considerable wage flexibility in periods of adjustment (see Levy and Newman 1989 on Côte d'Ivoire). Moreover, it is now apparent that in many countries, public servants have been unable to maintain their salaries above private-sector levels, reflecting a reduction in their bargaining power (see Stelcner et al. 1987 on Peru).

Governments, by and large, have taken the position that if devaluation is to encourage tradable production, then the unit cost of labor (reflected in the real product wage for tradables) must fall. Moreover, raising the money wage to compensate for increases in tradable prices runs counter to the urgent need to restrain government expenditures (because of the ramifications for the public wage bill). Raising the minimum wage following a devaluation has become an increasingly token gesture to labor since whatever adjustments are made usually fall far behind the rise in prices. Therefore, maintaining a fixed nominal minimum wage in the face of increases in tradable prices seems a reasonable model assumption.

A third source of wage rigidity, in the absence of government intervention, can lie in the profit-maximizing behavior of employers. Employers may gain higher productivity and lower recruitment costs by ensuring (through implicit contracts) risk-averse workers against the impact of demand-induced fluctuations in their marginal productivity by maintaining stable wages. Similarly, in efficiency-wage models, labor productivity is an increasing function of the wage, and there exists a wage level ("the efficiency wage") at which labor productivity is maximized (costs per unit of labor minimized). If the market-clearing wage is below the efficiency wage, then it is not profitable for employers to offer lower wages. Since workers would want insurance in their contracts against unexpected price rises, and since productivity is a function of consumption, these theories amount to propositions of real wage rigidity.

These explanations of wage rigidity are persuasive for developed countries with skilled industrial work forces. But aside from the newly industrialized countries, the predominance of informal employment contracts in developing countries, together with the dominance of unskilled employment, suggest a limited role for implicit contracts or efficiency-wage considerations in inducing wage rigidity.[44] A possible (and important) exception is where observed and real wages lie close to the nutritional minimum. This is featured in efficiency-wage models attempting to rationalize why rural labor markets do not clear despite high unemployment and the absence of institutional rigidities (Dasgupta and Ray 1986). Evidence on the existence of efficiency wages is so far lacking (Rosenzweig 1988), although a few tests have been undertaken. But the depth of recession in many developing countries, while it has undermined the incentive of firms to stabilize real wages for skilled workers, may have induced some real wage rigidity for the unskilled. This is because the real wages of the unskilled may have fallen near to the nutritional floor, so that there is now an incentive for employers to pay a wage above market-clearing levels in order to avoid a fall in productivity from malnutrition. If this is the case, then our assumption of a fixed nominal wage would have obvious limitations. During the early phase of adjustment, real wage declines in the covered sector would occur; once the nutritional floor is reached, an assumption of real-wage rigidity makes more sense.

Imposing nominal wage inflexibility in part of the labor market does not eliminate the ambiguity of the competitive neo-classical model over the real wage effect. However, with predictable changes in the level of unemployment, and with more certainty about differences

---

44. Lal (1989, p. 152) finds some evidence to support the theory that firms seek to reduce costly labor turnover by paying above-market wages in the case of skilled industrial wages in India.

in poverty between sectors, confident predictions can be made about the reallocative effects.[45]

An interesting result for policy is that the sector in which a minimum wage applies invariably experiences a real wage decline, regardless of whether it produces tradables or nontradables. But if the protection arises from barriers to entry, the tradables sector always experiences an increase in the real wage, while the real wage invariably falls in nontradables. The critical point is not so much whether tradables is predominantly a formal activity, but what form of labor market imperfection characterizes the formal sector.

Introducing labor market imperfections does make a difference in the poverty effects of adjustment, and this difference depends on the nature of the imperfection. Unfortunately, it does little to remove the awkward ambiguity found in the theory. At this stage, the policy debate would be well served by further empirical investigation.

References

Addison, T., and L. Demery. 1989. "The Social Dimensions of Structural Adjustment in Sub-Saharan Africa." Washington, D.C.: World Bank. January 9. Processed.

Aghevli, B.B., and J. Marquez-Ruarte. 1985. *A Case of Successful Adjustment: Korea's Experience During 1980-84.* Washington, D.C.: International Monetary Fund. Occasional Paper 39. August.

Barro, R.J., and H.I. Grossman. 1971. "A General Disequilibrium Model of Income and Employment." *American Economic Review* 61: 82-93.

Clower, R.W. 1965. "The Keynesian Counterrevolution: A Theoretical Appraisal." In F. Hahn and F. Brechling, eds., *The Theory of Interest Rates.* London: MacMillan.

Collier, P., and D. Lal. 1986. *Labour and Poverty in Kenya, 1900-1980.* Oxford: Clarendon Press.

Corden, W.M. 1985. *Inflation, Exchange Rates, and the World Economy.* 3d ed., Oxford: Clarendon Press.

---

45. Poverty in the covered sector is likely to be less than in the uncovered sector.

_____. 1986. *The Relevance for Developing Countries of Recent Developments in Macroeconomic Theory*. Canberra, Australian National University, Research School of Pacific Studies Working Paper 86/1.

Cornia, G.A., R. Jolly, and F. Stewart, eds. 1987. *Adjustment with a Human Face*. Vol. 1: Protecting the Vulnerable and Promoting Growth. Oxford: Clarendon Press for UNICEF.

Cuddington, J.T. 1980. "Fiscal and Exchange Rate Policies in a Fix-Price Trade Model with Export Rationing." *Journal of International Economics* 10, no.3 (August): 319-340.

_____. 1981. "Import Substitution Policies: A Two-Sector, Fix-Price Model." *Review of Economic Studies* 48: 327-342.

Cuddington, J.T., P. Johansson, and K.G. Löfgren. 1984. *Disequilibrium Macroeconomics in Open Economies*. Oxford: Basil Blackwell.

Dasgupta, P., and D. Ray. 1986. "Inequality as a Determinant of Malnutrition and Unemployment: Theory." *Economic Journal* 96: 1011-1034.

Demery, L. and T. Addison. 1987. "Stabilization Policy and Income Distribution in Developing Countries." *World Development* 15: 1483-1498.

Dixit, A. 1978. "The Balance of Trade in a Model of Temporary Equilibrium with Rationing." *Review of Economic Studies* 45: 393-404.

Dixon, H. 1988. "Unions, Oligopoly, and the Natural Range of Employment." *The Economic Journal* 98: 1127-1147.

Dornbusch, R. 1980. *Open Economy Macroeconomics*. New York: Basic Books.

Edwards, S. 1988. "Terms of Trade, Tariffs, and Labor Market Adjustment in Developing Countries." *World Bank Economic Review* 2: 165-185.

_____. 1989a. *Real Exchange Rates, Devaluation, and Adjustment*. Cambridge, Mass.: MIT Press.

_____. 1989b. "Tariffs, Capital Controls, and Equilibrium Real Exchange Rates." *Canadian Journal of Economics.*22, no. 1 (February): 79-92.

Foster, J., J. Greer, and E. Thorbecke. 1984. "A Class of Decomposable Poverty Measures." *Econometrica* 52: 761-766.

Harris, J., and M.P. Todaro. 1970. "Migration, Unemployment and Development: A Two-Sector Analysis." *American Economic Review* 60: 126-142.

ILO. 1987. *World Labour Report* 3. Geneva: International Labour Office.

Jamal, V. 1988. "Coping under Crisis in Uganda." *International Labour Review.* Special Issue: The African Crisis, Food Security and Structural Adjustment. Vol. 127, no. 6: 679-701.

_____. 1988b. "Somalia: Survival in a "Doomed" Economy." *International Labour Review.* Special Issue: The African Crisis, Food Security and Structural Adjustment. Vol. 127, no. 6: 783-812.

Kanbur, S.M.R. 1987. "Structural Adjustment, Macroeconomic Adjustment, and Poverty: A Methodology for Analysis." *World Development* 15: 1515-1526.

_____. 1990. *Poverty and the Social Dimensions of Structural Adjustment in Côte d'Ivoire.* Social Dimensions of Adjustment Working Paper 2. Washington, D.C.: World Bank. March.

Knight, J.B. 1976. "Devaluation and Income Distribution in Less-Developed Economies." *Oxford Economic Papers* 28 (July): 200-227.

Lal, D. 1984. *The Real Effects of Stabilization and Structural Adjustment Policies: An Extension of the Australian Adjustment Model.* Working Paper 636. Washington, D.C.: World Bank. March.

_____. 1988. "A Simple Framework for Analyzing Various Real Aspects of Stabilization and Structural

Adjustment Policies." *Journal of Development Studies* 25 (April): 291-312.

_____. 1989. *The Hindu Equilibrium*. Vol. 2. *Aspects of Indian Labour*. Oxford: Clarendon Press.

Levy, V., and J.L. Newman. 1989. "Wage Rigidity: Micro and Macro Evidence on Labor Market Adjustment in the Modern Sector." *World Bank Economic Review* 3 (January): 97-118.

Malinvaud, E. 1977. *The Theory of Unemployment Reconsidered*. Oxford: Basil Blackwell.

Mazumdar, D. 1983. "Segmented Labor Markets in LDCs." *American Economic Review* 73, no.2 (May): 254-259.

Mincer, J. 1976. "Unemployment Effects of Minimum Wages." *Journal of Political Economy* 84, no.4 , part 2 (August): S87-104.

Mussa, M.L. 1974. "Tariffs and Distribution of Income: Importance of Factor Specificity, Substitutability, and Intensity in Short and Long Run." *Journal of Political Economy* 82: 1191-1203.

Neary, P. 1978a. "Dynamic Stability and the Theory of Factor-Market Distortions." *American Economic Review*: 68, no.4 (September): 671-682.

_____. 1978b. "Short-Run Capital Specificity and the Pure Theory of International Trade." *Economic Journal* 88: 448-510.

_____. 1980. "Nontraded Goods and the Balance of Trade in a Neo-Keynesian Temporary Equilibrium." *Quarterly Journal of Economics* 95: 403-429.

Patinkin, D. 1965. *Money, Interest and Prices: An Integration of Monetary and Value Theory*. New York: Harper & Row.

Reisen, H. 1985. *Key Prices for Adjustment Towards Less External Indebtedness*. Development Centre paper. Paris: OECD.

Rosenzweig, M. 1988. "Labor Markets in Low-Income Countries." In H. Chenery and T.N. Srinivasan, eds., *Handbook of*

Development Economics, vols. 1 & 2. New York: North-Holland.

Stelcner, M., J. van der Gaag, and W. Vijverberg. 1987. *Public-Private Sector Wage Differentials in Peru: 1985-86.* LSMS Working Paper 41. Washington, D.C.: World Bank.

4

WAGE INDEXATION, ADJUSTMENT, AND INFLATION

Michael B. Devereux

Wage indexation, institutionalized in many developed economies since the Second World War, was of particular importance in the inflationary episodes of the 1970s and the early 1980s. In many developing economies, with high inflation, formal or informal cost of living allowances in wage contracts are unavoidable. However, in the economies of Argentina and Brazil, high and prolonged inflation led to indexation structures being deeply embedded in the system. There is a widespread belief that indexation—originally a good idea for dealing with inflation—has itself become part of the problem.

This paper surveys some issues involved in wage indexation, with particular reference to Argentina and Brazil. It focuses on the interaction between indexation and inflation. Also discussed is the effect of wage indexation on the real instability of the economy and the adjustment response.

With respect to wage indexation and inflation, one of the key questions is whether indexation perpetuates the inflationary process. There are a number of ways in which this might take place. First, by preventing real wage adjustment to supply or demand shocks, indexation can potentially destabilize the price response to these shocks. Second, wage contracts that tie wage adjustment to previous rates of inflation tend to be more persistent. This can greatly increase the real costs of disinflation and hence make continuing monetary

I thank participants at the Conference on Labor Markets in an Era of Adjustment, Warwick University, August 1989, for comments.

accommodation the less painful option, prolonging the inflation. Third, extensive indexation of government financial liabilities can raise the inflation rate required to generate a given level of seigniorage revenue. Fourth, widespread indexation, protecting the major political constituencies from real income losses due to inflation can erode the political will to follow stabilization programs.

Another concern is that extensive wage indexation may cause real allocational distortions. In an economy subject only to aggregate nominal disturbances, the natural and efficient method of adjusting wages would be to fully compensate for inflation. As long as there is no required adjustment in relative prices, there is no indexation dilemma at all. In the real world, prices change for all sorts of reasons, and wage indexation policies aimed at insulating real wages from any price movements may cause serious economic dislocation. Wage indexation that does not take account of the necessity of adjusting to real shocks, such as internal or external supply shocks, may thus prevent the normal adjustment of an economy. Similarly, wage indexation may erode the real effects of government policies, such as a devaluation. The extent to which indexation places such constraints on real adjustment depends on the flexibility with which the authorities can adjust the indexation scheme. This flexibility, in turn, is likely to be affected by the inflationary environment. In periods of very high inflation, it may be considerably more difficult to achieve discretionary adjustments in indexation policies.

The chapter examines the role and effect of wage indexation under both of these headings. The plan of the paper is as follows. There are three main parts. In the first part basic theory concerning wage indexation, inflation, and macroeconomic stability is reviewed. This section addresses issues such as the optimal degree of wage indexation, the appropriate contingencies in wage indexation plans, the dynamic effects of wage indexation, the effect of wage indexation in multisector economies, and the interaction between wage indexation, asset indexation, and inflation.

In the second part of the chapter I review the role of indexation in Argentina and Brazil, two countries that recently experienced high rates of inflation and anti-inflationary programs explicitly designed to counter the effects of widespread indexation. I describe the details of wage setting and the mechanics of wage indexation in these countries. Different views of the determinants of inflation in these countries are presented, and the role of wage and asset indexation in the inflationary process is discussed.

The third part of the paper is on key issues in the inflation/indexation debate. Some empirical evidence from the experience of the sample countries is examined. The Israeli case is also included. A crucial issue is the importance of indexation mechanisms in imparting inflationary "inertia" into the dynamics of these economies, and the relevance of this for the success of anti-inflation policies.

Wage Indexation: Basic Theory and Predictions

Aizenman (1987) defines wage indexation as "a mechanism designed to adjust wages to information that cannot be foreseen when the wage contract is negotiated." This is the sense in which wage indexation is understood in most of the theoretical literature of the last decade. In the real world indexation mechanisms of this type do exist, for instance in the form of "trigger-point" clauses whereby money wages are revised over the life of a contract if inflation exceeds a given rate.

Another implicit definition of wage indexation, however, arising frequently in discussion of the inflation experiences of developing economies, is the notion that contract wages, *at the time of renegotiation*, are adjusted partially or wholly for previous inflation. In this sense wage indexation is not a contract contingency but forms the basis for the structure of contracts at the time of renegotiation. Emerson (1983) observes that this is the more common practice among the European economies. While this does not fall into the strict category of wage indexation as defined above, I will devote some time to the analysis of wage adjustment schemes of this nature. Simonsen (1983) very forcefully argues for the importance of backward-looking wage adjustment schemes in the Brazilian inflationary process.

In keeping with my basic distinction between adjustment and inflationary aspects of indexation, I concentrate in the next section on adjustment problems, and in the following section on the theoretical relationship between indexation and inflation. As we will see, to some extent this distinction is artificial because inflation and adjustment problems are intimately interrelated.

Indexation and Adjustment

In a standard wage contract in a monetary economy, there are two conceptually distinct features of the contract. One is the real wage that can be agreed on between workers and firms. The other is the method of adjusting the actual money wages paid to take account of fluctuations in the average money price of commodities in the economy. The preserve of wage indexation schemes, at least ideally, is with the second factor.

If the aggregate price level were stable, money wages paid would accurately reflect the real value of these wages, and wage indexation is both irrelevant and unnecessary. When the aggregate price level fluctuates, however, the parties to a contract may find it useful to distinguish between the appropriate real wage, affected by aspects of productivity and costs, and a purely "inflationary" factor, generated by movements in the average price level. This second factor should not affect the real wage. One way to deal with this problem is to adjust money wages automatically in response to movements in the average price level by means of an indexation scheme. This can prevent inflation from distorting relative prices over the life of contracts during which some prices are fixed and some free to vary. The classic case for indexation in Friedman (1974) is based on this type of argument.

If contract structures can accommodate sophisticated contingency clauses that allow for adjustment of base wage rates as well as indexation to movements in the aggregate price level, then this rationale for indexed wages would be forceful. However, most labor contracts in developed economies, as well as in developing economies, have very simple contingencies for adjustment of wages during the life of the contract. In almost all cases the only such contingencies are Cost of Living Allowances, agreements that index wage rates to movements in the rate of inflation.

When contracts are thus restricted, it is unclear whether Friedman's argument still holds. The problem is that the two aspects of the contract—the appropriate real wage and the nominal wage to be paid to attain this—become intertwined. The best exposition of the difficulties of wage indexation in such environments is Gray (1976). Gray shows that in an economy subject only to nominal shocks, full indexation of wages to price movements is desirable. This insulates employment and output from the effects of the shocks, although it destabilizes the price level relative to a nonindexed economy.

More realistically, one might expect the economy to be prone to real shocks that require adjustments of *relative* prices. Commodity price fluctuations, terms-of-trade disturbances, and oil price changes are examples of such shocks. In this case, full indexation of wages to the price level is not desirable because it prevents the required adjustment of the real wage. A policy of full indexation may severely destabilize real output and employment in face of real shocks of this kind. In addition, it will destabilize the price level relative to the nonindexed economy. The best wage indexation scheme in face of real shocks, in the sense that it replicates the economy with freely flexible wages and prices, should allow for only partial compensation of wages to movements in the aggregate price level. This enables the real wage to adjust to the real shock in a desirable manner. In the presence of both types of shocks, nominal and real, the optimal rate of wage indexation is a linear combination of the two. This is a second-best strategy since it leaves the economy exposed to real effects of purely nominal shocks. Gray shows that indexation will be higher, the greater the variance of nominal disturbances relative to real disturbances.

In summary, wage indexation may be stabilizing or destabilizing, depending upon the disturbance hitting the economy. Note, however, that wage indexation tends to destabilize the price level in response to all shocks, whether real or nominal, in comparison to the fixed money wage, nonindexed system. This raises the question (addressed in the following section) of the inflationary effects of indexation.

Gray's paper was influential in pointing to the potentially damaging effects of full wage indexation as well as in suggesting the method for designing efficient wage indexation schemes. A large amount of theoretical work followed in the tradition of this paper, both extending the framework to more complex environments and criticizing some of its assumptions. One of the key questions addressed was why indexation schemes should stop at contingencies based on the price level alone. Karni (1983) showed that a scheme that ties nominal wages to movements in the price level as well as to movements in aggregate output can be designed that replicates the full employment, flexible-wage economy.

The problem of indexation in an open economy has been addressed by a number of authors.[1] One of the key issues here is the appropriate price index to use in wage indexation schemes. The two major choices are the Consumer Price Index, which includes the price of imported consumer goods, and the GNP deflator, which includes only the prices of home produced goods. Marston (1984) looks at the advantages of each type of indexation mechanism. In response to a terms of trade shock, indexing wages to the CPI is likely to destabilize employment and output since it allows fluctuations in imported goods prices to affect the real wage facing domestic firms. It will also inhibit the real effects of devaluation policies in their traditional role of reducing real wages. Therefore, the strong reaction to indexation of this type during the oil price increases of the 1970s is not surprising. Marston and Turnovsky (1985) examine the appropriate wage indexation policy in response to a rise in the price of an imported intermediate raw material, such as oil. Wages tied to domestic prices alone are likely to destabilize employment in this case because raw materials prices directly affect firm profitability, much as technology shocks do. They recommend an indexation to a "value added" price index, which is the domestic price index with the direct influence of the raw materials price netted out. Marston and Turnovsky argue that such a price index allows for a desirable fall in real wages after a raw materials price increase, restoring macroeconomic stability without unemployment. In fact, a wage policy of this sort was used in Japan after the second oil shock.

For economies facing problems of adjustment to internal or external shocks, wage indexation can be seen as an *impediment* to adjustment, or it can be used as a *tool* of adjustment. One strand of the

---

1. See, for instance, Turnovsky (1983), Aizenman and Frenkel (1985), and Marston and Turnovsky (1985).

literature has taken up the second point and focused on the interaction between monetary policies, exchange rate policies, and wage indexation policies in achieving optimal adjustment. Turnovsky (1983) shows that in certain cases wage indexation can lead exchange rate policy to be ineffective, while in other cases foreign exchange intervention policy can render wage indexation ineffective. Aizenman and Frenkel (1985) address this issue more fully; they outline a targets-instruments approach to the use of wage indexation, monetary feedback rules, and exchange rate intervention rules for macroeconomic objectives in a small open economy.

The alternative view, focusing on the impediments to macroeconomic adjustment presented by wage indexation, has also received a great deal of attention in the recent literature. Bruno and Sachs (1985) single out wage indexation policies that create real wage rigidity as one of the main reasons for the prolonged European unemployment in the 1970s in response to commodity price shocks and in the 1980s in response to high real interest rates. Their argument mirrors the implications of the Gray model; real wage rigidity becomes more serious in the face of supply shocks, which require an adjustment in real factor prices. A price increase of an imported intermediate good such as oil will shift the economy's aggregate supply curve to the left, at any given real wage. Even without accommodating demand policies, this will tend to be inflationary. With full wage indexation, none of this inflation can translate into reduced real wages, and the result is higher unemployment. Bruno and Sachs go further to argue that negative supply shocks in the face of widespread indexation will have magnified effects through reduced profitability and lower capital investment, thus leading to lower growth rates, exacerbating the initial unemployment. The result is "stagflation," high inflation combined with high unemployment. Moreover, the traditional aggregate demand policy instruments have diminished effects in the presence of indexation.

For developing economies, the most common type of external shock is a terms-of-trade shock. Edwards (1988) examines the labor market response of a multisector developing economy to terms-of-trade fluctuations, in the case where there are economy-wide or sector-specific minimum wages. This is comparable to a system of wage indexation, except in the latter the coverage is likely to be wider. In response to a terms-of-trade deterioration, wage indexation will cause (a) higher movements in unemployment, (b) less response of the real exchange rate, and (c) a worse position on the trade account. The presumption is that a high and inflexible degree of wage indexation will delay the adjustment to shocks, on the internal balance side and on the external balance side.

The key aspect of the adjustment problems arising from wage indexation is in the fact of real wage rigidities. But does wage indexation actually prevent real wage flexibility? Bruno and Sachs argue that this is the case for the European economies. Evidence from the high-inflation economies does not seem to support the argument that real wages have been inflexible. In fact, in Argentina, Brazil, and Israel, wage indexation coincided with a large degree of variability in measured real wages. One reason is because the method of indexation is quite different from that embedded in the theoretical models discussed earlier. In the Gray-type models, wage indexation can perfectly insulate against real wage fluctuations by adjusting wages instantly in response to unanticipated price increases. In practice, indexation adjusts wages for past inflation, and normally adjustment takes place at the time of contract renewal, rather than maintaining a constant real wage over the life of a contract.[2]

Fischer (1977) notes that lagged indexation can have quite different effects than those I have described. This type of indexation can be destabilizing, even in the absence of real disturbances, and it can inject long lags in the economy's response to disturbances. To see this, imagine that wages are set at the beginning of any contract period to equal the last period's price level. With instantaneous indexation, a

---

2. Even if indexation is based on intracontract contingencies, it is impossible to maintain a constant value of the real wage over the contract. Indexation must be conditioned on the reported price index, which will always reflect price conditions for a period before the wage is paid. Obviously, this problem is more acute, the more infrequent are indexation adjustments. Fischer (1988) distinguishes between three concepts of indexation: *ex ante, ex post,* and lagged *ex post*. In the first, which is rarely observed, indexation is made to a forecast of the price level. *Ex post* indexation holds when the wage for a period is adjusted to the price index for that period. Lagged *ex post* indexation adjusts the current wage to the last period's price index. The Gray model is then categorized as *ex post* indexation.

temporary demand shock may cause employment and output movements within the period (if indexation is incomplete) but will not persist beyond the life of the contract. With lagged indexation, however, the nominal and real wage in the period after the shock will increase, causing a shift in the supply curve to the left, reducing output and raising the price level. This, in turn, is translated into higher wages in future periods. Indexation builds inertia into the system, leading temporary disturbances to have prolonged effects. Rather than dampening real wage variability, this type of indexation actually causes it. In the face of accommodating monetary policy, the inertial features of this indexation may give rise to permanent inflation.

More elaborate models, including adjustment dynamics with backward-looking or lagged wage setting, have been constructed by Taylor (1980) and Dornbusch (1982). In Taylor's model, wage contracts are staggered over time, with each of two groups of wage setters setting wages every second period. Wages are partly based on expected aggregate demand pressure and partly on a desire to maintain a relative wage position against other wage setters. This second feature of the wage contract imparts a backward-looking element into the wage structure, similar to a lagged indexation scheme. Firms set prices to maintain constant markups over wages. Taylor shows that disturbances to demand or supply will have persistent effects on prices and output, as a result of the backward-looking features of wage setting. The more backward looking are wages, or the greater the degree of lagged indexation, the greater the inertia in price movements and the greater the variability of output. Dornbusch (1982) extends the Taylor model to look at the impact of exchange rate indexation. He shows that exchange rate indexation may increase or decrease the inertia in the system. It depends whether the stabilizing effects on demand of a more stable real exchange rate dominate, or are dominated by, the destabilizing effects of nominal exchange rate fluctuations being passed through to price markups via the domestic cost of intermediate imports.

Indexation and Inflation

The view that indexation is inherently inflationary has always been popular among policymakers. By adjusting wages and prices automatically in response to inflation, indexation may remove the natural forces for price stability. What is more, indexation reduces the social and economic costs of inflation, and so may lead to reduced political will to fight it. Yet Friedman (1974) proposed a system of widespread indexation precisely because it would lead to lower inflation rates. He argued that indexation allows prices and wages not only to rise with less social costs, but also to fall (by reducing the political costs of reducing inflation). By indexing tax brackets and government debt, Friedman claimed, the incentive for governments to generate revenue from surprise inflation is reduced, again leading to a lower average inflation rate.

Can indexation cause permanent inflation? Before addressing this question I would like to make two points. First, the structure of the indexation provisions are likely to be quite important. In particular, the distinction between current and lagged indexation is key. Second, permanent inflation requires corresponding money growth. This requires a hypothesis about the behavior of the monetary authorities. Indexation without money growth clearly cannot produce inflation on its own.

Fischer (1983) examines the link between wage indexation, asset indexation, and inflation. He distinguishes two ways in which indexation could be inflationary. First, wage or asset indexation could make the price level more responsive to shocks, so that price variability is increased in an indexed economy. Second, the average rate of change of prices could be higher in an indexed economy.

Fischer extends the simple theoretical model of Gray (1976) to allow for the effects of the government budget deficit. He assumes that part of the deficit is directly financed by money growth. Indexation can affect the government budget constraint for a number of reasons. First, indexed government debt ensures that unanticipated inflation cannot reduce the real value of debt repayments from government to the private sector. Unanticipated increases in the price level will then translate into an increase in government disbursements and a higher rate of money growth. In addition, wage indexation directly affects the real value of government spending, through its effects on public sector wages and salaries. Finally, indexation of the tax system has two conflicting effects. By indexing tax brackets in a progressive tax system to the rate of inflation, governments lose revenue otherwise generated by the effect of inflation pushing individuals into higher brackets. On the other hand, with delayed payment of taxes, inflation reduces real tax revenue when taxes are specified in nominal terms. This is the well-known "Olivera-Tanzi" effect. Indexing of tax liabilities reduces this loss. When government deficits are partly financed by money growth, all these effects are likely to have some influence on inflation.

Fischer concludes that in the first sense all types of indexing are inflationary. As in Gray's model, wage indexation increases the responsiveness of prices to shocks. Addition of the government budget to the model does not alter this result, as long as government finances at least part of the deficit by printing money. By increasing the responsiveness of money growth to current shocks, indexation of assets, taxes, or government spending will destabilize prices. Moreover, he concludes that the speed of adjustment of the price level to supply or demand shocks is unaffected by the extent of wage or asset indexation. This conflicts with Friedman (1974)—namely, that indexation would allow for a more rapid disinflation. The simple reason for the different result in Fischer's model is that indexation is of the *ex ante* type, correcting for unanticipated movements in the price level, and not in itself imparting or removing any inertia into the movement of the system.

In the second sense, however, there is no clear presumption that indexing is inflationary. What matters is the source of the inflation. If we take Fischer's model and allow for a constant real deficit financed by the inflation tax, then as long as output is stationary, the rate of inflation is not affected by the degree of wage indexation, since wage indexation does not affect the rate of money growth. If capital markets work efficiently so that the nominal interest rate adjusts to expected inflation, then the presence or absence of indexed assets is irrelevant for the long-run rate of inflation. The degree of indexation of taxes can be an important determinant of money growth, however, because it determines the share of government expenditures financed by direct taxation as opposed to seigniorage. Depending upon the strength of the two effects described above, the inflation rate may be higher or lower in the presence of tax indexation. But these conclusions are very sensitive to the type of monetary and fiscal policies followed. As noted by Fischer (1983), "Whether indexing is inflationary is thus not a question that can be answered a priori. The answer depends upon the types of policy being followed."

Despite the ambiguous nature of the links between indexing and inflation, politicians do seem to have a strong antipathy to embedding indexing provisions in contracts. For instance, in each of the disinflationary episodes of Argentina, Brazil, and Israel in 1985/86, de–indexation of wage contracts was a central plank in the policy. This may be because the indexation structures in those countries contain significant inertial features, unlike the models described in the past few paragraphs. Fischer and Summers (1989) give an intriguing, alternative explanation based on the differing incentives to create inflation that face policymakers in indexed as opposed to nonindexed economies.

Fischer and Summers adapt the framework of Barro and Gordon (1983). In the Barro and Gordon model, monetary authorities, in the absence of credible commitment, tend to overinflate in an attempt to reduce unemployment by the creation of inflation surprises. Fischer and Summers argue that indexation in capital markets will reduce the welfare costs of anticipated inflation, for any given rate of inflation, by removing the inflationary distortions in the tax system, and so on. This fall in the marginal cost of an extra percentage rate of inflation, however, increases the incentive for the policymaker to attempt to create surprise inflation and leads to a higher average inflation rate. It is quite possible for the second effect (the higher rate of inflation) to dominate the first (the lower average costs of inflation), so that, on balance, capital market indexation reduces welfare. The same argument does not apply to wage indexation, however. A higher rate of wage indexation in their model, by making the Phillips curve steeper, reduces the incentives to create surprise inflation. In fact, a simple way to eliminate the distortions from inflation in this framework is to institute 100 percent wage indexation.[3]

---

3. Ball and Stechetti (1989) reexamine the welfare benefits of wage indexation in an elaborated version of the Barro and Gordon framework. They argue that wage indexation may tend to be inflationary because it reduces the costs of inflation when these costs are based on the variability of relative prices generated by inflation in an

The traditional neo-classical view of the source of inflation ascribes a central role to aggregate demand factors, and in particular to the government fiscal imbalance. In this view, most strongly propounded by Sargent (1986), a necessary and sufficient condition for stopping inflation is to balance the government budget. This eliminates the source of current and future money growth that is the *fiscal* source of inflation and allows for an immediate fall in both inflation expectations as well as the rate of inflation. Fischer (1983) suggests only a very tenuous link between wage indexation and inflation in contexts where inflation is primarily driven by fiscal phenomena.

Many writers on Latin American inflation, however, believe wage indexation strongly influences inflation (Simonsen 1983; Williamson 1985. Theories of "inertial inflation" have been explicated by Simonsen (1983a; 1983b), Arida and Lara-Resende (1985), Dornbusch and Simonsen (1987), and others. These theories combine (a) wage contracts with lagged indexation provisions, automatically adjusting wages for previous rates of inflation, (b) staggered wage and price setting (sometimes with rigid mark-up pricing schemes), and (c) passive monetary policy. The combination of these three factors is said to produce an inflation process with a large degree of persistence, in which one-time shocks to the economy can lead to jump increases in the rate of inflation and to extremely high unemployment costs of inflation reduction. The primary mechanism for the continuation of inflation, in this view, is not fiscal imbalances. Rather, it is built into the structure of contracts and expectations.

The logic behind these theories can be explained as follows. With lagged or *ex post* indexation, in which wages are adjusted for past inflation rates at discrete intervals, the average real wage is *negatively* related to the rate of inflation. For any given group of workers, the real wage is highest at the time of readjustment and declines progressively through the life of the contract. This opens up a tradeoff

economy with built-in contractual rigidities. In their model wage indexation also will reduce the direct benefits of inflation by steepening the Phillips curve. They find that the first effect is likely to dominate and that wage indexation will be inflationary. On the other hand, they find that the welfare effects of indexation are likely to be positive since the direct benefits from inflation protection usually exceed the losses from a higher rate of inflation.

between unemployment and inflation, as long as the frequency of adjustment of wages stays relatively constant. Imagine that monetary policy is purely accommodative, with the authorities merely attempting to prevent any increase in unemployment. Then a shock that causes an increase in prices in one period will be reflected in higher wage demands next period, and will require increased money growth to prevent a rise in real wages. This in turn translates into future wages and prices. With 100 percent wage indexation, the rate of inflation can be permanently higher as a result of the shock. Any attempt to reduce the rate of inflation will cause an immediate (and permanent) increase in the average real wage and a large rise in unemployment. Moreover, the existence of staggering in wage setting between different industries means that changes in the rate of inflation will increase the variability in relative real wages during the adjustment period.

During periods of accelerating inflation, the frequency of wage adjustment is unlikely to stay fixed, however. As the frequency of adjustment falls in an environment as described here, the rate of inflation accelerates because higher inflation is required to maintain constant real wages. The only way to reduce inflation, without a large fall in employment, is to partially or fully de-index wages—in other words, eliminate the full compensation for past rates of inflation in new wage contracts.

Consider the following model.[4] Imagine an economy with a large number of groups of firms and workers, some of which set wages continuously and some of which set them at discrete intervals. For simplicity assume a continuum of groups, indexed by i and uniformly distributed on the unit interval so $0 \leq i \leq 1$. Thus, the number of total groups is one. Let all groups i for $i \leq \theta$ set wages every λ periods, where time is continuous. Wage setting is uniformly staggered, so λ/θ groups set wages at every instant. All groups i for $i > \theta$ set wages continuously. Let wages be set so as to achieve the real wage ω at the time of contracting. This assumption for the form of contracts is based on descriptive realism rather than theoretical correctness. Then for all

---

4. This model is somewhat similar to the model of Simonsen (1983).

groups i, $W_i(t)=P(t)$ at the time of wage setting. All variables are in logs. The economy-wide average wage is

$$W(t) = \theta\left(\frac{1}{\lambda}\right) \int\limits_{s=0}^{\lambda} P(t-s)ds + (1-\theta)P(t) + \omega$$

(1)

Write the economy-wide aggregate supply function as[5]

$$Y(t) = \delta\big(P(t) - W(t)\big)$$

(2)

and a simple unit velocity demand equation as

$$M(t) = P(t) + Y(t)$$

(3)

Combining equations (1) to (3) gives the following condition for the price level

$$P(t) = \alpha\left(\theta\left(\frac{1}{\lambda}\right) \int\limits_{s=0}^{\lambda} P(t-s)ds + (1-\theta)P(t) + \omega\right) + (1-\alpha)M(t)$$

(4)

where $\alpha = \sigma / (1+\sigma)$.

The critical assumption is the behavior of monetary policy. Assume the monetary authorities accommodate all shocks to the price level to achieve the target level of output k. Then the money stock is $M(t)=P(t)+k$. Substituting this into (4) and solving for the steady state rate of inflation, we get

$$\pi = \frac{2(\sigma\omega + k)}{\sigma\theta\lambda}$$

(5)

and using (1) the steady state real wage becomes

---

5. This can be done by assuming that each sector produces a single homogeneous good with immobile labor, and has supply function $y_i=\sigma(P(t)-W_i(t))$. Then integrating across sectors gives the supply function above.

$$W(t) - P(t) = -\frac{\theta\pi\lambda}{2} + \omega$$

(6)

In this economy, full indexation and passive monetary policy eliminates the presence of a "nominal anchor." There is nothing to tie down the long-run price level. Instead the rate of change in prices is determined by the demands of wage setters and the income target of the monetary authorities. Zero inflation is incompatible with the real wage claims being made by workers. This type of explanation for persistent inflation has been made by observers of the Argentinean and Brazilian situations. The model can be extended to allow for both wage and price setting.[6] In that situation inflexible price cost markups can lead to high inflation in the presence of passive monetary policy.

Consider again equations (5) and (6). Observe that the real wage is lower, the higher the rate of inflation and the less frequently wages in the contracting sectors are adjusted. An increase in the inflation rate, matched by a proportional increase in the frequency of adjustment, will leave the real wage unaltered. The equilibrium rate of inflation depends positively upon the monetary authority's desired output target k and on the workers' real wage target. Thus, with monetary policy reacting in this way, a rise in ω leads to a permanently higher rate of inflation. Moreover, as noted by Simonsen (1983), a doubling in the frequency of wage adjustment in the contracting sectors will cause a doubling in the rate of inflation. Finally, parameter $1-\theta$ can be interpreted as the fraction of sectors that engage in contemporaneous indexing (that is, immediately adjust the wage for price changes). Under this interpretation, and given the monetary policy rule, indexation clearly has a direct and significant (positive) effect on the rate of inflation. Indeed, as the economy becomes more and more indexed, inflation grows without bound in this simple model. This happens, not because of the direct effects of indexing itself, but indirectly. A higher fraction of indexed contracts reduces the size of the nonindexed sector, and this requires a higher inflation rate in order to achieve a given average real wage target.

---

6. For a model along these lines (but with a zero steady state inflation rate), see Blanchard (1986).

The inertial features of inflation in this economy are captured by the fact that with a passive monetary policy the proximate cause of the continued inflation is the continual increase in nominal wages by the readjusting sectors. At each readjustment, the nominal wage is increased to establish the real wage peak ω. This feeds into prices through its effect on the real wage and aggregate supply. In this model the orthodox recipe for stopping inflation will cause an immediate rise in the real wage and a fall in employment.[7] In a similar setting Fischer (1988) shows how the "sacrifice ratio" during a disinflation—the percentage loss in output for each percentage fall in the inflation rate—is significantly increased by backward-looking indexation. In fact, unless real wage cuts can be achieved, unemployment will rise permanently, and the sacrifice ratio is infinite. This reflects the fact that for given values of λ, ω, and θ, there exists a long-run tradeoff between inflation and output. This is not a particularly credible feature of the model, however. The value of ω should adjust over time to take account of inflationary developments; in other words, workers should be concerned with their average real wage and not just the real wage achieved at the readjustment time. The contracts that produce wage-setting equations like (1) could be improved by including forecasts of future price levels.

The constraints imposed by this backward-looking wage indexation were one of the main reasons for the renewed belief in a "heterodox" approach to disinflation. This combines the "orthodox" pillar of budget balance and reductions in money growth, with temporary freezes on wages and prices. In terms of our model, this involves reducing inflation without real wage increases. It is necessary to de-index wages in order to achieve a cut in inflation without output cost. If prices alone were frozen, then all new contracts would lead to a wage renegotiation to achieve the wage "peak," ω, and this would be the new average real wage for the economy. Thus, at the beginning of the freeze, it is necessary to reduce this peak, or equivalently, to index

---

7. Inertia here is most easily understood by taking the following experiment: start in a zero inflation steady state and assume a temporary demand shock that increases the price level. This is immediately translated into higher nominal wages and therefore higher prices in the future. Taylor's (1980) model is an alternative model with inertia arising from backward-looking wage setting.

wages to past inflation at less than 100 percent. In the present model, with uniformly distributed renegotiation the economy-wide average real wage is constant over time, and this deindexation is effectively achieved by a sudden freeze of all prices and wages. Start in a zero inflation steady state, and assume a temporary demand shock which increases the price level. This is immediately translated into higher nominal wages and therefore higher prices in the future.

The model by Taylor (1980), discussed in the last section, is an alternative model with inertia arising from backward-looking wage setting average real wage is constant over time, and this de-indexation is effectively achieved by a sudden freeze of all prices and wages. In practice, renegotiation is not uniformly staggered, and it might be necessary to actually reduce the real wage at the beginning of the disinflation program. In Argentina, this was done by allowing a jump in the prices of publicly controlled goods at the beginning of the freeze, without compensation for this in wages.

What happens after the freeze is lifted? Unless either the wage-setting equation (1) or the monetary policy rule (2) is adjusted then, the inflation rate will inevitably jump up to its old level. If monetary policy ceases to be accommodating but (1) is unchanged, then inflation will fall but employment must also fall permanently. To achieve a fall in inflation without a loss in output, we must have a permanent fall in ω. Note that a fall in ω can lead to a fall in the long-run rate of inflation without unemployment even in the absence of any alteration in monetary policy. Just as passive monetary policy may allow inflation to rise in the aftermath of real shocks, it can also allow it to fall if these shocks abate.

The interesting feature of the model is that it allows, at least conceptually, for two quite separate mechanisms for controlling inflation. The first is through conventional policy instruments by eliminating the accommodative stance of policy. The second is by altering the structural features of the labor market that give rise to high inflation.

This view of the inflationary process tends to downplay the role of the deficit and seigniorage in the creation of high inflation. In theory, we might see this type of inflation even in the absence of a central government budget deficit (Kiguel and Liviatan 1989).[8] Then, in principle at least, disinflation remedies can be designed that ignore the role of fiscal policy. Unfortunately, however, in most cases fiscal correction cannot be ignored.

A key problem with wage and price controls in the presence of staggering is the fact that they will freeze relative prices at the level they are at at the time of the freeze. In the model above, real wages of groups that have adjusted very recently are approximately ω, while real wages of those who adjusted farther in the past are lower. In fact, what is happening is that the de-indexation, caused automatically by the full wage and price freeze, is falling differentially on those who renegotiated farther in the past. Freezing all prices and wages without some initial adjustments to take account of this can thus cause major anomalies in the presence of staggering. The discrepancy in relative prices may lead to shortages and black markets, the classic pitfall of price controls. To equalize relative prices, the wages of those who have recently adjusted, must be reduced, and the wages of those who adjusted farther in the past must be raised, before the freeze takes effect. The idea is to jump to the equilibrium relative price vector for the economy and then continue along this path but now at zero inflation. As can be imagined, the difficulties this policy presents are manifold, and it becomes extremely important to lift the price controls at the earliest possible time.

Finally, we should caution that the interpretation of wage indexation as inflationary in this model is fundamentally dependent upon the assumption of passive, accommodating monetary policy. The advocates of these theories have argued that this does, in fact, characterize the Latin American experience since the nonaccommodation of wage increases would involve such large increases in unemployment that the political will to continue on a disinflation process would be eroded. However, even unorthodox views of inflation must be consistent with orthodox theories. Wage indexation alone cannot create inflation. The failure of the stabilization attempts in Brazil and Argentina attests to the

---

8. Note that it is possible to amend the model above to allow for the additional presence of the budget deficit as a source of inflation.

impossibility of success in the absence of correct "fundamentals." I now move on to explore the characteristics of indexation in these countries.

Indexation in Argentina and Brazil

Although Argentina and Brazil have had quite similar experiences in attempting to deal with high rates of inflation in the face of widespread indexation, they exhibit major differences in history and institutional structure. Therefore, I will discuss each country in turn before describing their common features with relation to the importance of indexation structures.

Argentina

Argentina has a long history of inflation and economic instability. This is due to external factors and to structural features of the economy as well as domestic policy response. Argentina is largely a closed economy. There is a heavy reliance on agriculture, mainly beef, for export revenue. Partly because of this, the country has traditionally experienced high terms-of-trade volatility. The manufacturing sector is relatively insulated from foreign competition, and it is dominated by powerful oligopolistic industries and large trade unions (Di Tella 1987). Since the mid 1970s, macroeconomic policy has been highly erratic. Successive regimes have imposed price freezes and disinflations, followed by excess stimulations and fiscal imbalances, followed by external sector liberalizations and overvaluations, followed by controls and massive devaluations. Since 1975, annual inflation has not dipped below 100 percent.

Macroeconomic experience in Argentina over the past decade is summarized. After this I discuss the role of indexation in the process of adjustment and inflation in Argentina.

Tables 4.1 and 4.2 give some relevant statistics for the time since the mid 1970s. One legacy of the Peronist regime that ended with the military coup of 1976 was a 400 percent annual inflation rate. This was partly a delayed response to the oil shocks of the early 1970s. Inflation remained intractable throughout the rest of the decade, and this precipitated a novel stabilization plan in 1978. The idea was based on an exchange rate freeze, followed by predetermined rates of devaluation of the exchange rate, in conjunction with a reduction of the monetization of the government budget deficit. The logic was based on the simple application of the law of one price; with a fixed exchange rate the rate of inflation in Argentina would converge to that of the United States. At the same time goods and capital markets were liberalized. While the inflation rate did decline somewhat, the fall was not nearly so great as expected. A huge real appreciation followed. The trade balance surplus of 1979 fell to a huge deficit in 1980. This, in conjunction with high real interest rates, led to a large increase in borrowing. Much of these funds ended up outside the country due to capital flight, and many private debts were taken over by the public sector in the ensuing years. This left a large debt overhang, with the servicing of this debt taking up to 8 percent of GNP annually (Di Tella and Dornbusch 1989). The debt has remained one of the most severe macroeconomic constraints since then.

Table 4.1 Argentina: The Relationship between Real Wages, Inflation, GDP Growth, and the Deficit, 1974-87

Year	Real Wages (1970=100)	CPI (% Change)	Deficit (%GNP)	GDP (%Change)
1974	126.4	24.2	7.9	5.4
1975	123.7	182.8	15.4	-0.6
1976	79.2	444.0	11.8	0.0
1977	75.6	176.1	5.0	6.4
1978	77.2	175.6	6.8	-3.2
1979	86.1	159.9	6.1	6.9
1980	100.0	100.8	7.5	1.6
1981	91.2	104.5	13.3	-6.8
1982	79.3	164.8	15.8	-4.6
1983	102.6	343.2	16.8	2.8
1984	124.8	627.7	12.7	2.6
1985	103.2	672.2	5.9	-4.5
1986	97.3	90.1	3.6	5.7
1987			2.51	

Sources: Di Tella and Dornbusch (1989), Argentina: World Bank Country Study (1987).

Table 4.2 Argentina
(% Monthly Change)

Year and month	CPI	Wages
1985		
January	25.1	20.4
February	20.7	15.1
March	26.5	21.4
April	29.5	24.9
May	25.1	31.7
June	30.5	28.7
July	6.2	-2.8
August	3.1	0.0
September	2.0	1.0
October	1.9	1.9
November	2.4	1.9
December	3.2	5.5
1986		
January	3.0	5.2
February	1.7	1.7
March	4.6	0.8
April	4.7	6.5
May	4.0	5.3
June	4.5	5.0
July	6.8	6.8
August	8.8	9.0
September	7.2	1.8
October	6.1	11.0
November	5.3	4.7
December	4.7	2.9
1987		
January	7.6	7.8
February	6.5	3.6
March	8.2	2.2
April	3.4	8.5
May	4.2	3.9

Source: Machinea and Fanelli (1988).

The constitutional government of Alfonsin took over in 1983, inheriting this large external debt, a severe deterioration in the terms of trade, an accelerating rate of inflation, and a high government budget deficit (16 percent of GNP). While having to deal with these problems, the government faced great social pressure to restore economic growth and increase incomes. A policy of gradualism was attempted, in which it was hoped to bring wages and prices down in tandem. Real wages were deliberately increased, and full indexing on a monthly basis began to maintain their purchasing power (Machinea and Fanelli 1988, p. 119). The attempt to deal simultaneously with internal and external pressures came unstuck, and by early 1985 inflation was at a historical high monthly rate of 25 percent. To lessen the threat of hyperinflation, the government in June 1985 instituted the Austral Plan. The plan combined wage de-indexation with orthodox budget cutting and an across-the-board wage and price freeze. In addition, a currency reform was instituted, with a conversion table from old to new currency for all contracts outstanding at the time of the freeze. Much of the inflation in Argentina was assumed to be internal—that is, built into the structure of the economy by expectations and contracts with backward-looking wage indexation. Cutting the fundamental source of inflation, the budget deficit, would reduce inflation only gradually and with large and politically unacceptable unemployment costs.

The results of the Austral plan were initially striking (Canavese and Di Tella 1988; Machinea and Fanelli 1988). Inflation rates fell from about 25 percent to 3 percent a month, and they stayed at this level for about a year. (All prices were not frozen, in particular food prices.) The budget deficit improved as a result of the increased real receipts in the wake of a fall in inflation. Real growth increased significantly in 1986. Money balances as a proportion of GDP more than doubled.

However, toward the middle of 1986, the prize freeze was relaxed, and inflation started to creep up again. The initial improvement in the budget deficit began to disappear. New freezes were attempted, but none had lasting success. The new government of Carlos Menem took power in 1989 during a hyperinflation crisis. None of the stabilization plans instituted since then has been successful.

What role does indexation have to play in the Argentinean economy? Unlike Brazil and Israel, Argentina did not have a legal structure for wage indexation at the outset of the high inflation era (McNelis 1987). Wage indexation for the most part was developed by the private sector in response to the experience of inflation. The importance of indexation to recent Argentinean macro experience has been argued forcefully by Vasena and Szewach (1985). They view the inflationary process in Argentina as the reflection of an economy beset with real rigidities and inflexible relative prices. The nonexport sector (basically all of manufacturing) is characterized by a "battle over shares," with large unions trying to maintain real wages and powerful oligopolistic firms setting inflexible markups over costs. Traditionally, there has also been exchange rate indexation linking the rate of exchange rate depreciation to the rate of change of domestic prices. This fixes the real exchange rate, preventing the relative price from acting as an equilibriating mechanism.

After 1982 the authorities attempted to increase real wages that had fallen during the military regime of the late 1970s. A system of full indexation was instituted. After 1984 there was overindexation, a result of the constitutional government's promise to raise real wages. In addition, prices of public utilities, an important part of the consumer basket, were fully indexed. The result appears to be a series of mutually incompatible rigidities in relative prices, inexorably leading to a rising inflation rate. The whole economy is in a wage-price-price spiral: one group gains temporarily at the expense of another, only to be losers on the next round of adjustments. Relative prices have a great short-term volatility, and the whole process drives up inflation. Monetary policy remains accommodating, allowing inflation to rise without increasing real interest rates. As inflation rises, the length of time between wage and price adjustments falls (Machinea and Fanelli 1988, p. 122). As we saw in the previous section, this just leads to further rises in inflation.

In the periods of price and wage freezes, this process is temporarily halted. But this prevents adjustment in relative prices, which takes place in normal times via inflation. Because all prices cannot be frozen, and because of the impossibility of freezing prices at an equilibrium relative price vector, this leads to increasing pressures to relax the price freeze over time. When the freeze is lifted, the required readjustment in relative prices leads quickly to a renewal of the inflation process (Di Tella 1987). This argument was used by Canavese and Di Tella (1988) to explain the sudden outburst of inflation at the end of the Austral price freezes.

This is a version of the inertial inflation model specific to the Argentinean case, and it has origins in the structuralist models of inflation. Distributive conflicts are placed squarely in front as the determinant of inflation. Fiscal imbalances and monetary policies are of secondary importance in the sense that they adjust to maintain consistency with the high inflation.

The importance of institutional structures allowing for full and rapid indexation of prices and wages will be discussed later in the paper. However, here I will survey some special features of the Argentinean case. First, in the discussions of the Austral plan there seems to be consensus that formal and informal indexation of private and public prices, wages, and the exchange rate made it extremely difficult or even impossible to halt inflation by means of an orthodox package of tight money and budget cutting. Evaluated in the very short run, the Austral plan, as with the similar episodes in Brazil and Israel, seems to indicate that de-indexation and price controls can be useful as part of an anti-inflation package.

However, there are reasons to be skeptical of an inertial inflation model in Argentina. First, inflation rates took a significant upward jump in 1975. It is unclear why this should have been associated with an increase in militancy of trade unions or powerful firms. Second, as pointed out by Rodriguez (1988) and Kiguel (1989), over a long data sample there is high correlation between inflation and the budget deficit. One of the significant failings of the Austral plan was to meet the fiscal projections. The underlying structural government budget deficit was not reduced significantly. Thus, while the particular propagation mechanism behind the inflationary cycles in Argentina are undoubtedly conditioned by the institutional features described above, it is unclear whether these features can provide a self-contained explanation for inflation.

How important has indexation been in Argentina's economic adjustment? The typical adjustment constraint, as described by Bruno and Sachs (1985), consists of inflexible real wages and an inability to correct the trade balance through real devaluation. There seems to be clear evidence that indexation has not been a constraint on adjustment along these dimensions. The real wage fell significantly between 1976 and 1978 during the first years of the new military regime, and it fell again following the failure of the exchange-rate-based stabilization from 1978 to 1980. A huge real devaluation was executed at that time, which succeeded in turning around the trade balance. These two events illustrate the ability of the economic authorities to alter relative prices despite the widespread presence of formal and informal indexation schemes. A related episode took place right after the 1982 war with Britain, in which the central bank deliberately controlled interest rates in face of inflation in order to reduce the total value of external debt, both public and private (Dornbusch 1989). Indexation does not seem to be a major constraint on the ability to engineer economic adjustment, at least in the short term.

Brazil

Table 4.3 provides some data relevant for the Brazilian case. Current inflationary problems in Brazil, as in Argentina, began in 1974 in the aftermath of the first OPEC oil price increase. Brazil by then had experienced five years of an "economic miracle" characterized by extremely high annual growth rates and rates of inflation low by Latin American standards. The negative effects of the oil shock on growth were avoided, largely by external borrowing, and annual growth rates, while declining somewhat from earlier times, remained high until 1980. Inflation rates, however, roughly doubled after 1974, and they remained in the 40 percent range until 1978. A high degree of asset and wage indexation prevented real income losses from this inflation, but the external debt rose significantly. Between 1978 and 1980, the inflation rate again doubled, coincident with a new wage law that halved the frequency of wage adjustment from one year to six months.

In 1980 the government attempted an exchange-rate-based stabilization similar to plans that had been tried in Argentina and Chile. The rate of growth of the exchange rate was fixed at a level below domestic inflation. The result was a massive overvaluation and a

Table 4.3 Brazil

Year	Inflation	GDP growth
1977	38.8	5.7
1978	40.8	5.0
1979	77.2	6.4
1980	110.2	7.2
1981	95.1	-1.6
1982	99.7	0.9
1983	210.9	-3.2
1984	223.8	4.5
1985	235.1	8.3
1986	65.0	8.2
1987	220.0	-

Source: World Bank: A Macroeconomic Evaluation of the Cruzado Plan (1988).

precipitous fall in the trade balance, causing the plan to be abandoned after less than a year. Following this, restrictive monetary and fiscal policies led to a fall in output in 1981 for the first time since the 1940s. The years 1981-83 were very unfavorable for the Brazilian economy since it had to adjust to the rise in real interest rates worldwide as well as to a cut-off in access to foreign capital. Inflation continued in the 100 percent range around this time and doubled again to over 200 percent in 1983. Brazil achieved a remarkable adjustment in its external accounts, and by 1984 it had begun again on a path of export-led growth.

The problem of inflation remained intractable, however. This was attributed both to the increased wage indexation of 1979 and to the widespread asset indexation in place since the 1970s. Many economists felt at the time that the inflation was not due to fiscal or monetary sources since the budget deficit had been brought down significantly after 1983. A new civilian government came to power in early 1985. At first it attempted a real wage increase by holding down prices and allowing wages to rise. However, by the end of 1985, it was clear that inflation was out of control, running then at around 15 percent a month. In February 1986, the government instituted the Cruzado plan. The plan included temporary price and wage controls, a currency reform, and an adjustment scale for converting all outstanding contracts made in the old currency, cruzeiros, to the new currency, the cruzado. To avoid the inequities of a general wage freeze in the presence of staggered contracts, wages were adjusted to equal their average value over the six months prior to the freeze, and then they were increased by 8 percent. In addition, a system of trigger-point indexation was instituted: wages would be indexed if inflation exceeded 8 percent. Unlike the Austral plan, the program included no objectives for fiscal correction.

The Cruzado plan succeeded immediately in bringing down inflation. However, an unexpectedly high budget deficit, severe imbalances in relative prices, and loose monetary policy meant that the prices of publicly produced goods had to be increased in late 1986 and indexed to the price level thereafter (Helpman and Liederman 1988; Modiano 1988; Simonsen 1988). The inflation rate for 1987 was once again at pre-Cruzado levels.

The role of indexation in the Brazilian economy has been widely discussed.[9] Like Israel, Brazil is one of the world's most highly indexed economies. Nowhere has the double-edged sword of indexation—making life with inflation less unpleasant, but perhaps causing so much more inflation that life is worse overall—been felt more than in Brazil.

The new military government of 1964 set out to eliminate some major distortions in financial and labor markets by a comprehensive system of wage and asset indexation. The wage indexation policy was quite unique in that it approximated an *ex ante* form of indexation, in Fischer's (1988) terminology. Wages were to be adjusted annually to the anticipated rate of change in prices for the year, in addition to a productivity factor. Both the price index and the productivity factor were determined by the government, however. In practice, inflation was consistently underpredicted (Simonsen 1983). This scheme actually achieved a fall in real wages during the late 1960s. Simonsen

---

9. The rest of this section draws heavily upon Simonsen (1983, 1988).

observes that in this way the indexation policy was really a disguised incomes policy. In any event, it was quite successful in bringing inflation down from 91 percent in 1964 to 24 percent in 1967. In 1968, the wage indexation policy was adjusted to include a backward-looking component, which became the main component in the indexation scheme in 1975.

Under a complete system of wage indexation, the country experienced five years of rapid growth and fairly stable prices up to 1975. After 1975, inflation began to rise progressively. In 1979, wage indexation policy was revised to allow for semiannual rather than annual adjustments. In addition, a policy of differential indexation was applied: wage earners in lower brackets were overcompensated, and those in higher brackets undercompensated for past inflation. There is widespread belief that this led to a jump up in the underlying rate of inflation (McNelis 1987). This system of indexation basically remained in place until it was superseded by the provisions of the Cruzado plan.

The reform of 1964 also introduced indexation into the capital market. The central feature of this was the ORTN, which are indexed treasury bonds. The face value of these bonds are adjusted every month to an index of past price increases. Many nominal contracts in the economy, rents, private financial assets, bank deposits, and mortgages are adjusted to the ORTN. Since capital market indexation involves maintaining a constant real value of government debt, in times of high inflation the government deficit is artificially raised by the "monetary correction factors," which compensate bondholders for the effects of inflation. The correct measure of the deficit (called the operational deficit) for economic purposes excludes this factor, however. Payments to maintain the real value of assets cannot be considered expansionary. In the early 1980s a large gap opened up between the operational deficit and the nominal deficit.[10]

---

10. This was the subject of some wrangling between the government and the IMF. The IMF wished to use the nominal deficit as the relevant measure in negotiations (Bauer 1987, p. 1021). Note that even in an economy without capital market indexation, if the nominal interest rate adjusts for anticipated inflation, the nominal deficit will be biased upward, and in fact will be exactly equal to the deficit in a perfectly indexed-bonds economy.

The role of indexation in perpetuating inflation in Brazil began to be a topic of debate in the early 1980s. The orthodox disinflation episode of 1981 led to a huge fall in output (industrial production fell 9.2 percent) with a very small gain in terms of reduced inflation. Brazilian writers on inertial inflation, such as Simonsen (1983), argued that was precisely what one would expect with lagged indexation. Lopes and Lara-Resende (1981), in an econometric study, argued that indexation alone could largely explain the process of inflation; adding on demand factors did not provide any additional explanation. These arguments were felt to be vindicated in 1984 and 1985, when inflation took off in the face of a declining government budget deficit, following the sharp external correction of 1983.

In an influential article Arida and Lara-Resende (1985) put forward a comprehensive proposal for stabilization through monetary reform based squarely on the view that Brazil's inflation was solely inertial. They proposed the introduction of a new "parallel" currency that would be at a fixed parity with the ORTN. Wages would be converted into this currency on the basis of the average real wage over the previous six months—to get around the problem of staggered wage setting. All contracts would be convertible into this currency at a rate that declined over time; the rate would be determined by the government. The rate of inflation in the new currency would be zero from the start, and the old currency would gradually (or quickly) become irrelevant. In fact, the same economic plan can be instituted with a price freeze that takes account of the staggering problem (Dornbusch 1985). However, the introduction of a new currency might be thought to provide additional psychological support for the stabilization objective. In fact, the Cruzado plan was based to a considerable extent on the framework laid out by Arida and Lara-Resende. (Possible flaws in the framework are evaluated later in this paper.)

An important factor in Brazilian indexation policy has been the objective of income redistribution. The wage policy of 1979 was explicit about this. If real wages had been determined only by the indexing policy, there would have been a convergence toward a common real wage. In the design of the Cruzado plan also, one can see popular pressure for protection of real wages, while prices were to be strictly controlled. Using wage indexation for income redistribution is likely to be inefficient. First, the 1979 law was likely to be highly inflationary, at least in the transition. If the law had been applied as written, average wages would have increased faster than the rate of inflation (World Bank Economic Memorandum 1984). Second, the disparities in relative prices will lead to resource misallocation, shortages, and black markets. Finally, it is impossible to enforce underindexation on one group over a long term. For instance, during the late stages of Cruzado I, price markups in defiance of the law were very common. Indexing to achieve income distribution goals is not a good idea.

Issues in the Indexation Debate

In contrast to the European experience in the 1980s, Brazil and Argentina achieved rapid adjustment in real wages, real exchange rates, and trade balances. There is little clear evidence that indexation policy unduly hampered the real macroeconomic adjustment process. However, one legacy of this adjustment is high and seemingly intractable inflation. There is clear evidence that indexation policy was important for the propagation of inflation. How large a part it played is still open to question.

Is inflation in Argentina and Brazil primarily inertial? Or is it primarily determined by expansionary fiscal and monetary policies with indexation magnifying and lengthening the inflation response? To understand what went wrong with the stabilization experiences and to design new anti-inflation policies, these questions must be addressed. First, I will review some empirical evidence, and then I will discuss the successful anti-inflation program of Israel by way of comparison. Finally, general questions about the role of indexation in disinflation are examined.

It is difficult to evaluate the importance of the inertial mechanism and full indexation in determining inflation. By contrast, in the neo-classical view of Sargent (1985), inflation is based purely on forward-looking behavior and expectations. With high budget deficits and monetization, there will be an ongoing high rate of inflation. But a credible announcement of the closing of the budget deficit can reduce inflation quickly and with no real cost. There is a completely flexible degree of indexation determined by expectations of future money growth and inflation. Establishing credibility, however, is the key difficulty.

Despite the apparently stark contrast between the theories, there is a great degree of observational equivalence between inertial inflations in which disinflation is difficult because of the structures of contracts and backward indexation, and an economy in which inflation is high and intractable because of the lack of credibility of disinflation programs. In the latter, real costs of disinflation can arise because inflationary expectations do not fall, maintaining high real interest rates. But with full credibility, inflation could fall quickly without any direct price controls. Sargent (1983) uses the examples of the rapid end to the European hyperinflations of the 1920s as evidence that restored credibility can cut inflation quickly, but it is well accepted that hyperinflation diminishes the delay between price changes so much that all contractual inertias are washed out of the economy. This allows for a quick restoration of price stability without the costs of raising real wages and unemployment.

Attempts to distinguish between theories have looked at the persistence of inflation and whether this changes over time. Inertial inflation predicts a large degree of persistence. As Dornbusch and Simonsen (1987) state, "The best guess is that ... inflation today will be what it was yesterday." This implies that the coefficient of autocorrelation from a regression of inflation on its past values is very high. Helpman and Liederman (1988) report a coefficient above 0.8 for monthly inflation in Argentina and Brazil, for the period of the early 1980s. Is this persistence related to the degree of indexation?

McNelis (1987) explores this question for a sample of Latin American countries. The method he uses is as follows. Take the autoregressive equation for inflation

$$\pi_t = \alpha_t + \beta_t \pi_{t-1} \tag{7}$$

If this is derived from a simple mark-up pricing rule, assuming accommodating monetary policy, then the parameter β_t is expected to be related to the degree of backward-looking indexation in wages and the exchange rate. In particular, changes in indexation—such as the Brazilian wage policy of 1979 or the Argentinean exchange-rate-based stabilization of 1980—should be associated with changes in the value of the coefficient β. McNelis tests for this by estimating equation (7) allowing for time varying coefficient estimates. He amends (7) in order to allow for direct effects of monetary and exchange rate policy on the rate of inflation. The results for Argentina and Brazil support the view that indexation is important in the inflation process. For Argentina the β coefficient falls after 1975, during the early years of the new military government when wage indexing was progressively reduced. The β coefficient then rises up until 1980, and levels off during the overvaluation period. Estimates for the post-Austral period are not given. In the Brazilian case, the persistence coefficient takes a sharp jump upward at the beginning of 1980, in response to the new wage indexing laws.

Similar studies on the properties of Brazilian indexation have been carried out in the Portuguese literature. Most argue that inflation displays characteristics that are primarily inertial (Baer 1987; McNelis 1987; Pereira 1987; Camargo and Ramos 1988).

For the Israeli case a study of inflation dynamics is carried out by Bruno and Fischer (1986). The economy of Israel is similar in many ways to that of Argentina and Brazil.[11] Like Argentina, it has had a growth crisis since the mid 1970s. Like Brazil, it has a long history of comprehensive indexation in wages and financial assets. Like both countries, it has suffered severe inflation. In 1985, Israel introduced a heterodox stabilization program consisting of price and wage controls combined with monetary and fiscal restraints and an exchange rate freeze. In contrast to the Argentinean and Brazilian cases, the Israeli plan was extremely successful in lowering inflation—from about 1,000 percent in 1984 and early 1985 to about 20 percent in 1986 and 1987. The same type of debate surrounding inflation in Argentina and Brazil took place in Israel in the early 1980s. It was felt that indexation gave inflation an inertial momentum and severely raised the costs of bringing down inflation. Bruno and Fischer (1986) presented evidence on inflationary inertia in Israel based on the sum

---

11. For references on the Israeli economy, see Fischer (1988).

of the first two coefficients in a regression of inflation on its own lagged values. If the period from 1965 to 1982 is broken into subperiods, then the sum of the estimated autoregressive coefficients are larger the later the subperiods. Inflation became more persistent over time as indexation structures became more deeply embedded in the Israeli economy.

Helpman and Liederman (1988) criticize the method of Bruno and Fischer and other studies that make inferences from regressions of inflation on its own past values. If inflation is nonstationary, then the results of these regressions cannot be given any reasonable interpretation, and any inferences are spurious. To account for this nonstationarity, they include a time trend in the regression equation, and they look at inflation equations for Argentina, Brazil, and Israel. They use the results to construct impulse response functions describing the effect of a one standard deviation increase in the standard deviation of inflation on future inflation. Without a time trend in the equation, they find, as implied by the findings reported above, that an inflationary shock carries a great deal of persistence. For all three countries a shock led to a permanent rise in inflation. However, with the inclusion of a time trend, the shock dies away very quickly. Removing the trend leads to a very small degree of inertia in inflation.

Why include a time trend? Helpman and Liederman argue that inflation may be determined by real factors in the economy in such a way as to make it appear to display high persistence. However, if one of these factors is altered, then inflation can rise or fall very quickly. They make a distinction between an environment where the rate of inflation is endogenously determined by the characteristics of firm and worker behavior, combined with accommodating demand policies, and one in which there is inflationary inertia. They construct a model where firms set prices and workers set wages in an overlapping manner, but in contrast to the model of backward-looking wage setting above, workers set wages based on expected future prices. Wage setting is purely forward looking. In this model there exists a constant steady state rate of inflation determined by the workers' required real wage, firms' cost parameters, and other variables, as long as governments follow accommodating policies. However, there is no inflationary inertia in their model. Credible announcements of future policy changes lead to immediate jumps in inflation. The key requirement for inertia is backward-looking behavior. Even if agents are forward looking, however, it is quite possible that observed dynamics will display persistence.

The Helpman and Liederman model is provocative because its policy implications are much closer to those of Sargent than those of inertial inflation theorists. Credibility, rather than institutional structures, becomes the key issue. Strictly speaking, in a model with only backward-looking behavior, such as a lagged indexation system, credibility is irrelevant for the success of an anti-inflationary strategy. The inertial component of inflation is all important. Once price and wage controls are applied and the fundamentals are put right, inflation should end. This probably led the 1985/86 plans to be overly concerned with the inertial mechanism and not concerned enough about the credibility aspects.[12] If credibility is important, then the possibility of a future breakdown of the plan because of missed fiscal targets or excessive money creation can have an important impact on current behavior. In fact, however, in the actual implementation of the plans, it was recognized that public confidence is a key ingredient. Probably in the real world, aspects of forward-looking and backward-looking behavior remain important for the dynamics of wages and inflation. The model of Taylor (1980), discussed earlier, is an elegant statement of this.

Is there any direct test of the importance of backward-looking indexation? One obvious one is the prediction of equation (1): the real wage should be negatively related to the rate of inflation in economies with backward indexation.[13] This prediction is clearly refuted in Argentina for the 1980s. Real wages increased dramatically after the Alfonsin government came to power as the inflation rate was accelerating. Brazilian data also fail to support this prediction. The suggestion is then that discretionary changes in wages (changes in ω)

---

12. A clear example of this is the discussion of Arida and Lara-Resende (1985).
13. One qualification to this is that the frequency of readjustments will be falling, tending to move the real wage in the opposite direction.

have been at least as important as the indexation system itself.[14] In fact, there is every reason to suspect that bargaining (at the industry level among firms and workers or at the level of the central government) will lead to changes over time in the negotiated real wage. The ability to achieve rapid real adjustment to external disturbances is evidence of this flexibility. But it is not clear how much wage indexation in and of itself has contributed to the inflationary experience.

The consensus view on the failure of the Argentinean and Brazilian disinflation plans is that the fiscal prerequisites for stopping inflation were not put into place in Brazil, and were based on transitory revenue gains without cuts in spending in Argentina (Helpman and Liederman 1988; Kiguel 1989; Martone 1989). This is contrasted with the experience of Israel, where significant deficit reductions did take place, and where the disinflation was by all accounts successful. It is hard to escape the fact that budget deficits played the key role in the eventual failure of both plans. However, the slippage of the Austral plan in the summer of 1986 took place before the data indicated any major increase in the deficit (Machinea and Fanelli 1988).[15] They argue that a re-indexation of the Argentinean economy was the main reason for the failure of the disinflation.

Even if we take the inertial inflation model at its face value, it is not hard to think of a reason for this. This model implies that with monetary accommodation and irreconcilable conflicts between sectors, inflation will take off. If monetary accommodation is taken as a constraint, on the assumption that large-scale unemployment is politically unacceptable in fledgling democracies, then an implication of the theory of inertial inflation is that unless the basic socioeconomic conflicts between sectors, between firms, and between workers and owners are resolved in some way, inflation will worsen as soon as the controls are lifted. Even if formal indexation is not restored, informal structures will be. Thus, even if the inertial theories

---

14. Fischer (1985) notes that this has been the case for Israel. Since wages in the early 1980s were indexed at less than 100 percent, direct negotiation was necessary to maintain real wages in the face of high inflation.

15. Granted the original projections for the deficit were not met over the course of the plan up to that time.

are accurate and the fiscal deficit is not the root cause of the inflation, it is still necessary to alter the fundamentals—the parameter ω in terms of our simple model above—in order to eliminate inflation dynamics from the economy. In fact, it might be argued that this alteration did take place in Israel, where great care was taken to enlist the support of the trade unions and employers' federations in the disinflation.

Conclusions

This essay has analyzed wage indexation and its relationship to inflation in Brazil and Argentina. How important is indexation in the process of inflation and in macroeconomic experience? Is indexation a help or a hindrance to policymakers? Questions of such broad implication can be answered only with detailed knowledge of the type of indexation, macroeconomic constraints, and behavior of macroeconomic authorities. Indexation schemes in themselves will not achieve macro objectives if other policy instruments are not correct. In particular, de-indexation may be helpful as part of an overall disinflation program, but it is no substitute for the required adjustment in the fiscal accounts.

References

Aizenman, J. 1987. "Wage Indexation." In J. Eatwell, M. Milgate, and P. Newman, eds., *The New Palgrave: A Dictionary of Economics.* London: MacMillan.

Aizenman, J., and J. A. Frenkel. 1985. "Optimal Wage Indexation, Foreign Exchange Market Intervention, and Monetary Policy." *American Economic Review* 75: 402-23.

Arida, P., and A. Lara-Resende. 1985. "Inertial Inflation and Monetary Reform: Brazil." In J. Williamson, ed., *Inflation and Indexation: Argentina, Brazil and Israel.* Washington, D.C.: Institute of International Economics.

Ball, L., and S. Cecchetti. 1989. "Time Consistent Wage Indexation." NBER mimeo. Cambridge, Mass.: National Bureau of Economic Research.

Baer, W. 1987. "The Resurgence of Inflation in Brazil 1974-86." *World Development* 15: 1007-1034

Barro, R. J., and D. Gordon. 1983. "A Positive Theory of Monetary Policy in a Natural Rate Model." *Journal of Political Economy* 91: 589-610.

Blanchard, O-J. 1986. "The Wage Price Spiral." *Quarterly Journal of Economics* 101: 543-565.

Bruno, M., and S. Fischer. 1986. "The Inflationary Process: Shocks and Accommodation" in Y. B. Porath, ed., *The Israeli Economy: Maturing Through Crises*. Cambridge, Mass.: Harvard University Press.

Bruno, M., and J. D. Sachs. 1985. "Economics of Worldwide Stagflation." Cambridge Mass.: Harvard University Press.

Camargo, J. M., and C. A. Ramos. 1988. "A Revolucao Indesejada: Conflicto Distributivo A Mercado De Trabalho." Rio de Janeiro, Brasil: Editora Campus.

Canavese, A. J,, and G. Di Tella. 1988. "Inflation Stabilization or Hyperinflation Avoidance? The Case of the Austral Plan in Argentina 1985-87." In M. Bruno, G. Di Tella, R. Dornbusch, and S. Fischer, eds., *Inflation Stabilization: The Experience of Israel, Argentina, Brazil, Bolivia, and Mexico*, Cambridge, Mass.: MIT Press.

Dornbusch, R. 1985, "Comments, Brazil." In J. Williamson, ed. *Inflation and Indexation: Argentina, Brazil and Israel.* Washington, D.C.: Institute of International Economics.

Dias C, Dionisio. 1987. "Long Run Adjustment, the Debt Crisis, and the Changing Role of Stabilization Policies in the Recent Brazilian Experience." In R. Thorp and L. Whitehead, eds., *Latin American Debt and the Adjustment Crisis*. Pittsburgh: University of Pittsburgh Press.

Di Tella, G. 1987. "Argentina's Most Recent Inflationary Cycle, 1975-85." In R. Thorp and L. Whitehead. ed., *Latin American Debt and the Adjustment Crisis.* Pittsburgh: University of Pittsburgh.

Di Tella, G., and R. Dornbusch, eds., 1989. The Political Economy of Argentina, 1946-83, Oxford: MacMillan Press.

Dornbusch, R. 1982. "PPP Exchange Rate Rules and Macro-economic Stability." *Journal of Political Economy* 90: 158-65

Dornbusch, R., and M. H. Simonsen. 1987. "Inflation Stabilization With an Incomes Policy Support: A Review of the Recent Experience in Argentina, Brazil, and Israel." New York: Group of Thirty.

Edwards, S. 1988. "Terms of Trade, Tariffs, and Labour Market Adjustment in Developing Countries." *World Bank Economic Review* 2: 165-85.

Emerson, M. 1983. "A View of Current European Indexation Experience." In R. Dornbusch and M. H. Simonsen, eds., *Inflation, Debt and Indexation,* Cambridge, Mass.: MIT Press

Epstein, E. C. 1987. "Recent Stabilization Programs in Argentina." *World Development* 15: 991-1005

Fischer, S. 1977 "Wage Indexation and Macroeconomic Stability." In K. Brunner, ed., "Stabilization of the Domestic and International Economy." Carnegie Rochester Conference Series on Public Policy.

_____. 1983. "Indexing and Inflation." *Journal of Monetary Economics* 12: 519-42

_____. 1988. "Real Balances, the Exchange Rate, and Indexation: Real Variables in Disinflation." *Quarterly Journal of Economics* 103: 27-50.

Fischer, S. and L. Summers. 1989. "Should Governments Learn to Live With Inflation?" *American Economic Review* Papers and Proceedings. 79: 382 - 387.

Friedman, M. 1974. "Monetary Correction" in H. Giersch et al *Essays on Inflation and Indexation*. Washington, D.C.: American Enterprise Institute.

Gray, J., 1976. "Wage Indexation: A Macroeconomic Approach." *Journal of Monetary Economics* 2: 221-35.

Helpman, E., and L. Liederman 1988. "Stabilization in High Inflation Countries: Analytical Foundations and Recent

Experience." Carnegie Rochester Conference Series on Public Policy 28, 9-84.

Karni, E. 1983. "On Optimal Wage Indexation." *Journal of Political Economy* 91: 282-92.

Kiguel, M. A. 1989. "Inflation in Argentina: Stop and Go Since the Austral Plan." Working Paper. Washington, D.C.: World Bank.

Kiguel, M. A., and N. Liviatan. 1989. "Inflation Rigidities and Orthodox Stabilization Policies: Lessons from Latin America." *World Bank Economic Review* 2: 273-98.

Lopes, F. L., and A. Lara-Resende. 1981. "On the Causes of the Recent Acceleration of Inflation." *Pesquisa e Planejamento Economico* 11: 599-616.

Macedo, R., 1983. "Wage Indexation and Inflation: The Recent Brazilian Experience." In R. Dornbusch and M. H. Simonsen, eds., *Inflation, Debt and Indexation.* Cambridge, Mass.: MIT Press.

Machinea, J. L., and J. M. Fanelli. 1988. "Stopping Hyperinflation, the Case of The Austral Plan in Argentina, 1985-87." In M. Bruno, G. Di Tella, R Dornbusch, and S. Fischer, eds., *Inflation Stabilization: The Experience of Israel, Argentina, Brazil, Bolivia, and Mexico,* Cambridge, Mass.: MIT Press.

Marston, R. 1984. "Real Wages and the Terms of Trade: Alternative Wage Indexation Rules for an Open Economy." *Journal of Money Credit and Banking* 16: 285-301.

Marston, R., and S. J. Turnovsky. 1985. "Imported Materials Prices, Wage Policy, and Macroeconomic Stabilization." *Canadian Journal of Economics* 18: 273-84.

Martone, C. L. 1989. "Fiscal Policy and Stabilization in Brazil." Washington, D.C.: World Bank.

McNelis, P. D. 1987. "Indexing, Exchange Rate Policy and Inflationary Feedback Effects in Latin America." *World Development* 15: 1107-1117.

_____. 1988. "Indexation and Stabilization: Theory and Experience." *World Bank Review of Research.* 3: 157-69.

Modiano, E. M. 1988. "The Cruzado First Attempt: The Brazilian Stabilization Program of February 1986." In M. Bruno, G. Di Tella, R. Dornbusch, and S. Fischer, eds., *Inflation Stabilization: The Experience of Israel, Argentina, Brazil, Bolivia, and Mexico,* Cambridge, Mass.: MIT Press.

Pereira, L. B. 1987. "Inertial Inflation and the Cruzado Plan." *World Development* 15: 1035-44.

Rodriguez, A. 1988. "Comments." In M. Bruno, G. Di Tella, R. Dornbusch, and S. Fischer, eds., *Inflation Stabilization: The Experience of Israel, Argentina, Brazil, Bolivia, and Mexico,* Cambridge, Mass.: MIT Press.

Sargent T. 1983a. "The Ends of Four Big Inflations." In R. E. Hall, ed., *Inflation.* Chicago: University of Chicago Press.

_____. 1983b. "Stopping Moderate Inflations: The Methods of Poincare and Thatcher." In R. Dornbusch and M. H. Simonsen, eds., *Inflation, Debt and Indexation.* Cambridge, Mass.: MIT Press.

Sargent, T. J. 1986. *Rational Expectations and Inflation.* New York: Harper and Row.

Simonsen, M. H. 1983. "Indexation: Current Theory and Brazilian Experience." In R. Dornbusch and M. H. Simonsen, eds., *Inflation, Debt and Indexation.* Cambridge, Mass.: MIT Press.

_____. 1988. "Price Stabilization and Incomes Policy: Theory and the Brazilian Case Study 1985-87." In M. Bruno, G. Di Tella, R. Dornbusch, and S. Fischer, eds., *Inflation Stabilization: The Experience of Israel, Argentina, Brazil, Bolivia, and Mexico,* Cambridge, Mass.: MIT Press.

Taylor, J. 1980. "Staggered Wage Setting in a Macro Model" *American Economic Review*, Papers and Proceedings, 69: 108-113.

Turnovsky S. J. 1983. "Wage Indexation and Exchange Market Intervention in a Small Open Economy," *Canadian Journal of Economics* 16: 574-92.

Vasena, A. K., and E. Szewach (1985). "Inflation and Indexation: Argentina." In J. Williamson, ed., *Inflation and Indexation: Argentina, Brazil and Israel.* Washington, D.C.: Institute of International Economics.

5

THE LONG-RUN CONSEQUENCES OF SHORT-RUN STABILIZATION POLICY

Edward F. Buffie

The central dilemma facing policymakers in much of the Third World today is how to revive economic growth while maintaining debt service. After the debt crisis struck in 1981-82, IMF-type stabilization programs were widely adopted. Austerity measures along with high interest rates and recession in the OECD countries led to sharp reductions in real output in most debtor nations. At the time many observers expected this contractionary phase to be short-lived (Sachs 1989), something on the order of two to three years. These hopes have not been borne out. The repercussions of macroeconomic austerity have cut deeper and been more damaging than anticipated. Despite recovery in the industrialized world and some easing in the burden of debt service, growth rates remain extremely low, often barely adequate to maintain the existing level of real per capita income.

The two most striking aspects of the post-1982 adjustment have been the collapse of investment (both public and private) and the sharp increase in underemployment. Table 5.1 provides some highly aggregated data on investment and per capita growth rates in the 15 major debtor nations and LDCs not burdened by debt service problems. The investment rate in the major debtor nations fell 32 percent between 1981 and 1984. Although it has increased slightly since 1984, it still stands some ten points below the average investment rate in countries not experiencing debt servicing difficulties.

I am indebted to Michael Walton and to participants in two conferences on labor markets at the University of Warwick for their helpful comments on an earlier draft of this paper.

Table 5.1 Per Capita Growth and Investment

Year	Per capita real GDP growth		Investment (% of GDP)	
	Major debtors	LDCs without debt-servicing problems	Major debtors	LDCs without debt-servicing problems
1980	3.1	3.5	24.2[a]	–
1981	-2.6	3.2	23.5	27.8
1982	-2.5	2.7	21.6	27.0
1983	-4.7	4.6	17.1	27.1
1984	–	5.4	16.0	27.0
1985	1.6	4.3	16.8	28.6
1986	1.9	3.8	17.2	28.3
1987	.1	4.3	17.4	27.7
1988	-1.1	6.7	17.0	27.9
1989[b]	-1.4	3.2	17.3	27.5

a. Average for 1970 to 1982.
b. Preliminary figures.

Source: International Monetary Fund, *World Economic Outlook.* 1989.

Low rates of growth and investment have been accompanied by rising underemployment. Public sector layoffs and stagnation in the industrial sector have greatly slowed or brought to a halt employment growth in the principal high-wage sectors of the economy. It is particularly noteworthy that higher underemployment has often occurred in conjunction with large decreases in real wages. As can be seen from from Tables 5.2 and 5.3, in a number of Latin American countries industrial employment remains below its 1980 level despite real wage cuts of 10 to 30 percent.

Though the adjustment process has proven to be quite lengthy, few development macromodels examine stabilization policy from a long-run perspective.[1] This chapter attempts to redress the balance by

---

1. Arida and Taylor (1989, p. 856) leave unanswered the "longer-term implications of short-run actions . . . for want of a framework." And neither the IMF nor the World Bank has an adequate framework for analyzing the medium- and long-

Table 5.2 Industrial Employment in Highly Indebted Latin American Countries (1980=100)

Country	1981	1982	1983	1984	1985	1986	1987	1988
Argentina	87.4	82.8	85.5	88.0	84.7	81.3	81.0	82.1
Brazil[a]	90.7	85.3	79.0	78.1	79.1	86.9	89.7	88.2
Colombia	95.4	90.4	84.4	83.4	81.6	81.3	83.8	86.1
Chile	98.5	71.3	74.3	81.8	86.6	93.1	100.3	111.2
Costa Rica	94.6	92.7	96.2	99.3	99.8	100.4	97.7	104.4
Mexico	105.6	103.0	93.1	92.2	94.3	90.5	87.4	–
Peru[b]	101.1	99.7	94.3	84.4	83.4	88.4	95.9	92.4
Venezuela	100.0	102.0	100.3	98.9	99.9	102.6	110.7	119.3

a. Industrial employment in the nine major metropolitan areas.
b. Manufacturing employment in the Lima metropolitan area.
Source: International Monetary Fund, *World Economic Outlook*.

developing a dynamic, dual-economy general equilibrium model that can be adapted to analyze the short- and long-run effects of fiscal policies on capital accumulation, underemployment, and real wages. I focus on fiscal policy for two reasons. First, fiscal adjustment has been a prominent part of many recent stabilization programs. Second, there appears to be a strong, direct link between labor market developments and certain types of fiscal policies.

The main purpose of the chapter is to show that the fiscal measures commonly adopted in highly indebted countries sometimes produce contractionary supply-side effects that could account for the adjustment pattern seen in the 1980s. An increase in the price of a publicly produced intermediate input is one policy likely to send the economy into a tailspin. If the price increase is combined with layoffs by state enterprises, the private sector is subjected to a joint supply

run consequences of stabilization cum structural adjustment programs (Khan, Montiel, and Haque 1990).

Table 5.3 Average Real Wages in Highly Indebted Latin American Countries (1980=100)

Country	1981	1982	1983	1984	1985	1986	1987	1988[a]
Argentina	89.4	80.1	100.5	127.1	107.8	109.5	103.0	97.3
Brazil[b]	108.5	121.6	112.7	105.1	112.7	121.8	102.4	107.1
Colombia	101.3	104.7	110.1	118.1	114.6	120.1	119.2	117.7
Chile	108.9	108.6	97.1	97.2	93.5	95.1	94.7	101.0
Costa Rica	88.3	70.8	78.5	84.7	92.2	97.8	89.2	87.5
Mexico	103.6	104.4	80.7	75.4	76.6	72.3	72.8	–
Peru	101.8	110.2	93.4	87.2	77.6	97.5	101.3	77.4
Uruguay	107.5	107.1	84.9	77.1	88.1	94.0	98.5	99.7

Note: Figures are usually for workers employed in manufacturing or industry. For more detailed descriptions of the individual wage series, see the notes to Table 11 in *Economic Survey of Latin America and the Carribean 1988*.

a. Preliminary figures.
b. Average real wage in basic industry in Rio de Janeiro.

Source: United Nations, *Economic Survey of Latin America and the Carribean 1988*.

shock (fewer intermediates versus more labor). While the nature of the shock depends in part on the government's layoff policy and the prevailing level of efficiency in the parastatal sector, there is a strong presumption the outcome will be contractionary. Under very weak conditions, employment in the high-wage manufacturing sector and the equilibrium capital stock decline. Labor bears the brunt of the adjustment process as, despite (possibly large) real wage cuts in both the formal and informal sectors, underemployment increases.

Cutbacks in human capital expenditures and infrastructure investment are another highly contractionary fiscal measure. Given that factors are usually complementary, a lower supply of skilled labor (or social infrastructure) reduces the productivity of both capital and unskilled labor. Private investment may increase temporarily, but over the medium run the adverse productivity effect becomes dominant and induces firms to decumulate capital. With smaller stocks of physical and human capital, the demand for unskilled labor in the formal sector is virtually certain to decline even if workers put up little resistance to real wage cuts. Again, real wage flexibility does not suffice to prevent a worsening in underemployment.

The chapter is organized into seven sections. Section 1-3 develop the basic model and analyze the impact of public sector price hikes and employment cuts while section 4 investigates the repercussions of reducing human capital expenditures. Section 5 contrasts the adjustment processes associated with the different fiscal measures and discusses the extent to which capital decumulation and greater underemployment increase the cost of adjustment. Section 6 discusses in a less formal and more conjectural fashion the potential relevance of endogenous skill acquisition, technological externalities and uncertainty. Finally, section 7 summarizes the main points and discusses the broad policy implications of the analysis.

A Pure Supply-Side Model

The models in this chapter highlight the supply-side effects of fiscal austerity. To abstract from demand-side complications, I assume the economy is small and completely open. Two traded goods are produced: an agricultural export good and a manufactured good. The price of each good is fixed at unity, and x and m refer, respectively, to the agricultural and manufacturing sectors. Production in the manufacturing sector requires labor L, capital K, and an intermediate input Z (gas, electricity, and so on) purchased from the public sector at a price P. The agricultural good is produced by just labor and land. Introducing capital and intermediates as factors in the agricultural sector does not substantively alter the results, provided the manufacturing sector is relatively capital intensive and intermediates intensive.

Numerous empirical studies conclude that sectoral wage differentials in LDCs are far too large to be explained by the payment of compensating differentials.[2] The labor market is highly dualistic:

---

2. See Gregory (1975), Mazumdar (1976, 1989a, 1989b), Squire (1981, chaps. 7 and 8), House (1984), and Portes, Blitzer, and Curtis (1986). Rosensweig (1989) cautions that many studies do not properly control for the differences in human capital characteristics when making wage comparisons. In his study of the Bombay city labor market, Mazumdar (1989b) controlled for all measurable human capital

wages in the modern formal sectors are sometimes more than double those paid elsewhere in the economy.[3] In keeping with the findings of these studies, sector x is equated with the low-wage agricultural or informal sector; the government and manufacturing comprise the high-wage formal sector. Following conventional usage, the term *underemployment* will refer to the fraction of the labor force employed in sector x. This terminology is somewhat imprecise. A genuine labor market distortion exists because there is too little employment in private manufacturing relative to agriculture. I do not assume, however, that the marginal product of labor is necessarily higher in the public sector than in agriculture.

Although the sectoral wage gap generates underemployment, there is no open unemployment. All those unable to obtain work in the government or manufacturing sectors are employed in sector x, where the wage w^x adjusts to clear the market

$$L^m + L^x + L^g = L. \qquad (1)$$

Total labor demand consists of private sector labor demand plus public sector employment L^g. The total supply of labor L is constant.

The most troublesome issue in modeling the labor market is the appropriate way to endogenize the manufacturing sector wage w^m. Theory offers numerous choices here: w^m may be set in implicit contracts to provide insurance to workers, by optimizing unions, by socio-political norms embodied in minimum wage laws, or according to efficiency wage considerations. Unfortunately, empirical work on the wage-setting process in LDCs is scarce and does not single out one theory as clearly superior. Furthermore, while the aforementioned theories may explain wage rigidity, they place few restrictions on how

---

factors. He found that the wages of unskilled labor in the largest enterprises were 2.5 times larger than were the earnings of casual labor. From their study of Uruguay, Porters, Blitzer, and Curtis (1986) also found that labor of the same sex and education level earned a wage in the informal sector that was only one-half that paid in the formal sector.

3. In 13 of the 23 countries in the survey by Gregory (1975), the wage for low-skill labor in manufacturing was between 30 percent and 108 percent higher than in agriculture. See also Mazumdar (1989a) and Portes, Blitzer, and Curtis (1986).

w^m changes in response to various shocks beyond that. *Ceteris paribus*, w^m should be positively related to w^x. As neither theory nor empirical studies offer much guidance, I choose a particularly simple specification

$$\hat{w}^m = b\hat{w}^x, 0 < b \leq 1,$$

(2)

where a circumflex indicates a percentage change in a variable ($\hat{X} = dX/X$) and b is constant.[4] This specification is consistent with the Solow condition (when b = 1) in efficiency wage models and with certain variants of the optimizing union model.[5] The parameter b plays a crucial role in the adjustment process as it determines the degree of real wage rigidity in manufacturing. If b = 1, the labor market is distorted by a sectoral wage gap, but both agriculture and manufacturing are flex-wage sectors. On the other hand, when b is small, the real wage in the formal sector is largely impervious to economy-wide employment conditions. More of the burden of adjustment to contractionary policies is then borne by wage cuts in the informal sector and increases in underemployment (that is, greater layoffs in sector m).

Firms are perfectly competitive and operate constant returns to scale technologies. The zero profit condition is therefore satisfied in each sector

$$1 = C^m\left(w^m, r, P\right),$$

(3)

$$1 = C^x(w^x, v),$$

(4)

---

4. A positive value of b is needed to ensure the existence of a steady state.

5. The major papers on efficiency wage theory are collected in Akerlof and Yellen (1986). See Calvo (1978), McDonald and Solow (1981), and Oswald (1985) on optimizing union models. I allow for b < 1 because b = 1 arises only in certain special cases. The Solow condition requires that effort enter the production function in a purely labor-augmenting manner. In optimizing union models, b = 1 obtains in a static setting when unions maximize the rents of existing employees [that is, Max $(w^n - w^x)L^n(w^n)$] and the perceived elasticity of labor demand is constant (Calvo 1978). In theory, b > 1 is possible. However, this contradicts the view that wages in the formal sector are generally less flexible, not more flexible, than in the informal sector.

where C^i is the unit cost function and r and v are the capital and land rentals.

With three factors present in the manufacturing sector, the algebra can quickly become messy. For simplicity, I assume technology in each sector can be represented by a (non-nested) CES production function. Private sector demands for labor and the intermediate input are then (in percentage changes)

$$\hat{L}^m = -\sigma^m \frac{1-\theta_Z}{\theta_K} \hat{w}^m - \sigma^m \frac{\theta_Z}{\theta_K} \hat{P} + \hat{K},$$

(5)

$$\hat{L}^x = -\frac{\sigma^x}{\theta_T} \hat{w}^x,$$

(6)

$$\hat{Z} = -\sigma^m \frac{\theta_L}{\theta_K} \hat{w}^m - \sigma^m \frac{1-\theta_L}{\theta_K} \hat{P} + \hat{K},$$

(7)

where σ^i is the elasticity of substitution in sector i; θ_T is the cost share of land in sector x; and θ_L, θ_Z, and θ_K are, respectively, the cost shares of labor, the intermediate input, and capital in sector m. The only characteristic of CES technology that is important for the results that follow is gross complementarity of factors (that is, an increase in P lowers L^m and the demand for capital). This is not a particularly strong restriction to place on technology. According to production theory, factors are normally gross complements (Rader 1968). Empirical studies also find, with rare exceptions, that complementarity holds.[6]

Capital accumulation is governed by factor returns and the intertemporal preferences of a representative, infinitely-lived family

---

6. This can be inferred from estimates of the Allen-Uzawa partial elasticities of substitution in studies that postulate a translog cost function. See Burgess (1974), Humphrey and Moroney (1975), Griffin and Gregory (1976), Ozatalay, Grubaugh, and Long II (1979), and Laumas and Williams (1981).

firm.[7] The firm is endowed with perfect foresight and chooses investment to maximize an additively separable utility function

$$\text{Max} \int_0^\infty V(E)e^{-\rho t}dt$$
$$\{E,I\}$$

(8)

subject to

$$E + I = R(K, L^m, L^g, P) + w^g L^g - T,$$

(9)

$$\dot{K} = I - \delta K,$$

(10)

where E is aggregate consumption expenditure: I is investment; T is a lump-sum tax; ρ is the pure rate of time preference; w^g is the public sector wage; δ is the depreciation rate, and an overdot signifies a time derivative. Current utility is represented by an increasing, strictly concave indirect utility function $V(\cdot)$: $V' > 0$, $V'' < 0$. Equation (9), the budget constraint, states that consumption and investment spending must equal disposable income. (Neither the private agent nor the government has access to foreign credit.) On the right side, private sector value-added is measured by the value-added function $R(\cdot)$.[8] R has the usual properties: $R_1 = r$ and $R_4 = -Z$. Also, since increases in L^m and L^g come at the expense of employment in sector x, $R_2 = w^m - w^x$ and $R_3 = -w^x$. The marginal gain from expanding employment in manufacturing is thus measured by the existing sectoral wage gap $w^m - w^x$.

Finally, the government must respect the budget constraint

$$w^g L^g + D = P Z + T.$$

(11)

---

7. The results do not change qualitatively if it is assumed instead that workers are too poor to save and hence only the capitalist-landlord class invests. The steady-state equilibrium is the same, and the system governing the dynamics is still saddlepoint stable.

8. The fixed total supplies of labor and land are suppressed in the value-added function.

Total public sector expenditure is the sum of the wage bill and debt service D (net of new capital flows). The profile of debt service, determined by negotiations with foreign creditors, is treated as strictly exogenous. The public sector wage is constant. Of the L^g workers hired by the government, L_1 are employed in producing the intermediate input: $Z=Z(L_1)$. But while L_1 is endogenous, the extent to which L^g varies with Z is a policy variable. When the demand for intermediates contracts, labor needed by the parastatal sector falls by $dL_1 = (Z / Z')\hat{Z}$, whereas the change in total public sector employment is

$$dL^g = \beta(Z / Z')\hat{Z},\ 0 \le \beta \le 1. \tag{12}$$

β defines the government's layoff policy. When $\beta < 1$, redundant labor is kept on the payroll or transferred to other activities where it produces something called "government services."[9]

Government revenue derives from two sources: a lump-sum tax T and sales of the intermediate input PZ. The unrealistic assumption of a lump-sum tax is made to simplify the analysis. In particular, the impact on the budget of variations in Z is offset by adjustments in T so that higher debt service can be dealt with by a one-time adjustment in P.[10] The complications caused by endogenous tax revenues are analyzed in Buffie (1991).

Equations (1)—(12) form the complete model. Since private sector saving and investment are equal, the trade balance is $PZ + T - w^gL^g = D$; thus, the overall balance of payments equals zero. In what follows, D increases from an initial value of zero, and some fiscal instrument is then adjusted in order to extract the required trade surplus.[11]

---

9. When the latter interpretation is adopted, none of the equations in the text need be modified if it is assumed that the government cannot charge for consumption of these services [so that no extra term appears in (10)] and that they enter the utility function in a separable fashion [so that the first-order conditions associated with (8) do not change]. Even without these assumptions, the explicit incorporation of government produced services affects only the slope of the saddle path in Figure 5.1. The short- and long-run results and the qualitative nature of the dynamics are unchanged.

10. T remains constant in the other fiscal policies analyzed.

11. One plausible interpretation is that the country for a certain period was borrowing to finance interest payments on the debt. New lending then ceases, and the country continues to meet its interest payments but does not retire any debt.

The manipulations involved in solving a perfect foresight general equilibrium model are straightforward but lengthy. To keep the main ideas clearly within view, the exposition in the text will be almost entirely verbal and graphical. Solution procedures for the short- and long-run outcomes, proofs of saddle point stability, and so on, may be found in a more technical version of the chapter that is available from the author upon request.

The Short-Run Impact of Public Sector Price Increases

An increase in the price of the intermediate input lowers labor demand in private manufacturing and in the parastatal sector at existing wages. Aggregate high-wage employment thus contracts, forcing a decrease in the agricultural wage.

Labor demand in the manufacturing sector is subject to two conflicting effects. While the decrease in w^x triggers a fall in w^m, the higher price of intermediates shifts the labor demand schedule to the left. Employment rises or falls depending on whether

$$\sigma^m \gtrless \sigma^x \frac{L^x(1-s)\theta_L}{L^m\theta_T b\beta} \tag{13}$$

where $s \equiv (w^m - PZ')/w^m$, the percentage gap between the marginal value product of labor in private manufacturing and in the parastatal sector. If $b\beta$ is small—either because the government maintains the level of public sector employment ($\beta = 0$) or because w^m responds weakly to changes in w^x(b is small)—the adverse productivity effect dominates and manufacturing sector employment declines. More generally, employment in both high-wage sectors is likely to contract unless technology is far more flexible in manufacturing than in agriculture. Since the share of the labor force employed in private manufacturing is small (L^x/L^m = 2–7), the term multiplying σ^x in (17) will usually be quite large.[12] Even when the government takes a tough line on layoffs ($\beta = 1$), real wages are equally flexible in the

---

12. In 1980, the employment share of the industrial sector (a rough proxy for the employment share of the formal sector) was 13 percent in low-income LDCs, 23 percent in middle-income LDCs, and 31 percent in upper middle-income LDCs. In our dual economy model, the corresponding values for L^x/L^m are 6.7, 3.4, and 2.3.

formal and informal sectors (b = 1), and the productivity gap between labor in the public and private manufacturing sectors is 50 percent (s = .5), σ^m has to be substantially larger than σ^x in order for L^m to increase.

Adjustment and the Long-Run Outcome

The adjustment process stretches beyond the short run because fiscal austerity affects the incentive to accumulate capital. As investment gradually alters the capital stock, the temporary equilibrium is displaced and further changes occur in real output, sectoral labor demands, and real wages.

The important qualitative features of the adjustment process are depicted in Figure 5.1. The steady-state is a saddle point with a unique convergent path to equilibrium. In the first quadrant, the positively sloped KK schedule shows the set of points for which net investment is zero. Above KK, net investment is positive and the capital stock is increasing; below the schedule, K is falling. The saddle path SS may be positively or negatively sloped.[13] Fortunately, the precise slope of the saddle path is not important. What is important is that, regardless of the slope of SS, K approaches its steady-state level monotonically.

The WW and LL schedules in the third and fourth quadrants complete the description of the equilibrium path. These schedules track the paths of w^x and high-wage sector employment as the economy traverses the saddle path SS. Both schedules are positively sloped since an increase in K bids up the market clearing value of w^x by raising labor demand in the high-wage sectors.

The dynamics of the adjustment process depend entirely on how the policy package affects the steady-state capital stock. Across steady states,

$$\hat{K} / \hat{P} = \left[\sigma^m (s + \beta - 1) - \sigma^x \frac{L^x(1-s)}{L^m \theta_T b} \right] \theta_z / N, \tag{14}$$

where $N \equiv \theta_L (1 - s) + \beta\, \theta_Z$.

---

13. The slope of the saddle path is $\lambda_2 + \delta$, where λ_2 is the system's negative eigenvalue. Thus, when SS is positively sloped as in Figure 5.1, it cuts KK from above.

Figure 5.1 The Adjustment to a Higher Intermediate Input Price when the Capital Stock Falls

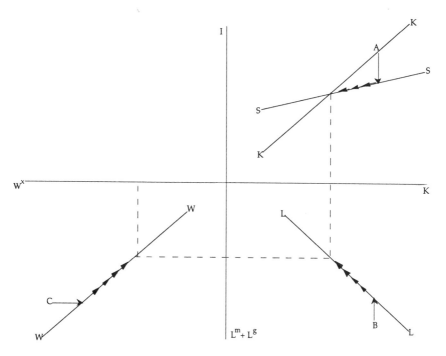

The impact on the equilibrium capital stock depends on whether the increase in P and the induced decrease in w^m combine to raise or lower the profitability of investment.[14] Although initial conditions (that is, L^x/L^m) and technology influence the outcome, equation (14) still yields several well-defined results. First, for small b, the potentially positive term involving σ^m is dominated by the second negative term; thus, K declines when there is a high degree of real wage rigidity in the manufacturing sector since w^m does not adjust enough to preserve profitability. Second, the capital stock always decreases when the parastatal sector "properly" belongs to the high-wage sector (s = 0). Third, capital decumulation occurs if the government resists making

---

14. In the short-run, r rises or falls according to the sign of the bracketed term in (14).

layoffs. More precisely, the larger the productivity gap between manufacturing and parastatal labor, the tougher must be the government layoff policy. There is no hope whatsoever of stimulating capital accumulation unless $\beta > 1 - s$.

In the most general case, there is a strong presumption that K will fall. Even when the productivity gap s is quite large, the government adopts a tough layoff policy, and the real wage in manufacturing is highly flexible, capital decumulation is to be expected. In the earlier example where the government lays off workers strictly as dictated by the decrease in demand for intermediates ($\beta = 1$), the productivity gap is 50 percent (s = .5), and labor in the formal sector accepts the same percentage wage cut as labor in the informal sector (b = 1), K still decreases if

$$\sigma^m < \sigma^x L^x / L^m \theta_T$$

As in the condition governing the short-run impact on manufacturing labor demand, K falls if σ^m is not many times larger than σ^x ($L^x/L^m\theta_T > 5$).

The high probability that the capital stock will decrease implies that manufacturing employment is more likely to fall in the long run than in the short run. The change in L^m across steady states is

$$\frac{\hat{L}^m}{\hat{P}} = \frac{\theta_Z}{\theta_L N}[\sigma^m\beta(1-\theta_K) - \sigma^x \frac{L^x(1-s)\theta_L}{L^m\theta_T b}]. \tag{15}$$

The critical value of σ^m required for L^m to increase is $(1 - \theta_K)^{-1}$ times larger than the critical value defined in (13). Hence, the condition for manufacturing employment to increase is roughly twice as demanding in the long run ($\theta_K \approx .50$) as it is in the short run.

The increase in P will usually provoke capital decumulation. Figure 5.1 describes the workings of the adjustment process in this the normal case. The initial equilibrium is (A,B,C). Immediately following the price increase, investment, employment in the high-wage sectors, w^x, and w^m all decline. As the capital stock decreases over time, underemployment continues to worsen and real wages and investment continue to fall.[15] The failure of repeated real wage cuts to forestall further reductions in investment and further increases in underemployment reflects an inherent feature of the adjustment process. Falling real wages on the transition path are an *induced* response to the weakening in labor demand brought on by capital decumulation. Consequently, they do not stimulate employment growth or investment spending.

When the productivity gap s is exceedingly large, the capital stock may increase, producing dynamics of the type shown in Figure 5.2.

Figure 5.2 The Adjustment to a Higher Intermediate Input Price when the Capital Stock Increases

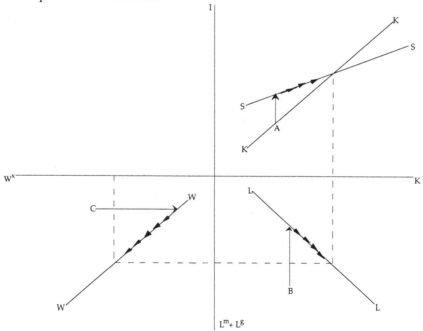

---

15. Recall that the lump-sum tax T adjusts to offset the fiscal effects of variations in L^g and Z. Real wages here are gross real wages (which differ from net real wages if some part of T falls on labor). Since Z falls with K, T is rising on the transition path if and only if $\beta w^g/PZ' < 1$. Net real wages, therefore, fall faster than do gross real wages if labor is paid its marginal product in the parastatal sector. In subsequent sections, T is constant, and it is not necessary to distinguish between variations in gross and net real wages.

After the initial shock, capital accumulation bolsters labor demand in the high-wage sectors, driving up w^x and w^m. Real output may eventually increase, but the labor market never fully recovers.[16] In the new steady state, underemployment is higher and real wages are lower.

The Micro-Macro Link

Parastatal price increases accompanied by production cutbacks often will be contractionary even when the productivity gap between the parastatal and private manufacturing sectors is large. This conclusion might seem to contradict basic microeconomic intuition in that production cutbacks in a highly inefficient sector would normally be expected to enhance overall economic efficiency.

The apparent conflict between the macro outcome and microeconomic logic is easily resolved once the term *efficiency* is properly defined. With the labor market distorted, the economy operates in a second-best equilibrium where constrained efficiency often entails a sizable productivity gap s. Consider the problem faced by a social planner who hires labor only to produce the intermediate input Z. When the parastatal hires extra labor, both w^x and w^m increase. The shadow wage for public labor is thus $w^* = -w^m dL^m/dL^g -w^x dL^x/dL^g < w^m$. Ignore for the moment the welfare effects arising from induced capital accumulation and concentrate on the marginal benefit yielded by increased production of Z. The latter consists of the direct output gain, PZ', plus the indirect gain obtained from reducing underemployment, $(w^m - w^x) (dL^m/dZ)Z'$. Current output reaches a maximum when the marginal benefit equals the shadow wage

$$PZ' + (w^m - w^x) \frac{dL^m}{dZ} Z' = w^* < w^m.$$

---

16. Real output always increases if the government lays off workers as dictated by the drop in demand for Z and the marginal product of public sector labor exceeds w^x.

To see what this condition implies, calculate how real output varies in the short run when the capital stock is fixed. For $\beta = 1$,[17] real output Y attains its maximum value at

$$s^* = \frac{1-\psi}{1 - \psi\theta_L + \sigma^m bL^m \theta_T / \sigma^x L^x}.$$

(16)

The other element weighed by the social planner is the welfare gain or loss stemming from induced capital accumulation. Setting $\beta = 1$ in (14) produces the conclusion that K reaches a maximum at

$$s^{**} = \frac{1}{1 + \sigma^m bL^m \theta_T / \sigma^x L^x}.$$

(17)

Straightforward calculations also show that the social return on capital exceeds the private return for all s smaller than

$$s^{***} = \frac{(1-\psi)(1-\theta_K)}{\theta_Z + \theta_L(1-\psi) + \sigma^m bL^m \theta_T \theta_Z / \sigma^x L^x}.$$

(18)

s^{***} may be larger or smaller than s^{**}. However, as shown in Figure 5.3, both s^{**} and s^{***} always exceed s^*. Thus, if s is initially below s^*, the policy shift is unambiguously welfare worsening; current output falls and the equilibrium capital stock decreases.

A far-sighted social planner would choose the s between s^* and s^{***} (or betweeen s^* and s^{**} if $s^{**} < s^{***}$) that balances the marginal utility loss from lower current output against the marginal present value gain realized by raising investment and the steady-state capital stock. In the present context, however, the point of interest is that policy "reform" often takes place from points on the upward sloping portion of the YY schedule. Table 5.4 shows how the values of s^* and $\bar{s} = \min(s^{**}, s^{***})$ vary with σ^m/σ^x (the solutions do not

---

17. $\beta < 1$ is not feasible (labor is hired only to produce the intermediate) and the planner will not, of course, accumulate redundant labor. The solutions for s^* and s^{**} are not altered when the planner hires labor to produce both intermediates and government services. The planner then equates the social marginal products of labor in the two different activities.

Figure 5.3 Critical Values of s

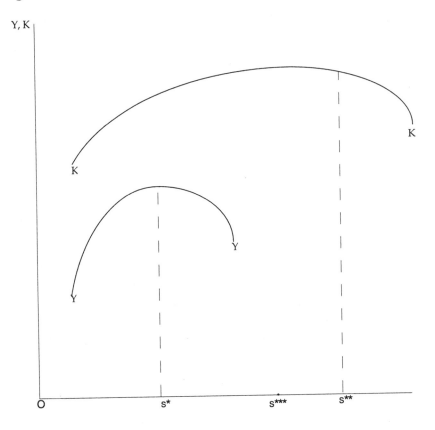

depend on the levels of σ^i), b, and w^m/w^x (= $1/\psi$) when θ_T = .475, θ_L = .40, and Q^x/Q^m = 1.7. The ratio of employment in manufacturing to employment in agriculture varies so as to be consistent with the values chosen for other parameters, viz.: $L^x/L^m = (1 - \theta_T)$ $Q^x w^m/\theta_L Q^m w^x = 2.23 w^m/x w^x.$[18] In selecting these parameter values, I was guided by the broad structural characteristics of the highly indebted countries (HICs) in 1980, the last year before the debt crisis. The share of sector m in GDP (37 percent) equals the weighted average output share of the industrialized sector in the HICs. The employment ratio L^x/L^m is higher, the more distorted the labor

18. This implies that the distribution parameter changes in the CES production functions. Technology differs across the cells in Table 5.4.

Table 5.4 Critical Values of s* and s̄

σ^m/σ^x	.5		1		2		3		4		5		
w^m/w^x	s*	s̄	s*	s̄	s*	s̄	s*	s̄	s*	s̄	s*	s̄	b
1.25	.29	.55	.28	.55	.27	.54	.26	.53	.25	.52	.24	.51	.2
	.27	.54	.26	.53	.23	.50	.20	.47	.18	.45	.17	.43	.6
	.26	.53	.24	.51	.20	.47	.17	.43	.15	.40	.13	.38	1.0
1.5	.45	.71	.44	.71	.42	.70	.41	.69	.39	.68	.38	.67	.2
	.43	.70	.41	.69	.37	.67	.34	.64	.31	.62	.29	.60	.6
	.41	.69	.38	.67	.33	.64	.29	.60	.26	.57	.23	.55	1.0
1.75	.55	.79	.54	.78	.52	.78	.51	.77	.49	.76	.48	.76	.2
	.53	.78	.51	.77	.47	.75	.43	.73	.40	.71	.38	.70	.6
	.51	.77	.48	.76	.42	.72	.38	.70	.34	.67	.31	.62	1.0
2.0	.62	.83	.61	.83	.59	.82	.58	.82	.56	.81	.55	.80	.2
	.60	.82	.58	.82	.54	.80	.50	.78	.47	.77	.45	.76	.6
	.59	.82	.55	.80	.49	.78	.45	.75	.41	.70	.38	.65	1.0

market. It rises from 2.79 when $w^m/w^x = 1.25$ to 4.46 when $w^m/w^x = 2$. At $w^m/w^x = 1.5$, the proportion of the private labor force employed in sector m assumes the same value (23 percent) as the weighted average employment share of the industrial sector in the HICs in 1980.[19]

For a wide range of plausible parameter values, s* is large. In fact, in exactly two-thirds of the cases, maximizing current output requires that the marginal product of parastatal labor be less than the marginal product of labor in the informal sector (s* > 1 − ψ). The corresponding figure is 83 percent (40 out of 48 cases) when σ^m/σ^x lies in the believable range of .5 to 3.

At some very general level, the orthodox rationale for parastatal price increases and employment cuts is valid. This policy package is all to the good *if* it generates an efficiency gain. But, as should be clear from Table 5.4, when the private labor market is highly dualistic, not much can be inferred about efficiency from the fact that the parastatal sector runs a large deficit or pays a wage (w^g) far above the marginal product of labor (PZ').

Public Sector Layoffs

There is always a supply dimension to public sector employment cuts since resources are released to the private sector. Layoffs connected with higher prices for intermediate inputs are part of a policy package that subjects the private sector to a joint supply shock. By contrast, layoffs in those branches of the government that produce final goods and "services" (broadly defined) combine the release of labor resources with a cut in consumption. Layoffs of this type can be analyzed by deleting Z from the model and letting Q(L^g) represent the value of government services measured in units of tradable goods. Assuming the government cannot charge for its services, a reduction in L^g of −dD/w^g maintains fiscal balance when debt service increases.

Figure 5.4 illustrates how the economy adjusts to a reduction in L^g. Initially, the supply of labor to sector x increases, thereby depressing w^x and w^m. Real output, on the other hand, may rise or fall in the short run depending on the productivity of public sector labor and the division of new hires between manufacturing and agriculture.

---

19. The figures for the 1980 output and employment shares of the industrial sector are from the *World Development Report, 1988*.

If there is an initial contractionary phase, it ultimately proves to be temporary. Lower real wages spur greater investment spending. As the capital stock grows, employment in manufacturing increases further and w^x starts rising. Over the long run, the capital stock increases enough that all of the laid-off workers are absorbed in the high-wage manufacturing sector without any lowering of real wages. To establish this, observe that in long-run equilibrium, the capital rental r is tied down by the rate of time preference $(r = \rho + \delta)$. It then follows from the zero profit conditions that real wages and the land rental are also constant across steady states. Thus, L^x is unchanged at the new long-run equilibrium, and clearing of the labor market implies $dL^m = -dL^g$.

Figure 5.4 The Adjustment to a Reduction in Public Sector Employment

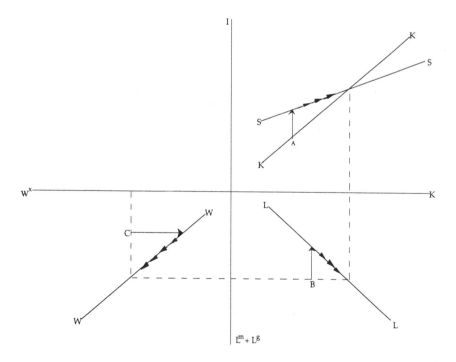

Eventually, higher debt service is financed partially or wholly by an expansion in economic capacity. But it is a long step from this to the conclusion that public sector layoffs (in the final goods and services sectors) are an easy remedy to the debt problem. A potentially difficult intertemporal tradeoff exists when output decreases in the short run. Furthermore, even if layoffs generate a favorable output path, the distributional repercussions may not be judged acceptable. Real wages are lower and underemployment is higher everywhere on the transition path until the new steady state is reached. A prolonged bout of great inequality is the price paid for higher output in the long run.

Reductions in Public Investment

Fiscal belt-tightening often takes its greatest toll on public investment. Cutbacks occur not only in planned infrastructure and industrial projects, but also in government spending to foster human capital formation. Typically, education, health, and training programs are cut severely. I investigate here the repercussions of reducing human capital expenditures.

Human capital is introduced into the model by distinguishing between skilled and unskilled labor in the manufacturing sector. I concentrate on the public sector contribution to skill formation, ignoring all other dimensions of the accumulation process. Skilled labor growth is assumed to be governed entirely by human capital investment of the government, I^S. The stock of skilled labor L^S is fixed in the short run and rises or falls over time depending on whether net public investment ($I^S - \delta L^S$) is positive or negative.[20]

Consider now what happens in the long run when greater debt service forces a cut in I^S. With factors being complementary, the productivity of unskilled labor in manufacturing declines at the same time that more of the work force becomes unskilled. Consequently, underemployment increases, and real wages for unskilled labor fall. Across steady states,

---

20. This specification implies a certain choice of units for labor. When the direct returns on physical and human capital (the returns obtained ignoring the impact on L^m) are equalized, $w^S - w^X = \rho + \delta$. Thus, labor is implicitly measured in very small units.

$$\hat{w}^m / b = \hat{w}^x = \frac{\theta_s \theta_T \left(L^m + L^s \right)}{\sigma^m L^m \theta_T b(1 - \theta_K) + \sigma^x L^x \theta_s} \hat{L}^s < 0 ,$$

(19)

where θ_s denotes the cost share of skilled labor.

In view of the countervailing effects exerted by a higher w^s and a lower w^m, it might appear that the impact on the incentive to accumulate physical capital is ambiguous. This is not the case. The decrease in the unskilled wage is an induced, second-round response: as such, it is too weak to offset the drop in the productivity of physical capital caused by the greater scarcity of skilled labor. Disinvestment in human capital thus leads to capital decumulation on a broad front. In the new steady state, K is lower by the amount

$$\frac{\hat{K}}{\hat{L}^s} = \frac{\theta_s \left[\sigma^x L^x + \sigma^m L^m b \theta_T (1 - w^m / w^s) \right]}{\sigma^m L^m \theta_T b(1 - \theta_K) + \sigma^x L^x \theta_s} .$$

(20)

It is not surprising that underemployment worsens when the human capital of the labor force is allowed to deteriorate. Equally important from a normative standpoint, allocative efficiency in the labor market is likely to decline. The demand for unskilled workers in manufacturing decreases, thereby worsening the labor market distortion, when

$$\sigma^m < \sigma^x L^x \alpha / L^s b \theta_T ,$$

(21)

where α is the share of wage payments to skilled labor in total wage payments in manufacturing. The scarcity of skilled labor and the large proportion of the work force employed in the informal sector ensure that $L^x \alpha / L^s \theta_T$ will be far above unity. Hence, as usual, L^m declines unless σ^m is much larger than σ^x and the real wage in manufacturing is highly flexible ($b \approx 1$).

With two capital stocks (physical and human) varying over time, the dynamics are intrinsically complex, and various adjustment paths are possible. On a "normal" adjustment path, private investment jumps downward on impact but does not overshoot its steady-state level. The physical capital stock, the supply of skilled labor, and real wages for unskilled labor all decline monotonically en route to the steady state.

In the normal case, the lower equilibrium capital stock elicits an immediate reduction in private investment. There is also the intriguing possibility that *I* will increase initially. When the government announces a reduction in I^S, the representative family firm foresees a declining path for future income and for the capital rental. The lower stream of quasi-rents earned by the capital stock implies that eventually investment will decline. But if the family firm has a strong preference for a smooth consumption path, it may increase I temporarily to shift some consumption from the present to the future. This gives rise to the dynamics shown in Figure 5.5. The possibility of this type of adjustment process underscores the importance of bringing the medium run and long run into view when evaluating stabilization policy. Over phase AB, private and public investment appear to be substitutes. If the economy experiences a downturn, it is

Figure 5.5 Path of the Private Capital Stock

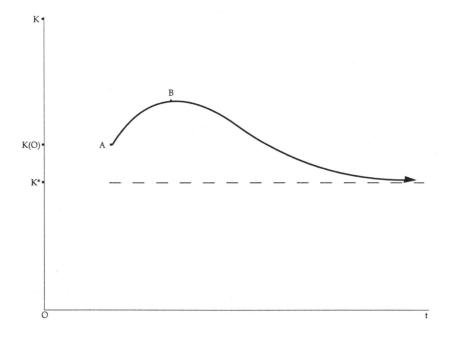

likely to be mild. The short-run response, however, is a faulty guide to how the policy affects the economy's growth prospects. Phase AB is only one part of a much longer adjustment process in which human and physical capital ultimately prove to be complementary.

The Adjustment Process and the Sacrifice Ratio

There are any number of ways of raising revenue and lowering expenditure to achieve a desired reduction in the fiscal deficit. The important point is that the real repercussions of fiscal austerity depend sensitively on how the fiscal deficit is lowered. A scorecard of the short- and long-run results is presented in Table 5.5. Employment cuts by parastatals producing final goods stimulate growth by expanding the resource base of the private sector. In the long run, real wages are unchanged and capital accumulation creates enough new jobs in high-wage manufacturing to absorb all of the discharged public sector workers. The major drawback of the policy is that real wages are lower and underemployment is higher throughout the adjustment process.

Price increases for publicly produced inputs and reductions in public expenditure to support human capital formation have very different consequences. Both policies depress real wages for unskilled labor and exacerbate underemployment. Moreover, these policy measures probably will induce capital decumulation and diminish allocative efficiency by reducing the demand for unskilled labor in private manufacturing (where its marginal product is highest). The economy manages to avert this outcome when prices of intermediate inputs are increased only if the real wage is highly flexible in the manufacturing sector, the government adopts a tough layoff policy, the productivity gap between parastatal and manufacturing sector labor is large, and technology is much more flexible in manufacturing than in agriculture. In the case of a cutback in human capital expenditure, the conclusions are somewhat stronger. The equilibrium capital stock always falls (though private investment may increase in the short run), and employment of unskilled labor in manufacturing declines unless, again, technology is far more flexible in manufacturing than in agriculture and real wages are almost equally flexible in the two sectors.

Table 5.5 Summary of the Short-Run (SR) and Long-Run (LR) Effects of Different Fiscal Policies

Policy	Real output		Capital stock		Underemployment	
	SR	LR	SR[a]	LR	SR	LR
Increase in prices of intermediates[b]	−	−	−	−	+	+
Layoffs in final goods sectors	?	+	+	+	+	0
Reductions in human capital expenditure[c]	0	−	?	−	0	+

	Unskilled employment in manufacturing		Real wages	
	SR	LR	SR	LR
Increase in prices of intermediates	−	−	−	−
Layoffs in final goods sectors	+	+	−	0
Reductions in human capital expenditure	0	−	0	−

a. The capital stock is fixed in the short run. The signs refer to the impact on investment spending.
b. Signs for real output, the capital stock, and unskilled employment in manufacturing are the presumptive outcomes based on equations 13 to 15 in the text.
c. A reduction in I^S does not affect real output, sectoral employment, or real wages in the short run because L^S is a predetermined variable. In signing the long-run effect on unskilled employment in manufacturing, it is assumed that equation 21 holds.

Tables 5.6 and 5.7 provide some additional evidence on the adjustment costs for public sector price increases and cutbacks in human capital expenditures. These tables show the decrease in net national income (NNI = Y − D) relative to the increase in debt service. I call this ratio the "sacrifice ratio" (SR). In a world where lump-sum taxes could be employed to service the debt, the SR would equal unity.

Table 5.6 The Sacrifice Ratio with Adjustment Through an Increase in the Price of the Intermediate Input (P)

σ^m w^m/w^x	.5	1.0	1.5	2.0	b
1.25	5.0	4.7	4.3	4.0	.50
	3.5	3.2	2.9	2.6	.75
	2.8	2.5	2.2	1.8	1.0
1.5	6.8	6.5	6.1	5.8	.50
	4.8	4.4	4.1	3.8	.75
	3.7	3.4	3.1	2.7	1.0
1.75	8.6	8.3	7.9	7.6	.50
	6.0	5.6	5.3	5.0	.75
	4.6	4.3	4.0	3.6	1.0
2.0	10.4	10.1	9.7	9.4	.50
	7.2	6.8	6.5	6.2	.75
	5.5	5.2	4.9	4.5	1.0

Table 5.7 The Sacrifice Ratio with Adjustment Through a Reduction in Human Capital Investment (I^s)

w^m/w^x \ σ^m	.5	1.0	1.5	2.0	b
1.25	11.9	10.6	9.7	9.1	.50
	11.2	9.7	8.8	8.1	.75
	10.6	9.1	8.1	7.5	1.0
1.50	13.1	11.7	10.7	9.9	.50
	12.3	10.7	9.5	8.7	.75
	11.7	9.9	8.7	7.9	1.0
1.75	13.9	12.5	11.4	10.5	.50
	13.2	11.4	10.2	9.2	.75
	12.5	10.5	9.2	8.3	1.0
2.0	14.6	13.2	12.0	11.1	.50
	13.9	12.0	10.7	9.7	.75
	13.2	11.1	9.7	8.7	1.0

In each table the elasticity of substitution in manufacturing (σ^m), the degree of labor market dualism ($w^m/w^x = 1/\psi$), and the degree of real wage rigidity (b) are allowed to vary. The other parameter values underlying the solution grids are

Table 5.6 $\sigma^X = .50, \theta_T = .475, \theta_L = .40, \theta_Z = .10, \rho = .10, \delta = .05,$
$Q^X / Q^m = 1.7, \beta = 1, s = .30;$

Table 5.7 $\sigma^X = .50, \theta_T = .475, \theta_L = .35, \theta_S = .15, \rho = .10, \delta = .05,$
$Q^X / Q^m = 1.7.$

As in Table 5.4, the values for Q^X/Q^m and the cost shares are set to yield output and employment shares for sector m that are close or equal to those of the industrial sector in the HICs in 1980.[21] In Table 5.6 it is assumed that the productivity gap between parastatal and private manufacturing labor is fairly large (s = .3) and that the government summons the political will to enforce a tough layoff policy (β = 1).[22] To generate the solution grid in Table 5.7, it was necessary to make some assumption about the return on investment in human capital. I assumed the initial direct return (the return ignoring the impact on L^m and the labor market distortion) equals the private return on investment in physical capital.[23]

What stands out to the eye in Tables 5.6 and 5.7 is that the SR is so far above unity. The large values reflect the fact that capital decumulation and greater allocative ineffiency in the labor market substantially increase the costs of adjustment. If K and L^m were unchanged, the SR would be unity in Table 5.6 and three in Table 5.7. The actual values for SR indicate that the real output loss attributable to adverse general equilibrium repercussions is usually several times larger than the combined loss owing to higher debt service and the direct contractionary effect produced by the policy shift. Real wage

---

21. The employment ratios are determined by the consistency conditions $L^X / L^m = (1-\theta_T)Q^X w^m / \theta_L Q^m w^X$ and $L^X / L^S = (1-\theta_T)Q^X w^S / \theta_S Q^m w^X$. (See note 23 for an explanation of how w^S is determined.) The private employment share for sector m varies from 26.4 percent (when $w^m/w^X = 1.25$) to 18.3 percent (when $w^m/w^X = 2$) in Table 5.6 and from 26.2 percent to 19.2 percent in Table 5.7.

22. Since $\beta = 1$, production of government services does not change, and the results measure the impact on total output, not just private sector value added.

23. The assumption of equal returns implies that $w^S - w^X = \rho + \delta$ and hence that $w^s / w^m = (\rho + \delta) / w^m + \psi$. To ensure that w^S/w^m takes on reasonable values, I set $w^S = .20$. The wage ratio w^S/w^m, therefore, ranges from 2 (when $w^m/w^X = 2$) to 3.2 (when $w^m/w^X = 1.25$).

flexibility helps a good deal in Table 5.6 but not much in Table 5.7.[24] The SR for an increase in public sector prices is roughly halved when the percentage wage cut in the formal sector is raised from 50 to 100 percent of the percentage wage cut in the informal sector. (Compare SR for b = .5 and b = 1.) In the case of a reduction in human capital investment, however, the same increase in wage flexibility lowers the SR by only 10 to 20 percent. Even with proportionate wage cuts in the formal and informal sectors, SR is often larger than 10.

Is it sensible to take seriously the quantitative predictions of a simple model? In this instance I believe the answer is yes. SRs on the order of 5 to 15 do not seem particularly unrealistic. Since the growth rate is zero across steady states in the model, a SR of 10 should be interpreted as saying that the adjustment to an increase in debt service equal to 3 percent of GNP would entail a cumulative output loss of 30 percent before the economy recovered its previous trend growth rate. This might take the form of the per capita growth rate being (approximately) 2.5 points lower for a period of ten years. In light of the deep contractions suffered by many debtor countries, it is not obvious whether the SRs in Tables 5.6 and 5.7 are too large or too small.

Other Stories

Thus far I have explored the linkages between different fiscal instruments, capital accumulation, and underemployment in models with no technical change and no uncertainty. In this section, I discuss informally the implications of relaxing these assumptions.

Endogenous Skill Acquisition

Earlier in this chapter human capital formation took the form of an increase in the general supply of skilled labor. More specialized human capital, however, seems to be generated directly by the firm's productive activity. The best known formalization of this idea is

---

24. This result agrees with the experience of Latin American debtors in the 1980s. It also appears to be consistent with the stabilization experience of a number of countries in Sub-Saharan Africa. In Côte d'Ivoire, for example, formal sector employment fell by 31 percent between 1979 and 1984 despite a 25 percent reduction in the real wage (Levy and Newman 1989). See also van Ginneken and van der Hoeven (1989).

Arrow's learning-by-doing hypothesis. In his original formulation Arrow (1962) argued in favor of the view that skill acquisition depends not on output *per se* but on labor's opportunities to work with new types of capital. Under the latter notion, labor-augmenting technical progress depends positively upon cumulative gross investment.

A related learning-by-doing hypothesis states that skill acquisition depends on the length of time on the job and, further, that the skills of laid-off workers deteriorate. There is limited empirical evidence that this phenomenon may be quantitatively important in the developed countries (Clark and Summers 1979; Dickens 1982), but, to the best of my knowledge, the hypothesis has not been investigated for any LDCs. About the only evidence one can point to of on-the-job learning is the universal finding of earnings studies that wages rise with experience.

Those two formulations treat technical progress as an exogenous by-product of investment in physical plant or length of employment. An alternative, perhaps more satisfactory formulation, is to postulate that firms add to their stock of skilled labor by developing training programs. Drazen (1985) has analyzed this case in a simple model where skilled labor is the only factor of production.

All of these methods of endogenizing skill acquisition have implications similar to my model. Physical and human capital decumulation will again be mutually reinforcing and capable of generating large multiplier effects. The learning-by-doing models produce the additional twist of hysteresis (Drazen 1979): the transition path will play a role in determining the long-run equilibrium. Hence, even temporary contractionary policies can have permanent adverse effects. In the Arrow formulation this is due to the fact that skill acquisition depends on the path of investment, as distinct from the capital stock itself. Temporary policies that lower investment can therefore drive the economy to a new steady state in which physical and human capital stocks are lower and underemployment is higher. Similarly, when the skills of the unemployed (or underemployed) atrophy, temporary policies that contract employment in the high-wage manufacturing sector inflict an irreversible loss of human capital on the transition path that lowers the equilibrium (physical) capital stock and raises the equilibrium level of underemployment.

Uncertainty

In the main body of this chapter I pursued the theme that certain fiscal policies might be partly responsible for the investment slump seen in the HICs. A second distinct explanation is based on policy uncertainty and irreversible investment. When information relevant to investment choices arrives over time, there is an *option value* to delaying an irreversible investment. By waiting a bit longer, a firm can gather additional information that might alter its optimal investment plan. Hence, if firm owners are risk neutral, the optimizing rule is to invest only when the value of an extra unit of capital exceeds its purchase cost *plus* the forgone option value. (In slightly different language, Tobin's q should exceed unity by an amount equal to the option value.) The cost of losing the option value can be large. According to calculations by Brennan and Schwartz (1985), McDonald and Siegel (1986), and Majd and Pindyck (1987), moderate levels of *permanent* uncertainty (that is, uncertainty that does not diminish over time) often imply that a project should not be undertaken unless its present value is double its direct cost. Similarly, Pindyck (1988) shows that for moderate levels of demand uncertainty, the optimal capacity of the firm may be only a half or a third of the capacity chosen under certainty. While the debt crisis will hopefully be behind us one day, figures of this magnitude suggest that ten or twelve years of policy uncertainty can strongly deter investment spending. The absence of large-scale private capital reflows is consistent with this conjecture.

An important point here concerns the asymmetric effects of good and bad news. The option value depends only on downside risk.[25] Potential good news does not affect the option value because unexpectedly high future returns can be appropriated equally well by investing today or in the future. No increase in potential good news, therefore, can offset a small increase in downside risk. Thus, downside risk is not necessarily bad news but rather any news that alters the

---

25. This is the bad news principle of Bernanke (1983).

ranking of project returns. Greater policy uncertainty may thus lower current investment even if all project returns will be higher in the future. For example, a policy package that lowers the future real wages by an uncertain amount will cause current investment to decline if the real wage cuts are large enough to reverse the relative profitability of capital-intensive and labor-intensive plants.

On its own, policy uncertainty can explain only investment cycles, not persistent low rates of investment. Following a major shock such as the debt crisis, investment may decline while the private sector awaits the government's response. But once the government decides on a new policy regime, the investment "pause" should be succeeded by an investment burst if the new policy regime does not lower the equilibrium capital stock. If policy uncertainty were the only factor that depressed investment in the 1980s, we should expect (with no change in policies) investment rates to climb above 25 percent in the HICs by the early 1990s. I do not think I am unduly pessimistic in saying that this is improbable. Nevertheless, policy uncertainty may be an important part of the larger story that explains the deep and protracted adjustment problems the HICs have experienced. Greater uncertainty was perhaps the major factor underlying the initial drop in investment spending, with more fundamental forces taking over in the ensuing years of slow growth. Low investment rates may now be a regular fact of life either because a coordination failure keeps the economy operating at low output levels where economies of scale cannot be realized (Kiyotaki 1988) or because the fiscal adjustments forced by falling tax revenues have lowered the return on capital. For the most part, the different explanations I have advanced for the post-1982 investment collapse are complementary.

New Theories of Growth

In the dual economy model developed earlier, capital accumulation reduces underemployment. Since private agents do not internalize the output gain stemming from lower underemployment, the social return on capital exceeds the private return. Recent advances in growth theory suggest other reasons why social and private returns on capital are likely to diverge. Romer (1986, 1989) conjectures that interdependence in the processes for accumulating knowledge and physical capital is a prominent source of external effects. If knowledge is embodied in physical capital and is partly a public good, capital accumulation generates a positive externality: when adding to its own capital stock, a firm overlooks the positive impact on the productivity of other firms.

Another possible source of strong externalities arises from the interdependence of market size and the extent of specialization, an idea that dates back to Adam Smith. Romer (1987a, 1989) develops a formal analysis along these lines. A single final good Q is produced under constant returns to scale by labor and a mix of intermediate inputs. The different intermediate inputs form a composite input having the Dixit-Stiglitz feature that greater variety (that is, greater specialization) yields greater output. Intermediates themselves are produced from capital and are subject to fixed costs. The need to spread fixed costs over a sufficiently large level of output creates the link between market size and the sustainable degree of specialization.

A basic externality is at work in this model that raises the social marginal product of capital above its private marginal product. As the capital stock increases, the market expands and greater economies of specialization are achieved. The interaction between scale economies and the gains from specialization can be surprisingly potent. Romer shows that with Cobb-Douglas technology in the final goods sector $Q = cKL^{\alpha}$, where c is a constant. The elasticity of output with respect to K is increased from the cost share of capital to unity.[26] Variations in the capital stock thus have a much larger effect on output and labor demand than in an otherwise comparable neoclassical model.

If the model just described is made dynamic by having a Ramsey agent accumulate capital, the economy experiences constant growth instead of converging to a steady state.[27] There is no stationary equilibrium for the simple reason that capital accumulation does not lower the return on capital.[28] Since the growth rate depends on only

---

26. Romer (1987b) suggests that the elasticity of output with respect to K ranges between .75 and 1. The estimates of Dervis and Petri (1987) for a cross-country sample of 20 middle-income LDCs are consistent with an elasticity close to unity (assuming a capital output ratio of 3) for the periods 1965 to 1973 and 1974 to 1979.

27. It is assumed here that the intertemporal elasticity of substitution is constant.

28. In models that allow for endogenous human capital formation, ongoing growth is possible when there are diminishing returns in K alone (but constant or

the private discount rate and the intertemporal elasticity of substitution, this does not substantively change the analysis of policies that lower the productivity of capital. The analysis of tax policy, however, *is* sharply altered. A proportional income tax raises the discount factor from ρ to $\rho/(1-t)$, and thus permanently lowers the growth rate.

Conclusion

One of the fundamental, unresolved puzzles in development macroeconomics is why austerity programs have produced such deep and prolonged recessions in many debtor nations. In this chapter I have argued that part of the answer to the puzzle may lie in the measures adopted to lower the fiscal deficit. There are sound reasons for thinking that fiscal policy exerts a stronger influence on private investment than is commonly believed. Cutbacks in government expenditures that promote human capital accumulation and higher prices for public sector inputs depress investment by lowering usage of factors complementary to capital. Once capital decumulation sets in, employment growth slows in the high-wage sectors of the economy. As a result, underemployment worsens at the same time as real wages are subject to general downward pressure.

Public sector wage cuts and layoffs in the final goods and services sectors can achieve an improvement in the external balance without sacrificing output and employment growth. Wage cuts are a pure absorption-reducing policy that need not have any lasting adverse impact on real output. Layoffs in the final goods and services sectors are actually conducive to adjustment through growth. The layoffs stimulate investment by returning real resources to the private sector. Private capital accumulation eventually creates enough new employment in the high-wage manufacturing sector to fully compensate for the loss of public sector jobs; in the long run, real output is higher and underemployment and real wages are unchanged.

While wage cuts and layoffs in the final goods sector appear to work better than other fiscal measures, neither policy can be

---

increasing returns in K and labor measured in efficiency units). For growth models of this type, see Uzawa (1965) and Lucas (1988).

recommended without qualifications. In the case of public sector layoffs, the adjustment process that brings gains over the long run also entails lower real wages and higher underemployment in the short and medium run. Given the valid concern of policymakers to minimize the impact of adjustment policies on the poor, layoffs will often have to be phased in slowly.

Public sector wage cuts are less objectionable on distributional grounds but have other drawbacks. In countries with a sizable nontradables industrial sector, a contraction in demand may trigger a coordination failure that shifts the economy to a low-output equilibrium. This problem can be handled by combining wage cuts with expenditure-switching policies to ensure that the contraction in demand falls mostly on tradable goods. A more fundamental problem is that after eight years of adjustment *further* wage cuts may no longer be a real policy option in some HICs. In a number of Latin American and African nations, real public sector wages have fallen to the point where moonlighting, long lunch breaks, and shirking have severely undermined the government's ability to carry on normal operations.

There are two broad lessons for policy in this analysis. First and most obviously, something must be done to revive investment. In addition to increased spending on social infrastructure and human capital formation, substantial investment subsidies are needed to lessen the divergence between social and private returns caused by underemployment and various technological externalities. In short, a "big push" in *productive* government expenditures is required. This points, of course, to the urgency of tax reform. Without a widening of the tax base and heavier taxation of factors in inelastic supply, the fiscal bind will not loosen enough to allow per capita growth rates to again reach respectable levels.

The second broad lesson is that adjustment should be gradual. No one denies that large-scale fiscal adjustments are often necessary. But if all adjustment is to take place within a year or two, a wide range of contractionary measures must be adopted, including many that are incompatible with policymakers' output and employment targets. With new capital inflows financing a longer timetable for reform, more of the burden of adjustment can be shifted onto the few fiscal instruments that do not damage the economy's long-run prospects for development.

References

Akerlof, G., and J. Yellen. 1985. "A near-Rational Model of the Business Cycle with Wage and Price Inertia." *Quarterly Journal of Economics* 100: 823-838.

——————. 1986. "Introduction." In G. Akerlof, and J. Yellen, eds., *Efficiency Wage Models of the Labor Market.* Cambridge: Cambridge University Press.

Arida, P., and L. Taylor. 1989. "Short-Run Macroeconomics." In H. Chenery and T.N. Srinivasan, eds. *Handbook of Development Economics.* New York: North-Holland.

Arrow, K. 1962. "The Economic Implications of Learning by Doing." *Review of Economic Studies* 29: 155-173.

Bernanke, B. 1983. "Irreversibility, Uncertainty, and Cyclical Investment." *Quarterly Journal of Economics* 98: 83-106.

Brennan, M., and E. Schwartz. 1985. "Evaluating Natural Resource Investments." *Journal of Business* 58: 135-157.

Burgess, D. 1974. "Production Theory and the Derived Demand for Imports." *Journal of International Economics* 4: 103-118.

Calvo, G.A. 1978. "Urban Unemployment and Wage Determination in LDCs: Trade Unions in the Harris-Todaro Model." *International Economic Review* 19: 65-81.

Clark, K., and L. Summers. 1979. "Labor Market Dynamics and Unemployment : A Reconsideration." *Brookings Papers on Economic Activity* 1: 13-60.

Dervis, K., and P. Petri. 1987. "The Macroeconomics of Successful Development: What Are the Lessons." In S. Fischer, ed., *NBER Macroeconomics Annual, 1987.* Cambridge, Mass.: MIT Press.

Dickens, W. 1982. "The Productivity Crisis." *Economic Letters* 9: 37-42.

Drazen, A. 1979. "On Permanent Effects of Transitory Phenomena in a Simple Growth Model." *Economics Letters* 3: 25-30.

_____. 1985. "Cyclical Determinants of the Natural Level of Economic Activity." *International Economic Review* 26: 387-397.

Gregory, P. 1975. "The Impact of Institutional Factors on Urban Labor Markets." Studies in Employment and Rural Development, No. 27. Washington, D.C.: World Bank.

Griffin, J. and P. Gregory. 1976. "An Intercountry Translog Model of Energy Substitution Responses." *American Economic review* 66: 845-857.

House, W.J. 1984. "Nairobi's Informal Sector: Dynamic Entrepreneurs or Surplus Labor?" *Economic Development and Cultural Change* 32: 277-302.

Humphrey, D., and J. Moroney. 1975. "Substitution Among Capital, Labor, and Natural Resource Products in American Manufacturing." *Journal of Political Economy* 83: 57-82.

Khan, M.S., P. Montiel, and N. Haque. 1990. "Adjustment with Growth: Relating the Analytical Approaches of the IMF and the World Bank." *Journal of Development Economics* 32: 155-179.

Kiyotaki, N. 1988. "Multiple Expectational Equilibria Under Monopolistic Competition." *Quarterly Journal of Economics* 103: 695-713.

Laumas, P., and M. Williams. 1981. "The Elasticity of Substitution in India's Manufacturing Sector." *Journal of Development Economics* 8: 325-337.

Levy, V., and J.L. Newman. 1989. "Wage Rigidity: Micro and Macro Evidence on Labor Market Adjustment in the Modern Sector." *World Bank Economic Review* 3 (January): 97-118.

Lucas, R.E., Jr. 1988. "On the Mechanics of Economic Development." *Journal of Monetary Economics* 22: 3-42.

Majd, S., and R. Pindyck. 1987. "Time to Build, Option Value, and Investment Decisions." *Journal of Financial Economics* 18: 7-27.

Mazumdar, D. 1976. "The Urban Informal Sector." *World Development* 4: 655-679.

_____. 1989a. "Government Intervention and Urban Labor Markets in Developing Countries." EDI Working Paper. Washington, D.C.: World Bank.

_____. 1989b. "Microeconomic Issues of Labor Markets in Developing Countries: Analysis and Policy Implications." EDI Seminar Paper 40. Washington, D.C.: World Bank.

McDonald, I.M., and R.M. Solow. 1981. "Wage Bargaining and Employment." *American Economic Review* 71: 896-908.

McDonald, R., and D. Siegel. 1986. "The Value of Waiting to Invest." *Quarterly Journal of Economics* 101: 707-728.

Oswald, A.J. 1985. "The Economic Theory of Trade Unions: An Introductory Survey." *Scandinavian Journal of Economics* 87: 160-193.

Ozatalay, S., S. Grubaugh, and T. Long II. 1979. "Energy Substitution and National Energy Policy." *American Economic Review* 69: 369-371.

Pindyck, R. 1988. "Irreversible Investment, Capacity Choice, and the Value of the Firm." *American Economic Review* 78: 969-985.

Portes, A., S. Blitzer, and J. Curtis. 1986. "The Urban Informal Sector in Uruguay: Its Internal Structure, Characteristics, and Effects." *World Development* 14: 727-741.

Rader, T. 1968. "Normally, Factors are Never Gross Substitutes." *Journal of Political Economy* 76: 38-43.

Romer, P. 1986. "Increasing Returns and Long-Run Growth." *Journal of Political Economy* 94: 1002-1037.

_____. 1987b. "Crazy Explanations for the Productivity Slowdown." In S. Fischer, ed., *NBER Macroeconomics Annual*. Cambridge, Mass.: MIT Press.

_____. 1989. "Capital Accumulation in the Theory of Long-Run Growth." In R. Barro, ed., *Modern Business Cycle Theory*. Cambridge: Harvard University Press.

Rosenzweig, M. 1989. "Labor Markets in Low-Income Countries." In H. Chenery and T.N. Srinivasan, eds., *Handbook of Development Economics,* vols. 1 & 2. New York: North-Holland.

Sachs, J.D. 1989a. "Social Conflict and Populist Policies n Latin America." Working Paper 2897. Cambridge, Mass.: National Bureau of Economic Research. Processed.

_____. 1989b. "Introduction." In J. Sachs, ed., *Developing Country Debt and the World Economy*. Chicago: University of Chicago Press.

Squire, L. 1981. *Employment Policy in Developing Countries*. New York: Oxford University Press.

Uzawa, H. 1965. "Optimum Technical Change in an Aggregative Model of Economic Growth." *International Economic Review* 6: 18-31.

van Ginneken, W., and R.van der Hoeven. 1989. "Industrialization, Employment and Earnings (1950-1987): An International Survey." *International Labour Review* 128: 571-596.

6

GENDER ASPECTS OF LABOR ALLOCATION DURING STRUCTURAL ADJUSTMENT

Paul Collier
A.C. Edwards and J. Roberts
Kalpana Bardhan

A THEORETICAL FRAMEWORK AND THE AFRICA EXPERIENCE

Gender relations are intrinsically specific to social context. Because of this, generalization across societies is problematic. This paper attempts to generalize across African societies and this is already heroic: matrilineal, patrilineal, monogamous, and polygamous systems form a patchwork across the continent. The paper does not attempt to generalize beyond this to other developing continents: some of the analysis may be applicable, but it may underplay considerations that are central in those societies.

Gender differences in skill acquisition and labor allocation are pronounced in Africa. Girls are less likely to go to school than boys; women are less likely to work for wages than men. These phenomena are of potential concern to policymakers because of their correlation with social and economic problems. At the social level, there are now good grounds for regarding maternal education as an effective means of improving the well-being of children.[1] Hence, the returns to girls' schooling may be greater than parents realize. At the economic level, structural adjustment is essentially about resource mobility, the labor market being one of the central processes for this mobility. If women do not participate in the market, the reallocation of their labor may be more difficult. Indeed, the central argument of this paper will be that women face particularly severe constraints upon reallocating both their labor and other resources under their control outside the context of the labor market. Our focus is thus not primarily on the labor market itself (where the issue is to explain women's absence) but on the various processes by which female-controlled resources (primarily their own labor) are allocated. At present the standard literature on structural adjustment, which is gender unspecific, coexists with a women-focused literature the thrust of which is often to present women as victims of structural adjustment. The focus of this paper is

This section was prepared by Paul Collier, Centre for the Study of African Economics, University of Oxford, United Kingdom.
1. See Lockwood and Collier (1988) for a survey of the literature.

on women as participants in, rather than as victims of, adjustment. Just as our understanding of the macroeconomics of adjustment has gained from the disaggregation of goods markets by their tradability, so our understanding of the microeconomics of adjustment can benefit from a disaggregation by gender.

Structural Adjustment and Intersectoral Resource Reallocation

It is useful to make a clear distinction between stabilization and structural adjustment because stabilization will lower living standards, and structural adjustment will raise them. Stabilization refers to the elimination of an initial unviable payments deficit (which might, for example, have been induced by a debt shock). Stabilization is not optional, and it often must be implemented with urgency. It is then quite likely that the government adopts a policy that achieves stabilization in a more costly way than might have been achieved. In this case there are two types of loss: the unavoidable loss involved in least-cost stabilization, and the avoidable loss involved in inefficient policies. Structural adjustment is the process whereby the economy recoups this second loss as the government undoes its policy errors. Many governments initially choose to stabilize their economies by means of tightened import quotas. Structural adjustment programs in such economies thus start from an external equilibrium in which binding import quotas give rise to allocative inefficiency. A key purpose of adjustment is to convert this quota-attained payments equilibrium into an exchange-rate-maintained payments equilibrium. Its objective is not to improve the balance of payments but rather to reduce trade restrictions. The rationale for this policy change is that trade restrictions, and especially quotas, give rise to deadweight inefficiencies that are avoided by appropriate use of the exchange rate. Hence, the policy switch should generate gains in living standards as these inefficiencies are removed.

The policy switch changes relative prices and thereby encourages resources to shift between sectors and also redistributes incomes. Table 6.1 illustrates the effects of a "debt shock" followed by structural adjustment. The space in which the figure is developed is defined on two relative prices: the domestic price of exports relative to

Table 6.1 Price Changes and Resource Shifts during Stabilization and Structural Adjustment

Relative Price	During Stabilization	During Structural Adjustment	Net
P_n/P_m	DOWN N→M	UP M→N	DOWN N→M
P_x/P_n	AMBIGUOUS	UP N→X	UP N→X
P_x/P_m	DOWN X→M	UP M→X	NO CHANGE

Notes:
N = nontradables;
M = protected importables;
X = exports and unprotected importables.
Arrows indicate direction of intersectoral resource shift.

importables on the vertical axis (world prices being given), and the domestic price of nontradables to importables on the horizontal axis. The N-N locus shows equilibrium in the nontradables sector. Its derivation is explained in Dornbusch (1974). The C-C locus depicts monetary equilibrium for a given nominal exchange rate. If some importable goods receive no protection prior to structural adjustment, then their domestic price will be altered in the same way as export goods. Hence, the export sector should be thought of to include all unprotected import substitute activities. The central analytic distinction within the set of tradable goods is not between importables and exportables but between protected and unprotected.

The need for stabilization is assumed to arise from a "debt shock": the economy has less disposable foreign exchange and so the nontradables equilibrium locus shifts to left. As disposable incomes fall, the demand for money falls, shifting the C-C locus) downwards. The government now has a choice between policies that further shift the schedules and policies that accommodate to the new schedules. The policy of accommodation is to tighten trade restrictions until domestic relative prices change to those at E2. At this point balance of payments equilibrium is restored. This was the most common policy response to the negative shocks of the early 1980s prior to structural adjustment. A structural adjustment program aims to shift the economy from E2 to E3 by a combination of trade liberalization, reductions in money supply (reducing the fiscal deficit), and raising money demand (devaluation). It thereby undoes the suboptimality of the initial response. Table 6.1 sets out the intersectoral resource shifts distinguishing between three time periods; that between El and E2, that between E2 and E3, and that between El and E3.

The price changes that occur as a result of structural adjustment are clear: the price of exportables rises relative to both other sectors and that of importables falls relative to both other sectors. The resource reallocations that should be induced during the structural adjustment period are not, however, quite so straightforward. If the program occurs soon after the debt shock, then the economy will not have fully adjusted to the price changes of the stabilization phase. This is particularly important with respect to the allocation of resources between the nontradables and import-substitute sectors. If the economy has fully adjusted to the stabilization phase, resources should shift from import substitutes to nontradables. If it has not adjusted at all, resources should shift in the other direction.

For some purposes it is important to distinguish within the nontradable sector between consumer and capital goods. Whereas the demand for consumer goods falls, the change in the demand for capital goods is ambiguous. There is likely to be some fall in the savings propensity, but since investment is the main mechanism for capital mobility, the change in relative prices raises the marginal efficiency of investment. Whereas structural adjustment will involve the contraction of the nontradable consumer goods sector, it may induce expansion in the nontradable capital goods sector.

The consequences of these price changes for income distribution depend upon whether there are any inflexibilities in either prices or quantities. These will be central to our subsequent discussion. In this section we consider only what would happen given complete flexibility. The change in relative prices will redistribute welfare through four routes: the squeezing of rents, the associated rise in government revenue, income generation, and the costs of expenditure.

Those agents who prior to structural adjustment received the rents on foreign exchange entitlements at below the market-clearing exchange rate will lose. These agents will include politically well-connected importers, but some of the rents may have been passed on to the consumers of importable products. The rise in the price that the government charges for foreign exchange increases its revenue. This enables the government to maintain a higher level of expenditure than it otherwise would have done (although the counterfactual may have been rapid decline). The beneficiaries depend upon which expenditures the government would have treated as marginal, and may therefore be either the users of health programs or public employees, for example. The redistribution of incomes through the change in marginal revenue products even with complete factor mobility depends upon which factors are used in which sectors but if all factors are used in each sector then the effect on factor prices is likely to involve a rise in the price of the factor used intensively in the export sector and a fall in that used intensively in the import sector. The fourth route by which a SAP will redistribute welfare is through the effect of relative price changes upon the costs of expenditure. The market-clearing price on importables relative to nontradables will fall, benefiting those whose consumption is skewed towards importables (though note that this effect must be taken in combination with the distribution of the loss of rents discussed above). The net effect of these four routes must be positive, in the sense that allocative efficiency has been improved. However, even in the absence of inflexibilities the effects of a structural adjustment program on living standards of various groups can be complex.

Many programs have had disappointing results to date. A common complaint is that contraction of some sectors gives rise to unemployment rather than the expansion of other sectors. The problems associated with adjustment center around two types of inflexibility: quantity and price. Quantity inflexibility, upon which we focus here, occurs to the extent that the allocation of factors between sectors at post-adjustment relative prices is not independent of their pre-adjustment allocation (so that there is some inertia). If all factors are completely immobile between sectors there is nothing to be gained from adjustment except a transfer from rents to government revenue:

there can be no improvement in allocative efficiency. (The N-N locus is vertical.) Hence, the extent of factor mobility between sectors is central to the rationale for SAPS. Price inflexibility both removes a principal mechanism for inducing voluntary mobility and replaces it with an ultimately greater amount of, and socially more costly, involuntary mobility.

Constraints upon Economic Activity by Women

An Introduction to Gender Differences in Mobility

Women face different constraints upon economic activity than do men. An obvious indication of this is that female-controlled resources are usually distributed between sectors very differently than are male-controlled resources. Women and men will usually have systematically different capacities to be mobile and systematically different requirements to be mobile. Programs designed to assist structural adjustment that fail to distinguish between the genders are flawed. They use a framework that is too highly aggregated for the problem. It is the same type of design error as treating exportables and importables as if they were a composite tradable commodity.

Let us take an example of how the intersectoral immobility of women can substantially impede structural adjustment. From table 6.1 recall that the sector that must unambiguously attract resources is the export sector. In much of Africa this is predominantly a component of smallholder agriculture, consisting primarily of tree crops such as cocoa, coffee, and tea. Hence, structural adjustment depends upon the entry of new resources into tree crops. Recent work on the adoption of tea in tea-growing parts of Kenya during 1975–82 (Bevan, Collier, and Gunning 1989) enables male- and female-headed households to be compared. Tea is arguably the most important export activity with potential for expansion in Kenya since unlike coffee it is not subject to international quotas. In investigating the determinants of tea adoption, we are at the heart of impediments to appropriate resource mobility. The study found that female-headed households had only half the propensity of male-headed households to adopt tea. Since in Kenya around a third of rural households are female-headed, this diminished propensity is in aggregate substantial. Further, the case of

Kenyan tea is particularly revealing because most of the labor of tea picking is done by females. This is reflected in the effects of the household labor endowment on the propensity to adopt tea. Holding other household characteristics constant, extra male labor has no effect upon the propensity to adopt tea, whereas extra female labor leads to a statistically significant increase. An additional female adult in an otherwise average household raises the propensity to adopt by around a quarter. Thus, in Kenya the key sector of tea is characterized by three apparently incompatible facts. Women do most of the work on tea, households with more women are more likely to adopt the crop, yet households headed by women are far less likely to do so. Why than are women at a disadvantage in taking up the economic opportunities that structural adjustment creates in the export sector? Although this example concerns the problems of female-headed households, male-headed households also have serious intrahousehold problems.

DIFFERENTIAL CONSTRAINTS UPON WOMEN. Four distinct processes account for why women face different constraints upon economic activity than do men. First, women may encounter discrimination outside the household. In developed countries the most emphasized example has probably been differential wage rates. In developing countries, however, discrimination in the labor market appears to take the form of differential access to wage employment. For example, in rural Tanzania (where formal sector employment is an elite occupation), men with secondary education had a 3-in-4 chance of such a job, whereas women with the same education had only half that chance.[2] Often a more important instance of discrimination is the credit market. Women usually do not own marketable land rights and as subordinates in the household cannot establish reputations for credit worthiness. As a result, their access to credit is markedly worse than men's. The credit problem for women is especially severe in economies subject to financial repression. The more acutely rationed by risk-bearing ability is the credit market, the more disadvantaged are women.

---

2. See Collier, Radwan, and Wangwe (1986).

The second process, which again operates outside the household, concerns a universal feature of human behavior: the tendency to imitate or copy role models. This tendency is a key way in which innovations spread over the population. Role models are usually gender specific: girls copy women, boys copy men. Thus, if some new economic opportunity is initially taken up by men, it may be diffused over the male population by a mechanism that will not transmit it to the female population.

The third process operates within the household and concerns the asymmetric rights and obligations of men and women. For example, in rural Africa women incur obligations to grow food crops for subsistence, to gather fuel and water, to cook, and to rear children. In return, men meet certain cash needs of the household and usually are responsible for the allocation of land. This pattern of reciprocal obligations is often unequal. In rural Africa women work for considerably longer hours than do men. Part of this work is on holdings the output of which is controlled by men. This gives rise to a classic "principal-agent" problem: the woman has little incentive to work well. For example, a survey in Kenya (Ongaro 1988) compared the effectiveness of weeding (a female obligation) on maize yields in male- and female-headed households. In both types of households, there were two weedings per season, and each weeding significantly raised yields. Whereas in female-headed households these weedings raised yields by 56 percent, in male-headed households the increase in yield was only 15 percent. Since other differences were controlled for, the most likely explanation is a systematic difference in effort due to differential incentives. Thus, the "incentives" argument, now so familiar in the World Bank, does not stop at the door of the household. To put Ongaro's findings about rural Kenya in perspective, the national maize loss from this disincentive effect would be roughly equal to the maize gain from the application of phosphate and nitrogen fertilizers.

The fourth process is the burden of reproduction. Because there is a phase during midlife when women's time is precommitted, certain activities are precluded. Skills decumulate, and long-term contracts such as are common in the labor market are terminated. The physical demands of child bearing and breast feeding strain health. Bevan,

Collier, and Gunning (1989) show that female health relative to male health goes through a trough in the child-rearing years. This health deterioration rebounds upon income earning opportunities, especially due to the uncertain discontinuities in the availability of labor. Women become confined to a range of economic activities in which such discontinuities are relatively unimportant.

These four differences between men and women tend to skew female labor allocation to certain sectors and to impair female mobility between sectors. Note that these consequences are distinct: if female labor is skewed between sectors differently from men, then the sectoral reallocations required for structural adjustment to succeed will impact differentially upon men and women. Even if capacities to be mobile are no different between the sexes, the requirements for mobility will differ, so that immobility might be a more serious problem for female than for male labor. Second, even were there no skew between sectors, if female mobility is less than male mobility then common requirements for mobility will encounter differential capacities so that again immobility becomes primarily a female phenomenon. Females tend to be located disproportionately in sectors that contract or expand, and they have less capacity to be mobile. First, consider how these four processes might give rise to differential capacities to be mobile.

CONSEQUENCES FOR MOBILITY AND IMPLICATIONS FOR POLICY. Intersectoral mobility in response to price changes, the essence of structural adjustment, depends upon the dissemination of information about opportunities and upon well-functioning labor and capital markets. The processes that disadvantage women impede their mobility. Labor and capital markets in the private sector and private processes of information dissemination make it likely that women will be less mobile than men. If private mechanisms of resource reallocation are systematically biased against women, public mechanisms should have an offsetting bias in order to compensate. Public interventions, however, usually reinforce private biases. We start with the labor market, showing that it is not the primary mechanism by which women's labor is allocated, and then we will consider nonmarket processes.

THE LABOR MARKET. Women's participation in the labor market is intimately bound up with their access to education (Appleton, Collier, and Horsnell 1990). It is uncertain to what extent the work by Appleton et al. on the Côte d'Ivoire applies across Africa, however. The labor market in Francophone Africa tends to be quite different from that in Anglophone Africa, and so we should be cautious about generalizations. In the Côte d'Ivoire, women are markedly less likely to work for wages and markedly less likely to go to school than are men. Extrapolating from developed-country experience, we might hypothesize that women participate less in the labor market partly because of child-bearing and child-rearing commitments and partly because of differentially low wage rates reflecting gender discrimination in wage setting. In turn, since the economic return to education depends upon participation and wage rates, the return to, and hence the extent of, female education would be lower than for male education. This plausible extrapolation turns out to be false.

Appleton et al. (1990) show that the limited participation of women in the Ivorian labor market is explained neither by child-related obligations, nor by differentially lower wage rates. It is partly the direct result of limited education for females: women are far more likely to participate in the labor market if they are educated. If the different educational endowments of women and men were fully to explain their differential participation in the labor market, then the entire focus of inquiry would shift to the determinants of access to education. We would be able to dismiss the labor market both as an arena of gender discrimination and as an explanation for differential investment in education. However, this is not the case: controlling for education, women are still markedly less likely than men to be in the labor market. This is the result either of gender discrimination at recruitment or of women having systematically lower employment aspirations than men. To the extent that it is the former, it may explain the preference parents reveal to invest in the education of boys. That is, discrimination in the labor market would give rise to three of the observed gender biases. First, controlling for education, women in the labor force are less likely to work for wages than are men. Second, parents are less likely to invest in the education of girls than in the education of boys. Third, women are less educated than men and hence are less likely to be in the labor market.

Appleton et al. are unable to distinguish between explanations based on discrimination on the part of employers and explanations based on the differential reluctance of women to enter the labor market. Just as the evidence can be interpreted as suggesting discrimination, so it can be interpreted as showing differences in preferences. This is unfortunate because the two types of explanation have somewhat different implications. Suppose that instead of discrimination by employers, the cause of the observed biases is that women tend to have lower career aspirations than men. Such differential aspirations would account for why women are underrepresented in the labor market: women are reluctant to apply for such high status work. Low female aspirations could explain why girls are less likely to go to school, as parents perceive that their daughters, because of lower aspirations, would make less good use of educational opportunities than would their sons. Finally, it might account for underperformance of girls once in the schooling system. A major reason why girls fail to continue to secondary schooling is that they perform less well in the primary school leaving examination used to ration state school places. If the underlying problem is low female aspirations, then the appropriate policy intervention is probably to improve girls' access to and performance in education. If the underlying problem is discrimination at recruitment, the solution must be in the labor market. In either case the problem can be diminished by increasing female access to and performance in education. This is because education powerfully reduces (although does not eliminate) the differential participation of women and men in the labor market. This can be interpreted either as education differentially raising female aspirations or as employers discriminating less against educated women than against the uneducated.

Appleton et al. (1990) find no evidence of gender biases in wage determination. Indeed, Ivorian labor markets are more equitable in returns than markets in developed countries. However, there are strikingly large gender-based differences in labor market participation: women are far less likely than men to work for wages. The two most superficially likely explanations for this turn out not to hold. First, it might have been that women are less likely than men to be waged simply because they are less likely to be in the labor force. However, restricting the analysis to adults already in the labor force, the powerful bias in labor market participation remains. Second, it might have been that women with children were less able than men to work the regular hours often required in wage employment and so participated in the labor force through self employment. This would have explained lower female participation in the labor market in terms of the differential household obligations of women. However, controlling for participation in the labor force, the presence of children had no significant effect upon whether women participated in the labor market. Further, child bearing does not reduce the potential duration of the working life of females relative to males. Evidently, social mechanisms for spreading the burden of child rearing are sufficient for children not to be a barrier to female labor supply to the market.

Clearly, there are substantial gender-related asymmetries in the Ivorian labor market. These relate not to wage discrimination, as in developed countries, but to differences in participation in the labor market, which in turn are strongly related to differential achievements in education.

In developed countries, public interventions in the labor market have focused upon equal pay legislation and upon the encouragement of provisions to make child-rearing compatible with employment. Neither of these interventions appears to be particularly appropriate in Africa based on the evidence from the Côte d'Ivoire. Once in the labor market, women earn equal pay to that of men, controlling for their characteristics such as age and education. Women's participation in the labor market, though low, does not appear to be explained by child-rearing obligations. Nevertheless, women are less likely than men with similar characteristics to enter the labor market. One interpretation of this is that employers discriminate against women. Public sector recruitment practices, an obvious point for policy intervention, appear to be unbiased. If the unions were male-dominated and excluded women, this might account for the bias in the private unionized sector.

Taking recruitment practices as given, the policy intervention that would increase the participation of women is the expansion of education. Gender differences in participation narrow as education is increased. This leads us to a discussion of policies aimed at increasing female access to education.

There are three points of access to the educational system: the entry to primary schooling, the entry to public secondary schooling, and, failing that, the entry to private secondary schooling. Of these, the gender bias in the first is the most severe: girls are 91 percent more likely not to go to primary school than boys. Indeed, the predominant reason why girls are less likely to go to secondary school is that many fewer of them have been to primary school (or have dropped out before completion). Having completed primary schooling, they are 37 percent less likely than boys to proceed to secondary school. Only at the level of upper secondary schooling does the differential become reasonably narrow: having completed lower secondary schooling girls are 14 percent more likely than boys not to proceed to upper secondary school.

Among the determinants of primary school enrollment, gender is the most significant. Nor does this bias against girls appear to be alleviated by household income. Increased household income increases the likelihood that children will be sent to school, but it actually widens the gender gap. At no income level does the chance of a girl being sent to school even reach the chance of a boy from the poorest household. Left to the "automatic" development processes— the diffusion of parental education, rising incomes, and urbanization—it will be a long time before the gender gap is eliminated. Left only to income growth, around a quarter of girls will receive no education even when all boys attend school. It will be girls who benefit differentially from the introduction of compulsory universal primary education, and without such government intervention a substantial group of the female population will remain uneducated under even the most favorable development scenarios.

The problems of access to secondary education are quite different. Conditional upon completed primary education, girls are less likely to attend secondary school because they perform markedly less well in the Certificat d'Etudes Primaires Elémentaire (CEPE) examination that rations entry. Among the determinants of exam performance, gender was the most significant variable. This is quite surprising. In many developed countries, girls tend to do better than boys at this stage in the educational system. But, quite unlike the gender gap in access to primary schooling, the gap in examination performance narrows dramatically as per capita consumption increases. Almost the entire problem of girls' underperformance is accounted for by the very wide gap between girls and boys from the poorest households. It is tempting to interpret this as indicating that when the household is driven in extremis to make agonizing priorities, a more generalized preference is given to boys over girls. Note, however, that Deaton (1989) did not find any tendency on average for households to favor boys over girls. This problem is amenable to policy in three distinct ways. First, the problem is evidently closely bound up with that of poverty. All those policies that raise the living standards of the poorest households will tend to reduce the problem of girls' underperformance in the CEPE. Second, underperformance is an educational production function. The government controls the inputs of teaching resources and the measurement of performance. Therefore, it can retarget teaching resources toward girls from poor households and/or revise the examination in such a way as differentially to increase their pass rate. Finally, girls' underperformance in the CEPE matters in particular because it is used by the government as the rationing device for a scarce public resource—namely, secondary school places. The government faces a problem only because its current rationing device differentially deselects girls from poor households. The government could, therefore, overcome the problem by supplementing the examination with other criteria so that the net effect was gender neutral.

Interventions in the labor market are mutually reinforcing. Improving the chances of women gaining employment in the private, unionized sector will enhance the incentives for parents to invest in their daughters' education and provide girls with role models for motivation in study. Improving the access of girls to schooling narrows the gender differential in participation in wage employment.

NON-MARKET ALLOCATION PROCESSES. We will now consider nonmarket allocation processes with a focus upon agriculture. We will begin with the role played by information dissemination in structural adjustment. The major expenditure on information in the economy as a whole is the formal education system. Within agriculture, however, other processes are also important.

Education is likely to ease structural adjustment into export agriculture because it appears to accelerate the transition to the new efficient pattern of resource allocation when prices or technology change (Lockheed, Jamieson, and Lau 1980). As discussed above, in rural Africa women are significantly less educated than are men; since they constitute the majority of agricultural labor, this educational bias is a potential drag on the pace of adjustment.

Within agriculture both public and private information processes are at work. The public process is the extension service, and the private process is imitation. Recent work on the imitation process in the adoption of tree crops suggests that it is very powerful (Bevan et al. 1989). Among contiguous groups of 200 households, on average every two households who adopted coffee induced a further household to follow suit. As discussed above, men copy male role models, women copy female role models. Whether such gender-specific imitation applies in agriculture has not been researched, but if it does, female-headed households would have a lower propensity to enter those sectors in which they were initially underrepresented. In much of Africa the export crops have traditionally been under male control so that female-headed households are indeed likely to be underrepresented. Biases in the private process of information transmission probably reduce the capacity of female-headed households, relative to male-headed households, to enter the agricultural export sector .

To offset this bias against women in the private process of information transmission, the public process, one could argue, should have an offsetting bias in favor of women. Yet in much of Africa, the public extension service has been heavily skewed toward contact with men. This is partly because the extension service is usually staffed by men and partly because it is largely targeted on existing growers rather than potential entrants (relying upon the imitation effect to take care of this key group). Structural adjustment thus has three policy implications for the extension service. First, as an instrument of resource mobility, the extension service may need to be expanded even if other public services are being reduced. Second, the service may need to be reoriented toward the adoption process rather than the improvement of the practices of existing growers. Third, within the group of potential adopters, the extension service needs to be targeted on women, whereas it is presently targeted on men.

Our analysis of why women might have a lower propensity than men to enter the export sector in response to structural adjustment concerned differences between female-headed and male-headed households. Intrahousehold asymmetries might have the same effect. It was noted earlier that disincentive effects appeared to be powerful: women's weeding of maize appeared to be markedly less well done in male-headed households than in female-headed households. This disincentive effect is likely to be more powerful for export crops than for food crops because the receipts from export crop sales tend to accrue to the male household head even though, as we shall see, the bulk of the work is done by females. This tendency for males to control the receipts of cash crops is partly the result of social convention: women often have responsibility for the provision of food, men for the provision of other purchased commodities. To the extent that this is the case, there would again be an argument for an offsetting bias in public policy. Since the major export crops are usually sold to public agencies (marketing boards), the scope for public intervention in the assignment of payments to household members is considerable. However, public policy powerfully reinforces the private bias of social convention since marketing boards credit the account in the name of the (male) household head.

Such public marketing channels contrast with the typical private markets for produce that is not internationally traded such as local vegetables: in this case, women commonly retail the produce that they grow, thereby directly handling the proceeds. A somewhat analogous retargeting of public payments within the household has been occurring in developed countries for child-related income benefits, with payment direct to the mother instead of through tax credits to the male household head. The underlying rational for such retargeting presupposes that women's expenditure priorities are not identical to those of their husbands, and if this is correct an incentive-compatibility problem must exist for the major cash crops.

Thus, for female-headed households there may be powerful informational barriers to resource reallocation toward export crops. For male-headed households the principal-agent problem may be particularly acute in the traditional export crops.

The second adjunct to resource mobility is investment. Much capital is intrinsically sector-specific once installed. Hence, the process of capital reallocation is at best through the redirection of new investment into the expanding sector. If there is a well-functioning financial market, this investment can be financed through credit. In conditions of financial repression there will be less intermediation, and so investment will require saving by the same agent. The private savings market in rural Africa is generally rudimentary since there are few informal deposit-taking agencies.[3]

Women are likely to be at a disadvantage in both the private savings and the private credit routes to the financing of investment. The acquisition of financial assets other than cash is subject to certain economies of scale: for example, minimum transaction levels in banks and fixed travel costs of transactions. Given that women's income is usually lower than men's, women will face higher unit costs of saving unless they have an offsetting higher savings propensity. To the extent that women in male-headed households have less autonomy than men, they may be forced to part with their savings, particularly if it is in the form of cash.

Nevertheless, female disadvantage in the private savings market is probably far less marked than in the private credit market. Access to credit requires the collateral of either assets or reputation. Women's limited autonomy implies that they control far fewer marketable assets than men and may lack the opportunity to acquire independent reputations for credit-worthiness. A symptom of female disadvantage in private savings and credit processes is that informal savings clubs (collusive arrangements between agents to make regular deposits into a common fund that lends in rotation) seem to be predominantly

---

3. Binswanger and McIntryre (1987) provide a convincing explanation of why private money lenders do not also act as deposit takers—namely, that local risks of deposit withdrawals are likely to be highly covariant, leading to default.

female. Such clubs are likely to be a response to female-specific problems.

Public interventions in financial markets are partly by way of the provision of services that compete with the private sector, and partly by way of the regulation and taxation of the private sector. Again there is a case for these public interventions to offset the male bias inherent in private financial markets. The public sector often provides the cheapest and most accessible deposit-taking agencies in rural areas through the post office network. However, the public credit program, like the extension service to which it is often formally connected, is heavily biased toward male heads of household. Public regulation of interest rates in the private sector gives rise to financial repression. One consequence of financial repression is that agents with relatively poor credit-worthiness get squeezed out of the credit market. It was suggested earlier that women tend to be disproportionately represented in this category. Finally, governments have typically imposed high implicit taxation on savings. Deficit financing, through the resulting inflation tax, falls disproportionately upon those agents who must rely upon cash-based savings rather than the credit market to finance their investments. Women are in precisely this position.

To conclude, women are at a disadvantage in financing investment because of biases in private savings and credit markets. Governments actively intervene in financial markets, so that they have the opportunity to offset these biases, yet on the whole public intervention either directly or indirectly reinforces private biases.

In this section we have discussed why the differential constraints upon women may make them less mobile intersectorally than men, and how public policies often exacerbate rather than offset this bias. Since mobility is the essence of structural adjustment, constraints upon the mobility of female labor are directly damaging. Further, the incentive for capital mobility is reduced by labor immobility. If labor is able to move into the export sector, then the marginal physical product of the capital stock in the sector is increased (and is reduced in those sectors from which labor has moved). These changes in marginal physical products of capital enhance the incentive to redirect capital (mainly through investment) into the export sector. Hence, the damaging consequences of constraints upon female labor mobility are geared up by this induced reduction in capital mobility. In conditions of financial repression, there will be less intermediation and so investment will tend to be undertaken by the agent who does the saving. This puts a premium on the intersectoral mobility of the agent: if the agent is immobile, investment cannot be reallocated between sectors. Since the returns to investment may be negative for agents in contracting sectors, savings by these agents will be discouraged.

SKEWNESS IN MALE AND FEMALE LABOR ALLOCATION BETWEEN SECTORS AND ITS CONSEQUENCES. The constraints that make women less mobile than men also concentrate their labor in distinct sectors. This is because the constraints often take the form of barriers to entry to an activity. Women's work is usually concentrated in two activities: food production and the provision of nontradable services such as marketing. Women are markedly underrepresented in the public sector, private formal employment, and formal export agriculture. Although there are variations between countries, Kenya serves as a good illustration (see table 6.2).

Gender skewness matters for structural adjustment. First, it implies a differential requirement for the genders to be mobile. If, for example, female labor is skewed away from the export sector (as it is in some countries), then the labor mobility into that sector, which structural adjustment requires, will place a higher requirement upon the mobility of women than of men. In such a case structural adjustment would be doubly impaired: the agents whose mobility is most required would be those who are the least mobile.

How likely is it that structural adjustment requires greater mobility by women? Recall from our discussion of the mobility requirements of structural adjustment that the protected import-substitute sector may contract or expand (depending upon the duration of prior protection), whereas the nontradable sector must unambiguously contract. The protected import-substitute sector is usually broadly coincident with the manufacturing sector, the labor force of which is generally heavily skewed toward males (see table 6.2). The nontradable sector, however, may be similarly skewed toward women. Within the nontradable sector the capital goods industry might behave differently from the consumer goods sector: the premium on

Table 6.2 Labor Allocation by Sector and Gender in Kenya, 1982 *(percent)*

Sector	Males	Females
Export agriculture		
estates[a]	76	24
smallholder[b]	42	58
Food agriculture[c]	37	63
Public sector[d]	81	19
Import substitute sector[e]	88	12
Nontradable capital goods[f]	96	4
Private service wage employment[g]	79	21

Notes and Sources:
a. Export agriculture: Estates include coffee, tea and sisal. Data are from the *Employment and Earnings Survey,* Nairobi, Government Printer, 1981, Table 8.
b. Smallholder labor allocation is from a rural household survey of 1982, see Bevan, Collier and Gunning (1989). The export crops included are coffee, tea and pyrethrum.
c. Food agriculture: smallholder only, source 1982 survey (Bevan and others, 1989).
d. Public sector employment is from the *Employment and Earnings Survey,* 1981, Table 1.
e. Import substitute sector employment is proxied by that in manufacturing, the source being the *Employment and Earnings Survey*, 1981, Table 8.
f. Nontradable capital goods employment is proxied by that in the construction sector, the source being the Employment and Earnings Survey, 1981, table 8.
g. Private Service Wage Employment is the residual of formal sector employment as measured by the *Employment and Earnings Survey*, 1981, minus the four sectors identified above.

investment as a mechanism of mobility might well prevent contraction in the capital goods industry. Whereas the labor force in the nontradables sector may be predominantly female, the labor force in the nontradable capital goods sector is overwhelmingly male. In Kenya, as shown in table 6.2 it is 96 percent male. Whether the nontradable consumer goods sector is skewed toward women critically depends upon the tradability of food, the production of which is generally dominated by women. If food is part of the unprotected tradable sector, then women are likely already to be disproportionately located in the sector that must expand. Labor relocation is then a problem directly concentrated among males, whereas capital relocation requires that women increase their access to credit at the expense of the sectors in which men predominate. Hence, the central women-in-structural-adjustment issue in such economies would be in the credit market rather than the labor markets. Conversely, if food is part of the nontraded sector, then the key resource relocation required in the economy is likely to be women's labor. Since most agricultural labor is not allocated through the market, this relocation is likely to involve women as entrepreneurs entering new activities, so the key constraints upon their labor mobility will lie outside the labor market.

In any particular economy it is generally straightforward to assign food to one of the three macroeconomic sectors, but this is not possible a priori. Food is sometimes part of the nontradable sector, sometimes part of the protected import-substitute sector and sometimes part of the unprotected tradable sector. For example, some staples, such as yams, are intrinsically nontradable. Although for the major grains there is an active world market, internal transport and storage costs within the rural economy can make food nontradable internationally. (While being tradable as far as much urban food supply is concerned, it is probably cheaper to transport food from Chicago to Lagos than from Kano.) Part of food production in many countries directly substitutes for imports. However, recall that the key analytic distinction within the set of tradable goods is whether they are protected or not. During the stabilization policies in Nigeria, food imports were banned. Hence, that part of Nigerian food production that substitutes for imports is protected, and a structural adjustment program will result in its contraction. However, in some countries, such as Zambia, although food production is an import substitute, it is not protected. Hence, as a result of structural adjustment the sector should expand just as the export sector. To summarize, there are three possibilities:

1) Food is nontradable and/or a protected import substitute. Its production should therefore contract as a result of structural adjustment. This can occur only if women are able to reallocate their resources into those nonfood sectors that should expand. If women face entry barriers to these sectors, then adjustment is impaired.

2) Food is an unprotected import-substitute or export. Its production should therefore expand. For this to happen, either male labor must shift into the activity, or female labor supply

must increase (a diversion of time from other activities), or females must be able to increase their labor productivity by investment.

3) Food is nontradable (rural consumption) and an unprotected import-substitute (urban consumption).The net effect of structural adjustment on production is ambiguous, but there should be a reallocation of consumption from rural areas (often subsistence) to urban areas. Thus, the sector which must unambiguously expand is the food marketing sector. This is commonly a female sector, which will require more resources.

Because of this variability in the classification of food, the skewness of male and female labor in the three analytically important sectors can differ radically from country to country. Sometimes successful structural adjustment will require women to reallocate their labor, sometimes it will require that land and capital be reallocated to the sector in which women are already concentrated.

Gender skewness gives rise to differential requirements for mobility. It also can generate powerful distributional and allocative inefficiency consequences. How skewness and immobility interact depends upon the specific pattern in which factors are skewed. A full taxonomy of possibilities is not developed here. Table 6.3 depicts a pertinent example in which skewness is stylized by considering its extreme form. Some factors are not used in all sectors.

Table 6.3 An Example of Structural Adjustment with Gender-Specificity

	Sector		
	N	*X*	*M*
Female labor	* |		
Male labor		* ⬅———	*
Land	* ——➤	*	

In the example of table 6.3, male labor is located in the import substitute and export sectors, and is mobile. Female labor is located in the nontradable sector and is immobile. Land can be used in either the nontradable sector or the export sector, and it can be reallocated between the two. Recall that structural adjustment will involve a rise in P_x/P_n and a rise in P_x/P_m. In this scenario the former induces a reallocation of land from N to X, and the latter induces a reallocation of male labor from M to X. The reallocation of land lowers the returns on female labor and raises the returns on male labor. The reallocation of male labor raises the returns to land deployed in the X sector. The latter induces a further reallocation of land from N to X. This further raises the returns to male labor and lowers the returns to female labor.

The above example has illustrated that in countries where women are concentrated in the nontradable sector and are less intersectorally mobile than male labor (or other factors of production), the returns to women's labor will fall as a result of structural adjustment despite the overall gains to the economy. This is simply the application of a standard result that a factor specific to a sector the relative price of which declines will suffer absolute losses of income in excess of the price decline.[4]

Such distributional effects may be important if the household is not an adequate intergender redistributional device (which, of course, is likely to be the case in female-headed households and may be the case more generally). However, even were changes in the intergender functional distribution of income to have no consequences for the personal distribution of income, the interaction of skewness and immobility would still be of significance because of the implications for allocative efficiency. Suppose that prior to structural adjustment, there were no differences in the returns to male and female labor so that the gender division of labor had no costs. After adjustment, the marginal product of male labor will be above that of female labor so that specialization by gender gives rise to allocative inefficiency. The social conventions that gave rise to gender specialization and female

---

4. For example, taking tradables as the numeraire, if nontradables fall in price by x percent then factors specific to the nontradables sector will suffer a loss of income in excess of x percent. A good exposition and development of the Ricardo-Viner model which underlies this is Neary (1978).

immobility can become more costly as prices (and hence opportunities) diverge further from those that prevailed when the conventions were formed.

GENDER DIFFERENCES IN PRICE INFLEXIBILITY AND INTERACTIONS WITH IMMOBILITY. Price inflexibilities, nominal or real, can occur because. of long-term contracts or because of bargaining power that creates reservation prices at certain levels. Such price inflexibilities are unlikely to be directly gender specific. However, because of the gender skewness between sectors and between self and wage employment, sector-specific price and formal labor market wage rigidities are liable to have gender-specific consequences.

Prices in Africa have proved markedly more flexible than in developed economies. However, there are significant differences between Francophone and Anglophone Africa (the former probably having more real price rigidities due to fixed exchange rates), and many markets display short-term nominal rigidities. Where these rigidities bind, the market will not clear and so involuntary nonfulfillment of the plans of some agents takes place. The main instance of this is in the formal wage labor market: real wages do not decline with sufficient speed for all quits to be voluntary and so redundancies occur. A sector subject to such a rigidity will contract more than if wages in the sector were fully flexible. Hence, wage rigidity in the import-substitute and nontraded sectors will accentuate their contraction. With price flexibility and induced voluntary quits, income losses are spread evenly among those who stay and those who relocate, but with price inflexibility, large losses are concentrated with those who involuntarily relocate. This can create powerful opposition to relocation.

An economy with price inflexibilities will require greater (involuntary) quantity mobility. If there are some barriers to mobility, these barriers are more likely to bind if the economy encounters binding price rigidities. Conversely, in an economy with binding quantity immobilities, the changes in relative goods prices, which constitute structural adjustment, will generate larger falls in the real incomes of those in declining price sectors. Hence, reservation wage rigidities are more likely to become binding. Thus, the damaging consequences of either type of inflexibility can include those of the other.

Because the allocation of women's labor is heavily skewed against the manufacturing and public sectors (see table 6.2), they are disproportionately in the flex-price part of the economy. The involuntary quits, which are the consequence of price inflexibility, will therefore be suffered directly by men. However, the short-term welfare consequences of such involuntary quits, and hence the intensity of opposition to them, will depend upon the capacity of the household to redeploy its resources so as to offset the income loss suffered by a male wage-earner member. To a significant extent the redeployment of women's labor represents the best opportunity for households to generate such offsetting increases in income. This is because the allocation of women's labor time between income generation and household activities is known to be considerably more sensitive to the income level of the household than is male labor. Thus, we would expect female labor supply to the market to increase in those households in which male wage earners lost their jobs. The scope for this income security strategy to reduce the short-term social costs of adjustment then depends upon the opportunities for women to earn incomes from this increase in labor supply. To date, public interventions to mitigate the social costs of adjustment have ignored the household as the natural unit of income security and instead have attempted to redeploy those who have lost their jobs through targeted credit and training. Often this has proved both costly and ineffective (Collier 1988). An alternative, or at least complementary intervention, would be to assist the household security strategy. But this amounts to easing the constraints that impede women from entering activities where their income might be enhanced. We are back, for example, to the credit market bias against women.

Conclusion

The price changes that constitute structural adjustment are designed to achieve reallocation of factors. Hence, factor immobility is a direct, central constraint. Price and wage rigidities increase the magnitude of required resource mobility. They also convert it from a voluntary to an involuntary process with potentially high short-term social costs borne by those households whose members lose their jobs. The macroeconomics of structural adjustment can be understood only by a more disaggregated model than that which had been used for most macroeconomic analysis: output must be disaggregated at least into three sectors. Analogously, the microeconomics of structural adjustment can benefit considerably from disaggregation of agents by gender. The capacity to be mobile, the requirement to be mobile, and the capacity to provide a household income security strategy are all likely to differ by gender.

References

Appleton, S., P. Collier, and P. H. Horsnell. 1990. *Gender Differences in Educational Attainment and in Labor Market Participation: An Analysis of the Côte d'Ivoire.* Working Paper, Centre for the Study of African Economies. Oxford University.

Bevan, D. L., P. Collier, and J. W. Gunning. 1989. *Peasants and Governments: An Economic Analysis.* Oxford: Oxford University Press.

Binswanger, H. P., and J. McIntire. 1987. "Behavioural and Material Determinants of Production Relations in Land-Abundant Tropical Agriculture." *Economic Development and Cultural Change*, vol. 37, p. i.

Bryson, J. 1981. "Women and Agriculture in Sub-Saharan Africa: Implications for Development." *Journal of Development Studies,* vol. 17, pp. 29–46.

Collier P., S. Radwan, and S. Wangwe. 1986. *Labor and Poverty in Rural Tanzania.* Oxford:Oxford University Press.

Collier, P. 1988. "African Public Sector Retrenchments: An Analytic Survey." Labor Market Analysis and Employment Planning Working Paper 27. Geneva: International Labour Organization.

Deaton, A. 1989. "Looking for Boy-Girl Discrimination in Household Expenditure Data." *World Bank Economic Review,* vol. 3, pp. 183-210.

Dey, J. 1981. "Gambian Women: Unequal Partners is Rice Development Projects?" *Journal of Development Studies,* vol. 17, pp. 109–122.

Dixon, R. B. 1982. "Women in Agriculture: Counting the Labor Force in Developing Countries." *Population and Development Review,* vol. 8, no. 3.

Dornbusch R. 1974. "Tariffs and Non-traded Goods." *Journal of International Economics,* vol. 4.

Folbre, N. 1986. "Hearts and Spades: Paradigms of Household Economics." *World Development,* vol. 14, pp. 245–255.

Gladwin, C., and D. McMillan. 1989. "Is a Turnaround in Africa Possible Without Helping African Women to Farm?" *Economic Development and Cultural Change.*

Horton, S., and B. D. Miller. 1987. "The Effect of Gender of Household Head on Expenditure: Evidence from Low Income Households in Jamaica." Mimeo, University of Toronto.

Joekes, S., et al. 1988. *Women and Structural Adjustment:* Part II Technical Document. Washington D.C.: International Center for Research on Women.

Jones, C. 1983."The Mobilization of Women's Labor for Cash Crop Production: A Game Theoretic Approach." *American Journal of Agricultural Economics,* vol. 65, pp. 1049–1054.

Koopman-Henn, J. 1983. "Feeding the Cities and Feeding the Peasants: What Role for Africa's Women Farmers?" *World Development,* vol. 11, no. 12.

Lele, U. 1985. "Women and Structural Transformation." *Economic Development and Cultural Change,* vol. 34.

Lockheed, N. I. E., D. T. Jamieson, and L. J. Lau. 1980. "Farmer Education and Firm Efficiency: A Survey." *Economic Development and Cultural Change,* vol. 29.

Lockwood, M. and P. Collier. 1988. Maternal Education and the Vicious Cycle of High Fertility and Malnutrition. Washington, D.C.: World Bank. Women in Development Working Paper 130.

Manser, M., and M. Brown. 1980. "Marriage and Household Decision-making: A Bargaining Analysis." *International Economic Review,* vol. 21, pp. 31–44.

Moock, P. 1976. "The Efficiency of Women as Farm Managers: Kenya." *American Journal of Agricultural Economics,* vol. 58, pp. 831–835.

Neary, J. P. 1978. "Short-run Capital Specificity and the Pure Theory of International Trade." *Economic Journal,* vol. 88.

Ongaro, W. A. 1988. "Adoption of New Farming Technology: A Case Study of Maize Production in Western Kenya." Ph.D. thesis, University of Gothenberg.

Pala, A. 1978. "Women's Access to Land and Their Role in Agriculture and Decision Making: Experiences of the Joluo of Kenya." Discussion Paper 263. Institute of Development Studies, University of Nairobi.

Palmer, I. 1988. "Gender Issues in Structural Adjustment of Sub-Saharan Agriculture." Working Paper, World Employment Programme. Geneva: International Labour Organization.

Ram, R., and R. D. Singh. 1988. "Farm Households in Rural Burkina Faso: Some Evidence on Allocative and Direct Return to Schooling and Male-Female Labor Productivity Differentials." *World Development,* vol. 16, pp. 419–424.

Safilios-Rothschild, C. 1985. "The Persistence of Women's Invisibility in Agriculture: Theoretical and Policy Lessons from Lesotho and Sierra Leone." *Economic Development and Cultural Change.*

Schultz, T. P. 1990. "Women's Changing Participation in the Labor Force: A World Perspective." *Economic Development and Cultural Change,* vol. 38, pp. 457–488.

Sen, A. 1985. "Women, Technology and Sexual Divisions." *Trade and Development,* no. 6, pp. 195–223.

Spring, A. 1988. "Women Farmers and Food in Africa." In *Coping with Africa's Food Crisis,* ed. N. Chazan and T. Shaw. Colorado: Lynne Rienner Press.

Staudt, K. 1977. Inequities in the Delivery of Services to a Female Farm Clientele: Some Implications for Policy." Discussion Paper 247. Institute for Development Studies, University of Nairobi.

Thomas, D. 1989. Intrahousehold Resource Allocation: An Inferential Approach." Yale University Working Paper.

THE EFFECTS OF STRUCTURAL ADJUSTMENT ON WOMEN IN LATIN AMERICA

Gender differences in the allocation of labor exist in Latin America, just as in Africa, but they are rather different. In Latin America women's labor force participation tends to be higher in urban areas than in rural areas, and it has thus tended to increase over time with urbanization. However, the impact of relatively high minimum wages and employee benefits in the formal sector has tended to concentrate women in the informal sector, particularly in family businesses and in domestic service (Schultz 1990).

Unlike in Africa, in Latin America there has been little analysis of the effects of women's mobility on structural adjustment. Most of the work for Latin America looks at women's labor market experiences as a dependent variable and focuses on the impact of structural adjustment on women, in particular on their participation rates. Much remains to be done to analyze the effects on their wages. This section examines the effects of structural adjustment on women in Latin America, and in particular on participation rates. Most of the discussion relates to urban areas, since women's labor force participation is higher in urban areas and since labor force surveys for Latin America are predominantly urban. It is important to bear in mind when analyzing the data that there have been trend increases in women's labor force participation in Latin America for many of the same reasons as in OECD countries—increased urbanization, education, and lower fertility.

There are at least three routes by which adjustment may affect women in the labor force. First, structural adjustment may affect women's participation as a result of temporary increases in unemployment. This has ambiguous effects on women's participation. It may increase it (added worker effect), as in Costa Rica (Gindling and Berry 1990). Or it may decrease it (discouraged worker effect), as in Bolivia (Horton 1990). Second, since structural adjustment also

This section was prepared by A.C. Edwards and J. Roberts, associate professors, California State University at Long Beach.

affects sectoral output, to the extent that men and women are differentially allocated across sectors, there may be differential employment responses. Lastly, following Standing's (1989) argument, trade liberalization will be associated with a reduction in the protection of workers, i.e., a reduction in employee benefits such as job security and an increasing reliance on part-time, temporary, or "flexible" labor. This third effect may tend to benefit women. We examine below some of the evidence for these predicted effects. The following decomposition exercise uses country-level data for Latin America. We then review evidence from individual Latin countries before presenting our conclusions and suggestions for further research.

Decomposition of Employment Changes

Our cross-country decomposition of the change in female employment is similar to the crossregion analysis undertaken by Schultz (1990). Growth in women's employment can be divided into two components. Firstly, women's share of total employment changes if the sectors that employ women expand or contract. This can be thought of as the effect of changes in aggregate demand on women's employment, and it is clearly related both to the development process and to structural adjustment. To take an obvious example, as a country develops, employment in the agricultural sector is likely to decline while that in manufacturing and services expands. In Latin America, women make up a disproportionately small share of the agricultural sector and a disproportionately large share of the manufacturing and services sectors. Therefore, women's employment will tend to expand in the course of development. Similar sectoral changes related to structural adjustment will affect women's employment.

The second component to changes in women's share of total employment consists of changes in the proportion of employees in each sector who are women. This proportion is likely to change in the course of development, with increases in urbanization, increases in women's education, and decreases in fertility. The proportion may also change due to structural adjustment if there is marginalization of the work force, i.e., a shift to more informalization and temporary labor.

We can express this decomposition algebraically, with WE_j, female employment in sector j; TE_j, total employment in sector j; WE, total female employment; and TE, total employment. Then the percentage of the work force that is female can be expressed as

$$\frac{WE}{TE} = \sum_j \frac{WE_j}{TE_j} \frac{TE_j}{TE} \tag{1}$$

$$w = \sum w_j s_j \tag{2}$$

where w represents the percentage of the work force that is female, w_j represents the percentage of sector j employment that is female, and s_j represents sector j's share of total employment. Then, the change in women's share of total employment can be decomposed as follows:

$$\Delta w = \sum_j w_j \Delta s_j + \sum_j s_j \Delta w_j + \sum_j \Delta w_j s_j$$

This decomposition relates to the foregoing discussion. The first term represents changes in women's share of total employment that can be attributed to changes in the structural composition of employment. The second term describes the effect of within-sector changes in the male/female ratio, holding constant the sectoral composition of total employment. This term captures the possible effect of increasing reliance on flexible labor as well as the global trend toward increased female labor force participation. The third term is the product of changes in two rates and is typically small.

The top panel of Table 6.4 shows the value of each term in equation (3) for ten Latin American countries. The employment data on which this table is based are from the *ILO Yearbook of Labor Statistics*. All Latin American countries for which the *Yearbook of Labor Statistics* reported employment by sector by sex for at least six years are included in Table 6.4 Since the time span covered varies by country, the figures in the table are standardized to represent changes per annum.

In most of these countries, the male labor force participation rate decreased over the period in question, while the female labor force participation rate increased. The only exception is Haiti, where the female participation rate declined.

Table 6.4 Changes in Women's Share of Total Employment
(average annual rates of change)

Country	Years	$w1 * \Delta s$ (1)	$s1 * \Delta w$ (2)	$\Delta s * \Delta w$ (3)	Total (4)	(2) / (1) (5)
Bolivia	1978–87	0.0009	0.0018	0.0001	0.0028	2.0498
Brazil	1970–85	0.0004	0.0068	0.0033	0.0106	15.814
Chile	1974–87	0.0015	0.0027	0.0001	0.0043	1.8138
Colombia	1975–87	-0.0008	0.0031	0.0005	0.0027	3.6394
Costa Rica	1980–86	0.0032	0.0010	-0.0000	0.0042	0.3130
Cuba	1978–86	0.0024	0.0077	-0.0001	0.0100	3.1866
Haiti	1970–83	0.0018	-0.0062	0.0005	-0.0039	3.5196
Puerto Rico	1978–87	0.0011	0.0035	0.0002	0.0048	3.2710
Panama	1974–87	0.0020	0.0017	-0.0001	0.0036	0.8519
Venezuela	1981–87	0.0013	0.0007	0.0000	0.0020	0.5909
Mean		0.0014	0.0023	0.0005	0.0041	3.505
Canada	1978–87	0.0017	0.0036	-0.0000	0.0054	2.0869
Japan	1976–87	0.0002	0.0020	0.0001	0.0024	8.2896
United Kingdom	1975–87	0.0024	0.0013	-0.0001	0.0036	0.5569
United States	1978–87	0.0011	0.0029	0.0001	0.0040	2.6888
Mean		0.0014	0.0025	0.0000	0.0039	3.4056

Source: Calculated from employment data reported in the ILO, *Yearbook of Labor Statistics*.

We turn now to the decomposition of these changes and look first at column 1, which represents the changes in women's share of employment that can be attributed to changes in the relative importance of various sectors of the economy. In nine of the ten countries considered, sectoral shifts have affected female employment positively. After looking at the data for each country, the only generalization we can make about the reasons for these positive effects is that, in most of these countries, the service sectors showed relative employment gains, and women are disproportionately represented in the service sectors. Colombia is the only exception, for reasons which are not clear.

Women's share of employment within sectors also has increased. The only exception to this is Haiti, where women's labor force participation declined. This is something that might be worth examining with country-level data.

The magnitude of column 2 relative to column 1 is reported in column 5 of Table 6.4. In 7 of the 10 countries, column 2 is larger (in absolute value) than column 1. This is especially true for Brazil, where women's labor force participation increased extremely fast. However, with the exceptions of Brazil and the three countries where column 1 dominates (Costa Rica, Panama, and Venezuela), another fairly consistent story emerges: the effects of within-sector change are about two to three times as large as the effects of changes in sectoral composition.

In sum, women's share of total employment grew throughout Latin America. This is in part due to increases in the importance of sectors that employ relatively more women than men. These increases can be attributed to economic development and to trade liberalization. However, bigger gains have come from increases in the proportion of women employed within each sector. Perhaps these are due to increased reliance on flexible labor, to increased education levels among women, or to decreases in work place discrimination.

Finally, it is useful to compare women's employment gains in Latin America with similar numbers for developed countries. The bottom panel of Table 6.4 contains a similar decomposition for Canada, Japan, the United Kingdom, and the United States. These figures are very similar to the numbers reported for Latin America. Women's shares of total employment (column 4) increased between .24 percent and .54 percent per year. These percentages are comparable to the typical values reported for Latin America. The gains have come about both because of changes in the sectoral composition of employment and because of gains to women within sectors. Finally, the second effect is two to three times as large as the first effect in both the top and bottom panels of Table 6.4.

In order to explain the crosscountry variations in women's labor force participation rates, we estimate a simple model of labor force participation using time-series/cross-section data provided by the World Bank (1989). The model is as follows:

$$FLFPR_{tj} = b_0 + b_1 (UPOPL)_{tj} + b_2 (FSEC_{-5})_{tj} + b_3 (TFRT)_{tj} + b_4 (D1 * CYCLE) +$$

$$b_5 (D2 * CYCLE) + b_6 (D3 * CYCLE) + b_7 (DJAMAICA)$$

The variable definitions and OLS estimates are reported in Table 6.5. Table 6.6 reports variable means for 1965 and 1987, the first and last years in our sample.

Table 6.5 OLS Regressions: Determinants of FLFPR Variations Across Countries in Latin America, 1966–87

Variable	Coefficient	T-Statistic	Sample Mean
FLFPR[a]			15.57
INTERCEPT	18.70	6.45	1.0
UPOPL[b]	0.038	2.61	54.762
FSEC$_{-5}$[c]	0.050	2.40	0.050
TFRT[d]	-1.62	-4.44	4.815
D1CYCLE[e]	-4.04	-2.15	0.005
D2CYCLE[e]	-1.60	-1.42	0.007
D3CYCLE[e]	0.72	0.67	0.006
DJAMAICA[f]	19.69	28.83	0.050

Note: Adjusted R squared = 0.818. Number of observations = 439 (20 countries, about 22 observations per country from 1966 to 1987).
a. Female labor force to female population ratio (used in preference to female labor force participation ratio, due to longer time series).
b. Urban as percentage of total population.
c. Female education level lagged 5 years (estimated from linear time trend).
d. Total fertility rate: average number of children that a woman would bear in her lifetime, at the prevailing age-specific fertility rates (instrumented here using the infant mortality rate).
e. CYCLE is the difference (in logs) between actual GNP per capita and its trend. D1 is the dummy for poorest 6 countries in group; D2, dummy for middle 7 countries in group; and D3, dummy for richest 7 countries in group.
f. Jamaica dummy: outlier.

The results of this regression are summarized as follows. Women's labor force participation increases with urbanization, with the level of education of women in the relevant age interval (measured by lagged values of female secondary education coverage), and with reductions in predicted fertility. The CYCLE variable suggests that an added worker effect seems to be significant in the low-income countries, to be present but not significant in middle-income countries, and not to be present in the richest group of countries.

Evidence from Individual Country Studies

Work on individual countries tends to focus on female participation rates. The interesting questions as to effects on relative wages and the

Table 6.6 Changes in Variables between 1965 and 1987

Country	FLFPR (percentage)	TFRT	FSEC$_{-5}$ (percentage)	UPOPL (percentage)	AGNP (US$)
Argentina	18.1/19.5	3.07/2.96	23/68	76.1/85.4	791
Bolivia	13.9/15.5	6.59/6.06	13/31	40.0/50.0	183
Brazil	12.6/19.5	5.65/3.46	9/40	50.4/74.8	538
Chile	13.9/20.3	4.78/2.73	25/66	71.7/84.6	635
Colombia	12.1/14.3	6.34/3.19	9/51	53.5/68.9	361
Costa Rica	10.2/15.3	6.26/3.26	23/50	38.1/44.5	503
Dominican Republic	5.9/9.0	6.93/3.75	8/53	35.1/58.1	299
Ecuador	10.4/11.8	6.78/4.33	16/53	37.2/54.6	340
El Salvador	12.2/16.7	6.71/4.86	14/24	38.9/43.6	260
Guatemala	7.9/9.1	6.70/5.77	5/17	34.3/32.7	337
Honduras	8.2/11.1	7.40/5.55	9/35	25.7/41.7	227
Jamaica	31.3/44.0	5.42/2.86	41/63	37.6/50.9	517
Mexico	9.5/18.3	6.71/3.78	12/51	54.9/71.1	667
Nicaragua	11.4/15.1	7.19/5.50	13/48	42.7/58.2	298
Panama	17.7/19.6	5.74/3.14	25/65	44.4/53.6	591
Paraguay	13.6/13.8	6.56/4.58	9/28	36.2/46.0	334
Peru	12.6/15.5	6.68/4.05	8/60	51.9/68.8	433
Trinidad	18.8/23.1	4.33/2.80	20/74	30.0/66.5	1252
Uruguay	20.1/23.6	2.84/2.61	14/69	81.1/85.1	722
Venezuela	11.8/19.0	6.12/3.77	24/48	69.8/83.0	1245

Note: AGNP is average per capita GNP in 1985 U.S. dollars. For explanation of other variables, see table 6.5.
Source: Own calculations based on World Bank (1989) data.

informalization hypothesis remain to be addressed. For Brazil, Sedlacek (1990) shows that the proportion of married women in the labor force increased from 34.5 percent to 39.7 percent from 1983 to 1988, while over the same period the proportion of female-headed households also increased from 7.7 percent to 9.2 percent. It is interesting to note that the rapid increase in female labor force participation in Brazil occurred at the same time as increased informalization (Edwards 1990). However, it is not known to what extent these trends are related.

For Chile, Pardo (1989) presents data on women's participation rates by age (Table 6.7). Labor force participation of prime-age women (24 to 44) increased between 1960 and 1987. (The decreases

Table 6.7 Chile: Women's Labor Force Participation by Age, Greater Santiago Area, 1960–1987

Year	14–19	20–24	25–44	45–54	55–64	65+	Total
1960	26.7	49.7	41.4	34.5	27.1	10.6	35.7
1970	16.8	50.1	44.0	36.3	21.0	9.8	34.3
1980	12.0	46.5	44.5	33.0	17.3	3.8	32.1
1987	12.4	46.1	53.9	37.0	25.9	4.9	38.4

Source: Pardo (1989).

in younger age groups are likely due to increased education.) Participation during the depressed labor market conditions of the mid-1970s and early 1980s appears to have declined.

In what follows, we analyze the effects of the severe structural adjustment in Chile. We use a rich data set from the Greater Santiago area, which represents about one-third of the country's labor market. These data consist of surveys undertaken by the University of Chile each June, combined with published data. The results for separate employment equations for men and women are presented in Table 6.8.

Evaluated at the means, each year of formal education increases a woman's probability of employment by 1.1 percent. The first child under age 6 decreases the probability of employment by 4 percent, additional children under age 6 decrease employment probability by an additional 3 percent, and absence of a husband increases the probability by 20 percent. If a woman's husband is present but unemployed, the probability of the woman being employed increases by 3 percent, as compared to the case where the husband is working. There is an additional time trend increase of women's employment probability of 0.14 percent per year. For men, additional years of education have similar effects as for women, but the presence of young children or a wife have no effect. However, if a wife is present, her work status does affect husband's participation. If she is present and working, the husband's probability of employment declines by 3.3 percent, and if she is present and unemployed, the husband's

Table 6.8 Chile: Determinants of Full-Time Employment—Probit Estimates

X	Women		Men	
	Xw	*dEMP/dX*	*Xm*	*dEMP/dX*
INTERCEPT	1.000	-0.7611**	1.000	-0.0451
YE[a]	8.169	0.0107**	9.007	0.0097**
AGE[b]	2.369	0.0267**	43.724	0.0264**
AGE2[c]	2003.810	-0.0004**	2113.330	-0.0004**
DNOKID[d]	0.193	0.0702**	0.198	-0.0232**
PCHILDL6[e]	0.346	0.0133	0.372	0.0122
NCHILDL6[f]	0.509	-0.0290**	0.552	-0.0002
YRSHOME[g]	1.506	-0.0330**	1.637	-0.0189**
YHXYE[h]	13.260	0.0023**	15.521	0.0013**
YHXEX[i]	9.852	0.0010**	26.819	0.0003*
SNOTPRES[j]	0.206	0.2031**	0.098	-0.0194
SLF[k]	0.692	0.0169*	0.225	-0.0326**
SUNEMP[l]	0.078	0.0312**	0.024	-0.1468**
SYE[m]	7.199	0.0006	7.502	0.0080**
T[n]	6.448	0.0014**	6.400	-0.0069**
TUNEMP[o]	15.419	-0.0015**	15.411	-0.0106**
# OBS	40222		35398	
DEP VAR MEAN	0.194		0.681	

**significant at the 1% level
* significant at the 5% level
Notes:
EMP: Dummy = 1 if individual is employed full time; = 0 else.
a. Years of education.
b. Age.
c. Age squared.
d. Dummy = 1 if individual has no children at home; = 0 else.
e. Dummy = 1 if individual has a child younger than 6; = 0 else.
f. Number of children younger than 6 years of age.
g. Years until youngest child reaches school age; = 0 if no children younger than 6.
h. YRSHOME multiplied by YE.
i. YRSHOME multiplied by (AGE-YE-6).
j. Dummy = 1 if spouse is not present; = 0 else.
k. Dummy = 1 if spouse is in the labor force; = 0 else.
l. Dummy = 1 if spouse is unemployed; = 0 else.
m. Spouse's years of education.
n. Time trend: 1974=1, 1975=2, 1987=14.
o. Aggregate unemployment rate.

employment probability declines by 15 percent, as compared to the case of wife present and not in the labor force. The additional time trend effect is a 0.7 percent per annum decrease in the probability of male employment.

We can interpret the coefficient on aggregate unemployment as telling us something about the effects of structural adjustment on men and women. The estimated coefficients imply that every 1 percent increase in the unemployment rate caused an average woman's employment probability to fall by .15 percent and an average man's employment probability to fall by 1.06 percent. However, the raw numbers do not tell exactly the right story. Rather, the relevant comparison is how changes in the unemployment rate affect the employed population. For example, if the work force contains three times as many men as women, increases in unemployment would be "sex neutral" if three times as many men as women lost their jobs. Algebraically, the effect is sex neutral if (.15/1.06) = (no. of women employed / no. of men employed) or if

$$\frac{.15}{\text{no. of women employed}} = \frac{1.06}{\text{no. of men employed}}$$

Assuming there are equal numbers of women and men in the population, we can substitute the proportions of women and men employed in the denominators, .194 and .681 respectively in our sample. Making these substitutions, the relative impact of changes in the unemployment rate on women is 0.77 and the relative impact on men is 1.56. Changes in unemployment had a proportionate effect on men that was twice as large as the effect on women.

In order to examine this effect further, we estimated a similar set of models, with male and female labor force participation rather than full-time employment as the dependent variables. A 1 percent increase in the unemployment rate caused an average woman's labor force participation probability to fall by .14 percent and an average man's participation probability to fall by .08 percent. Not surprisingly, women are more likely than men to withdraw from the work force during economic downturns. The effect is magnified if we take into account the fact that women are less likely to be in the labor force in the first place. Using a transformation similar to that employed in the previous paragraph, we find that the adjusted effect of changes in the unemployment rate on labor force participation is .48 for women and .10 for men.

The most important point, then, is that recent increases in Chilean unemployment had larger effects on male employment than on female employment (other things equal). However, women were more likely than men to be discouraged by high unemployment rates and to leave the labor force. Thus, a study that looked at unemployment rather than employment would understate the effect of cyclical swings on women.

For Colombia, Lardono and Maldonado and Guerreo-Lozano (in Ocampo and Ramirez 1987) document increased participation among married women, particularly in the 20-39 age group, between 1976 and 1984.

The most detailed analysis available is for Costa Rica (Gindling and Berry 1990; Gindling 1990). Gindling finds evidence of an added worker effect in the recession and stabilization of the early 1980s. Associated with this is a decline in average female earnings relative to average male earnings due to the entry of less educated and less experienced women into the labor force. Uthoff and Pollack (1985) confirm that women suffered a larger fall in real wages in the recession. If skill is controlled for, however, there was no difference in the real wage declines experienced by men and women.

Garcia and Gomariz (1989) report the evolution of women's labor force participation in Costa Rica, El Salvador, Guatemala, Honduras, and Nicaragua between 1950 and 1988 (see table 6.9). Female labor force participation increased faster in Costa Rica, El Salvador, and Nicaragua than in Guatemala and Honduras.

The rapid increase in Costa Rica was discussed earlier. An important factor in the cases of El Salvador and Nicaragua is military conflict, which led to large migration outflows. According to Funkhouser (1989), this outmigration has two effects: an income effect, due to remittances from migrants, and a wage effect, due to the decreased supply of labor. Funkhouser argues that the wage effect predominated in El Salvador, contributing to increased female labor force participation.

Conclusion

This paper reviews the existing literature on women's labor force participation in Latin America, paying special attention to changes through time. It also presents three new pieces of empirical evidence.

For the most part, the previous literature concentrates on the effects of human capital and demographic variables on labor force participation. It shows that, throughout most of Latin America, women's labor force participation is increasing. This is due to increasing educational opportunities and declining fertility. Both are worldwide trends.

By contrast, there is very little work on women's earnings relative to men's, with the notable exception of the empirical work based on Costa Rica (Gindling 1990; Uthoff and Pollack 1985).

By decomposing employment trends in Latin America using crosscountry data, we found that the effects of sectoral shifts on increasing women's employment are small relative to the effects of increasing female representation within each sector. Sectoral changes in Canada, Japan, the United Kingdom, and the United States (the only countries outside of Latin America that we considered) produced similar increases in women's employment during approximately the same period.

Using aggregate data for twenty countries and for the period 1965 to 1987, we attempted to explain variations in female labor force participation. Reductions in fertility, rising education levels, and rising urbanization explain a significant fraction of the variation. The effect of real GNP per capita variations from the trend seems to depend on income per capita. In particular, the coefficient turns out to be negative and significant for low-income countries and positive but insignificant among high-income countries.

Our access to survey data for Chile enabled us to look more directly at the employment effects of structural adjustment. We used a time-series/cross-section model to see how changes in the aggregate unemployment rate affected employment probabilities of men and women. We control for numerous other variables that can affect labor force participation. The effects of structural adjustment, as measured

Table 6.9 Central America: Labor Force Participation by Sex

Year	Costa Rica		El Salvador		Guatemala		Honduras		Nicaragua	
	Male	Female	Male	Female	Male	Female	Male	Female	Male	Female
1950	85.9	17.3	85.2	23.1	85.3	21.7	84.9	29.6	79.2	20.8
1960	80.2	17.5	81.8	23.6	82.4	20.5	84.2	23.9	79.6	26.0
1970	73.9	20.0	78.8	29.5	76.6	20.5	78.4	22.5	69.8	26.7
1977	n.a.	n.a.	76.6	32.4	n.a.	n.a.	n.a.	n.a.	68.8	28.6
1980	73.5	24.3	76.9	33.9	75.4	22.7	74.9	25.8	68.4	29.5
1985	78.8	27.7	76.2	34.7	74.6	23.9	73.7	27.6	68.0	31.3
1987	78.7	29.4	75.8	35.7	74.2	24.5	73.4	28.1	67.9	32.1
1988	78.7	30.2	75.6	36.0	74.1	24.6	73.3	28.5	67.9	32.5

n.a. indicates information not available
Source: Garcia and Gomariz (1989).

by changes in employment, are substantially larger for men than for women.

In summary, then, we present three new pieces of empirical evidence regarding the effects of structural adjustment in Latin America on men and women. First, the share of jobs that go to women has been increasing at about the same rate in Latin America as in our sample of developed countries. Second, as to any evidence regarding differential effects across countries, we find that variations in economic activity levels affect women's labor force participation differently depending on the income per capita. Third, at least in Santiago, changes in aggregate unemployment during the late 1970s and early 1980s were felt disproportionately by men.

There are several additional avenues that need to be explored. First, it would be useful to have empirical evidence about structural adjustment's effect on flexible labor (part-time employment and informal jobs.) Second, we should look at the effects of reform on women's earnings relative to men's, using a methodology similar to that employed in our study of Chilean employment. Since gender wage differentials are very sensitive to changes in the composition of the groups compared, and given the evidence presented here on Chile and on Costa Rica (Gindling's work on relative earnings), it would be very important to separate the evolution of gender wage differentials in its different components. That is, it would be useful to distinguish the effect on gender wage differentials of year to year variations in sample selection, labor force composition (by individual characteristics like education), employment composition (by occupation and sector), and returns to the individual characteristics.

References

Edwards, S., and A. Edwards. 1990. "Labor Market Distortions and Structural Adjustment in Developing Countries." NBER Working Paper 3346. Paper presented at the Warwick-EDI Conference on Labor Markets in an ERA of Adjustment, Warwick, England, May 21-24.

Funkhouser, E. 1990. "Mass Migration, Remittances, and Economic Adjustment: The Case of El Salvador in the 1980s." Paper presented at the NBER Conference on Immigration. Cancun, Mexico. January.

Garcia, I. and E. Gomariz. 1989. *Mujeres Centroamericanas.* Tomo I San Jose: FLACSO.

Gindling, T.H. 1990. "Women's Earnings and the Economic Crisis in Costa Rica." North-East Development Economics Conference. Economic Growth Center, Yale University, May 12.

Gindling, T.H., and A. Berry. 1990. "Labor Markets Adjustment in Costa Rica." Paper presented at the Warwick-EDI Conference on Labor Markets in an Era of Adjustment, Warwick, England, May 21-24.

Horton, S. 1990. "Labor Markets in an Era of Adjustment: Bolivia." Paper presented at the EDI-Warwick Conference on Labor Markets in an Era of Adjustment, Warwick, England, May 21-24.

ILO (International Labor Organization). various years. *Yearbook of Labor Statistics* Geneva: ILO.

Ocampo, J. A., and M., Ramirez. 1987. *El problema laboral colombiano: informes de la misión,* Chenery, vol. 1 and vol. 2. Bogota, Government of Colombia, Department of Planning.

Pardo, L. 1989. "Una Interpretación de la Evidencia en la Participación de las Mujeres en la Fuerza de Trabajo: Gran Santiago, 1957-1987." *Estudios de Economía,* vol. 16, no. 2, November, pp. 319-346.

Standing, G. 1989. "Global Feminization through Flexible Labor." *World Development,* vol. 17, no. 7, pp. 1077-1095.

Schultz, T.P. 1990. "Women's Changing Participation in the Labor Force: A World Perspective." *Economic Development and Cultural Change.* Vol. 38, no. 4, pp. 457-486.

Sedlacek, G. 1990. "Estrategias de Geracao de renda das familias Brasileiras: Um Estudo da participacao de mulher no mercado de trabalho." IPAE.

World Bank. 1989. *Social Indicators of Development*: *Data on Diskette.* Washington D.C.: World Bank.

Uthoff, A., and M. Pollack 1985. "Análisis Microeconómico del Ajuste del Mercado de Trabajo. Costa Rica 1979-82: Lecciones para un modelo macroeconómico." *Estudios de Economía* v.12, no. 2:83-111. September.

GENDER AND LABOR ALLOCATION IN STRUCTURAL ADJUSTMENT IN SOUTH ASIA

Widely different in the trade dependence of GDP and employment, the South Asian nations have experienced different external shocks since the mid-1970s and have responded with various macroadjustment policies. The weightiest problem of economic adjustment in this region is essentially a long-run demographic one, whereby a rapidly growing labor force presses against a slowly growing resource base (of cropped acreage, irrigation capacity, savings, and foreign exchange).

Whereas in Latin America, major investment cuts, causing unemployment and inflation, have been suffered on account of external shocks, in the Indian subcontinent the external crunch has been milder,[1] but it has compounded the longer-run problem of adjusting to the labor-force increases in the face of domestic capital constraints. In the past two decades, the pressures of unsustainable domestic and external deficits, aggravated by the oil shocks in the 1970s,[2] and by the terms-of-trade adversity in the 1980s, have

---

This section was prepared by Kalpana Bardhan, California State University at Berkeley.

1. The extent of external shocks and contractionary policy imposed by debt service costs has been less in South Asia than in Latin America and Africa, and softened by the surge in Gulf migration and remittance since the mid-1970s, which also relieved a little the flood of jobseekers for a while, but is petering out even as a marginal vent for surplus labor. The task of longer-term adjustment to the swollen net annual additions to labor force remains and will remain through the end of this century. The task involves mobilizing internal sources of financing investment—as Bangladesh cannot expect to move on to a higher growth path with under 5 percent savings rate simply by recycling external aid through the economy mostly as consumption and unproductive subsidies. Nor can Sri Lanka and India, even with a decent savings rate, combine the needed investment growth with escalating military budgets, cost of quelling unrest and "leaky bucket" welfare policies. The task also involves upgrading human resource, particularly girls' schooling and utilizing the underemployed, unemployed, and often discouraged female labor, which is important for equity, growth and the pace of fertility decline.

2. India's adjustment policy to the oil shocks of the 1970s took the form mainly of cutting back public investment in basic production sectors and infrastructure, the effect of which was to aggravate and prolong the growth crisis, especially the industrial stagnation of that period. Although India avoided becoming burdened with

coincided in South Asia with the peak of population growth and the lagged peak of labor-force growth (see Table 6.10).

The usual sources of labor force statistics, that is, sample household surveys like the extensive NSS in India, are often difficult to compare across countries, and even over time in the same country, due to changes in definitions. Participation rates change abruptly depending on the definition of unemployment and the classification of seasonal workers. But even allowing for such deficiencies, there seems to be a clear downward trend in the female participation rate in South Asia (Table 6.11). This also seems to have been the case in North Africa

Table 6.10 Demographic Shifts, South Asian Countries

	Bangladesh	India	Nepal	Pakistan	Sri Lanka
A. Persons aged 15-29 as percent of total population					
1985	27.5	26.8	26.2	28.3	30.4
1990	29.3	27.7	26.9	27.8	28.9
2000	30.3	28.9	26.8	27.4	26.9
B. Population growth rate (average annual percent)					
1980-89	2.6	2.1	2.6	3.2	1.5
1989-2000	2.1	1.7	2.5	3.2	1.1
C. Urban percentage of total population$_c$					
1960	5	18	3	22	18
1990	16	27	9	32	21
D. GNP per capita ($)					
1989	180	340	180	370	430

Sources: For item A, United Nations: *World Demographic Estimates and Projections, 1950-2025.* Report prepared jointly by the UN, the ILO and the FAO, 1988, pp. 296-310. For items B, C, and D, *World Development Report, 1991,* Tables 26, 31, 1.

the Latin American kind of commercial debt service costs, it was not achieved through an East Asian kind of export performance. The constrained import of raw materials and intermediate goods exacerbated the growth-depressing effects of the lowered public investment rate in response to the oil shocks.

Table 6.11 Aspects of the Female Participation in Economic Activities, South Asia

	Bangladesh	India	Nepal	Pakistan	Sri Lanka
Female LFPR (15+ years)					
1960	5.0	42.6	49.4	8.3	31.4
1980	9.8	32.2	63.8	10.6	30.7
Female LFPR (10+ years)*					
1960	4.8	40.0	47.6	7.9	27.1
1980	5.6**	29.7	43.6	9.3	26.5
Female % of total work force (10+ years)					
1960	4.6	31.6	35.4	8.0	24.8
1980	6.3	27.2	34.9	10.4	26.9
Female % of agricultural work force					
1960	4.4	35.8	36.6	9.3	29.0
1980	6.1	30.9	36.5	8.2	29.2
Female % of non-agricultural work force					
1960	5.8	19.9	15.7	6.0	19.3
1980	7.0	18.7	14.8	13.1	24.2
Agricultural % of all female workers					
1960	82.3	83.7	97.5	70.8	66.2
1980	72.0	79.2	97.0	43.0	58.0
No. of small children (male + female up to 9 years) per 100 female population of 10+years					
1960	93.0	84.0	75.0	104.0	92.0
1980	104.0	76.0	94.0	94.0	64.0

* These figures are higher than the activity rates published in the ILO and UN sources quoted below, because I have divided the economically active females aged ≥10 by female population aged ≥ 10, not by the total female population.

** 7.7 from 1984-85 LFS

Sources: ILO: *Economically Active Population: Estimates & Projections, 1950-2025.* Table 2. 1986.
UNESCO: *Development of Education in Asia and the Pacific: A Statistical Review*, 1985. The World Bank: *World Development Report*, 1981, 1989.

and the Middle East, but the trend in Latin America and Africa is upward (Schultz 1990). This paper examines some of the determinants of women's role in the labor force in South Asia, including changing macro-economic conditions, local infrastructure, education, women's reproductive role, and the new industrial division of labor.

Gender, Adjustment and Household Labor Allocation

Reported statistics on women's labor market participation do not cover women's non market work, and hence miss much of the changes in female time allocation necessitated by occupational or spatial mobility of other household members under adjustment. Most households in South Asia combine self-employment (or family employment) and wage employment in ways that, despite the seemingly rigid dictates of custom and culture, are quite sensitive to changes in economic pressures and in available options. Intrahousehold allocation of different members' labor and of investment in their human capital depend on the household budget constraint and the opportunities currently available in its environment as well as those expected to come within reach. Changes in the market supply of labor by sex and age in response to the changes generated by macro policy shifts cannot be fully understood and evaluated in isolation from what is going on in the nonmarket allocation of labor and the household level.

There is considerable evidence that in economically depressed times and regions, female participation in the work force undergoes both qualitative and quantitative changes (causing both women and children to resort to lower-yield subsistence activities and lower-wage labor under harsher conditions). For women particularly, economic stagnation means "not forced leisure but lower-paid work, and work more deleterious to their health and their children" (Mitra 1978). Stagnation of agriculture and industry relative to population worsens the female load of low-return work. Female share of work increases also with growth, but usually in better quality employment, accompanied by a lessening of sex gaps in wage and unemployment.

The largest increases in the female share of employment in India during the seventies were in agriculture and in urban sectors of cottaged-out, women-intensive industries, oriented mostly to the home market and partly to the export market. Within agriculture, the female ratio of wage-labor continued to rise, and unlike in the sixties, there was also a sharp increase in the female share of work as cultivators, due to men diversifying into other occupations locally or commuting to urban areas. Use of girls' labor increased alongside women's in smallholding agriculture, even as use of boys' labor decreased.

Labor Allocation and Local Economic Environment

Labor-time allocation for women tends to change much more than for men in response to economic growth and in accommodation to the needs of hard times and adverse local conditions. It changes with expanded opportunities arising from market changes, availability of growth infrastructure, and institutional innovations that lower access barriers to inputs (such as to credit and know-how). It changes also under conditions of local stagnation, deforestation, and technological obsolescence of former livelihoods—through differential resort to lower-return work (subsistence processing and gathering, generating goods and services for home use). It accommodates the labor redivision needs of household's migration strategies, in response to regional differences in growth. Although women now form a larger proportion of seasonal and circular work migrants, the greater constraints on women's mobility induce greater local adaptation.

In the slack season in infrastructurally depressed rural areas, without a nearby locus of nonagricultural employment, women of land-poor households do more low-return work inside and outside the labor market. The wage gap widens in the slack season and men tend to either migrate more for higher wage work or substitute more leisure, since they take a substantially smaller share of the subsistence gathering and processing work involved in scratching together some daily meal for the family. The fact that rural poor women in economically depressed environments do a lot more low-return work than do men means that the cost of generating family nutrition per unit of women's labor (calories spent) and time taken out of care-giving is very high in the slack season for the asset-poor families, particularly in areas that are poor in growth infrastructure and basic facilities. The hidden social costs of this are great in terms of the health, nutrition, care, and schooling of children, especially girls, who are drafted more than boys to help with the subsistence-processing work.

Some of these costs can be lessened by the public provision of certain basic facilities and social services, by more dispersed investment in infrastructure, and by counterseasonal employment schemes. In seasonal farm labor, landless women have constituted an increasing proportion over the past two decades in South Asia; likewise in construction and other low-wage casual labor. Women on the average form about 40 percent of the Employment Guarantee Scheme (EGS) workers in rural Maharashtra, a ratio very close to the female proportion of all rural workers in the state. Locally generated slack-season employment in the EGS public works has been promptly utilized by women, to an extent far exceeding the expectations of the scheme's architects. Without such locally generated wage employment, asset-poor rural women might have been forced into worse kinds of self-employment and/or into greater seasonal migration with possible adverse welfare effects. (This does not mean that self-employment under certain conditions, such as improved assets, would not have been better.)

Education and Female Participation in the Work Force

How participation in the work force varies with education level, and how female schooling is connected intergenerationally with female work conditions, are conditioned by a number of factors in the household's social and economic environment. Three interrelated factors are central here: the sex gap in educational access and attainment, which is wider toward the lower end of the socioeconomic scale; the relationship between formal schooling and labor market participation; and how the various markets for female labor differ by educational attainment. These three factors may also be shifting in the structural adjustment process.

In South Asia, the female work participation rate is generally high near the two ends of the socioeconomic scale, for uneducated women of assetless families and for highly educated women of affluent educated families. The two peaks are separated, by initial drop from large quantities of poor-quality employment and a rise in higher-quality employment for educated women. In between, there is a withdrawal into full time wife-and-motherhood in the primary to secondary education range (see Table 6.12). This pattern may be changing as more young, educated women migrate for jobs, and as new industries emerge, or old ones are restructured, to tap the cheaper

Table 6.12 Work Participation Rate (WPR) of Urban Women (≥15 Years) by Education, India and States, 1983

States	Education level					
	Not literate	Up to Primary	Middle	Secondary	> Graduate	All
Andhra Pradesh	36	16	11.5	14.7	35	26.7
Karnataka	39	29	14.8	19.4	35.5	29.7
Kerala	38	34	23.1	28.4	49	31.4
Tamil Nadu	39	26	14.1	24	35	29.7
Haryana	17	12	9.3	20	18	15.9
Punjab	20.5	14	18.9	14.6	40	19.4
Uttar Pradesh	19	10	5.4	8.7	19	15.3
Gujarat	28	14	13.8	10.2	25	19.8
Rajasthan	37	17	6.6	9.9	26	29.4
Maharashtra	33	19	8.7	15.8	35	22.8
Madhya Pradesh	31	15	9.8	11.4	19	22.7
Himachal Pradesh	28	11	12.8	31.7	49	25.2
Bihar	23	10	4.8	6.7	19	17.0
Orissa	25.5	7	2.8	5.7	36	16.6
West Bengal	23.5	15	9.7	13.8	32	17.5
Urban India	30	18	11.1	15.6	30	22.5

Source: NSS 38th round, *Sarvekshana*, April 1988, Table 13.1.

and more flexibly employable pool of semieducated female labor. From the latest 1987-88 NSS, however, the change seems to be minor in India.

The main reason for the modified U-shaped relation between education and women's labor force participation is that the paucity of male earnings, opportunities and assets amongst the landless has forced women with few marketable skills into the labor market. The jobs available are mainly in agricultural labor, hauling, petty trade, and domestic service, jobs filled by women from the bottom socioeconomic rung, and jobs that are socially denigrated as well as low in wage. The income elasticity of demand for withdrawing female labor from these kinds of low-wage labor to some form of home-based employment is very high. This is likely to change with the urban growth of employment in female-labor-intensive industries, the villageward spread of these industries in subcontracted small units or as cottaged-out work, and local linkages from agricultural growth into industry and services in the larger, diversified villages.

In Sri Lanka and Kerala, where the incidence of female education is already high and the culture of seclusion weak, growth-activating policies are likely to be particularly effective in expediting the labor market entry of the large pools of primary-to-secondary educated women (the currently discouraged workers). The female-male ratio in the rural work force in Sri Lanka is by far the highest in rural South Asia, and it is almost symmetrically distributed between wage employment and self-employment. In both Kerala and Sri Lanka, good transportation infrastructure has enabled rural residents, both male and female, to commute for urban jobs.

Since the mid-1970s, the Gulf migration of middle-educated women as nurses and domestics has served as an outlet for this underutilized pool of female labor in households that are poor, but not poor enough to have the women do the very low-wage menial jobs. That outlet was limited except for certain communities, and it has narrowed. It is now being outpaced by the option of working in export-processing zones, in electronics assembly and garment workshops, and in piece-wage contract homework in nontraditional industries, many of which also produce for the home market.

Reproductive Role and Employment Options as Determinants of Women's Work Patterns

Because of their housework and child-care responsibilities, women between 15 and 29 years of age often cannot work for wages away from home. Women's reported work participation goes up with the household asset base (land, livestock) since these assets provide the possibility for self-employment (Sundaram 1988). However, it is not that women in this age group in poor households do not work, merely that this work has low return in the absence of productive assets or of local job options.

This topic has been examined with data from the recent rounds of the Indian National Sample Survey (Sen and Sen 1985; P. Bardhan 1984). Within the large group of women classified as nonworkers (usual status), they distinguish between those usually doing just housework and those doing housework in combination with gathering fuel, fodder, and food and generating subsistence and maintenance uses. The incidence of the latter is lower in the states with higher incidence of landlessness, larger in the case of smallholders, and also systematically larger for young women aged 15 to 29. The data further indicate that the extent of these activities drops above the lowest landholding size and per capita consumption groups, and drops during the peak season, when labor markets are tighter and conventional employment options better.

The relative disadvantage of the female poor as self-employed producers, and especially in the labor market, is partly caused by poorer educational access and attainment (Table 6.13), and by cultural

Table 6.13 Sex Disparities in the Incidence of Education, South Asia

	Bangladesh	India	Nepal	Pakistan	Sri Lanka
A. Female percentage by education level: *1986*					
Primary	40	39	29	33	48
Secondary	31	32	23	28	52
B. Female percentage in total enrollment: *1980*					
First level	37	39	20	26	48
Second level	21	32	16	20	51
Third level	14	26	19	26	43
C. Percentage of age group enrolled by sex and school level: *1986*					
Primary level					
Female	50	76	47	32	102
Male	69	107	104	55	104
Secondary level					
Female	11	24	11	10	70
Male	24	45	35	25	63
D. Female literacy rate % (15 + years)					
1985	22	29	12	19	83

Sources: For items A, C, D, *World Development Report, 1989,* Appendix Tables 29, 32; 1990, Table 1. For item B, UNESCO (1985).

norms of dependency that inhibit women's ownership of income-yielding assets including marketable skills. It is partly caused by their worse access to organizational assets (collective bargaining, institutional credit, and productive infrastructure). In hard times, they are consequently forced into the low end of the labor market and in low-return subsistence work.

Improvement in the employment status of women relative to men (not only in terms of regularity and better wages, but better access to production credit and other inputs, and infrastructure that raises labor productivity in the customary female chores) may yield higher private returns as well as social returns in terms of nutritional improvement, investment in children's health and education, and decline in fertility. Economic growth does reduce the sex gaps in wage and employment intensity by tightening the labor market in agricultural slack seasons (K. Bardhan 1984). A number of factors, however, work against parity gain for female earners.

Quite a bit is known about the ways in which policy can ease the disadvantages facing women. Improved access to potable water and cooking fuel, local availability of slack-season work, and on-site child care for female wage-laborers are some of the things that can reduce female and juvenile workloads and help raise school enrollment and completion for girls, particularly from poor and disadvantaged communities. Extension services and public infrastructure and inputs can be made more accessible to women. Lack of land collateral as an obstacle to enterprise credit can be successfully overcome with peer-monitored group loans and with the help of nongovernmental organizations. Landholding disparity can be remedied partially by deliberate targeting of nonland asset distribution, like loans for animal husbandry, and by improving access to facilities like training programs for working women's organizations. Incentives can be given to firms to locate suitably, recruit and provide job training for young women from low-income communities, especially those affected by technological change and environmental depletion. There are several working examples of each of these.[3] However, these are still

---

3. In inventive forms of enterprise credit and input access for women, notable examples include: Grameen Bank, Self-Employed Women's Organization (SEWA), Working Women's Forum, Andhra Pradesh Women's Dairy Cooperatives. In job-

exceptions. Most existing programs generate little or relatively limited female access to training and employment, focus on males in most major programs for distribution of nonland assets for self-employment, and do not provide adequate amounts of coordinated inputs and know-how to sustain asset-poor women in viable self-employment.

Scale and Labor-Intensity in the New Industrial Division of Labor

Women workers in South Asia have tended to be employed predominantly in the informal sector. This part looks at the reasons for this pattern as well as some of the changes that are occurring with the shift of women's labor into growing export industries, and the increase in women's share of public sector employment. In India, labor laws and government policies of product reservation and subsidies for small-scale units have had certain (unintended) effects on women workers. Part of the proliferation of small units has been engineered by large companies in order to avoid (or deactivate) labor unions, evade the labor laws, and take advantage of the subsidies or tax breaks available for small units. A few of them became female-labor intensive in the process, but most reduced the number of organized female factory workers. This process has been accentuated by the existence of labor laws that were intended to benefit women, but ended up depressing the hiring of them. The female percentage of employment in the private organized sectors declined in India over the 1960s and 1970s.

More generally in South Asia, many industries oriented to domestic and/or export markets are vertically integrated structures of small units

---

training for needy young women, notable examples are: Ganosasthya Kendro, Bangladesh Rural Advancement Committee, SEWA. Examples of effective child care for low-wage laborer-mothers are India's mobile creche at public construction sites, low-cost schooling-cum-child-care organized at the community level in Bangkok's Klong Toey slums. Local provision of counter-seasonal employment through public works has invariably been utilized by the female land-poor, the most successful being Maharashtra's EGS in which the female share of employment is about half. Fish processing plants in Kerala have successfully hired young women from the fishing communities affected, while also setting up the basic facilities (tap water, transportation, electricity) for the communities.

that tap the scattered pools of cheap, unskilled or semiskilled female labor, who are less able to work in factories for reproductive or cultural reasons. Some of the industries are traditional (bidi, coir, lace, pickles, toys, sporting goods) and some are nontraditional. They all use combinations of home-based and workshop-based piecewage contract. Women get the employment, although at much less than the factory wage. The mutual benefits to the manufacturers and to groups of asset-poor women help keep the piecewage homework going. A more serious consequence of piecewage contract work is the inducement it offers to use child labor as helpers, thus hampering their school attendance and performance.

Interestingly, a number of feminist unions have risen successfully among small producers, traders, and certain sections of casual employees in the informal sectors, among women who have been at the work for years as earners of family subsistence. This has been happening at a time when new large export-processing and other manufacturing units are hiring young women on a temporary basis, and the mainstream unions in older factories have let the women workers' interests go. What is relevant for poverty alleviation and labor market adjustment is that the winners and the losers are often in different sets of families, from different socioeconomic backgrounds, and facing different needs and pressures.

Some demand has been voiced in recent years for protective legislation for contract workers and some attempts made at organizing them to this end. Case studies of piecewage homework structures have noted a variety of factors favoring their growth (Singh and Kelles-Viitanen 1987). In some cases, either sociocultural factors or the constraints of reproductive labor, or both favor piecewage homework from the labor supply side. In others, the extent to which piecewage homework is used is determined as a management question of saving supervision costs and wages. In still other cases, it is aimed at demobilizing or preventing trade unions. The ranks of piecewage workers in sweatshops and at home are likely to continue to grow. At the same time, attempts will continue to be made at organization for bargaining the terms and conditions.

The number of women laborers in the urban informal-sector has increased further in recent decades, though not just in India. At the same time there has been a rising female proportion of agricultural and construction laborers and piecewage homeworkers. More or less all over South Asia the private-sector economic growth process is being driven by a massive casual labor force, largely female, topped by a thin layer, largely male, of managerial and marketing personnel. As Schultz (1990, p. 481) has noted, given the gender asymmetry in union voice, "women are the main group that loses ground due to labor-market regulations in low-income countries. These may slow the transition of women from nonmarket to family-(based) market work and from family to firm employment, with consequences on the rate and structure of economic growth."

Only a quarter of the urban female work force in India in 1983 was made up of regular employees compared with nearly half of the male urban work force (Table 6.14). Three-tenths of all urban female workers (and half of urban female employees) were casual laborers compared with one-seventh of the male workers (and one-quarter of the male employees). Of the increasingly stratified labor markets, the lower tier has rapidly expanded to absorb the influx of female

Table 6.14 Distribution of Usual-Status Work Force (≥5 Years) by Mode of Employment, India 1972-73 and 1983

Worker/Year	Self(family-) employed	Casual employees	Regular employees	All workers
Rural Female				
1972-73	65	31	4	100
1983	62	35	3	100
Rural Male				
1972-73	66	22	12	100
1983	60	29	10	100
Urban Female				
1972-73	48	24	28	100
1983	46	28	26	100
Urban Male				
1972-73	39	10	51	100
1983	41	15	44	100

Source: *Sarvekshana*, April 1988, p. 39. Principal and subsidiary employment status.

labor, economically pressed and having limited options with lesser command over marketable skills. By and large, female participation at the low end of the informal sectors has tended to be of longer duration than male participations, even when the socioeconomic background of the men and women is similar.

Because the sex gap in wage rate is often wider in the unorganized sectors than in the organized sectors, the sex gap in earnings is possibly greater than what is indicated by the gap in the formal-informal distribution of employment. In South Asia, there is a cultural perception that women's earnings and education are primarily a means to further family goals. Under conditions of economic pressure, this is conducive to downward adjustment of women's work quality (in terms of wages, conditions, equipment, regularity, and scope for promotion). In poor households there may be adverse effects intergenerationally as daughters are recruited earlier as helpers in mothers' multiple duties, and thus attain less education.

A recent shift that has affected industrial hiring by age and sex is the tax incentives given to export industries, and the exemption of export processing zones from labor laws, inducing the past decade's growth in temporary hiring of young women for easy-to-train assembly operations. This has promoted a resurgence of large-scale units without organized labor, delinking large workplaces from the labor movement, in various combinations of preindustrial and postindustrial characteristics.

Since the early 1970s, electronics (an export industry heavily provided with incentives) has been a fast-growing employer of female first-timers in the labor markets in the ASEAN (Association of South-East Asian Nations) countries (Fong 1988). In South Asia and parts of Southeast Asia, textiles and garments (industries provided with fewer incentives and more oriented to domestic market) have grown, also heavily using mostly young women in factories, workshops, and contract homework. The phenomenal expansion of female-labor-based export processing of garments, electrical and electronic equipment, leather goods, and even cash crop growing has been taking place (more in Southeast than in South Asia) through subcontracting by corporations headquartered in the West and in Japan. This "new international division of labor" has been viewed with concern as a problem for organizing the industrial work force for negotiating the terms and the working conditions, particularly at the lower levels of the subcontract ladder (Pineda-Ofreneo 1988). Although home-based contract work has been increasing in both industrial and developing countries, in the former it is linked with home computers, whereas in the latter it spans a wide range of traditional and modern low-skill processes, and it has exploitative features. Although the boom in textiles and garments generates the much-needed employment and growth impetus, one can see why there is and will be a need for some degree of self-organization of the workers involved, especially in the case of workers at home and in workshops, and temporary employees, to improve their work conditions.

Government sectors and public services comprise by far the biggest employer in South Asia,[4] to some extent also of unskilled/uneducated labor, both male and female, particularly in public construction. The public (production and service) sectors' share in the economically active population has increased with particular rapidity in South Asia, with the shares of state and lower levels of local government particularly large in federally structured countries like India with a great many district-level development programs (ILO 1988, table 14). The female share in public sector employment in India in 1985 was 11 percent, while the female share of economically active population was 26 percent, a gap much larger than in Brazil, due perhaps to India's lower incidence of higher education, and fewer industrial and business opportunities for educated men (ILO 1988, table 17). However, the female percentage of educated public employees is higher than in the private organized sectors, and it has risen steadily with shrinking gender-disparity in higher education in South Asia, a trend likely to grow. Public sectors also employ many on a temporary and contractual basis, mostly in low-wage low-skill casual work in public construction and afforestation projects, some of which have large and increasing female proportions.

---

4. Public-sector employees are mostly in postal and telecommunication services (telephone, radio, television, railways and airways, and other public transport), health and medical services, water, gas and electricity supply services, teachers in school, colleges and universities, extension and training services, public construction, public production sectors, apart from administrative offices, planning bodies and the military. Many of these are unionized, especially in India.

Thus, the performance of the two major sectors of growing employment of more or less educated young women—the new semiskilled manufacturing and services in the private sector and the government and semigovernment services—from the standpoints of both equity and efficiency will depend largely upon the pace of expansion of girls' schooling particularly among the rural groups poorer in income and assets. In Sri Lanka, Kerala, Thailand, and Central and East Java, where the incidence of girls' schooling has been very high among the rural poor in the past ten years, so that the secondary or higher educated proportion is high among their young women, the expected growth of these two sectors is more likely to benefit them directly and contribute to both equity and efficiency. In most other cases, the direct and immediate beneficiaries will be from among the affluent farmer families and the urban middle classes, generating at best some indirect trickle-down effects for the rest.

In view of the history of counterproductivity of legislative intervention, India's recent deregulation in electronics and computer software industries—lifting restrictions on entry and enterprise growth, eliminating reservation for small-scale units in the production of certain electronic components in the presence of economies of scale, and rapid expansion of manpower training programs—seems likely to expand employment in these "sunrise sectors" and to make for better sex parity among employees.

While selective deregulation is a step in the right direction in terms of allowing reduction of sex disparity of workers in a few large-scale manufacturing units, it may not be correct to assume that most of the structural biases working against poor women would be automatically eliminated by the market mechanism and a growth spurt. The evidence from the freer-market cases in Southeast Asia and from the emerging evidence in the garments industry and similar vertically integrated industries in South Asia is mixed at best in this respect.

Conclusions

Demographic factors must be considered when examining structural adjustment processes in South Asia. Aside from the general contractionary effect and growth of labor force, demographic shifts affect the household labor allocation processes by age and sex via opportunity access differences.

Labor-market participation data do not cover women's nonmarket work, and hence understate some of the welfare costs entailed in economic adjustments via the impact on women's time.

The market-nonmarket ratio of work varies more for women than for men in response to cost-of-living increases, differences in local economic environment, and in local availability of social services and public infrastructure. Rural areas poor in growth environment tend to produce excessive loads of low-return work for asset-poor women and girls, both within and outside the labor market, with adverse consequences for health, nutrition, and education. The lack of basic infrastructure and the deterioration of the commons have generated additional low-return workloads in gathering and processing subsistence.

However, the new industries generated by recent deregulation and export promotion policies have offered opportunities for women with primary to secondary education. In South Asia, female labor-market participation has tended to be high at the two ends of the socioeconomic and educational scale—namely, for illiterate women of poor families and for highly educated women. The dip in the primary-to-secondary range derives in part from local scarcity of options for young women with middle levels of education. Growth of manufacturing sectors intensive in female labor with primary and secondary schooling is likely to level out this dip.

Several other changes are likely to occur in this process. The age distribution of female workers is likely to shift more than for male workers. Growth of jobs for semi-educated young women is likely to provide an incentive for girls' schooling in low-income families and also for delaying of marriage and first childbirth. The social and demographic benefits of these changes are obvious.

References

Acharya, S. 1990. *The Maharashtra Employment Guarantee Scheme: A Study of Labour-Market Intervention.* ILO/ARTEP working paper. May.

Banerjee, N. 1989. "Trends in Women's Employment, 1971-81: Some Macro-Level Observations." *Economic and Political Weekly.* Women Studies Issue, April 29.

Bardhan, K. 1990. "Women and Rural Poverty in Some Asian Countries." Unpublished paper for the Asian Development Bank Project on Rural Poverty. October.

————. 1984. "Work Patterns and Social Differentiation: Rural Women of West Bengal." In H.P. Binswanger and M.R. Rosenzweig, eds., *Contractual Arrangements, Employment, and Wages in Rural Labor Markets in Asia.* New Haven: Yale University Press.

————. 1989. "Poverty, Growth and Rural Labour Markets in India." *Economic and Political Weekly.* March 25.

Bardhan, P. 1984. *Land, Labor and Rural Poverty.* Oxford, Delhi: Oxford University Press.

Edwards, S., and A. Edwards. 1990. "Labor Market Distortions and Structural Adjustment in Developing Countries." NBER Working Paper 3346. Paper presented at the Warwick-EDI Conference on Labor Markets in an ERA of Adjustment, Warwick, England, May 21-24.

Fong, P.E., ed. 1988. *Labour Market Developments and Structural Change: The Experience of ASEAN and Australia.* Singapore University Press.

Funkhouser, E. 1990. "Mass Migration, Remittances, and Economic Adjustment: The Case of El Salvador in the 1980s." Paper presented at the NBER Conference on Immigration. Cancun, Mexico. January.

Garcia, I. and E. Gomariz, 1989. *Mujeres Centroamericanas.* Tomo I San Jose: FLACSO.

Garnsey, E., and L. Paukert. 1987. *Industrial Change and Women's Employment: Trends in the New International Division of Labour.* ILO Research Series Study No. 86.

Gindling, T.H. 1990. "Women's Earnings and the Economic Crisis in Costa Rica." North-East Development Economics

Conference. Economic Growth Center, Yale University, May 12.

Greenhalgh, S. 1985. "Sexual Stratification: The Other Side of 'Growth with Equity' in East Asia." *Population and Development Review*, vol. 11, no. 2, June.

Grown, C. A., ed. 1989. "Beyond Survival: Expanding Income-Earning Opportunities for Women in Developing Countries." *World Development*, vol. 17, no. 7, July.

Horton, S. 1990. "Labor Markets in an Era of Adjustment: bolivia." Paper presented at the EDI-Warwick Conference on Labor Markets in an Era of Adjustment, Warwick, England, May 21-24.

ILO (International Labor Organization). Various years. *Yearbook of Labor Statistics*. Geneva: ILO.

ILO. 1986. *Economically Active Population Estimates and Projections, 1950-2025.*

———. 1987. *World Labour Report--Incomes from Work: Between Equity and Efficiency,* no. 3. Geneva.

Little, I. M. D., D. Mazumdar, and J. M. Page Jr. 1987. *Small Manufacturing Enterprises: A Comparative Study of India and other Economies.* A World Bank Publication. Oxford University Press.

Mitra, Asok. 1980. *India's Population: Aspects of Quality and Control.* Delhi: Concept Publishing Co.

Ocampo, J.A., and M. Ramirez. 1987. *El problema laboral colombinao: informes de la mision,* Chenery, vol. 1 and vol. 2. Bogota, Government of Colombia, Department of Planning.

Pardo, L. 1989. "Una Interpretación de la Evidencia en la Participación de las Mujeres en la Furza de Trabajo: Gran Santiago, 1957-1987." *Estudios de Economia,* vol. 16, no. 2, November, pp. 319-346.

Pineda-Ofreneo, R. 1988. "Philippine Domestic Outwork: Subcontracting for Export-Oriented Industries." In J.G.

Taylor and A. Turton, eds., *Sociology of Developing Societies: Southeast Asia.* London: Monthly Review Press.

Schultz, T.P. 1990. "Women's Changing Participation in the Labor Force: A World Perspective." *Economic Development and Cultural Change.*

Schultz, T.P. 1990. "Women's Changing Participation in the Labor Force: A World Perspective." *Economic Development and Cultural Change,* vol. 38, no. 3, April.

Sedlacek, G. 1990. "Estrategias de Geracao de renda das familias Brasileiras: Um Estudo da participacao da mulher no mercado de trabalho." IPEA.

Sen, C., and G. Sen. 1985. "Women's Domestic Work and Economic Activity." *Economic and Political Weekly,* Women Studies Issue, April 27, WS 49-54.

Singh, A. Menefee, and A. Kelles-Viitanen, eds. 1987. *Invisible Hands: Women in Home-Based Production.* New Delhi: Sage Publications.

Standing, G. 1989. "Global Feminization through Flexible Labor." *World Development.* vol. 17, no. 7, pp. 1077-1095/

Sundaram, K. 1988. *Inter-State Variations in Work-Force Participation Rates of Women in India.* ILO/ARTEP Studies on Women Workers, No. 1. New Delhi.

UNESCO. 1985. *Towards Equality of Educational Opportunity: A Statistical Review.* Bangkok: UNESCO Regional Office for Development of Education in Asia and the Pacific.

————. 1988. *Report of the Asian Regional Seminar on Access of Girls to Primary Education, 1979.*

United Nations. 1988. *World Demographic Estimates and Projections, 1950-2025.* Report prepared jointly by the UN, the ILO and the FAO.

Uthoff, A., and M. Pollack. 1985. "Análisis Microeconomico del Ajuste del Mercado de Trabajo. Costa Rica 1979-82: Lecciones para un modelo macroeconomico." *Estudios de Economía* v.12, no.2: 83-111. Septiembre.

World Bank. 1989. *Social Indicators of Development*: *Data on Diskette.* Washington, D.C.: World Bank.

World Bank. Various years. *World Development Report.* Oxford University Press.

7

ORGANIZED LABOR, POLITICS, AND LABOR MARKET FLEXIBILITY IN DEVELOPING COUNTRIES

Joan M. Nelson

Organized labor is usually viewed as an obstacle to labor market adjustment. In fact, unions' responses to adjustment programs range from militant opposition to acquiescence or even explicit cooperation. Three sets of variables shape these responses: the strength and characteristics of the union movement itself, economic cycles, and political institutions and their ties to unions.

- *Strength of the labor movement.* In industrial democracies, an aggressive stance on wages tends to be associated with moderately strong unions. Small or weak unions are less militant, as might be expected; more surprisingly, large and powerful unions also tend to be more moderate, primarily because of their greater participation in consultation and decisionmaking at the national level. The experience in developing countries is somewhat different. Only a few developing countries have strong labor movements, and among them militancy is common. The large share of wage labor in the public sector complicates comparisons with industrial nations since governments as employers behave differently from private employers, particularly in hard times.
- *Economic cycles.* Depression almost invariably reduces militancy in developing nations as well as industrial nations.

- *Political institutions.* The nature of the political regime—democratic or authoritarian—is only roughly associated with how it handles labor relations, and correspondingly with the options available to unions. More important in shaping unions' behavior are political parties and how unions are connected with them. The conditions needed to gain workers' cooperation are analogous to those that encourage business to invest: political stability, a voice in policy that affects their interests, and, arising from these, the confidence that current sacrifices will ultimately yield a fair share of future benefits.

In developing as in industrial countries, the probable responses of unions are crucial to government decisions about wages, prices, and employment. Organized labor is usually seen as a potential obstacle to labor market adjustment, a source of rigidities impeding shifts in relative wages and reallocation of labor among sectors, and a center of resistance to stabilization measures that entail compression of demand. Yet in some countries, labor confederations have cooperated with the government and private employers to facilitate adjustment. What makes organized labor confront or cooperate, and what empowers it to slow or stall attempts to increase labor market flexibility? What political circumstances and approaches have persuaded organized labor to acquiesce in such attempts in the past?

Both theory and evidence on these questions are fragmentary. Partly because of poor data, much of the literature on organized labor in developing nations is too descriptive and narrowly focused to provide an adequate basis for comparative analysis. Most of the analytic and comparative research appropriate for the purpose is based on experience in industrial democracies. This chapter therefore reviews key findings from research on industrial countries and considers the extent to which they are relevant to developing nations. The focus is on two categories of variables that affect labor militancy; first, the size, strength, and structure of the union movement itself; second, the economic cycle. The discussion then turns to how political institutions and stability shape union behavior.

Union Structure and Union Militancy

Classic theory assumes that the free play of market forces will ensure flexibility in labor markets and that decentralized wage bargaining should restrain wage increases. Conversely, one expects strong unions and centralized wage bargaining to be associated with comparatively rapid growth of real wages in the organized sectors and with relatively high unemployment. Indeed, one influential line of analysis argues that over time, powerful organized interest groups (including but not confined to labor unions) may lead to such rigidities, such inability to adapt to changing circumstances, as to cause the decline of great powers (Olson 1982).

Evidence from Industrial Democracies

Recent research on labor movements in advanced industrial democracies calls into question these assumptions. This research finds that during the 1960s and 1970s countries with large, highly centralized union movements tended to experience low wage push, low unemployment, and low inflation.[1] Moreover, strike activity (as a measure of union militancy) was negatively correlated with strong labor movements and highly centralized wage bargaining. Using data from 1965 through the early 1980s, Cameron (1984) developed five indices of the power of organized labor in 18 industrial nations. The indices measured union membership relative to total labor force, concentration or fragmentation of union confederations, their power in collective bargaining, the scope of such bargaining, and the extent of arrangements for worker participation in decisions at the firm level (such as works councils and worker representation on company boards). Cameron found that each of these indices correlated negatively with strike activity, levels of unemployment, increases in both nominal and real earnings, and consumer prices between 1965 and 1982. Some of the correlations—with the organizational unity of labor and workers' participation in decisions in particular—were strong (Cameron 1984, Table 7.7).

---

1. Wage push is inflationary pressure largely generated by a pattern of increases in real wages outstripping increases in productivity.

More recent studies suggest that the relationship between centralized wage bargaining and militant wage demands may be humpbacked (shaped like an inverted U) rather than monotonic (decreasing steadily). Wage push is least evident where bargaining is highly decentralized (conducted largely at the level of individual firms), *and* where it is highly centralized; wage pressures seem strongest where bargaining is moderately centralized (at the sector or industry level). Calmfors and Driffill (1988, pp. 17-24) find a humpbacked relation between centralization—defined as "the extent of inter-union and inter-employer cooperation in wage bargaining with the other side"—and several indices of employment and inflation. Freeman (1988) uses the degree of wage dispersion across industries as a strong indicator of market structure. He finds that countries with very high or very low dispersion (usually the countries with highly centralized or highly decentralized bargaining in their labor markets) have increased employment more rapidly and wages less rapidly than have countries with intermediate degrees of centralization.

What mechanisms are at work here? Two different explanations are offered for these empirical findings. Calmfors and Driffill see shifts in incentives (rational expectations about gains and losses) as the principal impetus for intransigence in negotiations, depending on the degree to which wage bargaining is centralized. When bargaining is conducted at the firm level, unions have little market power. An increase in wages is likely to bring a large drop in employment because the isolated firm cannot raise output prices and remain competitive. The market power of unions increases if wage bargaining is conducted at the industry or sector level. But as the centralization of wage bargaining increases, greater power must be balanced against greater risk that wage gains will affect price levels, thus eroding the real value of nominal wage hikes. Increased centralization on the union side of the negotiating table usually goes along with correspondingly increased centralization on the employer side, and employers also face shifting incentives for resisting or accommodating union demands at different levels of aggregation. The outcome is a nonmonotonic or humpbacked relation between increased centralization and labor militancy: unions have the strongest incentives to bargain aggressively at intermediate levels of centralization.

An alternative explanation rests on the theory of democratic corporatist arrangements for determining wages and on broad social policies developed in the 1970s and 1980s mainly with reference to Western and Northern European nations. This use of the term *corporatist* may call for explanation. The same term often refers to political systems, including those in Latin America during the 1970s, in which relations between unions and governments are entirely different from those described in the following. Nevertheless, this is the label usually used to refer to the pattern of labor market arrangements discussed here, and I have followed this usage rather than compounding confusion by inventing a new label.[2]

Even when the concept of corporatism is used narrowly with reference to labor market arrangements, definitions and interpretations of its implications vary. Four characteristics, however, are common to most of the competing versions. First, in a corporatist system, each major interest in society is represented by one or a few central, or peak, associations (in the case of labor, confederations). Second, these associations include as members most of the relevant groups and individuals; in the case of labor, most of the labor force is unionized, and most or all unions belong to the peak confederations. Third, the peak associations have considerable control over their constituent organizations, and these in turn have considerable influence over their individual members. Fourth, peak association officials participate actively in government decisions affecting their constituents' interests. The arrangements for participation vary from country to country, but they entail discussion and bargaining among associations representing various interests and the state.

For labor, such arrangements mean that unions have sufficient economic and political muscle to encourage their incorporation into national decisionmaking circles. (They may have gained this strength historically, by gradual growth of unions and federations, or the government may have directly aided the growth of unions as part of

---

2. For an excellent brief discussion of democratic corporatism and its contrast with other meanings of the term *corporatism,* see Katzenstein (1985, pp. 30-37).

an elite strategy to preempt more radical influences.) Wage restraint and acquiescence in adjustment are a response to generous social security and welfare arrangements that buffer workers against the vicissitudes of adjustment and exchange the immediate advantage of a pay increase for employment security and a variety of longer term benefits.

At the same time, top labor leaders in a strong corporatist system have the authority within the unions to ensure that the rank and file will accept agreements made by the national elite. And discussion and bargaining with other decisionmakers lead labor leaders to recognize national interests that constrain pursuit of labor's narrow or short-term interests. (More radical interpretations would argue that not only rational persuasion, but also co-option—the desire to keep the material benefits and status of associating with the national elite—is a principal incentive to cooperate in such a case.) Recognition of broader national interests encourages acquiescence in policies of wage restraint to promote national economic stability and growth and thereby sustained employment and gradually rising real wages. Negotiating wage agreements at the national level also means that individual unions have less scope and need to worry about losses relative to other unions.[3]

In several of the smaller Northern and Western European nations, labor's cooperation with broader economic policies reflects the clear recognition that nations that are highly dependent on trade must maintain international competitiveness (Katzenstein 1985). Consider the case of Belgium. From February to March of 1982, labor agreed to skip an automatic indexed increase in wages following devaluation and to replace later indexed rounds with lower lump-sum wage adjustments to reach an agreed degree of deindexation. Further real wage increases were banned through 1984 and thereafter regulated by a norm of competitiveness taking into account the weighted average of

---

3. This description of corporatist arrangements for labor policies is, of course, stylized. Institutional arrangements, policies, and economic outcomes vary among the nations usually described as fitting the model, especially the Scandinavian nations, Austria, Belgium, the Netherlands, and Switzerland. Within specific countries, the approach has been more effective at some times than at others. For example, Sweden is often taken as the epitome of effective corporatist arrangements of this kind, yet recent trends in Sweden suggest that the model is no longer working very well.

Belgium's seven most important trade partners (Theo Peters in Williamson 1985, p. 99).

Virtually no developing country approximates the labor organization and wage negotiation arrangements of the corporatist model, but the principles that make the model work are useful in understanding problems of labor relations and labor market reform in developing nations. They also may suggest broad guidelines for improved labor relations. In essence, corporatist institutions affect the range of information and options available to all parties in the negotiations and thereby alter incentive structures. More specifically, they (1) broaden the options under negotiation to include a wide range of social policies along with wage and nonwage compensation; (2) lengthen time horizons, largely by increasing confidence in government economic management and in labor's continued access to decisions affecting its interests; and (3) increase the sophistication and complexity of economic implications taken into consideration by union, business, and government representatives.

Corporatist labor market arrangements cannot be replicated in most developing nations because the structure of labor markets and the larger economy bears no resemblance to the usually small industrial democracies in which these arrangements have evolved and because the arrangements have grown out of historical features quite unlike those of most developing nations. Moreover, most developing nations cannot afford the employment benefits and other social benefits that are key elements in the corporatist bargain. Indeed, in some developing countries the attempt to provide organized workers—a relatively small fraction of the labor force—with generous benefits modeled on those of industrial nations has exacerbated economic difficulties and social tensions.

For all these reasons the corporatist model is not a practical blueprint for emulation, though there may be a few developing countries that could evolve along these lines. Rather, it is a heuristic model that elucidates some of the mechanisms and relations that have helped certain nations channel the self-interest of a sizable and well-organized interest group in ways compatible with broader national interests. Where similar arrangements are unlikely to emerge, functional equivalents are needed—institutions, procedures, and policies that broaden the array of options, lengthen time horizons, and increase the sophistication of all key actors in labor markets.

Applicability of the Evidence to Developing Countries

Virtually no developing country replicates the features at the prototypical strong corporatist system with respect to labor. In many of the countries of Northern and Western Europe, unions claim as members two-thirds or more of the work force. Reliable and comparable data on union membership are missing for most developing countries, but those for which data are available suggest a span ranging downward from about a third of the labor force. In the mid-1980s Argentine and Venezuelan unions claimed about a third of the labor force, Jamaican unions a quarter, and Mexican unions a fifth.[4] Outside Latin America, save for Mauritius and Sri Lanka (both with roughly a third of the labor force unionized), union membership is much lower.

Some of the most industrialized (and rapidly industrializing) developing countries, above all the East Asian "tigers," have repressed union movements. Even the comparatively large union movements in some Latin American countries do not usually have the additional characteristics of strong centralized movements. In Brazil and Mexico, for example, rivalries among confederations are strong. The power of Mexico's largest confederation, the Confederation of Mexican Workers, is reduced, quite aside from the effects of aging leadership, by its structure: average union size is small (about 130 members), and less than half of the confederation's members are in powerful industrial unions such as railroads, petroleum, or mining. Nearly half are in enterprise-level unions, which are, in turn, parts of

---

4. The most extensive data on union members as a proportion of the labor force are found in Taylor and Jodice (1983) and the U.S. CIA (1989), but the former is now dated (referring to the mid-1970s), and some of the data from the latter are startlingly out of line with other sources. For example, U.S. CIA (1989) gives Mexican union membership as 35 percent of the work force, compared with Middlebrook's (1989) figure for 1979 of 16.3 percent and George Grayson's estimate (given at a conference on Mexican trade unions at the Overseas Development Council in 1989) for the late 1980s of 20 percent. Recent data for many countries are also available in the periodic U.S. embassy reports for individual countries (U.S. Department of Labor various years); this source is the main basis for the estimates in the text for Argentina, Jamaica, and Venezuela.

functionally diverse, regionally based federations. The Confederation of Mexican Workers must often compete with rival confederations active in the same geographic areas, and the government can manipulate these rivalries to undermine the confederation, as the government of Miguel de la Madrid did in 1983. Therefore, it is extremely difficult to coordinate labor action within an industry. Mexican unions rarely have strong representation, such as works councils, at the enterprise level (Middlebrook 1989, pp. 209-217). Similar weaknesses plague labor movements in many other countries. In short, few if any developing countries have labor movements able to play their side of the corporatist strategy in labor market policies.

If data were adequate to develop indices of union strength and centralization of wage bargaining for most developing nations, virtually all would fall in the low and moderate segments of a global scale arraying labor movements from weakest and least centralized to strongest and most centralized. (These dimensions do not necessarily covary neatly.) Classic liberal expectations as well as the forecasts of recent proponents of a humpbacked relationship based on the experience of industrial nations predict little militancy and wage push at the low end of this scale and greater militancy and wage push toward the center.[5] Evidence from developing countries accords with these expectations.

Walton and Ragin (1988, Table 10.3) found a strong correlation between the proportion of the labor force in unions (as of 1975) and the severity of protests against austerity between 1976 and 1987 in 26 countries in Latin America, Africa, and Asia. In many developing nations, labor movements are not only a small part of the labor force but are also weak and fragmented. Strikes (especially wildcat strikes) may be quite frequent, but they are likely to involve few workers and

---

5. A literal interpretation of the corporatist approach would not predict this outcome. But the corporatist line of explanation for unions and wage determination has concentrated on what was going on in the industrial democracies with very high degrees of centralization, and it has paid little attention to the range of incentives and strategies guiding union behavior where wage setting is decentralized. Had the focus been more on the decentralized cases (and, even more likely, had it been on developing-country cases), the assumed monotonic links among decentralization, labor militancy, and wage push might have been modified. It seems self-evident that very small and scattered unions are not likely to exercise effective wage push, and plausible that they will be only sporadically and briefly militant.

have little effect on broader wage levels. Unions in some developing countries, however, are strong enough to exercise considerable wage push in particular sectors or industries. Unions in strategic sectors may exercise tremendous economic and political leverage, even if the labor movement for the nation as a whole is not strong. Copper miners in Chile and Zambia, tin miners in Bolivia, oil workers in Mexico, Nigeria, Venezuela, and other countries, and, to a lesser degree, bauxite and alumina workers in Jamaica have been in a position to throttle a large fraction of national export earnings and government revenue. They have often used their leverage to maintain wages markedly out of line with the rest of the economy, with a variety of distorting effects on the industry and the economy as a whole.

In Mexico, despite the pattern of incorporation of Mexican labor confederations, especially the Confederation of Mexican Workers, their exclusion from economic decisions under the de la Madrid government, and their inability to block massive drops in real wages, certain Mexican unions were able to halt government reforms. For instance, the powerful petroleum union used threats of sabotage and massive resistance to force the government to back down on its plans to eliminate the union's control over subcontracting as part of a rationalization scheme. In a few developing countries with sizable industrial sectors, including several Latin American nations, Turkey, and Tunisia, not merely unions in strategic industries but labor movements more generally have periodically been militant, wielding considerable economic and political clout. In the framework of theories based on industrial democracies, these countries fall somewhere in the central range of the scale linking centralization to militancy and wage push: their militant behavior conforms with the hypothesis of a humpbacked relation.

A further characteristic of unions in developing countries may encourage a tendency toward militancy. The corporatist theories and Calmfors and Driffill's theory of union bargaining strategies implicitly assume that the unions have considerable analytic capacity to assess the implications for labor of current economic trends and alternative wage settlements. Few industry-level unions or national confederations in developing countries have economic staffs comparable to those in Western European countries. Moreover, available data are often unreliable, and analysis and forecasting are particularly difficult when inflation and other aspects of economic performance are highly volatile. The result may be to increase uncertainty and risk associated with wage restraint and reduce the attractiveness of trading off wage increases for social welfare benefits.[6]

The structure of labor movements in developing countries and in industrial democracies differs in another way: more of the labor force is in public service jobs in developing countries (see Table 7.1). At the end of the 1970s, in several African nations public sector workers made up 60 to 80 percent of nonagricultural workers; in India the figure was 72 percent (Heller and Tait 1984, Table 22).

The high proportion of wage labor in the public sector means that the sector's wage and employment policies are important both in their own right and also because of spillover effects into the private sector.

Table 7.1 Public Sector Workers as a Percentage of Nonagricultural Employment

| Category of countries | Number of countries[a] | Type of public employment | | | |
		Central government	State and local government	Nonfinancial public enterprise	Total public employment
OECD	16	8.7	11.6	4.1	24.2
Developing countries[b]	35	23.4	4.0	13.9	43.9
Africa	16	30.8	2.1	18.7	54.4
Asia	5	13.9	8.0	15.7	36.0
Latin America	10	20.7	4.2	5.5	27.4

OECD, Organization for Economic Cooperation and Development.
Note: Data are from 1979 or 1980.
a. The number for which data were available on central government employment. Not all countries had data for each category of workers. The number of observations therefore varies somewhat within each country category for different items.
b. Includes data for a few countries in the Middle East.
Source: Adapted from Heller and Tait (1984, Table 1).

6. This point was suggested by Kevin J. Middlebrook in correspondence with the author.

Heller and Tait (1984, p. 35) estimated that "central government decisions on wages and salaries in developing countries are likely to affect 15 to 40 percent of employed workers in the urban labor market and therefore have a pervasive 'leverage' effect on domestic unit wage costs."

How do large public sectors affect wage push and employment flexibility? The topic is little studied. Two questions are central. Are public sector unions intrinsically weaker (or stronger) than their private counterparts? And does government, in its role as employer, operate with different goals and constraints than do private employers? The answer to the first question is ambiguous. The answer to the second is clearly affirmative.

Public sector workers in industrial societies are often assumed to be in a weaker position to exert wage pressure that are private sector workers. Historically, they have often been restricted from forming unions. Even where employees' associations are legal and large, many categories of public sector workers are legally barred from striking, and workers risk dismissal and arrest if they do strike. Their position is weaker still if opportunities for alternative employment in the private sector are extremely limited, as is true in many of the poorest countries.

To balance these handicaps, do public sector workers and their associations have leverage that private workers do not? Freeman (1986, p. 42), discussing state and local government unions in the United States, argues, "A fundamental difference between public and private sector collective bargaining is that public sector unions, more so than private sector unions, can influence ... employer behavior through the political process."

But why? Public sector workers can form voting blocs or lobby or demonstrate for their demands, but so can organized private sector workers. Strikes, work stoppages, or slowdowns in vital public services hold the public hostage, generating strong political pressure on the government to hasten a settlement. The outcome may be repression rather than concessions to the strikers, depending on the political circumstances and particularly on the degree of public sympathy with the strikers.

A more convincing argument is based on patronage ties between politicians and public sector workers. Patronage implies a reciprocal commitment: the exchange of jobs for political support. Many national and local politicians have built up their support bases primarily through this mechanism. Sharp declines in real wages and, even more clearly, large-scale reductions in the work force mean the disintegration of support coalitions. In Africa, moreover, patronage often has tribal overtones and is endorsed, indeed mandated, by the strong traditional expectation that a "big man" protects and advances his ethnic brothers. A severe wage squeeze or extensive firings betray that trust.

Comparisons of public and private sector wage levels in developing countries offer ambiguous evidence as to whether public sector workers (and their unions or associations) are handicapped or advantaged. Any such comparisons must be approached with caution. Workers' compensation packages are complex, including base pay, varied bonuses, and nonwage compensation such as subsidized housing, insurance, and other benefits. And it is hard to control across sectors for differences in education and skill composition. There also may be important contrasts between the wages and security of civil servants and those of workers in state enterprises or local government.

Ehrenberg and Schwarz (1986), in their review of U.S. research on the issue, note considerable evidence that the relative wage gap between union and nonunion workers is smaller in the public sector than in the private sector, but they go on to suggest several considerations that cast doubt on the finding. Comparing public to private employees (without considering the union versus nonunion dimension), they note that U.S. federal government workers are paid somewhat better than are comparable private sector workers; this is particularly clear for women and for nonwhite males. The finding holds, but less strongly, for state and local employees, except perhaps for male local government workers. Taking into account nonwage compensation (which most studies ignore) would probably strengthen these findings.

For what they are worth, the "stylized facts" turn up geographical differences. In some Latin American countries in the mid-1980s, public sector workers seem to have been somewhat less well paid than were their private sector counterparts (Lopez and Riveros 1989; Riveros and Sanchez 1990). In Sub-Saharan Africa in the postindependence decades, public sector workers tended to be substantially better paid, but this advantage may have been erased or even reversed during the 1980s when real wages in the public sector fell dramatically (Lindauer, Meesook, and Suebsaeng 1988). The regional contrasts are probably attributable more to differences in the relative weight of public and private sector unions than to variation in the militancy of public sector unions. Private sector unions are large and important in a number of Latin American countries, presumably driving up private sector wage levels at least in highly unionized sectors; in Africa employment and unions in the private sector are much less important relative to their public counterparts.[7]

More broadly, it is surely the behavior of governments as employers more than the behavior of unions that distinguishes wage determination in the public sector from processes in the private sector, above all during hard times. Governments do not have to cope with profit and loss sheets but instead are constrained by fiscal and monetary considerations. Recession and fiscal crisis pit pressure from public sector workers to maintain wages and perquisites against political pressures for other uses of public funds. Trends in personnel costs as a percentage of total public expenditures could be viewed as a rough measure of the political priority accorded to public sector workers. In most of Latin America and Africa in the 1980s, that percentage rose substantially.

Under intense fiscal pressure, maintaining public employment has been given very high priority; indeed, especially early in the crisis, governments often tried to hire countercyclically (Lopez and Riveros 1989, p. 20; Riveros and Sanchez 1990, p. 35). As the need for long-

---

7. Heller and Tait's comparative study of public employment and pay is still the most comprehensive analysis available for developing nations, but it gives conflicting information regarding public and parastatal wage levels compared to private nonagricultural wages. Direct comparisons of wage levels suggested that central government employees and nonfinancial public enterprise employees tended to be better paid than were workers in private manufacturing (Heller and Tait 1984, Table 8, p. 18), but government employment constituted a larger share of total nonagricultural employment than did government wages as a share of total wages (p. 10).

term reform became inescapable, a few governments laid off large numbers of workers, but most such cases entailed generous compensation. Ghana, for example, paid the equivalent of roughly two years' total compensation to workers stripped from the notoriously overstaffed Cocoa Board. Guyana cut almost a quarter of its civil service and public enterprise workers but awarded severance pay so large that the government had to borrow heavily to cover the costs (Nunberg 1988, pp. 9-11). Buffering lower paid workers has also been stressed: not only have average real wages in the public sector dropped sharply, but, especially in Africa, differences between the highest and lowest paid workers have been cut dramatically. Union pressure obviously played a role in these patterns. But more fundamentally, the patterns reflected the different incentives and constraints motivating governments as employers, in contrast to those governing the actions of private employers.

Organized Labor and Its Social Allies

Before turning to the effects of economic cycles and political contexts on labor's role, I would like to consider how unionized workers are imbedded in their societies, and the implications for union militance. Kerr and Siegel (1954) observed in their crossnational comparisons that certain categories of workers (including miners, seamen, and lumber workers) are particularly prone to strike. Among their explanations for this pattern were similarities in the social setting of these types of workers: all tended to be geographically isolated from the larger social community, but tended to form close-knit social communities of their own.

A different line of inquiry focuses on the degree to which organized workers constitute a labor elite in developing countries. To what extent do organized workers enjoy privileged lifestyles, aspirations, and social and political ties? There may be broad contrasts among geographic regions. Organized industrial workers in some semi-industrialized countries may fit the labor elite pattern (viz. the description of Brazil as "Belindia," with a minority of the population similar to Belgian society while the remainder resembles India). Organized workers in less dualistic nations may be closely integrated with the remainder of the urban working classes, and as a result may receive considerable support in their industrial disputes. A very clearly described instance of this occurred in Sekondi-Takoradi, Ghana's third city, in the 1960s. At least half of the work force was unionized, including a large group of railway workers and other workers in the public and private sectors. These workers were integrated residentially and had strong family and other ties with the remainder of the working class. When the railway workers struck in 1961, the entire working-class population of the town supported their action. Other workers also went on strike, and market women dispensed free food. Similar broad social support occurred in Lagos in 1964 and again in 1971 (Nelson 1979, pp. 153-155).

It is worth taking a second look at the conflict or overlap of interests between organized labor and urban informal workers. High wages and nonwage compensation and tight constraints on firing in the formal sector undoubtedly reduce employment available in that sector, increasing competition and reducing earnings in the informal sector. But formal and informal sector workers share similar interests as consumers and as users of public services. Their interests are also intertwined in other ways: small-scale enterprises do special lot assignments or are otherwise linked to the formal sector. Market vendors, barbers, tailors, and other own-account service workers sell to unionized workers. Many households include formal and informal sector workers.

These overlapping interests in many cases ally unionized workers with much broader segments of the urban population. The result may be not only occasional community support for workers in industrial disputes, but union involvement in broader social protests against austerity and adjustment programs. For instance, unions were involved to varying degrees in initiating the massive protests against reduced food subsidies in Casablanca in 1981, in Santo Domingo in April 1984, and in Zambia at the end of 1986, but these (and similar cases elsewhere) were broad popular actions, not union actions. Stated a little differently, it may be easier for unions to defend their members' real wages on the consumption side than on the income side because the members are part of a broader popular coalition pressing for cheap consumer staples and improved government services.

The Economic Context and Labor Militancy

The most plausible and best-supported proposition about the effects of economic cycles on organized labor is that bargaining power and militancy decline in hard times and increase in prosperity. Strikes vary with economic cycles: when labor markets are slack and protracted unemployment looms, unions often consent to wage regulation; conversely, good times make labor more aggressive (Lange 1984; Kennan 1986). Labor militancy is likely to have higher payoffs in tight labor markets, and widespread wage drift (induced by workers or employers) and other forms of noncontracted gains are more probable. For instance, in Norway's postwar history of wage regulation, breakdowns were most likely during periods of rapid economic growth. Conversely, Epstein (1988) found fairly strong statistical links between rising unemployment and fewer and smaller strikes. He analyzed union responses to official austerity programs between 1976 and 1984 in seven Latin American countries with large and important labor movements.

The rapidity with which workers' priorities shift, during economic crises, from maintaining real wages to protecting their jobs tends to reflect the history of economic growth in the country in question. "The longer the time since the last structural crisis, the more workers are likely to expect that strong economic conditions ... will continue, and that downturns will be only temporary" (Lange 1984, p. 117). In Costa Rica the economic tailspin of 1979-82 broke a virtually uninterrupted span of growth from the early 1960s. After Alberto Monge's government's remarkably effective stabilization effort of 1982-83 had taken hold, popular pressure to restore real incomes to their precrisis peak mounted rapidly.

Lange's discussion of the rational bases of workers' consent to wage regulation adds one important modification. Although pessimism about short-term economic prospects usually encourages cooperation with wage regulation, the effect is less predictable when labor confronts "structurally bleak prospects." On the one hand, it might be thought that workers would be strongly inclined to regulate wages, for they would think that failing to do so would condemn the national economy to sustained recession or even depression, and their own wages to real decay. On the other hand, the bleak economic prospects might lead workers to think that there is little to be gained by restraint—things will not get better anyway without major disruptions to their economic lives—and that it is therefore best to try to get as much as possible while it can still be had (Lange 1984, p. 115).

In such situations, a key variable shaping workers' behavior is whether they believe that "the fruits of their restraint will redound to their future economic advantage" (Lange 1984, p. 116). This perception, in turn, rests on the credibility of the government's broader recovery program and on implicit or explicit assurances that workers' interests will be protected during industrial restructuring. In short, when the long-term economic outlook is grim, political relationships and expectations become much more important in determining labor's responses.

Political Structure, Labor Militancy, and Labor Influence

Power is relational. The strength of governments and their strategies toward labor markets are as important in shaping outcomes as the strength, autonomy, and orientation of labor movements. Unions adjust their actions to the political context. I will consider three dimensions of the political context: type of regime; the party system and the place of organized labor in that system; and more transitory political circumstances, particularly electoral cycles and changes in regime. These same factors may affect governments' commitment to adjustment in general and to labor market flexibility in particular. For this brief survey the discussion is simplified by assuming government commitment to measures (1) to contain wage increases to a significant degree, as an important element in a stabilization package, and (2) to encourage increased labor market flexibility in the medium term. In other words, government commitment to flexible labor markets is taken as a given here. The emphasis is on how varying political contexts shape government tactics and labor responses.

Regimes and Tactics

Most of the research reviewed earlier in this chapter is based on evidence from industrial democracies with governments widely accepted by their citizens as legitimate, with competition among two or more parties that constitute potential governments, and with broad legal and actual protection for civil and political rights. The type of regime, in effect, is held constant. In developing countries, types of regime vary widely. One would expect the type of regime to be most obviously reflected in the tactics governments choose, once convinced of the necessity of measures organized labor is likely to resist. To cope with that resistance, three basic types of tactics are available: persuasion, partial compensation, and containment. Social pacts combine persuasion and compensation. Compensation need not take the form of immediate wage increases; social pacts often trade short-run wage restraint for social benefits (in effect, deferred improvements in the security and quality of life). Another form of compensation is reform of labor laws to provide labor with assurances of greater freedom to organize or with better access to decisionmakers (in effect, improving prospects of later economic gains). Union pressure can be contained not only by repression (or the threat of repression) but also by coopting labor leaders or by encouraging internal divisions and the emergence of rival unions or federations.

Democratic governments rely primarily on persuasion and compensation. Authoritarian regimes are less reluctant than democratic governments to use containment in general and repression in particular. So unions in authoritarian systems—if they are permitted to operate legally at all—are likely to be more cautious and less militant.

But type of regime is too crude a variable to be a reliable predictor of governments' choice of tactics in dealing with labor. Authoritarian and democratic governments display a wide range of legal and institutional arrangements governing union activity. Some democracies have laws hedging union activity quite tightly, and many democratic governments have been willing to ignore or put down labor protests. In Sri Lanka in 1980 an attempted general strike was broken by dismissing large numbers of public sector strikers. In Bolivia in 1985 the newly elected government of Victor Paz Estenssoro acted promptly and decisively to squelch the miners' union that had repeatedly destroyed earlier stabilization efforts. In Jamaica in the same year Edward Seaga faced down an unprecedented general strike in which both major union confederations (each linked with one of the two major parties) protested his austerity program.

Conversely, some long-established, one-party or dominant-party governments grant unions considerable influence, despite episodes of tension or repression. Examples include the long history of Kenneth Kaunda's relations with the Zambian copper miners; the dominant Institutional Revolutionary Party's long-term management of labor relations and policies in Mexico; Neodestour's relationship with the major Tunisian labor federation; and Juan Velasco's military government's cultivation of support from Peruvian trade unions in the late 1960s and early 1970s. Electoral cycles clearly influence not only governments' willingness to launch or maintain unpopular wage and price measures but also organized labor's acquiescence in such measures. This pattern is not exclusive to competitive democracies. Ferdinand Marcos postponed stabilization measures until after the important Philippine legislative election of May 1984. The de la Madrid government, after five years of ignoring Mexican labor unions' anguished protests, entered into an Economic Solidarity Pact in December 1987, when it became increasingly clear that the elections scheduled for mid-1988 would pose an unprecedented challenge to the Institutional Revolutionary Party's control (Middlebrook 1989, pp. 207-208). In sum, the type of regime affects government handling of labor relations and, therefore, the options available to unions. But the more fine-grained features of the relation between organized labor and the government, including the channels and degree of access to decisionmaking circles, count more in how governments manage labor issues. These arrangements are not systematically related to the broad distinction between electorally competitive and noncompetitive regimes.

Party Systems and Labor's Political Role

Party systems and union ties with parties are particularly influential in shaping unions' political roles and their relations with governments. Labor movements occupy positions in party systems ranging from dominance in a ruling coalition to virtual exclusion. The examples that follow demonstrate the range of possible positions.

- Until quite recently, Peronist unions in Argentina dominated their party, and they have exercised tremendous power during periods of Peronist control of the government.
- A pattern more commonly found is incorporation of unions or segments of labor as subordinate parts of a ruling coalition, as in Mexico and Singapore.
- In several Latin American and Caribbean countries, unions have links with both of two centrist parties, which together dominate political processes. Colombia, Costa Rica, Jamaica, and Venezuela are examples. In these cases labor has access to (but does not dominate) the government regardless of the party in power.
- In Peru until quite recently, and in Argentina, labor has been linked to one strong party within a system divided by deep social and political cleavages. In Peru the result was to exclude the American Popular Revolutionary Alliance (APRA) and its labor allies for many decades. In Argentina Peronists periodically gained power. In both cases the political system was polarized and destabilized.
- In Uruguay and (less clearly) the Dominican Republic, unions have been linked mainly with weak radical parties: the result is semiexclusion.
- In the Republic of Korea until quite recently, and in Chile under Auguste Pinochet, organized labor was effectively excluded from tightly limited political arenas.

At any given time, different party systems and links between parties and organized labor strongly influence the options available to unions to defend or promote their interests. Over time, patterns of incorporation into the party system also affect the strength and orientation of the labor movement as a whole. Incorporation into an established dominant party, or links with parties that alternate in power, appear to encourage negotiation and compromise and dampen confrontation. But incentives for the party in power to make concessions to labor differ sharply in the two categories. The dominant party that incorporates major unions may assume that labor has no plausible alternative to cooperation. In more competitive two-party systems, access to both major parties ensures labor leaders that their interests will get a hearing—the kind of assurance Lange (1984) suggests is likely to moderate the militancy of desperation in very hard times. In contrast to both systems, the polarized pattern is likely to stimulate militancy, whether or not the party with which labor is affiliated stands a good chance of taking office.

Instability and Transitional Regimes

Just as research on the militancy of labor movements in high-income industrial democracies holds the type of regime constant, it also implicitly focuses on experience in stable political systems. Many developing countries are much less stable and predictable: governments frequently change through coups rather than scheduled elections, and not merely the people in power but the nature of the political system is prone to change. Unpredictable political settings have far-reaching implications for the politics of adjustment, including the politics of labor market adjustment.

In the short run, both elected and "irregular" new governments may have special opportunities to adopt needed economic reforms. The new government is likely to have a honeymoon period during which it can blame the need for unpopular economic measures on the legacy from its incompetent or dishonest predecessor. The honeymoon effect may be particularly strong both after a long period of political and economic decay and if the new government enters office with strong popular support. (New governments, of course, vary tremendously with respect to their sense of security and the clarity of their economic goals and program: both factors affect their ability to take advantage of the honeymoon period.) The effects of governmental turnover on the system as a whole over time are a different matter. Frequent turnover is likely to breed cynicism and to shorten drastically the period of time that all political players, including labor unions, are willing to take into account as they consider their strategies and tactics. The result in the realm of labor policy is diminished potential for trading deferred benefits for current wage moderation.

The current global wave of democratizing reforms and changes in regimes highlights the special question of interactions between democratization and economic liberalization, including labor market adjustments. A principal characteristic of democratization is rapid expansion of popular political participation. Popular demands for improved living conditions may be temporarily muted by widespread recognition that the country's economic problems require major reforms and will take time to carry out. That recognition seems to be particularly strong in some of the Eastern European countries now retreating from state socialism. But popular demands are likely to be more immediate and insistent in many of the nations of Latin America and Asia, and in some in Africa now turning or returning to democracy.

In short, new democracies often face considerable wage pressure. If the new government is viewed as a definitive break with the bad old days, workers are likely to look for speedy improvement in their situation. But if the new regime is viewed as fragile, labor may well seek to capitalize on the political opening while it lasts. From the government's perspective, too, the desire to consolidate or broaden popular support encourages wage increases and other populist measures.

Ups and downs in real wages obviously reflect not only government wage policies but other domestic policies and external trends, but it is striking how many of the new democracies of the past two decades illustrate the tendency to early wage concessions. In Portugal real manufacturing wages rose 13.7 percent in 1974 and 10.3 percent in 1975; nominal wages were hiked much more (Schmitt 1981, Appendix Table 1; Stallings 1981, pp. 108-109). In Spain real wages, which had been rising rapidly since the 1960s, accelerated after 1974 (Lopez-Claros 1988, p. 4 and chart 6). In Argentina real industrial wages dropped 11 percent in 1980 and 10 percent in 1981; the departing military government then raised real wages by at least 25 percent. (Diaz-Alejandro, in Williamson 1985, gives the increase as 29 percent. Later data in ECLAC 1989, Table 6, p. 17, record the increase as 25.4 percent.) Raul Alfonsin, campaigning for the presidency and probably basing his judgment on the 1980-81 data, promised to raise real wages. In 1984 real average manufacturing wages rose a further 26.4 percent (ECLAC 1989, Table 6). In Uruguay average real wages jumped 14.1 percent in 1985 with the return of civilian rule, after having fallen more than 30 percent between 1982 and 1984, although the new civilian government was firmly centrist and the unions were not traditionally powerful politically. In Bolivia Hernan Siles Zuazo's election in 1982 ended a long period of military rule, but Siles's attempts to gain control over the rapidly disintegrating economy were repeatedly blocked by militant unions. At least four times the government introduced austerity measures only to back off and raise nominal wages after general strikes.

In Turkey Turgut Ozal became head of the economic team when military rule was imposed in 1980, and he was later elected prime minister when civilian rule was restored in late 1983. Wage negotiations had become increasingly confrontational in the late 1970s as the economic and political crisis deepened, and the new military government cracked down on the labor unions. Real wages, already falling steeply in 1978 and 1979, dropped a further 25 percent in 1980. As the stabilization and adjustment program took effect, the rate of decline slowed to 7.4 percent in 1981 and 4 percent in 1982. In 1983, as elections to restore civilian rule approached, wage policy was eased and prices on key staples held in line; real wages increased 5.6 percent. The collective bargaining process was liberalized early in 1985 (internal World Bank report; Kopits 1987, p. 10).

Labor pressure on new democratic governments is not surprising. Much more interesting would be a semisystematic explanation for the experience of such governments in trying to bring wage policies back into line and to establish rules of the game to reduce conflict with organized labor while permitting stabilization and adjustment. The 1980s saw a wide array of strategies, including successful pacts (Spain), tactics to weaken or split labor (as Alfonsin initially tried to do), and straight union-breaking (under Paz Estenssoro in Bolivia). The results of such strategies in winning labor's cooperation with adjustment have ranged from considerable success to total failure. Explaining the results would go well beyond the scope of this chapter. But at the core of durable arrangements to encourage moderate labor demands must be a modicum of confidence.

Long-Haul Adjustment, Labor Cooperation, and Equity

Skillful government tactics can make a great difference to the effective or ineffective management of labor demands in the short run. But adjustment is a long-haul proposition, likely to extend over a decade in many countries, perhaps considerably longer in some. Resumed growth in those countries whose economies have stagnated or worsened in the past decade will facilitate labor's cooperation, but certainly in much of Latin America and Africa it is realistic to expect a long process of painful reorientation.

The crucial element in gaining workers' cooperation is the belief that their sacrifice will contribute to general gains and that those gains will be distributed fairly. That belief requires confidence in three respects. First, it requires confidence in the government's economic management and at least contingent hope that the government has a plausible game plan. In countries where external economic trends are very adverse, the plausibility of the government's game plan may hinge in part on the probability of substantial external support. Second, cooperation requires confidence that labor's interests will be fairly represented and that labor representatives will have access to and influence in decisionmaking circles. Third, as a prerequisite, reasonable confidence is needed in political stability—that is, assurance that changes in administration are not likely to bring dramatic change in labor's position or in the rules of the game.

These requirements are strikingly parallel to the conditions needed to get business to start investing again. Labor militancy—workers' main line of defense against declining incomes—can be seen as the counterpart to the business caution and capital flight that delayed supply response to partial reforms in many developing countries in the 1980s. Conversely, union acquiescence in wage restraint (to the extent that it is voluntary) is essentially an investment: current income and consumption are forgone in favor of expected greater returns later.

In some countries, cooperation might be encouraged by mechanisms to give labor fuller access to decisionmaking circles while ways are sought to broaden labor leaders' grasp of larger national problems. The corporatist arrangements of Northern and Western

Europe are suggestive but cannot be replicated—certainly not rapidly, or imposed primarily from above. The ruling elite has very limited ability to remold systems of party and interest intermediation, which are "the product of very lengthy and complex historical forces ... [and] are also subject to strong emergent organizational properties that guide their development and insulate them from ameliorative meddlings from above" (Schmitter 1981, p. 318). But what is widely perceived as a long-term crisis simultaneously increases the importance of political influences on labor relations and opens the possibility of dialogue.

Labor cooperation would also be encouraged if governments—and those advising them—balanced their insistence that labor make sacrifices in the public interest with practical steps to increase equity. Recent analyses of the self-destructive "populist cycle" evident during the past 40 years in several Latin American nations trace the roots of the cycle to marked and growing income inequalities and the resulting political pressures for redistributive policies to raise the incomes of poor groups. Sachs (1989) puts great emphasis on this point; it is less prominent but clear in Dornbusch and Edwards (1989, p. 5).

As the corporatist model suggests, institutional arrangements and policy outcomes must build up confidence that the benefits of economic reform and recovery will be widely shared. The modest measures likely to be feasible to increase equity in the 1990s—more progressive taxation (or simply the enforcement of taxes on the books) and reorientation of social services to better serve the working class and the poor—will not eliminate conflict over which groups bear the costs of adjustment. Such modest measures, however, might reduce anger and distrust and improve the chances for constructive dialogue and bargaining.

References

Calmfors, L., and J. Driffill. 1988. "Bargaining Structure, Corporatism, and Macroeconomic Performance." *Economic Policy 6* (April): 13-62.

Cameron, D.R. 1984. "Social Democracy, Corporatism, Labour Quiescence and the Representation of Economic Interest in Advanced Capitalist Society." In John H. Goldthorpe, ed.,

Order and Conflict in Contemporary Capitalism. Oxford: Oxford University Press.

Dornbusch, R., and S. Edwards. 1989. "The Macroeconomics of Populism in Latin America." Policy, Planning, and Research Working Paper 316. Washington, D.C.: World Bank. Processed.

ECLAC (Economic Commission for Latin America and the Caribbean). 1989. *Preliminary Overview of the Latin American Economy, 1988.* New York: United Nations.

Ehrenberg, R.G., and J.L. Schwarz. 1986. "Public Sector Labor Markets." In O. Ashenfelter and R. Layard, eds., *Handbook of Labor Economics.* New York: North-Holland.

Epstein, E.C. 1988. "Austerity and Trade Unions in Latin America." In W.L. Canak, ed., *Lost Promises: Debt Austerity and Development in Latin America.* Boulder, Colo.: Westview.

Freeman, R.B. 1986. "Unionism Comes to the Public Sector."*Journal of Economic Literature* 24 (March): 41-85.

_____. 1988. "Labour Market Institutions and Economic Performance." *Economic Policy* 6 (April): 63-80.

Heller, P.S., and A.A. Tait. 1984. *Government Employment and Pay: Some International Comparisons.* Occasional Paper 24. Washington, D.C.: International Monetary Fund.

Katzenstein, P. 1985. *Small States in World Markets: Industrial Policy in Europe.* Ithaca, N.Y.: Cornell University Press.

Kennan, J. 1986. "The Economics of Strikes." In O. Ashenfelter and R. Layard, eds., *Handbook of Labor Economics.* Amsterdam and New York: North-Holland.

Kerr, C., and A. Sicgel. 1954. "The Inter-Industry Propensity to Strike: An International Comparison." In A. Kornhauser, R. Dubin, and A. Ross, eds., *Industrial Conflict.* New York: McGraw-Hill.

Kopits, G. 1987. *Structural Reform Stabilization and Growth in Turkey.* Occasional Paper 52. Washington, D.C.: International Monetary Fund.

Lange, P. 1984. "Unions, Workers, and Wage Regulation: The Rational Bases of Consent." In J.H, Goldthorpe, ed., *Order and Conflict in Contemporary Capitalism.* Oxford: Oxford University Press.

Lindauer, D.L., O.A. Meesook, and P. Suebsaeng. 1988. "Government Wage Policy in Africa: Some Findings and Policy Issues." *World Bank Research Observer* 3: 1-25.

Lopez, R.E., and L.A. Riveros. 1989. "Macroeconomic Adjustment and the Labor Market in Four Latin American Countries." Policy, Planning, and Research Working Paper 33S. Washington, D.C.: World Bank. Processed.

Lopez-Claros, A. 1988. *The Search for Efficiency in the Adjustment Process: Spain in the 1980s.* Occasional Paper 57. Washington, D.C.: International Monetary Fund.

Middlebrook, K.J. 1989. "The Sounds of Silence: Organized Labour's Response to Economic Crisis in Mexico." *Journal of Latin American Studies* 21: 195-220.

Nelson, J.M. 1979. *Access to Power: Politics and the Urban Poor in Developing Nations.* Princeton, N.J.: Princeton University Press.

Nunberg, B. 1988. "Public Sector Pay and Employment Reform." Policy, Planning, and Research Working Paper 113. Washington, D.C.: World Bank. Processed.

Olson, M. 1982. *The Rise and Decline of Nations: Economic Growth, Stagflation, and Social Rigidities.* New Haven, Conn.: Yale University Press.

Riveros, L.A., and C.E. Sanchez. 1990. "Argentina's Labor Markets in an Era of Adjustment." Policy, Research, and External Affairs Working Paper 386. Washington, D.C.: World Bank. Processed.

Sachs, J.D. 1989a. "Social Conflict and Populist Policies in Latin America." Working Paper 2897. Cambridge, Mass.: National Bureau of Economic Research. Processed.

_____. 1989b. "Introduction." In J. Sachs, ed., *Developing Country Debt and the World Economy*. Chicago: University of Chicago Press.

Schmitt, H.O. 1981. *Economic Stabilization and Growth in Portugal.* Occasional Paper 2. Washington, D.C.: International Monetary Fund.

Schmitter, P.C. 1981. "Interest Intermediation and Regime Governability in Contemporary Western Europe and North America." In S. Berger, ed., *Organizing Interests in Western Europe: Pluralism, Corporatism, and the Transformation of Politics.* Cambridge: Cambridge University Press.

Stallings, B. 1981. "Portugal and the IMF: The Political Economy of Stabilization." In J. Braga de Macedo and S. Serfaty, eds., *Portugal Since the Revolution: Economic and Political Perspectives.* Westview Special Studies in West Europe Politics and Society. Boulder, Colo.: Westview.

Taylor, C.L., and D. Jodice. 1983. *World Bank Handbook of Political and Social Indicators.* 3d. ed. New Haven, Conn.: Yale University Press.

U.S. CIA (Central Intelligence Agency). 1989. *World Factbook 1989.* Washington, D.C.: Government Printing Office.

Walton, J., and C. Ragin. 1988. "Austerity and Dissent: Social Basis of Popular Struggle in Latin America." In W. L. Canak, ed., *Lost promises: Debt, Austerity, and Development in Latin America.* Boulder, Colo.: Westview.

Williamson, J., ed., 1985. *Inflation and Indexation: Argentina, Brazil, and Israel.* Washington, D.C.: Institute of International Economics.

NA →

INDEX

(Page numbers in italics indicate material in figures or tables)